D1241804

THE AMERICAN IMPACT ON RUSSIA
Diplomatic and Ideological
1784-1917

By MAX M. LASERSON

RUSSIA AND THE WESTERN WORLD
The Place of the Soviet Union in the Comity of Nations

THE AMERICAN IMPACT ON RUSSIA
Diplomatic and Ideological, 1784-1917

THE AMERICAN IMPACT ON RUSSIA — *Diplomatic and Ideological* — *1784-1917*

MAX M. LASERSON

THE MACMILLAN COMPANY - NEW YORK
1950

Permission has been granted by the respective publishers to quote from the following books:

Autobiography, Andrew D. White, published by Appleton-Century-Crofts, Inc., New York, 1905, Vol. I, pp. 550, 551. Copyright, 1905, by the Appleton-Century Company.

Elihu Root by Philip C. Jessup, published by Dodd, Mead & Company, New York, 1938, Vol. II, pp. 354-355, 356, 358. Copyright, 1938, by Dodd, Mead & Company, Inc.

Road to Teheran by Foster Rhea Dulles, published by Princeton University Press, Princeton, N.J., 1944, pp. 103, 104-105, 135. Copyright, 1944, by Princeton University Press.

Open Gates to Russia by Malcolm W. Davis, published by Harper & Brothers, New York, 1920, pp. 8-9, 24-29. Copyright, 1920, by Harper & Brothers.

Russia's Message by W. E. Walling, published by Doubleday & Company, Inc., New York, 1908, pp. 164-165, 420. Copyright, 1908, by Doubleday & Company.

The True Woodrow Wilson by H. G. Black, published by Fleming H. Revell Company, New York, 1946, p. 153. Copyright, 1946, by Fleming H. Revell Company.

Russia from the American Embassy by D. R. Francis, published by Charles Scribner's Sons, New York, 1921, pp. 107-108. Copyright, 1921, by Charles Scribner's Sons.

To the memory of
GEORGE KENNAN
the American fighter for Russia's freedom

Preface

THE IMPACT OF AMERICA ON RUSSIA HAS BEEN, QUALITATIVELY AND quantitatively, more substantial and more penetrating than one may at first be inclined to believe. The date of the beginning of this cultural and political interaction is difficult to determine. One might set it at the year 1781 when the official but unrecognized diplomat Francis Dana was sent by the American Congress to the court of Catherine II; or one might just as arbitrarily set it at the year 1784, when Benjamin Franklin was elected an honorary member of the Imperial Russian Academy of Sciences in St. Petersburg. Neither 1781 nor 1784 alone is correct. These two dates mark the start of separate threads of the story which in time became inextricably entangled. Therefore in diplomatic terms the book runs from Francis Dana to David Francis, ambassador to the last Czar, who remained in service through the democratic revolution of March–November, 1917, and the early months of the Soviet regime. In ideological terms the book reaches from Benjamin Franklin to Woodrow Wilson on the American side, and from Radishchev to Ostrogorski and Miliukov on the Russian.

It should be emphasized that the period from the age of Peter the Great (1700–1725) to the dawn of the October Revolution in 1917 represented eight long generations in which Russia absorbed, and recast, the cultural achievements of the West. The influence of the United States upon Russia was exerted roughly through the latter four of these generations—in all, about a hundred and thirty years.

This book is a pioneer attempt to elucidate and evaluate America's role in Russia's pre-Soviet history. Because of the very fact of this impact the successor government of Russia, in methodically reshaping its history, perforce must play down if not strike out completely the dramatic but little known phenomena here described. Of course American technical help in the industrialization and scientific improvement of Soviet Russia between the two World Wars and in arming, clothing, increase of production for victory against the common enemy was and is tangible—a daily reminder of America's contributions which cannot down or be downed. Hence the "American impact" remains for the Euro-Asian colossus, even beyond the terminal date of this volume, a stubborn and incontrovertible fact.

This work is limited to the field of international relations and diplomatic contacts on one hand, and cultural, political, socio-economic, and ideological relationships on the other. It tries to demonstrate how these two lines of influence have been mutually connected. It touches only casually upon literature and technology, and then only in so far as they express, illustrate, or explain diplomatic or ideological trends.

Throughout, the reader will find a plethora of direct quotations from American, Russian, and other documents as well as sources never before translated for English readers. Nevertheless a real handicap in the research was the limitation upon the use of the Russian daily press, particularly for crucial periods like the 1870's and early 1880's and the period from March to November, 1917: American libraries that the author was able to use had too few Russian newspapers of such periods. It has been necessary in some cases to describe in great detail events and trends of historic character in order better to estimate the influence of the United States. This was imperative in the agrarian problems, connected with slavery and serfdom, in problems of racial and religious minorities, and in political and constitutional reforms. Such material seemed worthy of inclusion, on the assumption that a knowledge of things Russian is still somewhat limited in America.

These remarks would not be complete without naming, among the Russian scholars whose views are more or less thoroughly described in this work, five who were my professors at the St. Petersburg University: V. Gessen, M. Kovalevski, Baron B. Nolde, I. Ozerov, and M. Tugan-Baranovski, in the seminars of whom I took an active part. The sixth, M. Ostrogorski, was the writer's personal guide and teacher in political science and institutions, particularly those of the United States, Great Britain, and France.

If this volume should be recognized as a segmental exploration in the hitherto neglected field of American influence on Europe, then its purpose will be fulfilled.

I am indebted to the Carnegie Endowment for International Peace for financial support which helped me to complete my present research. I am particularly grateful to Professor James T. Shotwell, the President of the Endowment, for giving me the benefit of his friendly criticisms within the broad field of American history and policy. My thanks go also to Professor Henry Graff of Columbia University, who read the manuscript and made valuable suggestions. I cannot mention all those of my colleagues who advised me on special points.

Mrs. Helen Steward Walcott and Miss Marion Kuhn edited different parts of the manuscript. To George H. Gibson I am grateful for his general polishing of the text and for the index. And to Miss Elizabeth Charney I am very much obliged for a free translation of Radishchev's poems.

Mrs. Jeanette Kennan Hotchkiss generously allowed me to use the photograph of her uncle George Kennan, and gave me biographical data on him. Colonel Stanley Washburn, Military Aide to Elihu Root, kindly made available the two photographs of Mr. Root's visit to Russia.

Finally I wish to mention the cooperation shown to me by the staffs of the American and Slavonic divisions of the New York Public Library, including Mrs. Anna Heifetz and Alfred Berlstein of the latter; to the Columbia University libraries and its International Law Library with Mrs. Florence Ferner Zagayko, and to the staff of the Woodrow Wilson Memorial Library.

MAX M. LASERSON

COLUMBIA UNIVERSITY
    July, 1950

Contents

Illustrations

THE AMERICAN IMPACT ON RUSSIA
Diplomatic and Ideological
1784-1917

I *The Three Circles of Foreign Cultural Influence in Russia: German, French, and English*

BEFORE WE BEGIN TO DESCRIBE THE CONTRIBUTION OF THE United States to Russia we must bear in mind that it was substantially conditioned by the knowledge of the English language and culture, and only in a lesser way by direct contact between Americans and Russians. For this reason we must know the approximate outlines of the three most influential foreign cultures in Russia throughout the last decades of the eighteenth century and the first of the nineteenth—the period of the emergence and the first steps of the United States. We are certainly not touching American influence upon Russian imaginative literature, which deserves special treatment. What we have predominantly in mind is the contacts and repercussions in the diplomatic, political, legal, social, and economic fields. In this relation, too, the extent of knowledge of foreign languages is important, although it cannot be denied that if, for instance, books written in English by Locke, Blackstone, Franklin, Smith, and Bentham reached Russia and influenced her in German or French translations, the repercussions might have been no less than if read by Russians in the original English. The same is true for constitutions, declarations, and other political or legal documents. And still the extent to which any foreign culture was known in Russia largely determined the depth of its penetration.

Except in the time preceding the Tartar yoke, the impact of Western culture and civilization upon Russia began basically with the father of Peter I in the middle of the seventeenth century, both through the mediation of Poland and by direct contact of Western foreigners. Already in Muscovite times the best represented foreigners in the German suburb of Moscow, Nemetskaya Sloboda—a special quarter for foreign merchants, officers, artisans, physicians, etc.—were the Germans, Dutch, and other Protestants.

Catholics, particularly after the invasion by Poland in the first decade of the seventeenth century, were scarcely tolerated by the Russian government; to the Russian Orthodox Church Protestantism was a lesser evil than the "Latin creed," whose champion, it seemed to the Russians at that time was Poland, the most persistent rival and invader of Russia. The general negative attitude to Catholicism could be reduced to the old Byzantine traditions which were transplanted to Russia after the decline of Byzantium, when Moscow was proclaimed the "Third Rome"; but Protestantism was a religious newcomer which, despite its heretical character, had nothing to do with Roman popery, the hereditary enemy.

German Influence

For almost two hundred years after Peter the Great, German culture was the most influential among the three foreign cultures in Russia. This was in part because of geographical conditions—namely, a certain closeness of western Russia and St. Petersburg to Prussia and the rest of Germany—but predominantly because of historical and political conditions. The Europeanization of Russia, which began seriously with the first secular reformation of Peter the Great, was carried out by him with the help not only of Germans, but also of other Western European mentors like the French, Dutch, and Scotch.

Two outstanding circumstances became manifest after the death of Peter in 1725. First, the conquest in 1710 of Livonia—covering modern Estonia and the central and northern parts of Latvia—led to the incorporation into Russia of two provinces in which the German nobility and the German town patricians and burghers had been the commanding strata since the thirteenth century. Secondly, under Catherine II in 1795 after the last partition of Poland, the former duchy of Courland was compulsorily incorporated into Russia; it was the westernmost part of modern Latvia, and since 1561 had been a vassal state of the Kingdom of Poland. The duchy, with a tiny but commanding German stratum, possessed two old harbors on the open Baltic Sea—Libau and Windau. During almost two hundred and fifty years (1561 to

1795) it had had virtual political independence and had actively participated in international politics, concluding commercial treaties with England and other countries, and stretching its colonial dependencies as far as the Caribbean Sea with the island of Tobago. Thus Courland reared a number of diplomats and statesmen; they all belonged to the German aristocracy, and many were the younger sons of the landed barons. In the duchy Germans were even more numerous than in the adjacent Livonian provinces.

The native nobility of Russia remained unaffected by Western influences until Peter I, and viewed as rivals and intruders these new Russian subjects of German extraction and aristocratic ascendancy, who were better trained and prepared. With the ascent to the Russian throne in 1730 of Empress Anne, the niece of Peter I, the predominance of the Germans became a well known fact, to endure almost to the bitter end of the Romanov dynasty.

But this ascent of Empress Anne became particularly important. The Supreme Privy Council (a kind of Star Chamber), in which the Russian aristocracy prevailed, decided to invite Anne, the widow of the Duke of Courland and a niece of Peter the Great, to the throne of Russia; but it instructed the Russian delegation which left for Mitau (capital of Courland) to obtain her signature to the so-called Conditions, limiting her powers by a kind of oligarchic constitution according to the Swedish pattern. Anne solemnly gave her signature to the document; but in Moscow her intentions suddenly changed when she found that the lower gentry and the higher Army officers were unwilling to consent to a regime under which they would inevitably be subordinated to the Supreme Council.

It was not hard to persuade the new Czarina to break her solemn promise: she simply tore up the Conditions and established herself as the absolute monarch of Russia, with the help of the Guards, the Army, and the lower gentry.

This meant not only a cancellation of the first legal overthrow of royal absolutism but also the establishment of what was later called, even by German scholars, Deutschenherrschaft.[1] Signs of German influence were noted in the last years of Peter the Great and Catherine I (his widow). But with the accession of Anne in

[1] Hans von Eckardt, *Russland* (Leipzig, 1930), pp. 72-79.

1730, and the decay of the high native Russian aristocracy, it became overwhelming, and German court favorites, chancellors, mar-
shals, and ministers directed Russian foreign and domestic policy.
Among these were Ostermann, Münnich, Biron (simultaneously
the Duke of Courland), the brothers Löwenwolde, and a host of
Courlanders and Livonians, almost exclusively aristocrats, and
foreign Germans of lesser ranks and titles. The period of German
predominance and arbitrariness went down in the memory of the
Russian people as the *Bironovshtshina*.[2] Literacy in German became a real prerequisite for everyone who dreamt about a political
career or even plain social contact. To such a degree was this the
case that the English ambassador to the Russian court of Empress
Anne, Lord George Forbes (afterwards Earl of Granard), complained of the necessity to learn German, "although this is very
difficult at my age."

Empress Catherine II, herself a German princess of Anhalt-
Zerbst, in a palace revolution of the officers displaced her later
murdered husband, Peter III, who was an admirer of Frederick
of Prussia (and presented to him the already conquered East Prussia); but she was inclined to diminish German influence out of
selfish dynastic considerations, and later out of patriotic motives.
In one respect, however, her patriotism was manifest: Her favorites and lovers were Russians and not Germans, and she held
a rather hostile attitude to Frederick II and Prusso-German frater-
nization with Imperial Russia.

In this she went so far as to write in one draft of her will:

For the good of the Russian Empire . . . I suggest barring from
any authority and counsel the Princes of Württemberg and communicating with them as rarely as possible and in equal degree setting aside
the counsel and advice of Germans of both sexes.[3]

However, the blunt honesty of her words could not change the
inertia favorable to the prevalence of the German element at the
court, in the diplomatic service, and in the tremendous and manifold administration of the vast country.

2 From the name of the Duke Ernst J. Biron.

3 *Sochineniya Imperatritsy Yekateriny* (Collected Works of Catherine II),
ed. Russian Imperial Acad. of Sciences, St. Petersburg, 1901–1907, Vol. XII,
p. 703.

In the intellectual field the dominant German influence was strengthened with the establishment of the Imperial Academy of Sciences in the year 1725. For a century and a half this highest body of learning was subject to a tremendous German influence, both in exact science and exploration and in philosophy, philology, and moral sciences—through members either of Baltic birth or coming from different states of Germany. Often German members pioneered in entirely new fields of scientific research. Throughout long decades physics, astronomy, mathematics were represented predominantly if not exclusively by German academicians. Geographic expeditions into Siberia and other remote parts of the Empire were also often led by Germans. Three of the best known academicians bore the family name Fuss: the mathematician and astronomer Nicholas Fuss, who entered the Russian academy in 1773 and died in 1824; his son Paul Heinrich (1797–1855), also a mathematician, and another son, the astronomer and geophysicist, Georg Albert (1806–1854). These three became the source of the sardonic, punning nickname given by Russian scholars to the Academy of Science: the *dreifüssige Akademie*, i. e., tripedal academy. It must be added that the tension between the German group among the academicians and the Russian minority frequently led to mutual charges and open clashes. During the first decades the leader of the Russian opposition was the vociferous anti-German and famous scholar Michael Lomonossov, a "rival" of Dr. Benjamin Franklin.[4]

A second very important vehicle of German influence was the University of Dorpat,[5] which was reestablished as an Imperial German University of Russia by Alexander I in 1802 upon the insistent petitions of the Baltic German gentry. This naturally supported a permanent liaison with its spiritual Fatherland Germany, whence it drew not only many holders of chairs but also German leading ideas, including, for instance, the early Pan-Germanism of Adolph Wagner. The famous German theologian

[4] Cf. P. Pekarsky, *Istoriya Imperatorskoi Akademii Nauk* (History of the Imperial Academy of Sciences), 2 vols., St. Petersburg, 1870, which contains abundant material about this rivalry between German and Russian members of the Academy.

[5] This was originally established as a German university in 1632 after the conquest of Livonia by the Swedes.

and church historian Adolf von Harnack, himself born in Dorpat, wrote in his article "Baltische Professoren":

In 1802 Alexander I had an outspoken intention to build a German university, he was far from any concealed thought of Russification. The uniqueness of the Dorpat University was achieved by the predominance of German Baltic scholars, who by their character, ways of social life, and convictions represented the type proper to Baltic Germandom— namely, the type of the *Herrenvolk*.[6]

Only in the late 1880's, with the Russification initiated by Alexander III, did this university become primarily Russian.

It cannot be denied that German representation in the Academy of Sciences and the University of Dorpat, as well as the many German professors delivering lectures in German at Russian universities like St. Petersburg, Moscow, and Kharkov, formed a body of gifted scientists extremely important not only in the exact sciences and medicine but also in the humanistic fields of history, philosophy, and law. In the humanities the German cultural influence worked mostly as a conservative factor. The Germans invited from Germany by the government or appointed from among Baltic subjects were politically the most reliable officials. This is why the number of Germans in the Army, Navy and different branches of the imperial civil service was disproportionate to their tiny percentage in the population.

Though noticeably diminished under Alexander III (1880–1894), this German dominance was felt up to the disastrous end of Czarist Russia. As long as the Baltic provinces—namely, Courland, Livonia, and Estonia—remained the strongholds of the German-speaking aristocracy and the leisure classes, there was no probability of the termination of German influence upon all phases of political and economic life of the huge country. At certain times, particularly under Nicholas 1 (1825–1855), Germans were preferred over native Russians for higher posts in diplomatic and military service.

There is an event which typifies the anti-German atmosphere created by the overwhelming predominance of Baltic and foreign Germans in the top military ranks. The famous general of artil-

[6] *Das Baltenbuch: Die baltischen Provinzen und ihre deutsche Kultur*, ed. Paul Rohrbach, Dachau, 1917, pp. 38, 40.

lery, hero in the Napoleonic Wars, and conqueror of the Caucasus, the native Russian Alexis Yermolov, was invited to the palace
of Nicholas I after one of his great victories. The Emperor, a
well known admirer of Germans, was in a very gracious mood and
asked Yermolov what reward he desired. Yermolov declined any
favor, saying he was satisfied with his regular salary and medals.
However, when the Emperor persisted he finally yielded with the
sarcastic reply: "If your Majesty insists, I would ask the favor of
being promoted to Germandom." To this the Czarist Military
Encyclopedia added that in those times, when such Germans as
Barclay, Wittgenstein, Adlerberg, Benckendorff, and Nesselrode
occupied the highest military and diplomatic posts, one had to be
an ardent Russian patriot and defender of Russian honor in order
to make such a remark to the Emperor.[7] Yermolov and Denis
Davydov attacked the Emperor, more or less *sub rosa*, for the
règne des allemands. In an outburst of bitterness Yermolov wrote
to Vorontzov: "Since 1814 I cannot understand why I am condemned to submit to constant annoyances and troubles. I detest
this cursed German *Coterie* and without any doubt I shall never
be rid of its continuous affronts." [8]

Even the native Russian and knighted general Arakcheyev, head
of the military colonies and the Emperor's right-hand man, was a
pro-Prussian reactionary showered with rich favors and honors by
Frederick William III, king of Prussia.

What the specific weight of Germandom signified in Russia
under Alexander I is conspicuously illustrated by the manufacture
of German lineage on the part of Russians in their own fatherland. A remarkable case is mentioned by Vigel.[9] The privy coun-

---

[7] *Voyennaya Entsiklopediya*, Vol. X, 1912, p. 346. Cf. also Pogodin's bio-
graphic materials about A. P. Yermolov in the review *Russkii Viestnik* (Russian
Herald), Vol. XLVI, Moscow, 1863, p. 670, in which the anecdote continues
with the question from the emperor, "Why?" Yermolov answered: "If I become a German, I can get anything I want by myself."

[8] Grand Duke Nicholas, in *L'Empereur Alexandre I*, St. Petersburg, 1912,
Vol. I, pp. 280-281, quotes from the lists of generals names like Pahlen, Essen,
Roth, Schwartz, Neidhardt, Rosen, Korff, Knorring, Oppermann, Bystrom,
Peucker, Oldekopp, Steinheil, and Kreutz to show the extent to which Ger-
mans had penetrated into the leading military posts of Russia.

[9] *Zapiski Filipa Filipovicha Vigelya* (Diaries of Philp Philipovitch Vigel),
Pt. III, Moscow, 1892, pp. 78-79.

cilor Ivan Andreyevitch Weidemeier, until the rise of Speranski a director of the chancellor's office of the Imperial State Council, was an illegitimate son of Russian parents of Greek Orthodox confession; but they had managed to give him the German-sounding family name as a lifelong talisman. This name led to a splendid and honorable career in which he was frustrated only by his own ineptitude. After Speranski replaced him as Secretary of State, this mediocrity continued his service as a member of the State council, Herr Weidemeier.

Under Nicholas I, the influence of the Germans reached its peak. The court looked askance at the Russian native nobility because of its broad participation in and friendly attitude toward the December upheaval of 1825.[10] To the end of his reign in 1855 a fight was waged clandestinely and often openly by the native nobility against German domination, including attempts to liquidate the provincial Baltic German landtags, courts, administrative offices, guilds, and schools in the three regions of Livonia, Estonia, and Courland. This fight was led by the Russian aristocrat Yurii Samarin (1819–1876), who visited Riga and the Baltic region in the 1840's. Samarin, a graduate of the Moscow University, was a nationalist writer, a rightist Hegelian, and a gifted disciple of the fathers of Russian Slavophilism, Khomiakov and Kireyevski. In a clandestine book *Letters from Riga* he demanded a sweeping change of Baltic aristocratic home rule that would level it down with the rest of Russia. He also asked for a thorough change in the attitude toward the Latvian and Estonian peasants, who were oppressed by the local German gentry. The provincial administration, headed by the Germanophile Baltic Governor General Prince Alexander Suvorov, regarded Samarin as a troublemaker and denounced him.

Nicholas read the *Letters from Riga* and on March 5, 1849, or-

[10] In the *Histoire de Russie* edited by Miliukov, Seignobos, and Eisenman, Paris, 1932, Vol. II, p. 737, a chapter on Nicholas I by Venedikt Miakotin describes the attitude of the monarch toward Count Alexander Benckendorff, chief of the corps of gendarmes and of the dread Third Division (secret police): "His Baltic origin was in the eyes of his master the highest merit. The Emperor said: 'The Russian nobles serve the State, but it is the Emperor that the German nobles serve.' Thus he underlined the kind of service which was most pleasant to him."

dered the incarceration of Samarin in the Peter-Paul fortress of St. Petersburg. Twelve days later he was brought from the fortress directly to the Emperor's private study in the Winter Palace for the cross-examination or dialogue which follows, in part:

Nicholas I: You obviously instigated the hatred of Germans against Russians. You stirred up quarrels between them instead of bringing them closer to each other. You condemn whole classes who served Russia loyally; beginning with Count Pahlen, I could enumerate some hundred and fifty devoted generals among the Germans. You want perforce to turn Germans into Russians. . . . But you also attack the government and myself because the government and I are one. True, I have heard of your attempt to separate my person from the government, but I do not recognize such a differentiation. . . . You directly aim at the government; you deliberately emphasize that from the time of Peter I down to myself we all have been surrounded by Germans and have therefore become ourselves German. Do you understand to what conclusions you have arrived? You have raised public opinion against the government; a repetition of December 14 thus has been prepared.

Samarin: I never had such intentions.

Nicholas I: I am sure that you did not have such intentions; but, nevertheless, this is where you are headed. Your book leads to something even worse than the 14th of December, because it tries to undermine confidence in the government and its links with the people by accusing it of having sacrificed Russian national interests to the Germans. . . . I sent you to the fortress so that you might think over what you have done. I did not turn you over to the court, but imprisoned you in order to save you. I did it in accordance with my despotic power against which you, I am sure, have revolted more than once.[11]

This half hostile, half paternal reprimand ended with the transfer of Samarin from St. Petersburg to Moscow. But he was not silenced by these measures; he continued his fight against the Baltic German nobility and for the Lettish and Estonian peasants up to his death. In Russian books and pamphlets prohibited in Russia and published in Germany, he polemized against Carl Schirren and Woldemar von Bock, the ideologists of German Baltic home rule.

He received a second imperial rebuke from the son of Nicholas

[11] Baron Boris E. Nolde, *Yurii Samarin i yego vryemya* (Yurii Samarin and His Time) Paris, 1926, p. 48.

I, the liberal Alexander II, who finally emancipated the Russian peasantry (1861) but remained as well disposed toward the Germans—including their half-feudal privileges—as his reactionary father. Official Petersburg sided with the Baltic Germans, and in November, 1868, Samarin was summoned to the Moscow Governor General, who conveyed to him the august dissatisfaction of Alexander with his anti-German publications.[12] Samarin refused to give up, and in December, 1868, he wrote in his "most devoted" letter to the Emperor some daring sentences, among them the following: "The Russian autocrat is bound by no rules in his actions and is not responsible to his subjects . . . but entirely apart from any constitutional provisions, there is still a moral responsibility which no power in the world can evade."

The struggle went on after the death of Samarin.[13] The Baltic Germans tightened their spiritual links with Imperial Germany after 1871, and the Russians steered toward the lessening of old Baltic German privileges granted since 1710, immediately after Peter's conquest of Livonia.

French Influence

An entirely different aura surrounded French culture and language in Russia.

First of all, in Russia as in the rest of continental Europe, French during the seventeenth and eighteenth centuries was regarded not only as the language of diplomacy and international relations but also as the language of true culture, social contacts, and good manners. Not only at imperial palaces but in every mansion of the higher nobles French was *the* language spoken and often the language written in everyday correspondence, always mixed in with the native language. (The "great" Prussian King, Frederick II, wrote all his works, including *Anti-Macchiavel*, in French—he

[12] Nolde, *op. cit.*, pp. 203-204. Cf. C. Schirren, *Livländische Antwort*, Leipzig, 1869.
[13] Friedrich Wilhelm Förster, professor of philosophy and pedagogics at the Munich University and an East Prussian by birth, felt called upon to point out the negative effect of the "German principle of mechanical coercion" on Russian and Baltic relations, in *Politische Ethik und politische Pädagogik,* Munich, 1918, pp. 236, 264, 374.

did not command literary German; and from his Berlin palace the famous Voltaire wrote in 1750: "I live here actually in France: all know our language. German is only for the horses and the soldiers.")

It is therefore little wonder that French became even more influential in Russia than in the countries to the west of her, except Poland. For long decades the aristocracy spoke and wrote French better than Russian. The same is true for political literature: for the leftist élite, Montesquieu, Mably, Rousseau, and Helvétius were teachers; for the rightists, the authorities were Bossuet, Count Joseph de Maistre, and Viscount Louis de Bonald.

The predominant role of the French culture and language in Russia scarcely needs elaboration. And if the field of our research starts with the last third of the eighteenth and the beginning of the nineteenth century we can safely say that in this period all Central and Western Europe, including Italy and Spain in the south and Scandinavia in the north, were under the same influence. In its last outgrowth French influence tended to negate the past and to carry out political reforms.

It cannot be denied that the lasting values of the creation of such geniuses as Pascal, Bossuet, Boileau, Racine, and Molière must have had also an indirect impact on the progress of morals and the extirpation of some vices in Russia as in other countries. But it cannot be asserted that French general literature always developed parallel to French political literature. True, general libertarian tendencies of Enlightenment which emanated from Racine or Molière were in full harmony with the rather tendentious writing of Voltaire; but Russia was also influenced by French writers and thinkers who were vehemently against enlightenment, against materialism, against secularity, and who regarded the whole eighteenth century as the most unfortunate dark age of history. It suffices to mention Maistre, who lived in Russia from 1803 to 1817 as a rather nominal envoy of Savoy, and who actually fought against the French Revolution and Russian liberalism and particularly against the Russian political reformer, Speranski. Hosts of French émigrés in Russia supported the "anti-French" policies of Catherine II and partly of Paul I against the new republican and antifeudal France. Paul I even granted to the refugee King of

France, Louis XVIII, together with his puppet court a royal asylum in the former ducal palace of Mitau. As for the period of Napoleonic Wars and their short-lived anti-Gallic mentality, the
French émigrés, being more or less established in Russia, were
often not less anti-French than the Russian patriots.

Still it cannot be denied that the spiritual climate of the second
half of the eighteenth century was that of the predomination of
French freethinking and of *volterianstvo*—Russian Voltairianism.
Not only the Empress Catherine II and Princess E. Dashkova, the
president of the Academy of Sciences (1743–1810), met Voltaire
and Diderot, but many representatives of the higher aristocracy
were in direct contact or correspondence with the two great Frenchmen as well as with Rousseau, Helvétius, and Alembert and the
dii minores of the Enlightenment and Encyclopedism.

Needless to say that political works of French writers beginning
with Montesquieu were imported into Russia, and many of them
were translated and published in Russian in one or several editions.
On the other hand the interest of the French to Russia was expressed in the fact that Voltaire himself with the help of some Russians wrote a *History of Russia Under Peter the Great,* and Pierre
Charles Lévesque who published in 1782–1783 five volumes of a
History of Russia. Blin de Sainmore published in 1797–1799 a History of Russia.

In Voltairianism the Russian aristocratic *fronde* and opposition
found its most conspicuous expression. It was not so much a written
Russian doctrine as an unwritten stage of mind, a typical *Zeitgeist,*
which was nourished by French political literature.

The most important and influential French political writer in
Russia was Montesquieu. His *Spirit of Laws* was published and republished. Strangely enough in the light of this French volume,
England became in the eyes of educated Russians the real pattern
of the rule of law. Montesquieu's theory of the separation of powers; the executive, legislative, and judicial, independently of
whether it was ever really materialized in English constitutional
law, became the most moderate and best camouflaged formula for
antiabsolutism. It became a secular credo of political trinity for all
those believers in oligarchic constitutionalism whose ideal was a
conservative monarchism opposed to the arbitrary autocracy of

Russian czarism. Even the popularity of the new American constitution was indebted to the unshakable faith of Russians in the
idea that the American constitution is the incarnation of the separation of powers. For Russians the father of this idea was not John
Locke but Baron de Montesquieu.

With this vogue of a modern political doctrine even the Russian
official circles, which never ceased to be autocratic, had to reckon.
Catherine II, particularly in the first period of her reign, admired
the theory of Montesquieu. In a letter to Marie Thérèse Jeoffrin
she wrote that his *Spirit of Laws* should be regarded as a breviary
of the sovereigns in so far as they had common sense.[14]

In another letter to Alembert in 1765 lauding him for his book
Sur la destruction des Jésuites en France, Catherine also emphasized how much she was obliged to Montesquieu and his great volume on *The Spirit of Laws* in compiling her Instruction. "You will
see," she wrote, "how much I plundered for the sake of my Empire President de Montesquieu, without mentioning his name. I
hope that if he will see me working hard in the other world he will
pardon me this plagiary for the benefit of twenty million men
which will be the result of it. Here, sir, an example is shown what
a destiny books of geniuses have, they serve the welfare of mankind." [15]

Voltaire was abundantly read not only in the original but also in
Russian translations. A collection of all the works of Voltaire translated into Russian was published in 1791, far away from the capital
in the province of Tambov. However, in the later years of Catherine's reign, after the suppression of the Pugachov rebellion but
particularly following the outbreak of the French Revolution, the
political weather turned strongly toward reaction, and the whole
Russian edition of Voltaire was confiscated by the government.

The Instruction of Catherine II, a compilation based on Montesquieu, Beccaria, Voltaire, and Blackstone, will always remain a
monument of political duality under European enlightenment.
Being herself an autocratic monarch, she still tried to harmonize

[14] "Son *Esprit des Lois* est le Bréviaire des Souverains pour peu qu'ils ayent
le sens commun." Quoted in *Sbornik Russkavo istoricheskavo obshchestva*
(Annals of the Russian Historical Society), Vol. I, St. Petersburg, 1867, p. 269.
[15] *Ibid.,* Vol. X, 1872, pp. 29-31.

the confused and backward positive law of her vast country with the generally recognized refined natural law of Western European culture.

One of the most important theses of her Instruction is the assertive dictum that Russia is a European power, "La Russie est une puissance européenne"—a thesis which was neglected by previous investigators of the august author. This thesis is of such great significance that in reality it remains the everlasting refrain of all rulers of Russia down to those of the Soviet Union, particularly during and after the Second World War. To a certain degree the mainly French-inspired Instruction is the first officially proclaimed shibboleth replete with the old juxtaposition of the Western or Eastern character of Russia. Catherine II pretended to be the Empress of a European, i.e., Western, Empire which had nothing in common with Asiatic despots and even with Byzantine autocracy. This idea was finally formulated by her in 1770 in her Instruction and became a stimulating slogan during the period of armed neutrality when the newly emerging United States became a factor in Russia's fight against Britain as a country on the Baltic Sea. But this alone would not explain the thesis of the European character of Russia in the Instruction. In order to understand it we have to go back to Montesquieu's *Spirit of Laws*, where we find in Book 16, in the chapter dealing with "the climate of Asia," the following: "The spirit of Europe has ever been contrary to these manners [of Tartary], and in all ages that which the people of Asia have called punishment those of Europe have deemed the most outrageous abuse." [16] And in the next chapter, entitled "A New Physical Cause of the Slavery of Asia, and of the Liberty of Europe," we find the most outspoken political contraposition between the Asiatic East and the European West based on quasi-geographic conditions. "In Asia," insists Montesquieu, "they have always had great empires; in Europe these could never subsist. Asia has larger plains; it is cut out into much more extensive divisions by mountains and seas . . . Power in Asia ought, then, to be always despotic: for if their slavery was not severe they would make a division [into different states] inconsistent with the nature of the country.

[16] Montesquieu, *The Spirit of Laws*, trans. Thomas Nugent, Colonial Press, 1900, Vol. I, p. 269.

In Europe the natural division forms many nations of a moderate extent, in which the ruling by laws is not incompatible with the maintenance of the state: on the contrary it is so favorable to it, that without this the state would fall into decay . . . It is this which has formed a genius for liberty . . . On the contrary, there reigns in Asia a servile spirit."

Catherine had to reckon with these views of her adored teacher, and she therefore rendered a rather confused explanation of her thesis of the European character of Russia. This is clearly demonstrated by the following Observations:

> The Alterations which Peter the Great undertook in Russia succeeded with the greater ease, because the Manners, which prevailed at that time, and had been introduced amongst us by a Mixture of different Nations, and the Conquest of foreign Territories, were quite unsuitable to the Climate. Peter the First, by introducing the Manners and Customs of Europe among the European People in his Dominions, found at that time such means as even he himself was not sanguine enough to expect.[17]

In so far, however, as inner legislative reforms in the fields of administration, criminal law, taxation, and agriculture, including serfdom, are concerned the Instruction was primarily meant as a basis for remaking the old anachronistic Russian law. Montesquieu, despite his libertarian views on serfdom, was unable to stop Catherine from extending serfdom to Ukraine in 1783 or from further strengthening the privileges of the landed gentry, particularly after the suppression of the Pugachov peasants' upheaval. Verily, Pushkin was right in calling the hypocritical Empress the "Tartufe in gown and crown."

Nevertheless, in the Instruction French influence found its most conspicuous expression with all the inconsistencies of Catherine II. This book became the official credo and the natural-law basis for the works of the Legislative Commission. Catherine, the autocrat of Imperial Russia, continued to work not on the basis of an autocratic doctrine. Such doctrines had existed in Russia in the times of Peter the Great. The Hobbeses and Filmers of old Russia

[17] Cf. *Documents of Catherine the Great: The Correspondence with Voltaire and the Instruction of 1767 in the English Text of 1768*, ed. W. F. Reddaway, Cambridge, 1931, p. 216.

such as Kotoshikhin and Theophan Prokopovitch were rejected by the Empress. Catherine's Instruction, a radical subversive book prohibited in monarchic France under the agonizing *ancien régime* of Louis XVI, remained the official breviary of Russian imperial legislation. All this, of course, did not give any better chance for real domestic political reform. The English brand is not the only hypocrisy in the world; Russian hypocrisy in French and American libertarian style during Catherine and Alexander I was no less pronounced.

Not only did Catherine reject the reform in the spirit of an aristocratic constitution proposed by Count Panin, but any real reform of a legislative character was reduced almost to zero after the dissolution of the Legislative Commission, excused as a necessary preparation for the Second Russo-Turkish War.

The enlightened Empress, after all her good intentions, shifted slowly and steadily backward with the ripening and development of the French Revolution and the necessity to suppress the Pugachov peasant rebellion. Steps were taken to stop the publishing of liberal literature. Radishchev, the first noble radical and friend of the young United States, was arrested and banished to Siberia. The books and the printing of the liberal and Masonic publishers, Novikov and Schwarz, were confiscated and the publishing houses closed. Even the further distribution of the Instruction was limited to the administrative and judicial bodies, and private persons were forbidden to use it for copying and reading.[18] Later, in 1795, Catherine II went so far as to blame the great French Encyclopedia for the entire French Revolution. "Helvétius and Alembert, said she, confessed to the late Prussian King that the Encyclopedia had only two aims: first, to exterminate the Christian religion and, second, to abolish the royal power. Already in 1777 this was mentioned." [19]

Nevertheless, French and English influence could not be stopped

[18] The writer owns a copy of the luxurious leather-bound edition of the Instruction printed in St. Petersburg in 1770 in four languages, Russian, French, German, and Latin, on the back of which appears: "Property of the Colomna merchant Vassily . . ." This shows that the Instruction was read and even owned by nonaristocratic liberally minded merchants of that time. Colomna is a provincial town of the Moscow district.

[19] Cf. Paul Miliukov, *Ocherki po istorii russkoi kultury* (Essays on the History of Russian Culture), Vol. III, Paris, 1930, p. 343.

even under the successors of Catherine; and with the ascent of her grandson, Alexander I, to the throne in 1801 French and partly English influence became even more significant.

As to the receptiveness of Russia toward French culture down to October, 1917, it seemingly was so manifold and so firmly rooted that it easily survived the hostility of the Russian aristocracy under Catherine II against the "poison of the French Revolution" and later, in Alexander's reign, against Napoleon before and after the invasion in Russia.

Under Alexander I, French was the language of the Russian Ministry of Foreign Affairs. Official memoranda were often written in French, the Russian text being merely a translation. Of the three imperial theaters in St. Petersburg, the Mikhailovsky, to the time of Nicholas II, was a French theater frequented only by French-speaking Russians.

On the extent to which a French language and culture were developed in the capitals of the Empire as late as the 1840's, an American engineer gives interesting testimony. In 1842, on the invitation of Czar Nicholas I, Major George Washington Whistler went to Russia with equipment furnished by the American firm of Winans, Harrison & Eastwick, to construct the first railroad in Russia joining the two capitals, St. Petersburg and Moscow.[20] His son James received his first systematic schooling in the Imperial Academy of Fine Arts. "He reveled," says Parry, "in the sound of the fluent French with which the Czar's courtiers and officers sprinkled their Russian talk—it was in the St. Petersburg of the 1840's that he learned the faultless French with which to dazzle his later world of London and to appear as a Gallicized American in Paris." [21]

A special chapter could be dedicated to the French emigrants in Russia from the end of the reign of Catherine II down to Alexander I. In this period, under the leadership of Armand, Duke of Richelieu—one of the highest aristocrats of France, who fled to Russia in 1790 with his friend Count Louis A. de Langeron—the whole newly conquered south, including the Crimea, and the en-

[20] To be exact, "Nicholas' Railroad" was the second Russian railroad. The first was a luxurious toy of some thirty kilometers connecting St. Petersburg with the magnificent imperial resort and cluster of palaces Tsarskoye Selo.

[21] Albert Parry, *Whistler's Father*, N.Y., 1939, p. xi.

tire northern coast of the Black Sea were opened to sea trade. Richelieu returned a few times to France and Europe for military and family reasons. However, with the help of a host of his earlier fellow émigrés, he dedicated himself to an outstanding work which brought about an entire change in, or rather the emergence of, regular Russian international commerce. New ports and cities were built, among them Odessa, which became the most important, shifting to a remarkable extent the direction of previous sea export through the largely icebound harbors of the Baltic Sea and its gulfs. The Ukraine, the Black Sea regions, and southern Poland, which had sent their hemp, flax, grain, wool, hides, and leather via Danzig and the Russian Baltic ports, now switched to Odessa and the other Black Sea ports. Despite Napoleon's continental system, pressed upon Russia, Odessa grew from almost nothing in 1802 to 35,000 population in 1813. Richelieu established a few French colonies in southern Russia. He also developed education, with the help of Abbé Nichol. The French Count Emmanuel Saint-Priest established the commercial court in Odessa, and the French architect Thomas de Thomon was helpful in planning cities and erecting public buildings, theaters, and so on. Richelieu was surrounded by many French emigrants for the political reliability of whom he took full responsibility before the Russian authorities during Napoleon's invasion of Russia. Many of the emigrants served as Russian officers against Napoleon.

Langeron, after 1815, continued the outstanding work of his friend Richelieu. Under him Odessa received the rights of a free port (1818), and a French newspaper appeared, the *Messager de la Russie méridionale*. The economic prosperity of the Black Sea region in the nineteenth century is to a very large extent due to the French émigrés in Russia.

The Russian novelist Turgenev, in 1878, described the French cultural influence upon Russia as follows:

Speaking here in the name of my compatriots . . . I shall limit myself to a significant connection which will clarify some enduring relations between our two peoples and the great influence which the genius of France has constantly exerted upon Russia. I will take three dates chosen at intervals of one hundred years. Two hundred years ago, in 1678, we did not yet have a national literature. Our books were written

in the Old Slavonic, and Russia, with good reason, could consider herself among the half-civilized nations, part European, part Asiatic.
Shortly before this year, Czar Alexis, already touched by the breath of
civilization, had built a theater in the Kremlin where performances of
humorous dramas of the mystery-play variety were given in the manner
of the Italian opera *Orfeo*. This theater, it is true, was closed after his
death; but one of the first plays performed at its restoration was your
Molière's *Le Médecin malgré lui*, presumably translated by the Grand
Duchess Sophia, daughter of Czar Alexis and regent of Russia during
the minority of her younger brother, who was to become Peter the
Great. Doubtless the audience at that time saw only the comedian in
the creator of *Le Misanthrope*, but we Russians are happy to have met
this great name at the dawn of our civilization. One hundred years
later, when our literature first dared to exist, in 1778, the author of
our first really original comedies, von Vizine, attended the celebration
for Voltaire at the Comédie-Française in Paris, and described the event
in a lavish public letter which revealed the most enthusiastic admiration
for the Patriarch of Ferney, then the master and model of our literature and that of all Europe. One hundred years flowed by again, and as
Voltaire had followed Molière, so Victor Hugo followed Voltaire. Russian letters finally came to life; they acquired rights of citizenship in
Europe. We can summon up before you, not without pride, names
which are no longer unknown to you, those of Gogol and Karamzin,
of the poets Pushkin and Lermontov; you have been willing to invite
several Russian writers to the International Congress of Literature. Two
centuries ago, without too much comprehension, we were proceeding
in your direction; one century ago, we were your disciples; today, you
accept us as colleagues, and it is indeed a singular and unusual fact in
the history of Russia that a simple and unassuming writer who is neither
soldier nor statesman, who has no rank in the official hierarchy, has the
honor to speak before you in the name of his country, to salute Paris and
France, those two promulgators of great thoughts and generous aspirations.[22]

The revolutions in France, particularly those of 1830, 1848, and
1871, gave much food for thought to the various Russian strata of
the non-satisfied. In the middle of the nineteenth century democrats and utopians like Tocqueville, Saint-Simon, Fourier, and

[22] Ivan Turgenev, To the International Congress of Literature, Paris, printed
in *Le Temps*, June, 1878, and reproduced in Turgenev, *Russkiye Propileyi*
(Russian Propylaea), Vol. III, Moscow, 1916, p. 253.

Proudhon became the spiritual guides. And until the beginning of the 1880's French orientation was so powerful that it held its ground against the frank and often cynical pro-Germanism of the government and the upper strata. And this so much so that under Alexander III the final reorientation of Russia against Germany and toward France, with a new Franco-Russian alliance, could be managed. To the end of the century and the first years of the twentieth century pro-German orientation in Russia became identical with reaction, while French, English, and particularly American alignments were characteristic of liberal thinking.

English Influence

The third sphere of foreign cultural influence—that of the English-speaking nations—was much more limited than the German and the French.

Direct contacts with England had been made as far back as Ivan the Terrible; English and Scottish merchants were living in the Niemeckaya Sloboda—the foreign quarter—of Moscow before Peter the Great. Some English and Scottish officers, both military and naval, were invited into the Russian imperial service, trade connections became well rooted, Russian *manufacturas* were sometimes built under English guidance, and invitations extended to English and later American engineers and other experts. And still the influence of English was limited to the highest aristocracy and the relatively small stratum connected with the navy and maritime trade. Patrick Gordon came to Russia in 1661, under Alexis, the father of Peter the Great, as a military expert. He served the father and the son, particularly in modernizing Peter's army. Four Bruces were of importance in Russian history. Roman Bruce, born in Russia in 1668, a son of a Scottish emigrant, William Bruce, was the first commandant of newly created St. Petersburg (in 1703) and was very active in defending it against Swedish onslaughts; he was also the builder of the St. Petersburg Fortress upon the Neva. His brother James later elevated to the rank of count, was the head of the Russian artillery in the historic victory of Poltava (1709) over the Swedish King, Charles XII. He was the best educated man of Peter's Russia, with a knowledge not only of

strategy but of astronomy and chemistry; besides, he was a translator of books. The second James Bruce, born in 1742, was a grandson of Roman. He led Catherine's wars against Turkey and Sweden. Lastly, a second cousin of the count entered Russian military
service in 1710 and left *Memoirs of Peter Henry Bruce, containing
an account of his travels in Germany, Russia, Tartary, Turkey, the
New Indies* (Leipzig, 1784).[23] The founder of the first Naval Academy in 1713, and its first teacher was an Englishman, Farwarson
(Farquharson?), who entered Russian service in 1698. Later, James
Bruce, brother of Roman, directed the schools of navigation, artillery, and military engineering.

John Paul Jones, the American naval officer, in December, 1787,
accepted an invitation from Catherine II to enter the Russian navy,
and lived for a time in Cronstadt. However, the numerous English
officers in the Russian Baltic navy declared that they regarded him
as a sworn enemy of England; under no circumstances would they
serve under him or with him. He was therefore assigned by imperial
order as a rear admiral to the Black Sea navy, which was then already
participating in the second war with Turkey (1787–1791). In May,
1788, he took command of a squadron of fourteen sailing ships.
According to Russian sources he contributed greatly to the annihilation of the Turkish fleet at Ochakov in June; but the victory
was officially ascribed to Prince Nassau-Siegen. Prince Potemkin,
the field marshal under whose command he served, even concealed the Jones's official report concerning the battle. He was
finally undermined by all these intrigues and left St. Petersburg—
and Russia—in September, 1789.[24]

We could continue enumerating English personages employed
in the Russian imperial military, civil, and educational service. But
they still would be outnumbered by Germans and French. And
these personal ties could not raise English culture to a level of

[23] P. Pekarski, *Nauka i literatura pri Petre Velikom* (Science and Literature
under Peter the Great), 2 vols., 1862. The Russian Brockhaus Encyclopedia,
Vol. III. Ernest J. Simmons, *English Literature and Culture in Russia, 1553–
1840*, Cambridge, Mass., 1935, the very interesting early chapters of which
give a report of cultural and political influences, but it does not go farther than
1762.

[24] *Voyennaya Entsiklopediya* (Military Encyclopedia), Vol. IX, St. Petersburg, 1912, p. 87.

influence comparable to that of German and French.

Of the three modern foreign languages only German and French were obligatory subjects in the curricula of all high schools—both

A UKASE TO OUR ADMIRALTIES COLLEGE

The Captain-Commodore Paul Jones is to be received into our service. Most graciously we have bestowed upon him a fleet captaincy with the rank of a major general and authorized his assignment to our Black Sea fleet. On this, our ukase has been issued to General Field Marshal Prince Potemkin of Tauris.

Catherine

At St. Petersburg,
The 15th of February, 1788

classic gymnasia and scientific high schools—until the fall of czarism. As to the cadet corps, it is noticeable that in the corps opened by Empress Anne two hundred forty-five Russian cadets took the following language courses in 1733: German, 237 cadets; French, 110; Russian, 18; Latin, 15.[25]

But later the same was true for all twenty-odd cadet corps of imperial Russia. Only in the Naval Academy and the Naval Cadet School and in the newly established commercial high schools in the nineteenth century was English not discriminated against; it became equally obligatory with German and French. Not less remarkable is the fact that according to Russian imperial code the full knowledge of English was obligatory for all seamen, beginning with the steersman's degrees.

Nevertheless, it cannot be denied that English, although incomparably less popular than the two other Western languages, was spoken and, more commonly, read by the highest aristocracy, among whom there was always a certain number of Anglophiles and admirers of the English constitutional law and liberal traditions as well as scholars who sought economic, juridical, and pedagogic knowledge in the works of English writers.

The masonic lodges appeared in Russia in the 1730's. The first lodges were in St. Petersburg and the Baltic region (Riga and Mitau). We know that in 1731 the Grand Master of the London Lodge (Lord Lowell?) appointed Captain John Philips provincial Grand Master of Russia; but Philips could not be regarded as the founder of Russian Masonry, because the order was originally established only for Britons living in Russia. Nine years later, in 1740, the English Grand Lodge ordained as Grand Master of Russia an Englishman, James Keith, who was a general in Russian service. It was then that the first Russians started to enter Masonry, and therefore the Russian brothers regarded Keith as the founder of Russian Masonry. With the high tide of German influence, Russian lodges mostly assumed German patterns.[26] The language of the residential lodges became predominantly German, and therefore Russian brothers had to learn German in order to take part in ceremonies, discussions, and activities. This was true for ten lodges of the "Astrea" and the Union of the Great Provincial Lodge. However, in others German and Russian were used. There

[25] Paul Miliukov, *op. cit.*, p. 342.
[26] See the symposium *Masonstvo v yego proshlom i nastoyashchem* (Masonry in Its Past and Present), 2 vols., Moscow, 1914–1915, Vol. II, pp. 64-65.

is no doubt that, despite the wide spread of German language and culture, the political thought of Russia under Catherine II and Alexander I was under the influence of French and English including American publicists and authors.[27]

Russian Masonry became more firmly established a few decades later, after the accession of Catherine II. An outstanding Mason was Ivan Yelagin, a historian and a high government official. He was the president of the St. Petersburg Lodge of the English system, established in 1770. In 1772 he received the diploma of "Provincial Grand Master of All Russian lodges" from the Grand Master of England, Henry Somerset, Duke of Beaufort.[28] He introduced in 1777 the Swedish-English system of strong observance.

Masonry, overwhelmingly of English character, was one of the first manifestations of Russian idealism. The mystic and religious romanticism of Freemasonry represented the antipode of materialism and the specific Russian Voltairianism. Russian Masonry found in Yelagin the father of early primitive Slavophilism, while materialism became connected with Westernism. Catherine herself was strictly antimasonic and fought against Masonry both as a ruler and as a writer, despite her moderate aristocratic Anglomania. Paul I here as in all other relations was in opposition to his mother, even accepting membership in the order according to some testimony.

English influence became particularly important for Russia in political and philosophic literature as well as in economic and agricultural research. Not only were Bacon, Locke, Blackstone, Benjamin Franklin, Adam Smith, Alexander Hamilton, and Bentham translated into Russian, but very often they were read in German or French translations. As has been shown by some writers, the main ideas of Adam Smith's *Wealth of Nations* were known in Russia prior to 1776, when it was first published in England.[29] Two graduates of the Moscow University, Simon Desnitski and Ivan Tretyakov, were sent in 1761 by Catherine II to the University of

[27] Maxim Kovalevski, "Bor'ba nemeckavo vliyaniya s francuzskim" (The Rivalry Between German and French Influence), in the monthly review *Vestnik Yevropy*, Oct. 1915, p. 128.

[28] See the symposium *Masonstvo, etc., loc. cit.*

[29] J. F. Normano, *The Spirit of Russian Economics*, N.Y., 1945, p. 16.

Glasgow to study law and mathematics; but both dedicated themselves entirely to law, then studied under Adam Smith and achieved the degree of *doctor legum*.

Desnitski was not long under the tutorship of Adam Smith, who left Glasgow in February, 1764, for France, and he concentrated on Smith's views on ethics, natural law, and politics. Tretyakov was interested mainly in Smith's economic doctrine, and published in 1772 a *Consideration of the Cause of Abundance and a Slow Enrichening of the State in Ancient as Well as Modern Nations*, based on his Glasgow notes. Four years later the famous *Wealth of Nations* appeared; the Russian translation was not issued until 1802–1806, but in the meantime Sartorius' German translation was widely read in Russia.[30]

After six years of study the two young scholars returned to Moscow in 1767, on the eve of Catherine's convocation of the Legislative Commission after completing her Instruction. According to Moroshkin, Desnitski in particular came back to Russia "full of scholarship and England." In their absence Karl Langer, an ardent admirer of John Locke, had taught law and politics at the Moscow University. After their return they both became professors of the University: Tretyakov in history of Roman and natural law, Desnitski in Roman and Russian positive law. Later, Blackstone's *Commentaries* were translated by Desnitski in 1780–1782 with his remarks "upon the august order of the great legislatress of all the Russias."

English thought influenced not only Russians who personally studied in England or traveled to England and the young United States, but others who were reared in French culture and even in German universities.

One detail is of great importance. It is well known that in the first years of the nineteenth century the Göttingen University became the spiritual center for the élite of foreign students, particularly Russian. In 1801 two-thirds of its seven hundred students were from outside Germany. The university, however, was far from promoting German nationalist doctrines. This was so because

[30] N. M. Korkunov, *Istoriya filosofii prava* (History of Legal Philosophy), St. Petersburg, 1898, pp. 290-295.

Göttingen was in Hanover, which was bound to England through a common ruler. Therefore, the university became, strangely enough, the conductor of English culture in addition to German.

УЧЕНІЕ

добродушнаго

РИХАРДА.

ВЪ Санктпетербургѣ

Печатано въ вольной типографіи у Карла
Шнора 1784 года

Benjamin Franklin's *Poor Richard's Almanack* appeared at Paris under the title, *La Science du Bonhomme Richard,* and was reissued at St. Petersburg in French and Russian (with a corresponding title, as shown above) in 1784.

Professor Sartorius read the *Wealth of Nations,* and through his mediation some later Decembrists and Russian writers became admirers of England in general and of its economic teachings in particular. Another professor, Heeren, delivered lectures on political, social, and administrative institutions of England, France, and the United States.[31]

Count Nicholas Mordvinov, son of an admiral and himself in

ОТРЫВОКЪ

изъ

ЗАПИСОКЪ

ФРАНКЛИНОВЫХЪ

Съ присовокупленіемъ

Краткаго описанія его жизни

и

нѣкоторыхъ его сочиненій,

Перевелъ съ Французскаго
А. Т.

МОСКВА.
Въ Университетской Типографіи,
у Ридигера и Клаудія.
1799.

Title page of the first volume of Franklin's collected works in Russian (Moscow, 1799), reading as follows: "Excerpts from Franklin's Notes and a Short Description of His Life and Some of His Works, translated from the French by A.T. [Andrei Turgenev]."

the navy for a time, was sent to England in 1774 to complete his naval education and developed a sympathy for British ideas and institutions. In 1802, under Alexander I, he became Minister of the Navy. He was very well educated in economics and was a follower of Adam Smith. In Russia, both in the Department of Economy of the State Council and as a president of the Free Economic Society, he defended protectionism and tended to promote a de-

[31] Kovalevsky, *op. cit.*, p. 135.

gree of industrialization. By some Russian economists he was re-
garded as the Alexander Hamilton of Russia;[32] but, like Catherine
II, he regarded the landed nobility as the proper administrator of
Russian economy.

He was also for a moderate and steady emancipation of serfs;
but when Nicholas Turgenev, an enthusiastic advocate of the
sweeping abolition of serfdom, asked whether he would approve of
that reform he answered: "No, we have to begin with the throne
and not with the serfs; the Russian proverb says a staircase must be
swept from above."[33] Politically he was close to the Decembrist
reformers.

Mordvinov corresponded on a high scholarly level with Jeremy
Bentham. They were introduced by Jeremy's brother, Samuel Bentham, who returned to England after having been a steward of the
estates of Prince Grigory Potiomkin in White Russia. In 1806
Mordvinov quitted his civil service, shifting his interest to self-
government. His intention was "to spread the light which ema-
nates from the works of Bentham," for which he had already collected some money. One of his highest dreams, he wrote to Samuel
Bentham, was

to settle in England, and once there I want to be the acquaintance of
your brother. *In my eyes he is one of the four geniuses who did and will
do the utmost for the happiness of mankind—Bacon, Newton, Smith
and Bentham: every one a founder of a new science, every one a creator.*

This admiration for English culture, civilization, and creativeness existed long in Russia after the death of Mordvinov. It goes
without saying that friendliness toward English culture was not
diminished by the American Revolution. Cromwell and Washington, Newton and Franklin, Adam Smith and Hamilton were personalities who in the eyes of the Russian élite held the English-
speaking peoples together, in spite of temporary tensions.
Significantly enough, Mordvinov was a shareholder and a leading
figure in the Russian-American Trade Company, and so were some
Decembrists, as we will see.

[32] Cf. Normano, *op. cit.*, pp. 21-23.
[33] N. I. Turgenev, *Rossiya i Russkiye* (Russia and the Russians), St. Petersburg, 1915, p. 90.

From 1825 through the 1850's—the years of reaction, equivalent to the reign of Nicholas I—English and French influence remained dominant in politics while German culture was most influential in philosophy. With the epoch of the Great Reforms under Alexander II (1860–1865) and in the liberal decade ended by his violent death (1881) English and French influence overwhelmed the German.

After 1881 two wings of Russian political thought took on a German slant. These were the extreme right—the monarchists, Slavophiles, and nationalist conservatives—and the leftists of "legal" and illegal Marxism. For the first the polestar was Prussianism, with prevalence of the state over the individual citizen, limited self-government, if any, and Hegel as the leading philosopher. For the second camp, the final ideal and goal was the organization of the proletariat on the basis of class-consciousness and class struggle, maximal concessions for welfare in the legal frames of capitalism, democracy as the best way to socialism—with Hegel as the leading philosopher. True, for the rightist Germans and Russians Hegel was the philosopher of royal absolutism, of the Absolute Idea incarnated in different leading nations, of "the state as the reality of the moral idea," while for the leftist Germans and Russians, including the Marxist social democrats, Hegel was the philosopher of dialectics and of freedom as the perceived necessity.

English culture, particularly in economic, political, and jural thinking, was prevalent during the reforms of Alexander II; and it became more so after 1905 with the appearance of Russian constitutionalism, among the moderate and radical democrats of idealist and non-Marxian mentality. It is characteristic that in this sequence of periods and groups all three circles of influence—German, French, and English—had their ups and downs from Peter the Great to Stalin. Some leading personalities were of longer endurance, some of shorter, and some stars declined in order to reappear later.

A point in case is Jeremy Bentham with all his encyclopedic creativeness from abstract philosophy through civil, criminal, constitutional, and international law to political economy. The first of Bentham's writings in Russian translation appeared in 1804 in the official review of the Ministry of the Interior, *St. Peterburgski*

Journal. These were articles on the knowledge of laws, on the advantage of education, on security, etc. In 1805–1811, by order of Emperor Alexander I and with the participation of Etienne Dumont and Speranski, three volumes of his works in Dumont's French edition were translated and published; they were the *Traités de législation, civile et pénale.* In 1860 a translation of Bentham's work on the judiciary system appeared. The first volume of the *Selected Works of Jeremy Bentham* appeared in 1867, including the *Introduction to the Principles of Morals and Legislation* in Bowring's edition as well as the *Principles of the Civil Code* and *Principles of the Penal Code.*

There has been a relatively weighty literature on Bentham published in Russia, including important works by legal and political philosophers like Boris Chicherin (*History of Political Doctrines*), Yarosh (*Jeremy Bentham and His Relation to Natural Law*, Kharkov, 1886) and the very learned and thorough Peter Pokrovski (*Bentham and His Time*, Petrograd, 1916—covering Bentham's entire system).

We will discover in the coming chapters the specific weight of American thought in Russia as a branch of English culture.

II *Catherine II, and the Emergence of the United States*

W<small>E HAVE TRIED TO DESCRIBE THE ATMOSPHERE OF IMPERIAL</small> Russia in the last three decades of the eighteenth century in so far as it was influenced by the three leading cultures of the West. If it was ever true that "the Enlightenment began in complacency and ended in fear," [1] it is especially true for the Catherinian period of Russian history. Still, in general we may say that the soil was well prepared in Russia of Catherine II and Alexander I for the ideas of the American Revolution, particularly for its political ideas and views on constitutional law. This cannot be doubted if we consider that the early authorities and forerunners of the American Revolution were approximately identical with the inspirers of Western European Revolution. If there are some differences they are conditioned by the lesser radicalism of young America and England in religion, ethics, and philosophy. The English and American revolutions emanated from a different social and spiritual milieu with a certain prevalence of the middle-class Roundheads over the Cavaliers, while in the later, French Revolution and the rebellious opposition of Catherine's Russia the repentant and disappointed aristocrats and not the bourgeois were the instigators. From Cromwell to Jefferson revolution in England and America was freer from aristocratic skepticism and atheism than the French and Russian political philosophies.

Despite the fact that France was incomparably higher in culture, civilization, and economics than Russia of the eighteenth century, the revolutionary spirit in both countries did often exist in approximately the same social strata. These were the disappointed aristocracy inclined to a full negation of the bases of their previous social being, to religious skepticism if not atheism, and to a relative independence of and negligence toward all kinds of tradition, and

[1] Herbert W. Schneider, A *History of American Philosophy*, N.Y., 1946, p. 37.

the intelligentsia. The intelligentsia could have been human splinters from the declassified families of the lower aristocracy or sons
of the middle class, merchants or lower clergy and bureaucracy.
The ramifications and nuances were so complex and so delicate that
no exact Marxist approach to this specific phenomenon would
give any definite clue to their origin, although it must be admitted
that long after Catherine II a Russian bourgeoisie developed as a
political factor. Even as late as in the upheaval of 1825 ideals defended in the West mainly by the middle class were courageously
fought for by representatives of the privileged aristocracy.

The Empress Catherine and her immediate environment became less liberal as those doctrines were materialized which she at
first had hailed enthusiastically.

As for America it should be taken into consideration that the
official commanding circles of Russia perceived the American "colonies" first of all in the lines of foreign and not of domestic policy.
They belonged to England, they were her rich "provinces" in
America. Russia itself, an empire of tremendous expansion, fighting two wars with Turkey, conquering the shores of the Black Sea,
parts of Turkey, and the half-independent Crimea, trying to get
the most important Asiatic regions and rounding out its expansion
to the west—in the Ukraine, White Russia, and the Baltic regions
of Courland and Finland—it might be expected to be far from
sympathetic toward the secession of the American colonies from
their British motherland. Basically to official Russia the Americans
would be rebels against their legal rulers.

This essentially negative attitude toward young America was
changed only by foreign policy considerations. In the first years of
Catherine's reign the relations between England and Russia were
excellent. In 1766 a commercial treaty was concluded between the
countries. The hostility between France and England was advantageous for Russia, and the Anglo-French war during the fight for
American independence was regarded as favoring the Russian expansion in Europe and Asia.

Nevertheless, Catherine blamed England for her inability to retain her American colonies and to punish her rebels. In different
letters during the years 1775–1779 she made a series of frank statements about the matter. The successful suppression of the Puga-

chov peasants' rebellion partly explained her complacency. Although professionally, as we have remarked, on the side of the British ruler against his non-abiding subjects in the overseas dependencies, she was politically educated enough to understand that the rebellious Americans with their sober bourgeois leadership had a better chance of reaching independence than her closest neighbors, the Poles and the Courlanders, led by their unreliable aristocrats.

One of Catherine's most clever and prophetic remarks was in a letter to Madame Bielke dated June 30, 1775:

The English king is an excellent citizen, a good husband, a good father and brother. Such a man will never consider it luck to lose a sister of no value.[2] I will wager he is mourning more over the loss of his sister than over the defeat of his troops in America. You know that his excellent citizens feel themselves very much bored and that often they even . . . But we shall do better not to finish. I wish from the depths of my heart that my friends, the English, should come to terms with their American colonies. But as so many of my prophecies have materialized I am afraid that I shall live to see America break away from Europe.[3]

In April, 1778, Catherine wrote to this same lady:

As to your friends the English, one wants to tell them what Molière so often repeated to George Dandin: "Vous l'avez voulu—You have asked for it, George Dandin."

Hinting at the domestic democratic tensions, the letters of Junius and the Wilkes trial, she added:

Those men always do things which do not enter the mind of anybody. For fifteen years they have been on the wrong road.

In June, 1778, she wrote in part to Baron Grimm:

England has lost her most happy and flourishing stage; when one recalls the brilliant situation in which this kingdom was nineteen years ago and her present case, one's heart bleeds! This constitution, this government which was regarded as the best in Europe, and which—

[2] Caroline Matilda, Queen of Denmark, who had recently died.
[3] *Sbornik Russkavo istoricheskavo obshchestva*, Vol. XXVII, St. Petersburg, 1880, p. 44.

what is worse—does not dare to punish the guilty! All her deliberations, her arrangements, even her projects are made public, and the rebels retard everything by making all steps of the government difficult; this makes one gnash his teeth, and all is lost if you think about it. . . . George II and his predecessors acted differently; it is not, therefore, the form but the actors that are at fault.[4]

About the "wool merchants" (Britons fighting in America and Europe) Catherine wrote to Grimm on July 5, 1779:

Let us say something about the cloth-merchants: it seems to me they never have been in a more inconvenient and vexing situation; they have now on their necks a double squabble which must render them more compliant, particularly if they are going finally to understand that for long years they were doing nothing else than stumble.[5]

And in December, 1781, she writes to the same person about the king of England:

My brother, the woolen-draper, tried all the thirty-six mishaps of the harlequin; it is good at least not to succumb after it. That's all there is to say about it.[6]

And finally on June 7, 1778, Catherine writes to an unknown lady:

But I tremble about what you are telling me concerning England. How did that happen? You believed once it had the best government in Europe and now you think it has the worst. I cannot agree with your last assertion. In wrong hands all becomes wrong. Franklin and Deane for having said what the things really were when they stayed in England did by no means deserve to be hanged. They must have been heard and acted upon *en anglais*, there was no necessity to provoke the Americans in order to tip the scales in favor of the king. This I say in short and for all times.[7]

Armed neutrality was a stage in the very clever foreign policy of Catherine. The most severe critique of England, expressed in the remarks just quoted, was the spiritual background against which Catherine's attitude toward England became negative and grew rapidly more and more so. To the extent that the criticism involved indirectly a positive attitude first toward the colonies and after

---

[4] *Sbornik, etc.,* Vol. XXIII, 1878, pp. 92-93.   [5] *Ibid.,* p. 149.
[6] *Ibid.,* p. 224.   [7] *Ibid.,* Vol. XXVII, pp. 153-154.

1776 toward the United States, it is worth while to dwell on it.

This anti-British and pro-American trend of Catherine's Russia had behind it important considerations of an economic and particularly a commercial character. In her Instruction she defends freedom of trade and particularly of maritime trade. Recognizing that agriculture is the most important branch of economics, she nevertheless recognizes that the second branch is *manufacture*, which must be based on the country's own production. The trade ought to be free, and no country should consent to sell all its commodities to only one nation under the pretext that this will purchase them at a certain price. The true principle of a state is not to shut off any nation from its commerce except for very important reasons. From these general considerations Catherine turns toward England, criticizes its "jealous attitude" in trade and its unwillingness to bind itself to other nations with trade treaties, and makes the following complaint:

England prohibits the Exportation of her wool: she has ordained Coals to be imported to the capital by sea; . . . she obliges Ships, which trade from her colonies in America into Europe, to anchor first in no other harbours than those of England.[8]

As time passed and the play of opposites grew, this undertone became more audible and articulate. Russia's economic interest, which required the Black Sea ports through which the whole agricultural production but particularly wheat of the fertile south-central Russia and the Ukraine could be shipped, led to cooperation and partly to competition with England. But there is no doubt that in her criticism of the British sea trade the first roots of her later idea of armed neutrality can be discovered. According to the dominating opinion it was Count Nikita Panin who drafted the project of armed neutrality. This act granting freedom of sea trade to neutral countries during the American Revolution was supported by France and Spain—against Britain. The act became favorable

[8] Instruction, chap. xiii, par. 321. I have made a slight correction in the 1768 translation which is here wrong. This is virtually the only place where Catherine mentions the American colonies, but it must be admitted that the indirect and slight reproach is made in a way which was not repugnant to Russia's good relations with Britain. The writing of the Instruction was completed in July, 1767, except for some additions.

to the United States. Denmark, Sweden, Prussia, Austria, Portugal, and the Kingdom of the Two Sicilies joined the alliance.

In order to understand the attitude of some countries to the American-British conflict, which involved not only interests but even more ideologies and political regimes, the lines which divide internal policies from foreign policies must be kept in mind.

Prerevolutionary France of Louis XVI and imperial Russia of Catherine II are cases in point. Both countries were influenced, in their attitude toward the American Revolution, by considerations of foreign politics. This was overwhelmingly true of France, where the sympathy in conservative and monarchistic circles for the United States was based on hatred of England. France could not forget the Seven Years' War, which had ended with the terrific defeat of her navy and the loss of Canada. To weaken England was the goal, for which internal principles were sacrificed. Louis XVI, by joining the thirteen colonies in their war against England, recognized not only the secession of the rebellious colonies but also the Declaration of Independence of 1776, in which the right of the people to alter or to abolish a form of government is set forth. The king of a France based on serfdom gave his assent to the "self-evident" truth that "all men are created equal." The famous Mirabeau said of the Declaration of Philadelphia:

The great manifesto of the American United States was welcomed here by everyone with enthusiasm. . . . But I am asking myself, Did the governments which joined them in fighting England dare to read all this manifesto and, having read it through, did they turn to their conscience? I ask, Is there at present in Europe even one single government, except Switzerland, Holland, and the British Isles, which according to this declaration would not have to be ousted?

A contemporary pamphlet printed in England addressed itself to the French King Louis XVI as follows:

Imprudent king! You look to arms to support the independence of America and the principles proclaimed by the Congress. There is a power which at present rises over the law, the power of ambitious thinking. It provoked a revolution in America *and perhaps it prepares one in France.*[9]

[9] Cf. Félix Rocquain, L'Esprit révolutionnaire avant la révolution (1715–1798) Paris, 1878, pp. 370-371.

Certain conservatives and friends of the old regime, like Abbé Raynal, blamed the French government for its pro-American decision; nevertheless Louis XVI was inconsistent enough to receive Dr. Benjamin Franklin as the American envoy and to disrupt diplomatic relations with England. Certainly Catherine was incomparably less friendly to the United States, this in direct proportion to the degree in which monarchic Russia saw advantages in an Anglo-American conflict. If Russia was directly interested, it was mainly from the viewpoint of her maritime trade.

At that time Russia, as has been said above, was eager to have her products and commodities exported at the right time and through her own outlets. Her ambitions in the Black Sea were partially covered by the two successful wars with Turkey which led to a full establishment of Russia on the northern shores of that sea. A few figures will show how rapidly her export through the new ports developed: 1764, 59,000 roubles; 1776, 369,000 roubles; 1793, 1,295,000 roubles.

Following these Russian successes on the Black Sea the British foreign secretary wrote to the ambassador in St. Petersburg on February 14, 1775, in connection with the need of Russia to dispose of a certain number of ships that Britain must get the rights of free navigation to all the Russian Black Sea ports.[10]

Thus England was a hindrance to and competitor of Russia in the Black Sea. In the Baltic Sea Russia was the organizing center of other northern European states, including Denmark, against which England became most aggressive. The open hostility which came close to a maritime war with England was on a basis which looks very modern—particularly in terms of international law—but which at the bottom remained the old clash between the traditional English doctrine of the closed sea and the originally Dutch and later Dutch-Scandinavian-Prusso-Russian doctrine of the open sea. At the same time this armed neutrality gave an excellent platform for the support of the young United States and the weakening of England.

If one takes into account Catherine's complaint in her Instruction about the subordination of the American colonies in sea trade

[10] Cf. M. N. Pokrovski, *Russkaya Istoriya* (Russian History), Vol. III, Moscow, 1924, pp. 114-115.

to England, already quoted, one can understand that the armed neutrality was a very important *point d'honneur* to her. She was anxious to have this modern doctrine connected with her name as the author. Reacting to Abbé Denina's *Essai sur la vie et le règne de Frédéric II, roi de Prusse*, which appeared in Berlin in 1788, she categorically denied that the idea was originally conceived by Frederick and wrote:

This is not true, the armed neutrality came from the brain of Catherine II and from nobody else's. Count Besborodko might testify that this idea was one morning by inspiration formulated by this Empress. As to Count Panin, he did not even wish to hear about it . . . and it took much pain to explain this idea to him; it was Bakounin to whom this task was intrusted, and finally he [Panin] put his signature on it.[11]

It goes without saying that both republican young America and monarchic France accepted enthusiastically Catherine's views on sea trade. To this extent Louis XVI was associated with his fellow autocrat in the support of the new nation to the very year of the French Revolution.

But it was no accident that imperial Russia did not go so far as France in her sympathies and commitments toward the United States; successful in both external and municipal policy, she could afford to refrain from fighting shoulder to shoulder with a republican and rebellious country against its legal sovereign. For the agonizing French *ancien régime* the American war was approximately the same kind of safety valve to divert inner prerevolutionary tension as the war of the Russian *ancien régime* against Japan in 1904.

It is an entirely different question whether the American Congress and the leaders of American foreign policy were fully acquainted with the European political circumstances, intricacies, and shades of opinion which influenced the extent of help which the new nation could expect from different European governments, varying from active belligerent coparticipation in the war against England to indirect diplomatic or commercial assistance.

But from the outset it should have been clear at a glance that Catherine's Russia really had little more in common with France of the *ancien régime* than a monarchic form of government based

[11] *Sochineniya imperatritsy Yekateriny*, Vol XII, p. 684.

on serfdom. Behind these sociological and structural similarities in contour there were deep differences, and the most important was the presence in France of an active politically impatient pushing third estate—the bourgeoisie—which knocked at the doors of the palaces, undermined the authority of the king, and fraternized with the American rebels. To the French bourgeoisie America was rather a political ally, while to the monarchy it was only an external ally against a common enemy—perfidious Albion. In 1778 Louis XVI refused to receive at Versailles the aged Voltaire on his return to France shortly before his death. Voltaire and Benjamin Franklin were equally admired by the subversive Frenchmen in Paris—and who was not subversive then and there?—but only the foreigner Franklin was frankly admitted to the court.

Contacts could not develop along the same lines between imperial Russia and the United States as between France and the United States.

In this relationship one diplomatic incident deserves to be mentioned. In May, 1782, when Benjamin Franklin was resident at Passy, the son of Catherine II and heir presumptive to the throne (later, Emperor Paul I) visited incognito the French capital under the name of Comte du Nord. He ordered cards sent to all the ambassadors, and one arrived at the American legation bearing the names of Comte du Nord and of Prince Bariatinsky (Russian ambassador to France). As was customary Franklin stopped at the door of the Russian embassy and had his name written in the visitors' book. The next day a servant came to Passy, greatly disturbed, saying his mistake in bringing the card there was likely to be his ruin.[12]

Franklin never met the august traveler, whose son, Alexander I, was the first Russian ruler to receive an official envoy of the young United States.

[12] Benjamin Franklin, Autobiographical Writings, selected and ed. by Carl Van Doren, N.Y., 1945, pp. 654-655.

III *First Contacts—*
Francis Dana's Mission

IT SHOULD NEVER BE FORGOTTEN THAT THERE WAS ALWAYS A certain social and economic incompatibility if not estrangement between the United States and Russia from their earliest contact, in the last quarter of the eighteenth century. Briefly, it can be said that America, a country without feudalism in the past and with a bourgeoisie of tremendous vitality in the present, faced Russia, a country endowed with feudalism as a going concern and lacking any well established, postfeudal bourgeoisie.

The two countries "met" in the 1860's, in a simultaneous emancipation of slaves and serfs, and followed together for a few decades the same capitalist lines of enrichment and industrialization—on very different levels, of course—only to part again in 1918. Then America was "left behind" in capitalism when her former feudal friend in the armed neutrality, after a short capitalist apprenticeship, became with the October Revolution the first socialist state in the world.

Already at the time of that earliest contact with America, Catherine II was well informed about the lack of a middle class in Russia. In her correspondence with Diderot she even promised to help establish in Russia a kind of third estate. She became particularly concerned about it before the convocation of the Legislative Commission at which all her subjects were to have been represented except the serfs. In order to direct the work of the Commission, she compiled her Instruction, in which she came to the conclusion that in the absence of a regular trading class the nobility must engage in the conduct of commerce and trade. Without naming Montesquieu she mentioned what "one of the best writers upon laws" had said:

In a monarchical government, it is contrary to the spirit of commerce that any of the nobility should be merchants. "This," said the Emperors Honorius and Theodosius, "would be pernicious to cities and would remove the facility of buying and selling between the merchants and

40

the plebeians." It is contrary to the spirit of monarchy to admit the nobility into commerce. The custom of suffering the nobility of England to trade is one of those things which have there mostly contributed to weaken the monarchical government.

With impartiality she added in the next paragraph:

There are people, however, of a different opinion, who judge that such noblemen may be permitted to trade as are not actually in the service of the government; but still with the restriction that they conform themselves in everything to the laws of commerce.[1]

These were approximately the views of Catherine on commerce and the role which the noblemen should be allowed to play in a nonaristocratic profession.

It certainly must be understood that Montesquieu, who wrote at a time when the French merchants were an efficient and ambitious social class with traditions of self-government, had a very different attitude from that of Catherine II, in whose time urban self-government was to be established from above in the form of a ready-made Charter of Townships (Gorodovoye Polozheniye).

All the remnants of medieval urban freedom and democracy of genuine Russian character had been extirpated as early as 1488 by Ivan III, who put an end to the Hanseatic towns of Novgorod and Pskov and their tremendous northeastern dependencies. So much were Russian merchants subdued by the central state power that it was not difficult for Alexis, the second Romanov czar and father of Peter the Great, after the peace treaty of Kardis in 1661 to introduce a full-fledged monopoly of foreign trade—a remote forerunner of the similar Soviet monopoly. The Russian merchants were compelled to sell all their goods and commodities to the Czar and to buy from him all the foreign commodities.[2] Thus

[1] Paragraphs 330 and 331 in the English text of 1768 as given in *Documents of Catherine the Great*, ed. W. F. Reddaway. In the original Montesquieu spoke of England but Catherine substituted for the name "a certain country," obviously to avoid offending the government of that country. Cf. the English translation of Thomas Nugent, p. 327.

[2] Cf. W. Chr. Friebe, *Handbuch der Geschichte Lief-, Esth- und Kurlands*, Riga, 1794, Vol. V, pp. 97-98. The author shows that Narva, Reval (Tallin), and Dorpat were the Livonian (now Estonian) towns that most energetically protested against this foreign trade monopoly because they had the largest share in the trade with neighboring Russia.

foreign free trade was arbitrarily abolished. Only after insistent protests from Sweden, which was victorious over Russia at that time and ruled Livonia, was this monopoly repealed. In the century which separated the merchants of Alexis from those of Catherine II, the economic development was not enough to turn the tables. The most important claims of the Russian bourgeoisie in the sessions of Catherine's Legislative Commission centered on equality with the nobility in the ownership of serfs and the purchase of lands. She was not threatened by a revolutionary "third estate" which tended to become a decisive political stratum in Russia. This was the extraordinary difference between Catherine's bourgeoisie on one hand and those of France and America on the other.

Commerce, sea trade, and all the other vocations of the middle class of the West were much less developed in Russia. Willy-nilly the nobility had to a certain degree to take over the task of the not ripened bourgeoisie. And this is why, if Catherine II was an ardent herald of armed neutrality, she was influenced much more by foreign political considerations than by the pressure of a seagoing bourgeoisie which asked for free trade, as in France, the Netherlands, and North America.

A memorandum on the establishment of a trading company like the British East India Company was submitted to the Empress in 1768 (?), on which she made the following notation:

It is up to the merchants to trade where they think best; as for me, I will furnish them neither men, nor ships, nor money, and I renounce in perpetuity all territories and possessions in the East Indies and America.[3]

This apparently antiexpansionist statement by Catherine obviously excluded, however, the Aleutian Islands and Alaska, which both the government and the merchants considered as far back as 1740 to be "Russian America." Moreover, it openly contradicted Catherine's own secret ukase of 1764 to the Admiralties College

[3] "Pisma Yekateriny II k grafu N. I. Paninu" (Letters of Catherine II to Count N. I. Panin), in *Chteniya v Imperatorskom Obshchestve istorii i drevnostei rossiskikh* (Proceedings of the Imperial Society of Russian History and Antiquities), Moscow, 1863, Vol. II, pp. 141-142.

(Navy Ministry) for equipping and sending a naval expedition into the North Pacific, to "hitherto unknown islands from which all possible resources ought to be used"—the expedition of Captain-Lieutenant P. Krenitsin to the Aleutians and mainly to Kodiak Island, to define its exact distance from the "renounced" American continent. Not even the "Ruling" Senate of the Empire had been informed of the plan.

Catherine's unwillingness to establish a regular company under the general control of the government, for colonial trade in the North Pacific, may be explained by apprehension of an open clash with Great Britain, which was eager to retain predominance in these regions of furs and fish but was ready to compromise and come to a settlement with both Spain and the much more aggressive Russia. However, the Russians were jealous of the explorations and discoveries of Captain James Cook and sent out expeditions of their own. In this connection a newly found letter of States Secretary P. Soimonov to the Empress is revealing:

Finding herself on the borders of Europe, Russia can well continue her trade with Asiatic peoples without fearing any harmful competition. And judging by the present circumstances we may long remain secure. But this has ceased to be true of the fisheries and hunting grounds in the Eastern Ocean, which up to now have been exclusively in our hands. The newest discoveries of Cook are the best reason for no longer regarding ourselves as without rivals.[4]

In 1799, three years after the death of Catherine, her successor and opponent, Paul I, issued the charter for the new Russian-American Company—a charter requested by a group of Siberian merchants and shipowners.

Only during and after the Continental Blockade (1806–1812) did Russia's interest in sea trade grow definitely; and Americans at the time of their first contacts with Russia overestimated the economic and commercial alertness of an agrarian country dominated by an easy-going gentry with a mild interest in trade.

---

[4] Quoted without any date in S. B. Okun, *Rossiisko-Amerikanskaya Kompaniya* (The Russian-American Company), Moscow, 1939, pp. 14-15, which states only that it is taken from the Soviet Archives of Internal Politics and Culture.

After the Russian naval expeditions of Bering and Chirikov finally determined that Siberia was separated from the American continent by water the first American "minister" went to the court of the Empress Catherine II. He was sent to St. Petersburg on the basis of the resolution of December 15, 1780, by the Congress. In the instructions of the Congress to him on December 19 we read:

> You are to manifest on all proper occasions the high respect which Congress entertain for her Imperial Majesty; for the lustre of her character and the liberality of her sentiments and her views; and particularly you are, in the strongest terms, to testify our approbation of the measures which her Imperial Majesty has suggested and matured for the protection of commerce against the arbitrary violations of the British court. You will present the act of Congress herewith transmitted, declaring our assent to her Imperial Majesty's regulations on this subject, and use every means which can be devised to obtain the consent and influence of that court that these United States shall be formally invited or admitted to accede as principals and as an independent nation to the said convention. In that event, you are authorized to subscribe the treaty or convention for the protection of commerce in behalf of these United States.[5]

It can be imagined what chance this diplomatic outcast had to present the views of the Congress of the American Confederation to the liberally minded autocratic Empress or to sign any treaties or conventions with her. The man went to St. Petersburg as a legally unrecognized envoy of a group of colonies which were daring enough to sever their historic ties with Great Britain and to rebel successfully with arms against their mother country.

Francis Dana was the name of this daring man. But already in March–April, 1781, it became obvious from his conferences in Paris with Dr. Benjamin Franklin and particularly with Count de Vergennes, the foreign minister of Louis XVI, that his arrival in St. Petersburg would be without any diplomatic character. He wrote to the President of the Congress April 4, 1781, about Vergennes:

[5] Francis Wharton, *The Revolutionary Diplomatic Correspondence of the United States*, Washington, Govt. Printing Office, 1889, Vol. IV, p. 202. Designated in later references as "Wharton, *Correspondence.*"

He inquired whether I had received any assurances from [Russia] that my residence in it would be acceptable. I told him a gentleman not a native of the country had written from thence that some persons of rank, whether they were connected with the court at all I could not say, had expressed their wishes that some person should be sent there from America capable of giving information of the state of our affairs.

He observed that Russia had not acknowledged the independence of America, that British influence was not done away at St. Petersburg. . . . I answered to this effect: That I should appear as a mere private gentleman travelling with a view of obtaining some knowledge of that country; that whatever suppositions of the sort might be made, the court would always have it in their power to deny they knew anything about me.[6]

The very fact that such quasi-ministers as Dana were sent by the Congress of rising America was not, as some writers think, sheer impetuosity which prompted diplomatic campaigns without regard to the rules of diplomacy. Nor was it the arbitrary and wild notion that money could be got by sending ministers to ask for it wherever there was a foreign court.[7] It was also not sheer legal ignorance of a revolutionary parvenu state that led the American Congress to the wishful and pretentious step toward St. Petersburg.

Wherever the specific interests of France in her support of young America against England may have been, it is a fact that the Most Christian King, Louis XVI, was the ally and creditor of the revolutionary Americans in their fight of secession against their legitimate monarch. True, in the 1770's and 1780's there was no Holy Alliance or other international body to hamper any legitimate monarch in his desire to support the subjects of another monarch in an illegitimate rebellion.

If Louis XVI—this argument of the Americans went on—was courageous enough to receive an American diplomat at his court and to support the Confederation, why should not the "more liberal" Catherine II be inspired to the same attitude, with the maritime interests of Russia as well as the neutral maritime governments of northern Europe so obviously opposed to the interest of the British sea-tyrant? If French political, maritime, and colonial interests were interpreted in favor of the new emerging common-

[6] *Ibid.*, pp. 348-351.   [7] *Ibid.*, Vol. I, pp. 290-291, 574-575.

wealth, why should not similar Russian interests—equally anti-British—help the American cause?

These were more than abstract considerations. If the above-mentioned resolution of the Congress characterizing Catherine II refers to "the liberality of her sentiments and her views," this was not merely diplomatic courtesy as we have already seen.

Dana's visit to St. Petersburg lasted from August, 1781, to September, 1783. But he remained in the Russian capital unknowing and unknown. "His position was one of the most mortifying isolation"—not only because he had to knock patiently and hopelessly for admittance to the palace but because he did not find the bridge to the Russian liberal society of that time. In purely official contacts he was not entirely helpless, he still found a way to communicate with the Russian minister Ostermann.[8]

To Livingston in December, 1782, Dana wrote these words of self-consolation and patriotic decency: "The United States have acquired too much consideration in Europe to be lightly offended by any sovereign, and I do not believe the illustrious sovereign of this empire has the least disposition to offend them." As a matter of fact when he left America, being first chosen secretary to Franklin and later diverted to Russia, he might have thought of himself as an American diplomat with a difficult burden on his shoulders. Even his mission to St. Petersburg based upon the December, 1780, resolution of the Congress was not to be considered as an illegal adventure. His quality "as a mere private gentleman" and traveler interested in Russian trade and other conditions was finally decided in April, 1781, on the eve of his departure to St. Petersburg and received his consent. His position became specifically precarious only after his arrival in the Russian capital.

Besides, Dana was not prepared for his responsible diplomatic commission. True when in Paris in contact with Lafayette he took upon himself "to acquire the language of this country by the time I shall quit it. . . . What I suffer every day for want of the language, will, I hope, quicken my diligence." [9] In St. Petersburg of Catherine II French was a vernacular in court circles and among the cultured elite. But Dana all through his stay was dependent upon the dubious knowledge of French of his young secretary John

[8] *Ibid.*, Vol VI, pp. 411 ff.   [9] Cf. W. P. Cresson, *Francis Dana*, p. 101.

Quincy Adams and even more so upon the dubious and distorted information of his hired agents or spies. Not only did he lack any knowledge of languages but he was insufficiently prepared in geography and international relations. Maria Theresa was for him "the late Empress of Hungary and Bohemia" and not the Roman-German Empress; he also evaluated wrongly Catherine's role in the armed neutrality. He overestimated the importance of commercial and economic considerations for Catherine and her aristocratic milieu. Only so can we understand his insistence in his rare meetings with the minister Ostermann on the commercial interests of Russia.

We have already seen how weak the middle class of Russia was at the time Dana lived in St. Petersburg. A regular bourgeoisie developed very slowly. The interests of trade and commerce were represented essentially by the landed gentry, which was to a notable degree interested in regular export—mainly of grain, flour, hemp, etc.

Dana did not show much comprehension of Russian interest in external trade, particularly in the Baltic Sea. As he himself admitted in his letter of September, 1782, to Livingston he did not know "what the consequences of the measures taken by her Imperial majesty to restore the deposed Khan of the Crimea might be." He could not foresee that the Russian intervention in the Crimea would be of the same character as that in Poland, i.e., the incorporation of the country, with the effect of extending Russian sovereignty over the whole northern shore of the Black Sea and diverting export trade through the warm ports of that sea and into the main seaways of the Mediterranean. This meant sending through the Black Sea all the grain exported from the central and southern parts of the country including the Ukraine. It also meant that, without harming the Baltic ports' trade, the Black Sea harbors would serve for a free export of Russian corn and hemp, the latter competing in the western market with American hemp. Besides, while the profits from the trade with the West through Riga and other Russian Baltic outlets went to these harbors and to the Baltic and Polish landlords of the near hinterland, the southern Black Sea trade would be more profitable for the exporting landlords of central and southern Russia.[10]

[10] M. N. Pokrovski, *op. cit.*, p. 113.

Exactly at the time when Dana was residing in St. Petersburg the American issue and even the armed neutrality were overshadowed for Russian diplomats by Crimea and the nearing second war with Turkey.

Dana certainly did not allow for the basic fact that Russia would be less receptive to his proposals about profitable commercial treaties than a country possessing an energetic bourgeoisie or at least an established stratum of noble merchants and patricians. This is also true of his proposals to furnish Russia with the commodities of the West Indies at a cheaper rate than any of the European countries could offer, because they had to carry the products to their respective ports, unload them, and load them again for shipment to Russia,[11] while America could bring the products to Russia directly, without transshipment.

After George III's proclamation in February, 1783, declaring the cessation of warfare Dana wrote a splendid memorial to the Russian vice chancellor Count Ivan Ostermann using this proclamation to show that her Imperial Majesty as a neutral sovereign had no other course than to recognize the United States as an independent state and receive him, Dana, as its minister. Particularly convincing is the juridically well founded reply of Dana to the cautious and protracting excuse of the Russian empress that she could not receive him as the minister plenipotentiary while his letter of credence bore a date earlier than George III's acknowledgment of America's independence.[12]

Meanwhile the Congress rapidly lost interest in Dana's mission. On May 21, 1783, a motion made by Hamilton and seconded by Madison stated in part:

That Mr. Dana be informed that the treaties lately entered into for restoring peace have caused such an alteration in the affairs of these States as to have removed the primary object of his mission to the court of Russia. . . .

[11] Wharton, *op. cit.*, Vol. V, p. 841, Vol. VI, p. 249.
[12] *Ibid.*, Vol. VI, pp. 414, 415. Dana wrote: "This objection seems deeply to affect the rights and interests of the United States. The United Colonies, on the 4th of July 1776, erected themselves into an independent sovereign power. . . . The United States have not, therefore, acquired the rights of sovereignty in consequence of this acknowledgment of their independence [which] necessarily have existed prior to the acknowledgment of it by the King of Great Britain."

Not much importance was ascribed in this motion to the commercial treaty with Russia:

That in this view, unless Mr. Dana shall have already formed engagements or made proposals, from which he cannot easily recede, of a more indefinite and extensive nature, before this reaches him, he be instructed to confine the duration of the proposed treaty of commerce to fifteen years. . . .

And as to the lasting principles of a confederation by which the independence of the United States would be supported the motion stated:

That though Congress approved the principles of armed neutrality, founded on the liberal basis of a maintenance of the rights of neutral nations and of the privileges of commerce, yet they are unwilling, at this juncture, to become a party to a confederacy which may hereafter too far complicate the interests of the United States with the politics of Europe, and therefore, if such a progress is not yet made in this business as may make it dishonorable to recede, it is their desire that no further measures may be taken at present towards the admission of the United States with that confederacy.[13]

Had Dana made the contacts with the Russian society which, primarily because of his nonofficial and basically private position, should not have been so difficult, his stay throughout two years might have resulted in the creation of a lasting rapprochement.

The Russian aristocratic society and the higher intelligentsia were, as we will see, more than favorably inclined toward the United States. But Dana remained unknown, isolated from any contact with them as well as with the English around their embassy, for whom he was the crazy political adventurer trying to trickle through by all means in diplomatic and court circles.

Left thus to his own meditations and observations, he was fascinated by the architectural beauty, not entirely original, of the young capital, which rose steadily to a classical perfection under the guidance of foreign and native masters like J. B. Vallin de la Mothe, A. F. Kokorinov, Antonio Rinaldi, F. Veldten, V. Bazhenov, and the English palace builder Charles Cameron. Dana wrote from St. Petersburg in August, 1781: "This is the finest city I have seen

[13] *Ibid.*, pp. 437-438.

in Europe, and far surpasses all my expectations. Alone, it is sufficient to immortalize the memory of Peter the First." [14]

As a somewhat romantic newcomer under the influence of masterpieces of architecture on the banks of the majestic Neva, Dana
vaguely felt the grandeur of the city and the vastness of the empire it represented. But, alas, he did not perceive beyond its grandeur and the magnificence of its new avenues and the splendor of
its palaces and monuments that St. Petersburg had begun to be
divided against itself, with a slowly growing opposition against the
privileged malefactors, an opposition which made this division effective not only in the capital but also among the most enlightened
and educated in the rest of the country.

It is most remarkable that Dana, so eager to carry out all his
diplomatic obligations and particularly his task "to sound out the
disposition" and get the support of Catherine to the recognition
of the independence and sovereignty of the United States as well
as to conclude a treaty for the protection of commerce, neglected
entirely the second part of his great object—social contacts with
the Russian society. The original first paragraph of his Instructions runs as follows:

> The great object of your negotiation is to engage her Imperial Majesty
> to favor the support the sovereignty and independence of these United
> States, and *to lay a foundation for a good understanding and friendly
> intercourse between the subjects of her Imperial Majesty and the citi-
> zens of these United States, to the mutual advantage of both nations.*[15]

The Congress appreciated rightly the importance of gaining the
sympathies of the Russian high society for the American cause
and charged Dana to be not only its plenipotentiary or "public
minister" but also the daring pioneer of good will to the Russian
society and find in it friends for the cause of "promoting the happiness of mankind and . . . disarming tyrants of the power of doing mischief." After one hundred and sixty years we fairly say
that the puritanical lawyer did not fulfill this part of his duties—
maybe more because he was merely a lawyer than because he had
puritanical views and approaches.

[14] *Ibid.*, Vol. IV, pp. 680-681.
[15] *Ibid.*, p. 201. The italics are mine.

Some modern writers including Cresson wrongly explain the failure of Dana by the fantastic policies of Catherine's ministers and favorites or by her "alcove diplomacy." [16]

No doubt Dana, as a lawyer and a Puritan, was disturbed by the frequent delay and procrastination caused by irregular programs of nonchalant Russian ministers and the changing of political schemes and plans with the capricious rotation of the Empress's favorites or lovers. But this was not a specific Russian phenomenon in the age of powdered wigs and rococo courtesans. Nor were bribes essentially Russian. For the puritanical Dana the courts of the Bourbons and Hapsburgs might have appeared not less frivolous, vicious, and sinful than the court of the Romanovs or quasi-Romanovs. To be exact, Dana never was a diplomat "at the court" of St. Petersburg. He never entered even an antechamber. Had he been recognized as a regular diplomat he might have been led into temptation to practice the usual methods of other diplomats on the banks of the Neva. And who knows whether he would have stood the test?

There might have been a specific reason for Dana's timidity. He had been connected too long with law and judiciary not to have a kind of inferiority complex in being an illegal agent who therefore was not entitled to any diplomatic quality in Russia.

Had foreign relations meant something more than pure diplomacy to him Francis Dana could have found a rich field for contact and work with Russian circles favorable to any rapprochement with the new Republic beyond the seas, so real but so far away. Vis-à-vis the obstinacy of the imperial court toward the United States, the young Russian society at the outset represented enthusiastic devotion to America and the Americans, as the forerunners of a successful fight against royal despotism.

And although, according to our best knowledge, Dana departed from St. Petersburg in August, 1783, without having made any personal and social contacts with the Russian opposition, the newly created United States became a very influential factor in the Russian opposition to Czarist autocracy. Its influence inspired

[16] W. P. Cresson, *Francis Dana: A Puritan Diplomat at the Court of Catherine the Great*, N.Y., 1930, pp. xiv, 199, 205-207.

the first political works of Russian thinkers such as Radishchev and subsequently the Decembrists, despite the fact that the United States itself, eager to disrupt its links with the "controversies of European nations" made in 1783 a full retreat from its earlier international approaches [17] and plans of world confederacy to home policies, a retreat most conspicuously illustrated under Monroe in 1823 and under Woodrow Wilson in 1919.

[17] Foster Rhea Dulles, *The Road to Teheran*, Princeton, 1944, p. 15.

IV *Radishchev, Admirer of the Transatlantic Republic*

> Radishchev is worse than Pugachov, he hails Benjamin Franklin.—Catherine II.
>
> Northern America with her Washington and Franklin was invoked by the Russian inexperienced youth to turn their wonderful dreams of freedom and human perfection into reality.—*Memoirs of Philip Vigel* (Part III).

AT THE VERY TIME WHEN DANA WAS IN ST. PETERSBURG UNKNOWN and unknowing, isolated as an unrecognized diplomat and separated from those Russian radical circles which admired America, the young fighting pioneer country, a Russian poet, writer, and political thinker from among the best educated aristocrats wrote his Ode to Freedom hailing Cromwell and Washington as the heroes of freedom and preaching the right of revolution in somewhat pompous stanzas. This was Alexander Radishchev.

In the early 1780's, St. Petersburg was a relatively small capital with 300,000 inhabitants. The quarters of the élite were mainly along the English Quay, the magnificent newly granite-clad Neva riverside, and the downtown parts of the Neva Prospect. On the opposite bank of the Neva was the Russian Quartier Latin with the Academies of the Sciences and of the Arts. In all these better quarters were interspersed urban mansions, sometimes even private palaces, of the aristocracy as well as a few hotels, in one of which— Hôtel de Paris—Dana resided with the young John Quincy Adams, the future American Minister to Russia.

Probably Dana and Radishchev passed each other and rubbed shoulders on some of the avenues or squares of the brand-new capital of the old empire without knowing that they were spiritual brothers with the same political creed. Dana could even have spoken to Radishchev, because he was one of the few Russians who had some command of English, reading freely Milton and Shakespeare in the original and discussing with the pro-British president of the Ministry of Commerce, Count Alexander Vorontzoff, the problems of English tariffs and customs when he was working on state projects. Dana and Radishchev, both interested in politics and economics, both convinced republicans, and both idealists, could have established a lasting friendship. Without having been introduced to each other officially at a diplomatic rout or a secret Masonic gathering—strangely enough, neither was a Mason—they could have met on some occasion of public significance, such as the unveiling of Etienne Falconet's world-famous monument to Peter the Great in August, 1782.[1] But obviously they missed each other.

*   *   *

In the year 1766 after graduation from the Russian Eton College of that time, the Imperial Corps of Pages in St. Petersburg, Radishchev was sent abroad by Catherine II with a dozen other aristocratic youngsters to perfect himself for the service of the state. The University of Leipzig was their destination.

Their program of study was arranged by the Empress herself with "moral philosophy, history, and predominantly natural and international law" as the main subjects; and it should be said at the outset that one of the most inspiring and motivating forces in all Radishchev's writings is the idea of natural law. The dictation of the heart was for him, as for Locke, the highest law.

We cannot dwell here on the details of Radishchev's spiritual, almost Voltairean many-sidedness. We have to concentrate on him as a political thinker of the first degree in the eighteenth century and mediator between young America and imperial Russia.

Having a variety of interests, going through philosophy under Plattner, a disciple of Leibnitz, and *en passant* graduating from the medical school, Radishchev must be regarded as a typical thinker of the enlightened eighteenth century, when many-sidedness was a virtue and when a famous writer had to have a Weltanschauung, or general outlook on the world, in which moral and political principles formed only a part of the whole edifice.

It cannot be denied that Radishchev was much influenced by the French materialists, particularly Helvétius and Holbach for whom

---

[1] This event made a deep impression both on Dana, in whose letters St. Petersburg is the incarnation of the will of the great God, and on Radishchev, evident in his essay, "A Letter to a Friend in Tobolsk," discussed later.

ALEXANDER RADISHCHEV

Sunday morning in front of the Philadelphia
Arch Street Meetinghouse (built 1804)
painted by Paul Svinyin

matter and movement were the basic notions and man had to be reduced to nature. But he was not subject to these influences alone. The school of Leibnitz left its imprint on him when in Leipzig. He of course remained far from Christianity as a positive religion; nevertheless, he cannot be regarded as a materialist. He was far from mysticism, he was not a Mason, although most of his friends were Masons. He was an enemy of the established church, particularly of the Orthodox Russian church, which he considered as the spiritual armorbearer of the Russian monarchic despotism. In spite of all these qualifications and inclinations toward natural science Radishchev was a worldly, universalistically minded deist like Voltaire.[2] Being so ardent an advocate of natural law that he came sometimes close to the defenders of tyrannicide, he could not possibly be merely a follower of Helvétius, whose system was not less hostile to natural law of the eighteenth century than the systems of Hobbes or Spinoza. As a reformer not only of the political order but also of punishment, he evaluated the Pennsylvania Quakers, "the peaceful haters of bloodshed," too highly to be simply registered as a materialist.

In the Ode to Freedom Radishchev notes that after the unmasking of bigotry Reason commands us to sing a hymn of praise to the "Eternal Father of all visible." Martin Luther is for him "the man who reconciled the Heaven and the Earth." More than that, his philosophical treatise "Man, His Mortality and Immortality" shows that he is influenced by Holbach, Diderot, and Helvétius but also by Joseph Priestley's *Disquisitions Relating to Matter and Spirit* and—last but not least—by John Locke's *Essay Concerning Human Understanding*. Under the impact of Adam Smith's *Theory of Moral Sentiments* he became an adherent of the theory of fellow feelings as a basis of social contacts of human beings. He definitely fights against Helvétius' views on the milieu as the exclusive factor in the development of mental abilities and rejects his theory about the innate equality of our men in spirit.[3]

[2] B. S. Osherovich in his book *Ocherki po istorii russkoi ugolovno-pravovoi mysli* (Essays on the History of Russian Thought on Criminal Law), Moscow, 1946, p. 151, tries to show that Radishchev was a materialist of the Helvétius type and therefore a predecessor of Marxism.
[3] A. N. Radishchev, *Polnoye sobraniye sochinenii* (Collected Works), Moscow-Leningrad, 1938, Vol. II, pp. 59, 65, 372-373.

The somewhat sectarian inclination of Radishchev to English culture, because of the high political standards of Britain and America, found expression in a naïve statement: "I have tried to bring the English language closer to you because in it the flexibility of the spirit of freedom receives its best expression; this language affects the Reason to produce rigid notions which are so necessary under all forms of government." The real reason for this statement, as already hinted, was the existence of the English constitution, and the English and American revolutions led by Cromwell and Washington. It should never be forgotten that the "Journey" was written and concluded before the outbreak of the French Revolution of 1789.

This same inclination found even more conspicuous manifestation in the preference which he gave to Benjamin Franklin in the well known discussion of Lomonosov versus Franklin, which took place in the Russian Academy of Sciences.

Lomonosov was at that time one of the most loved men in Russia. Because he was a Russian Da Vinci, combining gifts as an investigator in natural science, as a mosaicist, and as a writer of mathematics, prose and poetry and a translator with a deep knowledge of history, he was tremendously popular. He was a very rare if not a unique personality, able to rise from the peasantry of Russia in the early eighteenth century to membership in the Academy of Sciences—an equivalent of the American self-made man in the environment of rigid feudal regimentation. He was the pride and, to a certain degree, the guide of the early Russian élite who had at that time to risk the first steps of spiritual independence surrounded by the foreign teachers and experts who inundated the capital and continued to pour into it, attracted by Russian generosity.

Even against this extraordinarily popular personality Radishchev was courageous enough to raise his voice for the sake of truth and impartiality.

"Let us follow the truth," he said of Lomonosov, "without trying to seek in him the great historian and to compare him with Tacitus, Raynal, or Robertson.

". . . Is it possible for us to put Lomonosov close to the man Benjamin Franklin who was honored with a most flattering inscription under his bust? This inscription engraved not by simple flattery but by truth which dares to be violent runs as follows:

"He snatched the thunderbolt from heaven, the scepter from tyrants. (Eripuit caelo fulmen, mox sceptra tyrannis.)[4]

"Can we confront Lomonosov with Franklin only because he investigated the electrical power in its action, only because he did not disrupt his research of electricity after his teacher was killed by the electrical power of lightning artificially conducted into his laboratory?[5] Lomonosov knew well how to conduct electrical power, he knew how to divert the thunderbolts, but Franklin was in this science an architect while Lomonosov was nothing else than an artisan."

This rather one-sided and extremely unjust evaluation of his countryman Lomonosov as a simple artisan in comparison with Dr. Benjamin Franklin as the real creator in science, probably is to be explained rather by Radishchev's emotional admiration of America and his founding father than by purely scientific considerations.[6] Besides, Radishchev, an amateur in physics and chemistry, was unable to appreciate correctly the creative powers of Lomonosov, who was recognized as the predecessor of modern

[4] The inscription for the Houdon bust of Franklin, ascribed to A. R. J. Turgot. In a letter to Felix Nogaret, Franklin commented on the inscription: "Notwithstanding my experiments with electricity the thunderbolt continues to fall under our noses and beards; and as for the tyrant, there are a million of us still engaged at snatching away his sceptre." (Cf. *The Home Book of Quotations*, ed. Burton Stevenson, 1934, p. 722.) But Radishchev was an ardent Russian Westerner and therefore very far from the ironic skepticism of Franklin who "knew better."

[5] Prof. G. Richmann, academician and senior colleague of Lomonosov, started his experiments of aerial electricity in 1752, immediately after the experiments of Benjamin Franklin became known in St. Petersburg.

[6] The Russian physicist N. Liubimov in his essay on *Lomonosov as a Physicist*, Moscow, 1855, ascribed to Franklin the role of an initiator of Lomonosov's theory in so far as the latter, successfully "guessing" on the basis of vague information about Franklin's discoveries, developed his own far-going theory of aerial electricity before he received letters from Franklin.

Postwar Soviet patriotism emphasizes the originality of Lomonosov in atomistics, in the idea of conservation of energy, in the kinetic theory of gases, and in chemistry and evolutionary geology (B. G. Kuznetsov, *Lomonosov, Lobatchevskii, Mendeleyev*, Moscow, 1945, pp. 5-6). In the third edition of N. A. Menshutkin's biography of Lomonosov (Moscow, 1947, preface) the editors find it necessary to quote a western authority, Alexander Smith, president of the American Chemical Society, as a crown witness to the effect that Lomonosov belongs to "the small group of chemists of first magnitude in the world."

physical chemistry, and as a forerunner of the world-famous Lavoisier.

The opinion of Radishchev is connected with the well known discussions in the Russian Imperial Academy concerning the first authorship of the idea of aerial electricity connected with Franklin's invention of the lightning rod. In November, 1753, Mikhail Lomonosov delivered a speech on electrical power at a solemn session of the Academy. A few academicians expressed doubts about the originality of Lomonosov's theory on the formation of electricity in the atmosphere thanks to the upward and downward flows of air. Suspicions were even voiced as to whether Lomonosov's ideas had not developed under the influence of Benjamin Franklin's discovery of aerial electricity in 1752.

Lomonosov was anxious to disprove such suspicions, and asserted in an official explanatory memorandum that his theory of the origin of electrical power in the air was by no means based on any borrowing from Franklin; he had not seen Franklin's letters until his academic speech (report) was almost completed, and he quoted some of his colleagues who had been acquainted with his experiments before the report.[7]

Radishchev's education in politics and legal ideas had begun very early in his boyhood, under an extremely well prepared tutor, a French refugee and former member of the Parliament of Rouen, who had fled from the persecution of the government of Louis XV.

*   *   *

Strangely enough the first political writing of Radishchev was a very long and somewhat pompous Ode to Freedom. It was inspired mainly by the American Revolution and was written between 1781 and 1783. The boldness of this poem is so much the more amazing because the author, who attacked monarchic tyranny and serfdom and hailed Cromwell and Washington as leaders of people's revolutions against the kings and tyrants, was himself an aristocrat and a member of the imperial Russian government. Besides, it was written in the second half of Catherine's reign, when her liberalism and benevolence toward French Encyclopedism had

---

[7] Cf. P. Pekarski, *Istoriya Imperatorskoi Akademii Nauk* (The History of the Imperial Academy of Sciences), St. Petersburg, 1873, Vol. II, pp. 524-532.

turned into crass defense of the Russian autocracy and to an intensive foreign policy of expansion and conquest involving the extermination of that limited constitutional monarchism which she had once encouraged. Although aware of the punishment which awaited him, he did not try in the prefaces of his subversive writings, the Ode and the essays that followed, to evade responsibility before the authorities by asserting that no mischief could follow from his reasoning as did such great thinkers as Grotius, Spinoza, and Abbé Raynal, his direct predecessor. Defending democracy and freedom in the very citadel of Russian autocracy and rejecting at the outset any compromises with the almighty ruler, he became the noblest forerunner of the daring Decembrists.

Credit must be given to Semennikov for noting that some stanzas of the Ode were inspired by Abbé Raynal's book *The Revolution of America*.[8] Radishchev himself testified that Raynal's *A Philosophical and Political History of the British Settlements and Trade in North-America* (1776) inspired him; but he did not mention the *Revolution of America*.[9] Raynal's enthusiastic address to America may have moved the Russian author of the Ode to Freedom. It runs in part as follows:

Heroic country, my advanced age permits me not to visit thee. Never shall I see myself amongst the respectable personages of Areopagus; never shall I be present at the deliberations of thy congress. I shall die without having seen the fulfilment of toleration, of manners, of laws, of virtue, and of freedom. My ashes will not be covered by a free and holy earth: but I shall have desired it; and my last breath shall bear to heaven an ejaculation for thy prosperity.

We find the reference to ashes repeated in Stanza 46 of the Ode, quoted in the following pages. Radishchev opens his Ode thus:

[8] V. P. Semennikov, *Radishchev: Ocherki i izsledovaniya* (Radishchev: Essays and Investigations), Moscow and Petrograd, 1923, pp. 5-7. *The Revolution of America*, by the Abbé Raynal, Dublin, 1781. The same printer issued this book in French in London in the same year. It is not known whether Radishchev used the French original or the perfect English translation. The address is printed on p. 122 of the Dublin edition.

[9] Radishchev wrote that he considered this book to be the beginning of his "unfortunate mood"—an expression which he used when brutally cross-examined by the political police of Catherine.

O blessed gift of heaven,
O good eternal nave,
O freedom previous leaven,
Hear greetings from a slave.
Embrace my heart with fire.
From bondage, darkness shake.
Oh, answer my desire.
Let Brutus and let Tell awake
Thy thunder kings must hear
And, trembling, know the hand of fear.

Stanza 17 mirrors very well the fight against serfdom and the dream of Europe's enslaved tenants. Here the people address themselves to the tyrant:

We covered the sea with ships,
We built harbors on its shores
To bring treasures to the cities.
But tears will wet the golden crop
Until the day dawns
When Europe's peasant says:
"I am not a tenant on my land
A prisoner on the field,
I prosper on my soil
And sow for me alone."

The poet addresses himself to Cromwell—whom he does not consider as free from ambition, from suppression of England's freedom, from bigotry and arbitrariness—almost in the style of the old Scotch and French "monarchomacs" who preached the killing of tyrants:

I see evil in you, Cromwell.
With power heavy in your hand
You crushed the country's freedom
But you did once and forever
Teach the people the way to vengeance
By the court death of King Charles.

Aiming at the beaten armies of England compulsorily herded and conscripted for battles against young America's forces, he jubilantly hails the rebellious country and her leader Washington:

Gaze on this boundless field.
The armies of evil lie crushed,
Crushed by a mighty foe.
Not mercenaries, not Redcoats
But by an army of free men,
Leaders all and unafraid.
O Washington, invincible warrior,
Thou art and wast unconquerable,
Thy guide being freedom.

In conclusion Radishchev with an ardent zeal and romantic nostalgia bids farewell to young republican America. This forty-sixth stanza goes on thus:

My soul yearns towards thee,
O famed land!
Where once the yoke pressed hard
And freedom was enchained.
But now thy joy sings out,
Yet we still suffer, still striving
To achieve thy goal.
It may not be my fate
To reach thy free and happy shores,
But let my ashes rest beneath your earth.

The first daring political essay which Radishchev published was "A Letter to a friend living in Tobolsk." It was written immediately after the unveiling in 1782 of the monument to Peter the Great, the sculptor of which, Falconet, a member of the French Academy of Painting and Sculpture, was recommended by the Encyclopedist Diderot to Catherine's ambassador in France, Prince D. Galitzin, as early as 1766. The solemn unveiling took place in the presence of the Empress, high officials, diplomats, and thousands of cheering inhabitants.

Radishchev used this occasion to criticize royal power which is directed against the personal liberty of the subjects, and wrote:

Peter upon common recognition was given the title "the Great." But just what for was he called so? Alexander, the destroyer of half of the globe, was styled the Great; Constantine who bathed in the blood of his son, too, was called "the Great"; Charles I, the first renewer of the Roman Empire, was called so; Leo, the Pope of Rome, the protector of sciences and arts, was proclaimed "the Great"; Cosimo I Medici, the duke of Tuscany, was recognized as "the Great"; the good-hearted French King Henry IV was called "the Great"; Louis XIV, the vain and proud ruler, was given the title of "Great"; Frederick II, the king of Prussia, in his own lifetime became "the Great." All these rulers, not to mention hosts of others whom servile flattery called "the great," received this title because of having rendered outstanding services to their fatherlands, though possessing great vices. . . . Despite the citizen of Geneva [Rousseau] Peter was correctly and of merit called the Great, being an unusual and outstanding man.

Following this sober eulogy of the worldly Russian reformer was a paragraph which caused Catherine later to characterize Radishchev as "the first advocate of the French Revolution in Russia":

> Let me not diminish myself in your eyes, my beloved friend, if I extol such an ambitious autocrat, who exterminated the last signs of his fatherland's wild freedom. He is dead, and one dead cannot be flattered. But he could have been much more glorious had he lifted himself and elevated his fatherland to the freedom of persons. Though there are some cases in which kings have abdicated their thrones . . . there is no instance and will not be to the end of time in which a king voluntarily gives up even a part of his power as long as he is sitting on his throne.

To which the author added an ominous little footnote: "If this had been written in the year 1790 the instance of Louis XVI could have given the author different thoughts." [10]

Needless to say that the "instance" meant the execution of the king, which could not be expressly mentioned under the Czarist censorship. Nevertheless Peter I remained in the eyes of Radishchev a monarch who established necessary institutions and introduced reforms which were favorable to the needs of the people.

The Ode to Freedom was a part of Radishchev's most important work, *A Journey from St. Petersburg to Moscow*, in which more subjects concerning America's new-established political and social order were elaborated.

One important circumstance has to be taken in consideration. When the Ode was written there had been only one successful

[10] Cf. A. N. Radishchev, *Polnoye sobraniye sochinenii*, Vol. I, pp. 150-151, 461.

revolution outside England. The French Revolution was only in stage of preparation. France encouraged the American Revolution without knowing that it itself would follow the example and would exceed America in sweeping away the old regime. It was Jefferson who would reproach the French Revolution for the execution of Louis XVI and Marie Antoinette. But when Radishchev wrote his *Journey* the French Revolution had not yet emerged. When the book appeared in 1790 Catherine was horrified by the "deeds" of the French rebellion and took all steps to fight against France and to support her counterrevolutionary enemies. She certainly was compelled to suppress the book and to punish the author.

The pro-American feelings of Radishchev might have appeared even more subversive than his moral support of the French Revolution. America at the end of the 1780's and the beginning of the 1790's became the fortress of well established "Jacobins," while the results of the French rebellion may have seemed to be uncertain. The changing fortunes of the revolutionary and counterrevolutionary wars before and after the execution of Louis XVI did not produce any stable situation. In America, however, any restoration was unthinkable. And the only way to get the United States back in the counsels of the counterrevolution was through the nets of foreign relations.

This is why the pro-American Radishchev was doubly hated.

He began with criticisms of the stages of conquest which had preceded and partly accompanied the emergence of a free America. He was doubtless under the influence of Abbé Raynal's *History of the Settlements and Trade of the Europeans* when he wrote about the acts of the "Europeans who have destroyed and ruined America, irrigated her plains with the blood of the natives. But they replaced their murder by new acquisitiveness. The devastated fields of this suffering hemisphere began to feel the plow which turns up the clod."

However, there was a great difference between Raynal and Radishchev. While Raynal defended the American interests of France of the Bourbons in contrast to Great Britain and her minister Pitt, mentioning only in passing that justice and humanity had been neglected in the conquest of America, Radishchev, as a writer educated in natural law and as an ardent humanist, wrote of the conquest of America:

Having killed off most of the Indians, the wicked Europeans, preachers of the love of peace in the name of the true God, teachers of meekness and of love for mankind, expanded their ferocious and murderous conquest through the purchase of slaves. These unfortunate victims from the burning banks of Niger and Senegal, torn from their homes and families, transferred to lands unknown to them, and put under the heavy scepter of order, now till the prolific cornfields of America, which despises their toil. Should we call this country of desolation a blessed one only because her fields are covered not by bramble bush but by various plants? Shall we call her blessed because hundreds of her citizens loll in luxury while thousands are deprived of a secure livelihood and of a roof against heat and frost? Oh, that they may be devastated, these abundant countries! that thorns and thistles may sink their roots deeply to extinguish all the precious fruits of America!

And hinting at the Russian serf-owning landlords he concluded his emphatic paragraph:

Tremble, my beloved ones, that no one shall say about you: "Change the name, and the story applies to yourself" (Mutato nomine de te fabula narratur).

Despite the sins of the conquerors and the invasion of the rights of the native Indians, Radishchev emphasized the difference between the period of conquest and that of the new established American colonies turning to an independent political existence. Here he followed the general tradition of the enlightened eighteenth century literature, which regarded the United States as a continuation and development of European political history.[11]

Most remarkable is the role which Radishchev ascribed to the idea of liberty in general and particularly to the freedom of press. In the first stages of the fight of Russian freethinkers and liberals the freedom of the press was the most important freedom. Without it no dispersion of antiautocratic views could be accomplished. Milton in England, Voltaire in France, and Radishchev in Russia wrote on their shields the freedom of press in order to have it materialized in legislation created by a national revolution.

[11] A *Journey*, etc.—the chapter entitled "Khotilov," pp. 249-251 of the original Russian edition.

Young republican America was the pattern for the élite of enlightened Russia, and Radishchev the mediator between the American ideal and the sad Russian reality. In his *Journey* a whole chapter was devoted to the history of suppression of freedom of thought. America was the country which had found the just and correct result in this field in a long and twisting course of mankind since ancient Greece. In a subchapter entitled "A Short Narration of the Genesis of Censorship" he began with the priests' instigation of the people of Athens to prohibit the writings of Protagoras, to collect all the copies of them for burning. He insisted that censorship had common roots with the Inquisition:

While cowardly mistrust of things affirmed compelled the monks to establish censorship and to extirpate thought at its very birth, Columbus dared to pierce the incertitude of the seas to discover America, and Kepler foresaw the existence of the natural power of gravitation finally proved by Newton. Simultaneously Copernicus was born, who described the movement of the celestial bodies in space. But with deep regret at the fate of human reasoning we have to say that grand ideas frequently begot ignorance. Letterpress printing gave birth to censorship; the rationalist philosophy of the eighteenth century produced the teaching of the Illuminates.[12]

Continuing, he took up the most important western countries since mediaeval times, describing the deadening effects of clerical and secular censorship. He dwelt upon Luther's Reformation and emphasized that with the weakening of the Roman Church and the falling away of certain confessions from Rome, particularly during the Thirty Years' War, many books were printed free from censorship; but in France and other countries the press continued to be restricted. England after its Glorious Revolution and particularly the "united governments of America" forever had ended the domination of violence over reason.

Here, too, Radishchev showed his admiration for the Anglo-American ideals of press freedom and liberty in general. It is most remarkable that in an insertion to the *Journey* added by the author after the whole of the *Journey* had been set, and approved by the censor, Radishchev expressed the vehement protest:

[12] In the chapter "Torzhok" of *A Journey*, etc.

Now, when in France all applaud liberty, censorship is not abolished. Recently we read that the people of France has imitated its former monarch by confiscating books and arresting authors who dare to write against the National Assembly. And Lafayette was the performer of such decisions! O France, thou art still standing on the brink of the Bastille abyss.

He concluded this chapter with a very picturesque interruption:

As to Russia . . . What happened with the censorship in Russia, you will learn another time. And now, not performing any censorship on the post-horses, let me hasten to continue my journey.

The American governments laid down freedom of the press as one of the fundamental laws granting civil liberty. Radishchev's book was the first in Russia to quote articles and sections of American constitutional law as models of political justice and toleration. Catherine had dared only to apostrophize, plagiarize, and vaguely stylize Western authors; Radishchev, her former "page" and protégé, went some steps farther, importing exact dicta of Western, particularly American, constitutional law in an autocratic country in defiance of its censorship.

Radishchev quoted the preamble to the Constitution of Pennsylvania (1776) and particularly Paragraph 12 of its Declaration of Rights, running as follows: "That the people have a right to freedom of speech, and of writing, and publishing their sentiments; therefore the freedom of press ought not to be restrained." Also Section 35 of its "Plan or Frame of Government," which proclaimed: "The printing presses shall be free to every person who undertakes to examine the proceedings of the legislature, or any part of government."

He quoted further the Constitution of Maryland (1776), particularly Article 38 ("That the liberty of press ought to be inviolably preserved"), the similar principle of the Delaware Constitution and Section 12 of the Virginia Declaration of Rights of June 12, 1776, reading: "That the freedom of the press is one of the great bulwarks of liberty and can never be restrained but by despotic government." And in conclusion the important Delaware's declaration (Article 1, Section 5) where his cherished idea of the jury determining the facts and the law concerning libels was apostrophized:

> The press shall be free to every citizen who undertakes to examine the official conduct of men acting in a public capacity, and any citizen may print on any subject, being responsible for the abuse of that liberty. In prosecution for publications investigating the proceedings of officers, or where the matter published is proper for public information, the truth thereof may be given in evidence; and in all indictments for libels, the jury may determine the facts and the law, as in other cases.

There can be no doubt that the political elements of Radishchev's writings, and especially his defense of resistance against the king as well as his vehement argument for freedom of press, were most abhorred by Catherine and her administration. Even his attack upon serfdom and the selling of serfs like cattle in regular deeds and in auctions was less painful to the regime than his political claims, particularly his blunt confronting of backward autocratic Russia with young republican America. It speaks volumes that in the subsequent periods of more liberal attitude under Alexander I (1801–1825) and Alexander II (1856–1880) other works of Radishchev were allowed to be published but not the *Journey*. This book remained prohibited but was sometimes eagerly read, published abroad as far away as London and illegally imported into Russia as well as often clandestinely copied down to the period following the revolution of 1905 when it finally could be printed in the second half of the last Czar's reign.

Nor was Radishchev sufficiently appreciated under the Soviets for his political views. He was admired for his materialism or closeness to it, for his hostility to the established church, for his unselfish and ardent defense of the emancipation of peasants, even for his Western ideas of penitentiary reforms and his suggestions toward an improvement of the judiciary, including criminal procedure; but his political ideas, so much influenced by the successful Revolution in America, and particularly his Western constitutional ideas remained undesirable and tainted with suspicion.[13]

---

[13] Semennikov's book on Radishchev, published in 1923 during the "liberal" period of New Economic Policy, is much more objective than Osherovich's *Ocherki po istorii russkoi ugolovno-pravovoi mysli* and is free from the stylization so noticeable in that book. Osherovich omits all Radishchev's quotations

Having described the United States as the palladium of freedom of thought and of the press in history and constitutional law, Radishchev tended to show that in actual political life, too, America was the country of press freedom. How did he do that?

He quoted in the same chapter John Dickinson, "who took part in the 'change.'" "Change" was the misleading word which had to replace "revolution"—a word not tolerated by the czarist censors from Catherine II down to 1905. Dickinson, the elected president of the Supreme Executive Council of Pennsylvania, was called by Radishchev intentionally the "highest executive authority in the province" in order to bring him in Russian eyes into sharp contrast with the Russian governors of provinces (gubernatory) who were appointed by the Empress. The governor represented the person of the Czar in the province and was high above common mortals or even scribes or journalists. Radishchev, having described Dickinson in his administrative functions as the closest analogy to a Russian *gubernator*, noted that when he was scurrilously attacked in a series of sharp articles he "did not abhor" to answer to the scurrilous sheets with his printed *Vindication*, in which he "not only defended himself but also refuted his opponents, making them ashamed." This, added Radishchev, was a model worthy of imita-

---

from the American constitutions and passages bearing on his fight for freedom of the press. This cannot be regarded as accidental because he shows a thorough acquaintance with the *Journey*, as well as the less important political essays of Radishchev. The Ode to Freedom is quoted, but not the more substantial essays elaborating Radishchev's political ideas.

But this was obviously not anti-Western enough for the newest vogue of 1949, and Osherovich, with other Soviet authors, was criticized for pro-Western cosmopolitanism and failure to recognize Radishchev's originality and independence of Western Europe and America. See S. A. Pokrovski, "Politicheskiye vzglady A. N. Radishcheva" (The Political Views of A. N. R.) in *Izvestiya Akademii Nauk SSSR: Otdeleniye ekonomiki i prava* (Journal of the Academy of Sciences: Section of Economics and Law), 4, 1949, pp. 241-254. V. S. Pokrovski too insists on R.'s absolute originality in his article "Gosudarstvenno-pravoviye vzglady A. N. Radishcheva" (The Constitutional Views of A. N. R.), *Sovietskoye gosudarstvo i pravo* (Soviet State and Law), Oct., 1949, pp. 28-42. The peak, however, was reached in a preposterously chauvinistic unsigned article which was published on the bicentenary of Radishchev's birth: "R.: Vershina obshchestvennoi nauki XVIII veka" (R.: The Summit of Social Science of the XVIIIth Century) in *Sovietskoye gosudarstvo i pravo*, Sept., 1949, pp. 1-7. This lauds Radishchev above Rousseau and Montesquieu, and all French encyclopedists.

tion as to how accusations should be avenged which are publicly made in a printed pamphlet. "If, however, somebody grows furious against every printed line, he induces us to think that the printed story was true, and that the avenger is exactly the man characterized in the printed sheets."

Needless to say that in comparison with this American model of a righteous and courageously liberal administrator the arbitrary Russian governor not controlled or limited by any higher administrative body became the incarnation of stupid despotism.

Radishchev not only admired the incarnation of natural law in the American bills of rights and the various declarations included in the constitutions of the particular states and endorsed American constitutional law but also idealized to a high degree the criminal law of the United States. In his memorandum "On Legislation" for the Commission to Draft New Laws, after his return to Russia from Siberia in 1801,[14] he emphasized that the Russian legislators who tended to establish new codes should follow the precedents of Greece (Solon, Lycurgus, and Pythagoras) and Rome and travel to countries where good laws were enacted in order to reenact them in the younger countries. He asked, for instance, the introduction of "trial by jury" and freedom of press in Russia. But the proper elaboration of all the legal details would require a journey to England, with a study of the details that would not be limited to general principles.[15] An "exact picture" of the new American criminal law was also desirable. It was not possible to trust different authors in all they wrote about these matters, and therefore a visit to America was needed:

It is already known that the peaceful Quakers who hate bloodshed have initiated the abolishment in Pennsylvania of capital punishment; even physical discipline or flogging for any category of crime is done

---

[14] It was not discovered until 1916. Cf. *Golos Minuvshavo*, Dec., 1916, with an introduction by A. Popelnicki.

[15] He dreamed even of himself visiting England (and America). Cf. M. I. Sukhomlinov, "A. N. Radishchev, avtor Puteshestviya iz Peterburga v Moskvu" (A. N. R., the author of "A Journey from St. Petersburg to Moscow"), in *Akademiya Nauk, Sbornik Otdeleniya russkavo yazyka i slovesnosti* (Academy of Sciences, Collection of the Section for Russian Language and Literature), Vol. XXXII, No. 6, St. Petersburg, 1883, pp. 84 ff.

away with, and imprisonment is introduced instead. But it is not yet known exactly what are the results of this law. Not long ago one of the travelers published information about the forms of imprisonment in Pennsylvania; it has been asserted that this new kind of punishment is most effective, and that there are already instances in which the worst criminals have left jail entirely transformed.

These were in short the basic features of the American myth which Radishchev began to spin in a kind of prophetic vision, and which reached its full display only when the Decembrist upheaval took place in 1825.

It is really imposing to discover that the first Russian modern political thinker who became a political martyr, despite the fact that he was a chosen child of monarchic generosity, developed into a spirit perfectly emancipated from prejudice, commonplace and obligatory, law-abiding official patriotism. Some of his contemporaries went the way of partial reforms, avoiding direct attack upon the main fortress of Czarism, and were more successful than he. But he passionately despised half-measures, and after coming back from his Siberian *intermezzo* he began anew where he had left a decade before when he was deported from St. Petersburg. This holy quixotism which inspired Radishchev to fight all the windmills from St. Petersburg by way of Moscow to Siberia and back, later became the predominant state of mind of the Russian intelligentsia, which was always inclined to self-criticism and to the divination of the foreign. But remaining to a certain degree domestically isolated, deprived of a third estate, be it the urban bourgeoisie or the peasant masses, this noble élite secluded itself, developing an ineptitude to exercise a real power in the Russian society and in the Russian people.

Radishchev began to spin Russia's myth of America at the dawn of America's independence. This was not the myth produced by the land-hungry peasants or half-serfs of Italy, Poland, Ireland, and Germany, a myth produced by the dream of peasants living in poverty and wrath, and longing for the United States as an enchanted land of riches and fertile plains. Ethnic Russia had its own America in the vast confines of her territory. This Russian myth of

America was created by repentant aristocrats fond of a brand-new, genuine democracy.

In Radishchev's head fermented all the humanitarian and libertarian ideas of the eighteenth century; and he was permeated and vivified by them, they supported him throughout a decade in icy Siberia. But his tragedy was less due to his personal mischief-making than to the emergence of the early-ripe Russian revolutionary aristocrats with nobleness of soul and character. Radishchev certainly exaggerated if he dreamt of a sudden change-over from the quasi-leadership of Catherine with her plagiarized Instruction and helpless Legislative Commissions to regular parliaments, and from the arbitrariness of Russian autocracy to the English habeas corpus and American bills of rights. But neither Milton and Locke nor Blackstone and Jefferson would have succeeded without the great middle class in England and the powerful burgher-colonists of America. Radishchev's myth of America could not be generally accepted because of social reasons. There was no middle class in the Russia of Catherine II and Alexander I ripe to perceive and apply his doctrine.

The signal attempt of Radishchev was made too early, the emergence of a Russian bourgeoisie as the kernel of the nation came too late. This was the first act of the tragedy, of which the second was played before and during the 1825 Decembrist revolt.

V Constitutional Reforms: Alexander I, Jefferson, and Speranski

THE EIGHTEENTH CENTURY PRODUCED IN RUSSIA ONLY ONE REAL attempt to limit constitutionally the autocracy of the Czarist power. This was the conditions signed in 1730 by Duchess Anna of Courland prior to her ascent to the Russian throne. All the other coups and political changes were caused by praetorian revolts.

After the last pronunciamento which led to the murder of Paul I in 1801, Alexander I, his liberal son and the beloved grandson of Catherine, initiated some constitutional drafts, projects, and actual reforms. The same Alexander defeated Napoleon I and was a historical figure of the greatest importance in the international relations of the first quarter of the nineteenth century. Both in domestic reforms and in foreign relations, Alexander and his closest friends and helpers had a significant contact with young America; and under him regular diplomatic intercourse was established between the two countries.

Only a brief sketch can be given here of Russia's domestic and foreign policies, in so far as they were connected with America and American ideas.

The domestic field, embracing internal developments and shifts, was for Russia of a more organic and lasting character than the foreign relations. So far as the world at large is concerned, Alexander's foreign policy from its very liberal beginning down to the establishment of the anti-American Holy Alliance left a much deeper imprint upon the future generations than his domestic policy. Even for America, the remote country which fought Britain when France attacked Russia, while Britain and Russia were in relative friendship—even for America the Russian Emperor, the adversary of Napoleon, was Alexander the Deliverer.[1] Little wonder, therefore, that for Britain, the old enemy and "victim" of Napo-

[1] See *Correspondence Respecting Russia Between Robert Goodloe Harper and R. Walsh, Jr.*, ed. Robert Walsh, Philadelphia, 1813.

leon, for the whole of Germany and the rest of Central Europe and Russia, Alexander was a real Deliverer and Liberator from general suppression and partition and even from total national destruction.

It is reasonable that in both fields Russia was eager to come into contact with young republican America. The letter of Alexander to Jefferson dated November 7, 1804, furnishes the best testimony for this. It has two parts, the first of which speaks of the establishment of regular commercial relations between the two countries, and the second is concerned with constitutional reforms and the American constitution as the wisest and most liberal one.

The domestic reforms of Alexander I were much discussed, negotiated, and partly materialized in the first years of his reign predominantly with the help of the Unofficial or Intimate Committee, which consisted of Count Victor Kotchubey, Nicholas Novosiltsev, Prince Adam Czartoryski and particularly Count Paul Stroganov.

While Alexander I had a very good "press" abroad even in the first years of his reign, a press which hailed him as a great monarch and reformer, the Russians were much more sober about him. Even the Russian historian Grand Duke Nicholas Mikhailovitch a bit too bluntly states: "Emperor Alexander I never was a reformer, and in the first years of his reign he was more conservative than all the advisers around him." One of these advisers, Stroganov, described well the means by which the Emperor could be influenced:

The Emperor ascended the throne with the best intentions to introduce the possibly best improvements. Only his lack of experience, and his weak and lazy character, are opposed to this. To straighten him out one has to overcome these three obstacles. Because he has a meek character it is necessary to enslave him in order to have any influence upon him.[2]

There is no doubt that his friends knew under what contradictory influences the young Emperor was educated. They knew it much better than his American and European admirers and correspondents.

It is interesting to quote Prince Adam about the worry of the Unofficial Committee, which he calls the Secret Council:

[2] Grand Duke Nicholas Mikhailovitch, *Graf Pavel Alexandrovitch Stroganov*, St. Petersburg, 1903, Vol. II, pp. ix-x.

Various plans of reform were debated; each member brought his ideas, and sometimes his work, and information . . . as to what was passing in the existing administration. . . . The Emperor freely expressed his thoughts and sentiments, and although the discussions . . . had no practical result, no useful reform was tried or carried out during Alexander's reign which did not originate in them. Meanwhile the Official Council, namely, the Senate and the Ministers, governed the country in the old way. . . . In our Council Stroganov was the most ardent, Novosiltsev the most prudent, Kotchubey the most time-serving, and I the most disinterested. . . . the Emperor's character inclined him . . . to compromises and concessions, and moreover he did not yet feel sufficiently master of the position to risk measures which he thought too violent.[3]

In the first stage, which began in April, 1801, Stroganov was the most industrious and active member of the Committee.

This moderate reformer had been a "Jacobin" and as a youth under the guidance of his French tutor Romm had visited Paris in the very first stormy years of the Revolution. During the first conversation which he had with his august friend Alexander, he developed a very moderate plan of legal changes in Russian public and administrative law. The leading principle of Stroganov was to begin with changes in the administration of the vast country and not in the constitution as such. The latter ought to be only the logical sequence of administrative reforms. Alexander approved his approach but added that the enactment of the famous rights of citizens (la fixation des trop fameux droits de citoyen) should remain the most essential part of the work of the Committee.[4]

Alexander, who had been educated by the well known Swiss statesman, jurist, and general, Frédéric César de La Harpe, preferred constitutional acts and declarations to sober codification of administrative law in a country which, according to his words in a conversation with John Quincy Adams, was much too big to be administered in a very centralized way.

Pro-Americanism was a logical result of the interests of Russia among the nations and, of course, of the lessons Alexander had received from his Swiss tutor. His idea of a constitution was the

[3] Prince Adam Czartoryski, *Memoirs*, 2 vols., London, 1888, Vol. I, pp. 260-261.
[4] Grand Duke Nicholas, *op. cit.*, pp. 8, 9.

concoction of the ideas of Jean-Jacques Rousseau, the famous countryman of La Harpe, of the acts and demands of two English revolutions and finally of the American and the French Revolution.
Alexander's intention before his ascent to the throne and in the first
years after it was to establish a just order and prosperity in Russia,
and then to abdicate. But events were more powerful than good intentions, and Alexander remained Emperor of all the Russias. Later,
his second set of ideas, the reactionary ones, were rooted not in
Switzerland or America but in the cadet corps and barracks of military Russia. His predilection for parades was invoked to balance
the abstract radicalism. The figure of General Arakcheyeff, one of
the darkest figures of Russian reaction, had not yet appeared on the
horizon. All this relates to the opening years of Alexander's reign.
As if to tip the scales back toward pure republicanism, La Harpe,
after his revolutionary attempts in the canton of Vaud, undertook
a journey back to Russia and stayed there with his former august
pupil in 1801 and 1802 exactly when the Unofficial Committee
was at work. Alexander did not invite his tutor to be a member of
this Committee, which half ironically and half out of French revolutionary tradition was called by him Comité de Salut Publique
(Committee of Public Welfare); but it frequently consulted him.

Count Stroganov knew well the untrustworthiness of the august
republican on the Russian throne. He wished to get from this committee first of all a decent moderate constitution in order to tame
and fetter the orthodox Russian variety of Hobbes's Leviathan;
and at the outset he gave his own description of what he understood by "constitution."

A constitution, said Stroganov, is the legal recognition of the
rights of a nation and of the forms in which they can be materialized. In order to insure their validity a guarantee must be given
to stop any extraneous power from interfering with their realization.

And in accordance with the American doctrine of democracy as
the government of laws he added:

The constitution is the law which regulates the method by which
administrative statutes . . . have to be changed. Such changes should
be made in a known, fixed, and invariable way which prevents any
arbitrariness. Consequently, the evil is diminished which arises from the

different abilities of those persons who are on the top of the state-nation.[5]

Stroganov therefore tried to bind the committee and its chairman, the Czar, to the concrete Russian earth and its daily administrative necessities. But slowly the committee, not having enough "fodder" for permanent work in domestic policies, began to slide over to foreign policies, toward which Novosiltsev alone was relatively indifferent.

Stroganov was primarily interested in the separation of powers and secondarily in representative government. This shows that basically the most active member of the committee had some rigid and stable principles besides a general inclination toward France of 1789. He favored a cautious transplantation of English political traditions and English self-government, which at that time was also predominantly aristocratic, to imperial Russia, where the gentry alone had limited self-government. The Russian modestly liberal statesmen were all "great Anglomaniacs," rightly remarked Count Rumiantzev to John Quincy Adams in 1809 on his arrival as the American minister to Russia.[6] As for these Russian liberals, theirs was not the "American doctrine" which helped to move and push the French Revolution, but a kind of conservative and compromised rule of law in the tracks of which Russia could be peacefully transferred over to the ways of concessions and slow reforms.

Every one of the members of the committee was under the influence of England. Alexander's closest and most esteemed friend the Polish Prince Adam Czartoryski had gone in 1789, as a youngster of nineteen years to London by way of Paris to complete his political education by studying the English constitution. He witnessed there the trial of Warren Hastings. He returned to Poland, and in 1793 he again went to England. During this stay he wrote two treatises on English law and civilian administration. After he

[5] *Ibid.,* pp. 40-41.
[6] *Memoirs of John Quincy Adams,* Vol. II, p. 65: Said Rumiantzev: "Je dois vous prévenir que nous sommes ici de grands anglomanes." After warning Adams of the pro-English orientation of the liberal aristocrats, based "upon old habits and long established commercial intercourse," he emphasized, however, that these same circles were against "English exclusive maritime pretensions," and that Russia would willingly support the United States as the rival of England.

participated in the Polish Kosciuszko insurrection against Russia he was rather compulsively invited by Empress Catherine to come to St. Petersburg in 1795 and to enter Russian service, during which his only leading star was the restoration of Poland.[7] Counts Kotchubey and Novosiltsev, too, had lived and worked in England, and the latter was there twice—during the reign of Paul I, 1799–1801, and after 1805. Stroganov was sent to London as an extraordinary envoy to soft-pedal the too Anglophile and pro-Pitt ambassador Count Simon Vorontzov, and resided there from 1805 to 1807. Thus all of them were convinced adherers of English constitutional ideas and British anti-Napoleonism.

All these pro-English "habits" could not stop the same gentlemen from being in favor of America as a newly stabilized country the system of which was founded on the separation of powers and the rights of the individual.

There were no direct political results of the works and discussions of the Unofficial Committee which coexisted with the very official Council and Senate of Imperial Russia. Alexander, in order to prevent too great duality, appointed his friends to high office. And still the direct task of elaborating a future constitution was handed over to Speranski and Baron Rosenkampf and not to any higher official body.

Among nonpolitical ideas, the Unofficial Committee discussed very broadly the status of the peasants.

This question was not only social but political. In theory there was no doubt that something had to be done for the realization of the natural rights of the peasant, and that deliverance from the absolute political arbitrariness of old Czarism had to be accompanied by a colossal social reform in agrarian relations. This is what Jefferson expected of Alexander when he wrote to Priestley on November 29, 1802:

Alexander will doubtless begin at the right end, by taking means for diffusing instruction and a sense of their natural rights through the mass of his people, and for relieving them in the meantime from actual oppression.[8]

[7] Czartoryski, *Memoirs*, Vol. I, pp. 49-52.
[8] Thomas Jefferson, *Writings*, ed. Paul Leicester Ford, New York, 1897, Vol. VIII, p. 179.

This relief "from actual oppression" meant the abolition of serf-dom in Russia based upon the unalienable rights of liberty. Such a conclusion, harmonized with the Declaration of Independence, was natural, nay, inevitable for Thomas Jefferson, as it was for all ideologists of humanitarian liberalism in that era; but, righteous as it sounds, it could not take shape in Alexander's Russia with an actually existing privileged stratum of landlords.

About 1800 every layer of the Russian aristocracy was first of all interested in the reduction and limitation of the autocratic power and arbitrariness of its august master.

Before Jefferson's letter was written—to be exact, a year and a half earlier—Alexander had begun perhaps "at the right end"—not the end Jefferson had in mind, exactly the opposite. Alexander I and his young friends of the Unofficial Committee being afraid of stirring up the gentry, terrorized by the American and French revolutions, decided that the "right end" to begin with reforms was the confirmation of the old privileges of the nobility. By a special manifesto of April 2, 1801, Alexander solemnly restored the charter granted by Catherine to the Russian nobility in 1785.[9]

This maneuver accomplished and the rear secured, some reforms could be started. The Unofficial Committee was reluctant to take general measures of outstanding importance. Such measures were particularly difficult to carry out because among the landed gentry there were two conflicting approaches. The members of the higher aristocracy were mostly interested in the rent (*obrok*) paid by the peasants, and were more inclined toward the personal emancipa-tion of the peasants if their own income did not suffer. They were therefore not against an agrarian reform by which the greatest part of their land should be cultivated by free peasants. The lower strata of the provincial gentry, on the contrary, were mostly interested in the actual husbandry service or "average" (*barshchina*) of the serfs. No wonder that they were much less abolitionists than their richer

[9] *Polnoe sobraniye zakonov Rossiisskoi Imperii* (Collection of Laws of the Russian Empire), Vol. XXVI, No. 19,810. It is entitled "On the Restoration of the Charter Granted to the Nobility" and speaks about the "justice, holiness, and inviolability of the prerogatives of the nobility." Simultaneously the Charter of the Townships protecting commerce, industry, and the handicrafts was also restored. These two measures followed immediately an act establishing a relative freedom of prints, abolished by Paul.

brethren, the great lords around the throne. But both groups should have been handled carefully without offending or provoking them by radicalism. This was well understood by Stroganov:

The task consists in the necessity of carrying out the liberation of peasants without violent shocks. If this condition cannot be fulfilled, it is better not to do anything. The owners should be spared. We have to proceed toward our goal by the way of a series of decrees, which, not harming the owners, will improve the situation of the peasants.

Later the same principle of slowness and moderation in the abolition of serfdom was introduced in Speranski's constitutional "Plan." So Jefferson's advice was not adopted.

Some basic principles for future legislation were laid down by the committee, principles which recall the early United States:

Freedom and ownership of land ought to be the basis of agricultural work.

They [the peasants] must get the right to enjoy the fruits of this freedom and this property, i.e., they should really have such freedom and property, and the free use of it, which constitutes real happiness.

These measures shall be combined with the interests of their masters.

But if there are no outlets for the products of the agriculturists, it is in vain to try to encourage agriculture, it will not prosper anyhow.[10]

Two decrees were enacted in December, 1801, and February, 1803. By the first, merchants, burghers (*meshtshane*) and peasants of crown lands (who were not serfs) were entitled to purchase land. By the second, landlords became entitled, on the basis of mutually agreed-upon conditions, to free their peasants. This decree became known as the "law of the free farmers"—a law hated by the advocates of serfdom.

In 1803, after two and a half years' work, the Unofficial Committee was canceled, having had only eleven months of regular meetings.

In that year Michael Speranski was invited to elaborate a Russian constitution. Like his predecessor, Stroganov, he was not inclined

[10] *Ibid.*, pp. 43-48.

to recommend the immediate establishment of a full written constitution. His basic task was "to prepare Russia for the acceptance
of the genuine forms of monarchy" by a series of gradual reforms.
Already in the discussions of the Unofficial Committee which
adopted the terminology of those times, the "true monarchy" was
a limited constitutional monarchy, while an autocratic monarchy
was regarded in the terms of Montesquieu as despotism. Catherine,
the author of the Instruction, had disliked appearing before the
world as a despot; and the feeling of her grandson, Alexander, educated by the Swiss republican La Harpe, was stronger. Speranski
was an ardent advocate of limited monarchy, and in this had the
full support of the Emperor. The first step to be taken was the reform of the Senate, in which legislative and administrative functions were united with judicial. Speranski's idea was to divide it
into two parts: the Legislative and the Executive Senate, the latter
to have the judicial and administrative functions. The idea was
that, after the people got acquainted with this division of powers,
the Legislative Senate could be turned into a representative body
of a parliamentarian type.

Speranski's very moderate plan did not meet fully the wishes of
the reigning "republican" Emperor, and he appointed Rosenkampf,
a Baltic baron who scarcely could read Russian, to work on the constitution. Being well educated in German law, particularly civil and
criminal law, he was unable to draft a regular constitution for Russia. He concentrated on comparative law and translated a series of
constitutions of different countries, and it is probable that in connection with his work and Speranski's the Emperor formed the wish
to be informed about the new constitution of the United States.

Here a part of Jefferson's letter of April 18, 1806, to Lovett Harris,
the American consul at St. Petersburg, is of interest:

A little before Dr. Priestley's death, he informed me that he had
received intimations, through a channel he confided in, that the Emperor entertained a wish to know something of our Constitution. I have
therefore selected the two best works we have on that subject, for which
I pray you to ask a place in his library. They are too much in detail to
occupy his time; but they will furnish materials for an abstract, to be
made by others, on such a scale as may bring the matter within the

compass of the time which his higher callings can yield to such an object.[11]

Which exactly these "two best works" were, we indirectly discover when we turn to a letter written by Jefferson to Dr. Joseph Priestley on November 29, 1802. In the second half of this letter we read:

I should be puzzled to find a person capable of preparing for him [Alexander] the short analytical view of our constitution which you propose. It would be a short work, but a difficult one. Mr. Cooper's Propositions respecting the foundation of civil government; your own piece on the First principles of government; Chipman's Sketches on the principles of government, and the Federalist would furnish the principles of our constitution and their practical development in the several parts of that instrument. I question whether such a work can be so well executed for his purpose by any other, as by a Russian presenting exactly that view of it which that people would seize with advantage.[12]

There is no doubt that all four works mentioned, only two of which were books, were sent to Alexander in Russia, where the Unofficial Committee was at work. It is improbable that they were read by the Emperor, but they may well have been used by Speranski and other members of the committee for the drafting of laws.

Jefferson was much more enthusiastic about Alexander's constitutional and legislative attempts than Stroganov, the official constitutionalist of the Unofficial Committee who, as we have already seen, was mostly interested in the negative limitation of monarchic arbitrariness than in all the refined legal niceties of the people's natural rights. That Jefferson's enthusiasm was genuine we may see from the first part of November 29, 1802, letter to Dr. Priestley— a private letter of a thinker to a thinker:

. . . I am very thankful for the extract of Mr. Stone's letter on the subject of Alexander. The apparition of such a man on a throne is one of the phænomena which will distinguish the present epoch so remarkable in the history of man. But he must have an herculean task to devise and establish the means of securing freedom and happiness to those

[11] Jefferson, *Writings*, Monticello ed., Washington, 1904, Vol. XI, pp. 101-102.
[12] Jefferson, *Writings*, ed. P. L. Ford, Vol. VIII, p. 179.

who are not capable of taking care of themselves. Some preparation seems necessary to qualify the body of a nation for self-government. Who could have thought the French nation incapable of it? Alexander will doubtless begin at the right end, by taking means for diffusing instruction and a sense of their natural rights through the mass of his people, and for relieving them in the meantime from actual oppression.

After this letter was written Jefferson received the text of a letter of La Harpe to Stone dated October 20, 1803. Stone had approached Joel Barlow, who at that time lived in France as a mediator, in order to hand it over to Jefferson. The letter written in French quotes an excerpt from Alexander's letter to La Harpe, as follows: "I would be extremely thankful to you, if you could be helpful to make my closest acquaintance with Jefferson, I would be much flattered by that." [13] La Harpe commented: "It would be a good thing if you could find a secure and suitable way to let Jefferson know about it." It was therefore only natural that Jefferson should react in the most friendly way to this attempt of Alexander, who behaved rather as a modest beginning writer eager to get a prominent correspondent than as the Emperor of Russia. And, nevertheless, it is much more than usual courtesy that Jefferson's letter of June 15, 1804, to Alexander contains, in the part dealing with the Russian domestic reforms:

I avail myself of this occasion of expressing the exalted pleasure I have felt in observing the various acts of your administration during the short time you have yet been on the throne of your country, and seeing in them manifestations of the virtue and wisdom from which they flow. What has not your country to hope from a career which has begun from such auspicious developments! Sound principles, pursued with a steady step, dealing out good progressively as your people are prepared to receive and to hold it fast, cannot fail to carry them and yourself far in the improvement of their condition during the course of your life.[14]

Alexander answered in a letter of November 7, 1804, of which the second part reads as follows:

[13] V. M. Kozlovski, "Imperator Alexander I i Dzhefferson" in the Russian review *Russkaya Mysl*, 1910, No. 10 (Pt. 2), p. 84. He quotes as a source The Manuscripts of Jefferson, Series 2, vol. 2, No. 12.
[14] Jefferson, *Writings*, Monticello ed., Vol. XIX, p. 144.

At all times I nourished a very high esteem for your nation which knew well enough how to use its independence particularly by giving itself a free and wise constitution which insures the happiness of all and that of every one in particular.

Being extremely sensitive to the interest you have shown in the welfare and prosperity of Russia, I believe I cannot better express my feelings toward the United States than by stating that they are reciprocal in this relation, and that I express the wish that the United States may retain for a long time at the head of their administration as virtuous and enlightened a Chief as you are.[15]

In a letter dated August 20, 1805,[16] he acknowledges Jefferson's thanks for the rescue by the Russians of some American sailors who were fighting against pirates of Tripoli, and once more repeats his esteem for America for having created an outstanding constitution. Of greater importance is his letter of August 10, 1806, which covers in its first half constitutional problems. At that time the Unofficial Committee had ceased to work; but constitutional problems were not dropped by Alexander despite the unhappy defeats suffered by the Russian armies in fighting Napoleon. The letter continues:

Mr. Harris brought to me the letter which you entrusted him to hand over to me, as well as the interesting works on the Constitution of your country which you sent to me at the same time. I hasten to convey to you, by the channel of the messenger whom Mr. Harris is sending, how much I am touched by these new tokens of your friendship. You have shown me a fair appreciation, which flatters me very much, proving by the very choice of the works on your country which you are sending me that you are aware of the extent of the interest I have for it.

If my reading of these works could increase this interest it would only double the satisfaction with which I observe its happiness entrusted to your patriotism and wisdom. . . . It is very satisfying for me to be able to add to the testimony of my own conscience, the fairness with which you consider my intentions, and this feeling should be for you a sure guarantee that these intentions will never change. If they should be crowned with the success towards which my most serious efforts are

15 The French original of this letter is preserved in the Pierpont Morgan Library, New York.
16 Library of Congress, Jefferson Papers, Vol. 152, pp. 26550-26551.

directed, it is partly in your approval that I shall seek my reward; because the nation at the head of which you are placed will equally be instrumental in the general good which these intentions shall have brought about.[17]

The results of the work of the Legislative Commission were, as we have seen, not of great importance.

Rosenkampf was not the person who could give a clear blueprint of an imperial constitution; he showed his full inability for creative legislative work, and in August, 1808, an order of Alexander I virtually put Speranski in his place. Speranski's Plan for a Political Reform was completed in 1809.[18]

The Francophile Michael Speranski was invited to work before Rosenkampf and continued to work after him. The books on the American constitution that Jefferson had sent in April, 1806, were used by the Legislative Commission and may have had some influence on the formulation of the shortened bill of rights and the separation of powers included in Speranski's project which was completed in October, 1809, and in the Constitutional Charter of 1819 prepared by Novosiltsev.

The federal character of the United States was partially mirrored in Novosiltsev's project of 1819, while Speranski's project built upon French models was strictly centralistic.

Already at that time, in the eyes of European reformers, the three most conspicuous features of the American Constitution were the bill of rights, the separation of powers, and the federal structure.

The American bill of rights was very popular in the whole of Europe from the time the French Declaration of 1789 became obsolete under Napoleon, and particularly after the restoration of the Bourbons in 1814. The level of democratism of different European states was determined mainly by the degree to which they adopted the principles of the American bills of rights, and of course of the Declaration of Independence. Of peculiar importance was the principle of the right to revolution. This was in general too radical to be enacted as positive public law in Europe, particularly in Russia. It was expressly formulated in the most radical French

[17] *Ibid.*, Vol. 160, pp. 28175-28176.
[18] Cf. Baron M. Korff, *Zhisn grafa Speranskavo* (Life of Count Speranski) St. Petersburg, 1861, pp. 146 ff.

declaration of 1793, but in general Europeans did not go so far as to justify resistance against the established constitutional order. The supporters of the old regimes did not have the courage to fight for their rights of rebellion, and the promoters of the new democracy were not sure enough of the new regime to grant such a right. And with the decline of natural law it became old-fashioned to insist upon such an outmoded subversive dictum. The United States alone did not change this dictum of the right and duty to throw off despotic governments as formulated in 1776. This country educated generation after generation in a secular unholiness of the state order as such and in a secular belief that political changes might be undertaken if the pursuit of happiness or the "higher rights" required it.

But what imperial Russia took from America was the minor usual rights and guarantees: toleration, freedom of religion and the press, and the inviolability of the person. The right of habeas corpus was included not only in the criminal procedure but also in the constitution—the fundamental law of the country. No other country than the United States appeared as a model. England had no written constitution, and therefore offered no ready pattern. The French constitutions following one after another at short intervals became, according to the winged words of a famous Frenchman, "daily literature," i.e. of an extremely transient value. Among the sixty German sovereignties there was no constitution worthy of mention. So Russian liberal thought was bound to recognize the United States as the basic source for constitutional reform.

Speranski, an adherer of Montesquieu and Beccaria but even more of Bentham, showed a very independent and rationalistic way of thinking. The general introduction to his Plan tries to find the right place of Russia in the political frame of Europe. It distinguishes three political systems: the republican, in which the sovereign power is moderated by the laws, in the passing of which the citizens more or less participate as in the ancient Greek republics; the feudal system based on autocratic power, which is not limited by the law but rather by its material division; and the despotic system, mostly in the Orient, which does not know any restriction or limits. All the political transmutations of Europe present a permanent clash between the republican system and the feudal one. With the unfolding enlightenment the first system became stronger; the second, feebler. The enlightenment and growing trade asked for the construction of a new order, in which the motivating idea remained the same; namely, the attainment of political freedom. The present turn from the feudal regime to a republican one is the third period. England was the first country to make the turn, and the states which followed were Switzerland, Holland, "the United Provinces of America," and, finally, France.[19]

As necessary prerequisites of any Russian constitution Speranski mentioned: all the estates (classes) of the state which were free should participate to a certain degree in legislation; the constitution was not only written law but must express the national spirit; freedom of the press in certain limits must be established; full independence of judiciary must be established, with the exclusion of the competence of the Emperor; all acts of the administration should be made public, except certain cases.[20]

Of no less importance was the American principle of separation of powers. True, this was not a purely American product. Montesquieu had styled the English body politic the home of the separation of powers. But England, too rich in common law, could not serve well the constitutional reformers of Europe. America, on the contrary, had a clearly fixed, constitutionally formulated separation of powers, which nobody could doubt. The President, for instance, as the head of the executive power, who was authorized to approach the legislative power, the Congress, only through written messages, became an unextinguishable symbol and a fascinating pattern of American freedom and separation of powers. The same was true for the outstanding, nay, overwhelming independence of the American judicial power, headed by the Supreme Court.

These features could easily have been combined with the Russian somewhat reformed monarchy. Speranski first tried to introduce the separation of powers into his Plan, along the following lines: the legislative power was to be exercised by the All-Russian State Duma (the parliament) together with the Emperor, this feature finally materialized a century later, in 1906; the executive

[19] M. M. Speranski, *Plan gosudarstvennavo preobrazovania* (Plan for a Political Reform), Moscow, 1905, p. 19.
[20] *Ibid.*, pp. 175-176.

power belonged to the monarch; the judicial power was handed over to the courts and judges, elected by the people. This principle of the separation of powers had to be carried out not only in the central bodies but also in the local ones, from the top to the bottom. The organs of the legislative were: the State Duma, the gubernial (provincial), regional and district dumas. The organs of the administration were the ministries in the capital, and the subordinated governors and other executives down to the village district (*volost*). The judiciary organs reached from the Supreme Court (*Senat*) down to the local district courts.[21]

Only one important feature proposed by Speranski differed from the American pattern; this was the functioning of the executive powers as vested in the Emperor and his ministers. Liberal Russia was inclined to lean upon the English pattern, i.e., on the responsibility of the ministers to the legislative body. Here, obviously in a serious effort to prevent any transgressions by the ministers, the legislative Duma was endowed with the important role of making "remonstrances" against ministers if by any measure of the government an open violation were committed of the fundamental law of the State—namely, against personal or political freedom—and if the government should not present in due time the obligatory accounts and budgets. This problem of the responsibility of the ministers was not solved in the Constitution of 1906; it remained crucial in the Czarist regime, and became the reason if not the main cause of the democratic March Revolution of 1917.

Of exceeding importance was the independence of the judiciary as fixed in Speranski's Plan. While according to the old, and almost universal practice of the absolute royal power the Emperor had the right to intervene in trials and to give his decisions on appeals, the idea of the Plan was to extend the judicial power to all cases and to preclude any royal interference in judiciary: a principle which became Russian positive law in 1864 under Alexander II.

The only parts of the Plan which were carried out were: the establishment in 1810 of the State Council with a character of an advisory legislative council, appointed by the Emperor and turned in 1906 into a regular parliamentary upper house; and the intro-

[21] N. I. Lasarevski, *Russkoye gosudarstvennoye pravo* (Russian Constitutional Law), St. Petersburg, 1913, Vol. I, p. 176.

duction on June 1, 1811, of Ministries. In establishing the State Council the autocracy recognized the political virtue of the separation of powers. Later it gave the possibility to Russian constitutionalists to distinguish between an imperial decree (ukase) and a statute.

All the other and most important parts of Speranski's Plan were canceled, partly under the pretext of the nearing clash with Napoleon. More serious was the estrangement between the Emperor and his most active helper, Speranski, who was detested by the reactionary circles of the highest court gentry and of the bureaucracy who finally denounced him as an agent of Napoleon. Speranski fell in disgrace; he was compelled to resign and was exiled to the Ural regions.

Speranski's Plan was finally given up, but still Alexander did not give up the idea of less radical constitutional reforms. Strangely enough the western border provinces of Russia were much better treated by the Emperor than Russia proper. Poland received a moderate constitution in 1818 with its own diet and a broad home rule. In 1817–1819 the Latvian and Estonian serf-peasants of Livonia, Courland, and Estonia were emancipated from their German Baltic barons. In 1809 Finland received a far-going autonomy although Russia proper had only the insignificant decree about the free farmers of 1803. In his opening throne speech to the Polish diet Alexander undertook to establish a similar institution for his own fatherland; but this promise made in a solemn speech of a Polish king who happened simultaneously to be a Russian emperor was never fulfilled. In 1819 Novosiltsev was ordered to draft another project of a State Constitutional Charter (Ustavnaya Gramota) for Russia. This was after the victory over Napoleon and the reestablishment of peace, and after the western provinces of Russia had been endowed with constitutional and administrative reforms. The second official project of a constitution for Russia proper was this Constitutional Charter of the Russian Empire.[22]

In this project French influences prevail; the text of the Charter

---

[22] The Russian and the French texts were published together in full in Berlin, 1903. An introduction by Prof. Th. Schiemann precedes the text. This project remained a concealed document for almost a century, because of czarist mistrust of liberal political ideas.

has much in common with the Polish Constitutional Charter of 1815 both in some articles, which coincide, and in the political terminology used for the representative and other bodies. Most remarkably the Polish constitution proclaims, "The Polish people shall have forever a national representation in its Sejm," and the Russian project repeats it literally (Art. 91).

American influences are most conspicuous in Articles 1 to 8 and 148 to 151 of the Charter, which deal with the division of the Russian Empire into provinces. Like the American states, these not only are administrative regions but have their own legislative bodies divided in two classes: one half of the seats to be vacated after the first three years and the second half after six years. Like Washington, D.C., St. Petersburg and Moscow, the two capitals, and their regions are exempt from the general division into provinces. As in America, the central and provincial parliaments consist of two chambers. The exact number of provinces is not mentioned in the project, but from a document not directly associated with the Charter we get the following list of twelve capitals: Riga, Vitebsk, Kiev, Odessa, Archangel, Tver, Tula, Orenburg, Kazan, Tiflis, Tomsk, and Vilna.[23] The Charter is a forerunner of Muraviev's full-fledged federal constitution which enumerates thirteen states but includes Finland as the Bothnic state, while Novosiltsev's project excludes Finland as a province enjoying the highest degree of autonomy.[24] Strictly, according to its constitution, Finland was not a part of Russia.

Other similarities to the American constitution can be found in the articles devoted to the bill of rights. In a country of established serfdom Article 80 runs as follows: "The law protects equally all the citizens without any discrimination." This is reminiscent of the Declaration of Independence of 1776. But the term "citizen," introduced by Nicholas Novosiltsev, was not used in Russian law, being a republican term in contradistinction to the traditional "subject." The project was thus an early forerunner of the Russian democratic revolution of 1917 which finally substituted "citizen" for "subject." All the procedural guarantees, of indictment, trial,

[23] G. Vernadsky, "Reform Under Czar Alexander I: French and American Influences," in *Review of Politics*, Vol. IX, p. 59 (Jan., 1947).
[24] See below, chapter VII.

judgment, and punishment, as well as the principles of *habeas corpus* are laid down in Articles 81 to 88. Article 89 grants freedom of press. Article 94 gives the right to every domiciled person of good behavior, after five years of residence, to acquire Russian citizenship with the right to be appointed to public office. Articles 97 and 98 proclaim the inviolability of private property, which is not to be taken for public use by the government without just compensation.

Needless to say that, if such a constitution could have been enacted in the second decade of the nineteenth century, it would have been a real political emancipation. While the project of Speranski was more exact in reference to the conservation of serfdom, Novosiltsev's project somehow tried to circumvene the question by creating—*nolens volens*—a position in which serfdom would not fit into the general picture of his proposed constitution. Alexander's position in regard to Novosiltsev's constitutional project was a difficult and ambiguous one. After having "given" two constitutions to Finland and Poland he could not openly reject the Russian constitution without insulting the intelligence and good will of the Russian élite represented by the best strata of the Russian aristocracy. On the other hand the reactionary atmosphere was growing in and around the Holy Alliance in which he was the initiator and to which he tried to invite even the United States of America. The influential Metternich and lesser German reactionaries of Austria and Prussia were terrified by the liberal intention of the Czar to constitutionalize his huge autocratic empire. Vienna and Berlin took all possible steps of friendly intervention to prevent the enactment of Novosiltsev's project. To this Russian historians add another, internal event. In 1820, when Alexander was at the Congress of Troppau, riots broke out in the Semionov Guard Regiment against the severity and brutal disciplinary actions of the regiment's commander, Schwartz. A part of the regiment was jailed in the Peter-Paul fortress. From Troppau, Alexander ordered the dismissal of Schwartz and the dissolution of the regiment. Many soldiers were flogged and banished to Siberia. Simultaneously, however, these riots erased the last remnants of Alexander's constitutionalism, and he did not sign the ready project.

The well prepared project was buried—and constitutional reform in Russia was postponed for an entire century with all those fatal consequences which necessarily derive from an infinitely postponed reform.

This meant at least for a certain time the official refutation of the American doctrine in Russia sanctioned by Alexander I, who himself in his first letters to Jefferson had been ready to regard the American Constitution as a pattern for his own country. However, if even in France, which collaborated with the young United States in its difficult emergence, the American doctrine was abandoned with the rise of Napoleon to power, a similar betrayal was more natural for imperial Russia. And still the Decembrist movement in the first half of the 1820's and the later restitution of the American doctrine in the Russian constitutional doctrine during and after the 1860's shows that the blow of 1819 was not a fatal one and could not stop an extraordinary impact of American political ideas upon Czarist Russia.

Nevertheless it cannot be denied that the Holy Alliance brought disaster to European countries both in their domestic progress, which was influenced to a marked degree by American patterns, and in their foreign policies. It is worth while to notice what Marquis de Lafayette wrote to Thomas Jefferson about the European reaction of that time and about Alexander I:

You have been a sharer, my dear friend, in my enthusiastic French hopes; you have seen the people of France truly a great nation, when the rights of mankind, proclaimed, conquered, supported by a whole population, were set up as a new imported American doctrine, for the instruction and example of Europe, when they might have been the sole object and the glorious price of a first irresistible impulsion, which has since been spent into other purposes by the subsequent vicissitudes of government. The triple counter revolution of Jacobinism, Bonapartism, and Bourbonism, in the first of which disguised Aristocracy had also a great part, has worn out the springs of energetic patriotism. . . . In the meanwhile all adversaries of mankind,—coalesced kings, British aristocrats, Continental nobles, Coblentz emigrants, restored Jesuits, are pushing their plot with as much fury but more cunning than they had hitherto evinced. Emperor Alexander I is now the chief of European counter revolution; what he and his allies will do, either in concert or in competition with England, to spoil the game of Greece, and to annoy the new republics of America, I do not know; but although the policy of the United States has been hitherto very prudent, it seems to me they cannot remain wholly indifferent to the destruction, on the American Continent, of every right proclaimed in the immortal Declaration of Independence.[25]

We shall see in Chapter VII that the "imported American doctrine" was influential in the 1820's in Russia, too; but the rebels' courage in convictions and their self-denial were not enough to prevent the brutal suppression of upheavals in an autocratic subcontinent. There was a very interesting attempt to reawaken and bring back to life the buried Russian constitution. This was made by the revolutionary government of Poland, which found the French and Russian texts of the constitution left by Novosiltsev in Warsaw, and published them on July 30, 1831, with a foreword by Andrew Horodyski, the foreign minister of the revolutionary government, which invited the Russians to rise against Czar Nicholas I:

We leave it to the Russian nation to re-appreciate the motives out of which such a great idea and such an important work have fallen into oblivion. The Poles ardently wish that this casual discovery may remind the Russian government that it is high time for the nation over which it rules, and which long has been eager to improve its political condition, with so many millions of human beings oppressed by despotism, so that it shall finally begin to enjoy the fruits of a constitutional monarchy.

This clever address and the republished constitution were a slap in the face of Nicholas I before the whole world, five years after his brutal suppression of the Decembrist revolution. The reaction to the revelation was characteristic of this most tyrannical Russian despot. He wrote to Prince Paskevitch after the capture of revolutionary Warsaw:

The printing of this charter is extremely disagreeable: out of a hundred Russian officers there [in Warsaw] ninety will read it, not understand or despise it, but ten will well remember it and discuss it, and, what is most important, *they will never forget it*. And this troubles me to the utmost.[26]

[25] Jefferson, *Writings*, Monticello ed., Vol. XVIII, pp. 325-326. The letter is dated Dec. 20, 1823.

[26] V. E. Yakushkin, *Gosudarstvennaya vlast i proyekti gosudarstvennoi reformy v Rossii* (The State Power and Projects of Russian Constitutional Reforms), St. Petersburg, 1906, pp. 95, 96.

Only Nicholas I, who suppressed the Decembrist upheaval in the first days of his reign, a movement for which "constitution" was the popular slogan, could be so terrified by the discovery of a constitutional project written by the august order of his late brother, the friend of Thomas Jefferson and John Quincy Adams. It was natural for such a convinced autocrat to order the purchase of all 1,578 copies found in Warsaw and their secret burning in Moscow.

VI *International Contacts: Alexander I,*
Jefferson, and John Quincy Adams

IT IS PECULIAR THAT THE FOREIGN POLICIES OF BOTH CATHERINE II and Alexander I were closely connected with their domestic policies. Moreover, their reigns represent the period when Russia gradually became a center around which Europe often revolved. In spite of well deserved skepticism in regard to the political sincerity of these monarchs, who began by accepting and admiring that which they later denied and despised, the years from 1762 to 1825 (with the short dim-out of Paul I, 1796–1801) were the most magnificent period of the St. Petersburg stage of Russian history (1703–1917). The general foreign policy and diplomacy are not necessarily applied according to domestic standards. Outwardly both the grandmother and the grandson were enlightened rulers and supported rather more liberal views in international relations and municipal legislation than some of their Western august "cousins." Catherine II was not only more daring and freethinking than her immediate and remote German neighbor-potentates but also more enlightened than George III of England. Alexander, until the Vienna Congress was more "progressive" than King Frederick William III of Prussia, Emperor Francis and Prince Metternich of Vienna, and was not less liberal than Castlereagh and other leading English conservative statesmen of that time.

This, of course, does not mean that these Russian monarchs were free from tendencies of aggression—and aggrandizement. They, after Peter I, were the greatest augmenters of the Empire. Moreover, while the Western powers were pushed to their conquests by the interests of a very active bourgeoisie, the Russian monarchs were without the link between crown and town and, therefore, the support of a mighty middle class eager to expand its foreign markets. Adventurous traders or hunters in the vast dependencies were no substitute for a middle class. We have seen that Catherine was eager to "establish" a third estate, an urban bourgeoisie; but the replacement of trading and manufacturing landlords seriously interested in a monetary economic system by a regular bourgeoisie was very slow. The postponed and long overdue emancipation of the peasantry had so frozen this otherwise "natural development" that only after 1880 did the Russian bourgeoisie become politically active. Thus the augmentation and territorial growth of Russia— at least in the St. Petersburg period (1700–1917)—was a matter of routine for the new body politic established by Peter I.

The Russian monarchic state of and after Peter I, in the machinery of which external wars constituted a heavy budgetary item, had great need of money. This was particularly true during the reign of Alexander I, who conducted bloody and costly land and sea wars against Napoleon and Sweden and Turkey. After 1814 the diplomatic service, and the lavish expenditure on the congresses of the Holy Alliance and the standing army of 1,200,000 swallowed tremendous amounts of money. The poll tax (capitation) of the poor serfs and the urban masses and the profits from the wine and spirit monopoly of the state could not meet these tremendous expenses. Therefore the extraordinary new income from navigation and sea trade was welcome; and to that extent Russia was interested in its own sea trade and in the destruction of the British maritime pretensions. Its antagonism to England coincided with the interests of the United States, the country of a blooming new bourgeoisie, the two were not necessarily the same. A growing commercial state like the United States was more interested in the rights of an open sea and neutrality than the Russian mainly continental leviathan, but there was, no doubt, a clear common anti-British denominator between Russia and America.

When one adds to all this the well known fact that even after the conquest of the outlets in the Baltic and Black Seas the Russian fleet could be always bottled up by its seagoing enemies in straits and sounds surrounded by foreign countries, the importance, or rather nuisance value, of the Russian resistance to British sea power grows considerably. It was a constant factor during the nineteenth century, and was very advantageous to the United States, particularly during the Civil War.

In this atmosphere the cooperation between the United States and imperial Russia can be well understood.

This was also the social and domestic background behind imperial Russia's attempts to reshape established international relations to which she was a typical belated newcomer, bare of any traditions, prejudices, or maritime experience. The armed neutrality of Catherine which endured under Alexander I was therefore a means of changing the mutual correlations of the older seafaring nations.

This was also the bridge upon which Jefferson's "distant and infant nation" could meet the predominantly agrarian Russia.

Russia from the time of Catherine was very jealous of her territorial conquests. To insist on the inviolability of her vast territories was a military necessity, independent of the question to what degree she was able to exploit her legendary riches. Even the young nonfeudal United States was for a long time unable to produce its own iron and steel.

In the early period of diplomatic contact between Russia of Catherine II and the United States, John Ledyard of Connecticut arrived in Paris, where Jefferson was American Minister, in the interest of a mercantile company in the fur trade of the western coast of America. When he failed Jefferson in 1787 proposed to him "to go by land to Kamchatka, cross in some of the Russian vessels to Nootka Sound, fall down into the latitude of the Missouri, and penetrate to and through that to the United States." Through the Russian Embassy in Paris the permission of Catherine to cross her territories was obtained; and Ledyard reached a point "two hundred miles from Kamchatka" where he had to pass the winter. As "he was preparing in the spring to resume his journey, . . . he was arrested by an officer of the Empress who, by this time, had changed her mind." He was brought back to Poland from which he had to return to Paris. This was the consciousness of imperial sovereignty in the days of Catherine.

To this Jefferson epically adds: "In 1792 I proposed to the A.P.S. [American Philosophical Society] that we should set on foot a subscription to engage some competent person to explore that region in the opposite direction, that is, by ascending the Missouri, crossing the Stony mountains, and descending the nearest river to the Pacific." [1]

Reconsidering this picturesque incident, one comes necessarily to the conclusion that Jefferson's proposal that the region of Kamchatka and Alaska be explored "in the opposite direction" found its final realization in "Seward's folly"—the American purchase of Alaska as late as 1867. In the meantime this buffer province on the American continent never became a serious cause of discord between the two vast countries despite a few attacks of Russian activity in the Western Hemisphere.

On the other hand commercial relations between the two countries, during the whole of the nineteenth century, were at no time of great importance to either. Even in the years preceding the First World War, when Russia became much more industrialized and bought from the United States large quantities of machinery, cotton, and fuel, she sold in return only small quantities of raw materials.[2] This—in addition to the tremendous distance from Philadelphia or Washington to St. Petersburg—prevented the diplomatic relations between the countries from being disturbed too much by the export-import business or by exclusively economic and commercial differences. It may be right to say that this slightness of economic contact led to a heightening of political factors in their relations, with specific times of a sharpened interest in commercial and naval communications and issues. Such were the periods of Francis Dana's residence under Catherine II, of John Quincy Adams's residence under Alexander I, and before the conclusion of the 1832 commercial treaty between the countries under Nicholas I.

The predominance of purely political considerations and factors in Russo-American diplomatic relations is illustrated in the last two decades of the eighteenth century, particularly in the reign of Paul I. Around 1798–1799 the trade of the United States with Rus-

[1] *The Complete Jefferson*, ed. Saul K. Padover, New York, 1943, pp. 909-910. On p. 1164 Padover makes the correction that the Empress actually refused the permission, but Ledyard proceeded on his journey, hoping to obtain this later.

[2] Cf. Mikhail V. Condoide, *Russian-American Trade*, Columbus, O., 1946, p. 5.

sia was at an exceedingly low ebb.[3] Nevertheless, Russia became very eager to establish closer relations. Certainly not out of mere economic or commercial reasons, although trade often appears as an outer pretext in diplomatic correspondence. The real cause was a political event; namely, the rupture in 1798 of diplomatic relations with the French Directory as a result of which the United States began great preparations for war. In Europe a coalition was formed against France by Russia, Austria, England, Turkey, and Naples. Russia's aim was to get the help of the United States for the complete isolation of France, a precedent and antidote to Napoleon's later continental blockade. In connection with this in November, 1799, Count Simon Vorontzov, the Russian ambassador at London, approached Rufus King, the American minister to Great Britain on the subject of closer relations between Russia and the United States. Vorontzov emphasized the trade interests of America in the whole of the Baltic Sea and suggested not only a commercial treaty with Russia but also offered his help in concluding an American-Turkish treaty to extend American trade in the Levant. The United States remained reluctant.

Throughout the first years of the reign of Alexander I, until 1812, there was a much greater harmony between the inner and the outer Russian policy than after Napoleon's unsuccessful invasion of that year.

True, there was no sharp line between the early liberal years and the later mystic and reactionary years of Alexander I. There were always diversions and sudden twists and turns forward and backward. Some of them were amazing. In September, 1807, after the conclusion of the Tilsit peace with Napoleon and the inevitable materialization of a Franco-Russian alliance, Alexander stopped at Mitau for a night on his way to St. Petersburg—because in Mitau lived the émigré Louis, Count of Provence and heir of the executed King Louis XVI, with his puppet court. The Russian liberal Emperor and official ally of the subversive Napoleon stopped in Mitau

---

[3] John C. Hildt, *Early Diplomatic Negotiations of the United States with Russia* (Johns Hopkins Univ. Studies in Hist. and Polit. Sci., Series 24, Nos. 5-6), Baltimore, 1906, pp. 30 ff. Quoting Pitkin's *Statistical View of the Commerce of the United States of America* (1817), Hildt states that "at that time the exports of the United States to Russia were less than to any other European nation."

to assure the future King Louis XVIII, open adversary of Napoleon, of his own continued good will in spite of his alliance with Napoleon.[4] On the other hand during the reactionary period of Alexander's reign a no less amazing instance of hypocrisy than this treacherous visit was a confession made by this crowned mystic reactionary and most active builder of international monarchic legitimism throughout Europe, in the last weeks of his life, to a courtier before whom there was no point in showing off: "Whatever will be said about me, but I lived and I will die as a republican." [5]

Although Jefferson was not acquainted with the Russian background of his august correspondent, he became conscious of the Emperor's ambiguous role only in the last years of his reign. In the first years of the nineteenth century Alexander was the only liberal sovereign of Europe equally progressive in the field of constitutional reforms and in the international field of world pacification.

Only in the light of a forgotten Russian document can we understand the most important theme which repeats itself in the correspondence between Jefferson and Alexander on diplomatic relations; namely, the issues of "general intercourse of nations" and their "pacification."

The whole character of the correspondence between Thomas Jefferson and Alexander I in diplomatic matters (particularly, the constant underscoring of Russia's role in the universal pacification, which is ascribed by the great American to the Czar) is clarified by an important document in which is expressed the whole conception of Alexander's foreign policies in the first seven or eight years of his reign.

This document is a directive from the Czar which introduces the negotiations of Russia with England in the early autumn of 1804, proposing a collective struggle of some European countries against

[4] See C. Joyneville, *Life and Times of Alexander I*, London, 1875, Vol. II, p. 4.
[5] See M. N. Pokrovski, "Alexander I" in *Istoriya Rossii v XIX vyeke* (History of Russia in the Nineteenth Century), Moscow, 1907–1911, Vol. I, p. 33. Pokrovski comments that despite the open contrast of this confession to the actual political situation of the Russian Empire he does not doubt the sincerity of Alexander. He ascribes these and similar inconsistencies not to the hypocrisy of Alexander but to the conflicting conditions of Russia in the first quarter of the century.

France. Alexander needed a broad program for such a fight. He tried to derive some conclusions from the revolutionary wars of France and the early monarchic counterrevolution. Because of his liberal education by La Harpe he was able to understand that the old dynastic and *ancien régime* views could not serve the cause of a new struggle against Napoleon, the child of the Revolution. He put the principles of the great French Revolutionary wars which recognized the right of peoples to their national liberty against Napoleonic France itself.[6] Simultaneously the liberal tendencies in the internal and external relations of Russia were underlined. Alexander I in his first liberal years was skeptical enough not to put the burden of such negotiations upon the old conservative Anglomaniac ambassador, Count Alexander Vorontzov. He chose the younger Novosiltsev, his "intimate" friend who was thoroughly "acquainted (as we have seen) with the views and opinions" of his august master and who was more likely to succeed in this responsible diplomatic job.

The document which we have in mind is the Secret Instructions from the Emperor of Russia to M. de Novosiltsev signed September 11, 1804, by the Emperor and countersigned by his intimate friend Prince A. Czartoryski.[7] The Instructions point out in part:

The most powerful weapon hitherto used by the French, and still threatening the other European states, is the general opinion . . . that her cause is the cause of national liberty and prosperity. . . . It would be dangerous for all the powers any longer to leave to France the great advantage of seeming to occupy such a position. . . .

Being repugnant to any reaction, I would wish the two governments to agree that, far from attempting to reestablish old abuses in the countries which will have to be emancipated from the yoke of Buonaparte, they should, on the contrary, be assured of liberties founded on a solid basis.

[6] Cf. the very instructive article of B. S. Mirkine-Guetzevitch, "Russki proyekt mezhdunarodnoi organizatzii Yevropy 1804 goda" (A Russian Project of the International Organization of Europe in 1804) printed in the *Sbornik* devoted to P. N. Miliukov, Prague, 1929, pp. 435-449.

[7] *Memoirs of Prince Adam Czartoryski*, ed. Adam Gielgud, London, 1888, Vol. II, pp. 41-51. The text of the Instructions is somewhat shortened in comparison with the French original.

In the Instructions views expressed are on particular countries: Sardinia, Switzerland, Holland, and the whole of the motley Germany of those times. Alexander urges for all these countries free and wise constitutions and, wisely enough, is against the absorption of all the various German states by Austria and Prussia and for the establishment of a "more concentrated federal government." As to France, says Alexander, "we should declare to the French nation that our efforts are directed not against her, but only against her government, which is as tyrannical for France as for the rest of Europe." The Instructions actually ask for an establishment of what could be called in modern terms an international organization of nations—a scheme of pacification which was much admired by Jefferson, and in which he saw the greatest merit of the Russian monarch; and they continue:

The object would be, first, to attach nations to their governments, by making it only possible for the latter to act for the benefit of their subjects, and secondly, to fix the relations of the various states toward one another on more precise rules, which would be so drawn up as to make it the interest of each state to respect them. The internal social order will be founded on wise liberty . . . and at the same time on international law, which regulates the mutual relations of a European federation which will be established on sound principles. . . . It is not the dream of a permanent peace that we are going to materialize. . . . Why should not the general rules of international law be imposed upon the positive law of nations? . . . When peace is made, a new treaty should be drawn up as a basis for the reciprocal relations of the European states. Such a treaty might secure the privileges of neutrality, bind the powers who take part in it never to begin a war until after exhausting every means of mediation by a third power. . . . On such principles we should proceed toward general pacification and lay down a sort of new code of international law which, being sanctioned by the greater part of the European states, would, if violated by any of them, bind the others to turn against the offender and make good the evil he has committed.

In order to remain consistent in continuing the traditions of Catherine's armed neutrality, and maybe in order to strengthen Russian ties with the United States, which at those times was rather apprehensive about the maritime preponderance of Britain, the Instructions conclude cleverly:

Among the important points of which you will have to treat with the English government the most difficult will be that of making it feel the propriety and necessity, at a moment when it would reestablish order and justice in Europe in concert with Russia, also to consent to make some change in its maritime code—the only matter as to which the British cabinet is not free from reproach, and which enables its enemies to injure it by exasperating the neutral powers. Some concessions on this point, not of a character to do any real damage to the commerce of England or to her preponderance on the sea, would destroy the fears and the mistrust of the neutral states. . . .

Only by comparing these Instructions with the later views developed in the documentation of the Vienna Congress can we measure the great contrast between the internal and the external policies of Russia. The Vienna Congress of 1815 did not inaugurate any permanent international organization nor universal pacification. Here and there in the instruments of this Congress a vague verbiage and terminology recall the old formulas used by the almost forgotten Instructions of Alexander and Czartoryski. But in general the made-in-Vienna European system based on "political balancing" was the ruin of a splendid edifice originally built in a French-Russian Directory style. None the less, there is no doubt that in 1804 autocratic Russia was much more progressive in its international policies than parliamentary England. This—whether completely known or only vaguely felt by the young United States —was an important pillar of Russo-American friendship, so conspicuously and colorfully expressed in the correspondence between Jefferson and Alexander. The smashing defeat of Alexander by Napoleon in and after Austerlitz (December, 1805) was the knell of the principles of a new international organization laid down in the Instructions.

The American friendship with Russia survived all the blows suffered by her after Austerlitz. Among these we must mention the Tilsit treaty with Napoleon in July, 1807, and the establishment of a Franco-Russian alliance. In November, 1807, England took its measures of blockade against Russia as a part of Napoleon's continental system. This time Russia was not only politically but economically interested in the support of the United States. The Russian landowners—exporters of grain—had to look for a substitute for the English market. The immense Russian war machine needed money and exchange. As a large producer of raw materials Russia required an alliance with a nation largely devoted to the carrying trade,[8] and she turned to the United States. In June, 1808, Count Rumiantzev wrote to the American consul at St. Petersburg, Levett Harris, asking him to inform his government of the appointment, in order to strengthen the friendship between Russia and the United States, of André Dashkoff as consul-general at Philadelphia and *"chargé d'affaires* near the Congress of the United States."* This rapprochement led a year later to the appointment of John Quincy Adams as the first American minister at the court in St. Petersburg.

After having established the first connection with Thomas Jefferson, Alexander [9] wrote him a letter August 20, 1805, in which he dwelt on the new diplomatic relations with the United States, ascribing particular importance to the establishment and growth of commercial relations between the countries and promising special hospitality and privileges to Americans in Russia. He added:

I share your opinion about an instrument [sur un acte] which could add nothing new, but I place more value upon the reciprocity on the part of the government of the United States regarding my subjects. I have not the least doubt about the sincerity of the assurances which you have given me in this regard.

Obviously in view of the delicate diplomatic relations of the two countries with Great Britain, an exactly formulated treaty between Russia and the United States would have been regarded askance in London.

Jefferson's answering letter of April 19, 1806, deserves to be quoted *in extenso*. Even with the slow communication of the time, this answer was belated. Between August, 1805, and April, 1806, tremendous events had taken place in Europe. Russia was beaten

[8] *Ibid.*, p. 38. Hildt quotes here the letter of Gen. Armstrong to the Secretary of State, Paris, Nov. 24, 1808.

[9] See Chap. V.

by Napoleon in the famous battle of Austerlitz, with the annihilation of the Russian and Austrian armies so that the Austrian Emperor Francis and the Russian Emperor Alexander fled from the field in different directions. This battle deeply changed the correlation of the leading powers. Despite Nelson's triumph at Trafalgar over the Franco-Spanish navy, William Pitt was terrified by the successes of Napoleon's land forces. When Pitt, the most obstinate and talented enemy of Napoleon, received the fatal news about Austerlitz, he succumbed. The next British cabinet of Fox proposed peace to Napoleon in February, 1806.

Doubtless all this news had reached President Jefferson long before he wrote his letter to the beaten Russian Emperor, whose way went downhill to the Tilsit negotiations of summer, 1807. Nevertheless, he wrote to Alexander in his former tone, still addressing him as on the same level as the victorious Napoleon, calling them the "two personages of Europe" who had in their power to establish a new international order and pacification.

Washington, April 19, 1806

I owe an acknowledgment to your Imperial Majesty for the great satisfaction I have received from your letter of August the 20th, 1805, and embrace the opportunity it affords of giving expression to the sincere respect and veneration I entertain for your character. It will be among the latest and most soothing comforts of my life, to have seen advanced to the government of so extensive a portion of the earth, and at so early a period of his life, a sovereign whose ruling passion is the advancement of the happiness and prosperity of his people; and not of his own people only, but who can extend his eye and his good will to a distant and infant nation, unoffending in its course, unambitious in its views.

The events of Europe come to us so late, and so suspiciously, that observations on them would certainly be stale, and possibly wide of their actual state. From their general aspect, however, I collect that your Majesty's interposition in them has been disinterested and generous, and having in view only the general good of the great European family. When you shall proceed to the pacification which is to re-establish peace and commerce, the same dispositions of mind will lead you to think of the general intercourse of nations, and to make that provision for its future maintenance which, in times past, it has so much needed. The northern nations of Europe, at the head of which your Majesty is distinguished, are habitually peaceable. The United States of America, like them, are attached to peace. We have then with them a common interest in the neutral rights. Every nation indeed, on the continent of Europe, belligerent as well as neutral, is interested in maintaining these rights, in liberalizing them progressively with the progress of science and refinement of morality, and in relieving them from restrictions which the extension of the arts has long since rendered unreasonable and vexatious.

Two personages in Europe, of which your Majesty is one, have it in their power, at the approaching pacification, to render eminent service to nations in general, by incorporating into the act of pacification, a correct definition of the rights of neutrals on the high seas. Such a definition, declared by all the powers lately or still belligerent, would give to those rights a precision and notoriety, and cover them with an authority, which would protect them in an important degree against future violation; and should any further sanction be necessary, that of an exclusion of the violating nation from commercial intercourse with all the others, would be preferred to war, as more analogous to the offence, more easy and likely to be executed with good faith. The essential articles of these rights, too, are so few and simple as easily to be defined.

Having taken no part in the past or existing troubles of Europe, we have no part to act in its pacification. But as principles may then be settled in which we have a deep interest, it is a great happiness for us that they are placed under the protection of an umpire, who, looking beyond the narrow bounds of an individual nation, will take under the cover of his equity the rights of the absent and unrepresented. It is only by a happy concurrence of good characters and good occasions, that a step can now and then be taken to advance the well-being of nations. If the present occasion be good, I am sure your Majesty's character will not be wanting to avail the world of it. By monuments of such good offices, may your life become an epoch in the history of the condition of man; and may He who called it into being, for the good of the human family, give it length of days and success, and have it always in His holy keeping.[10]

In his second letter to Jefferson, August 10, 1806, Alexander is anxious to bind his American correspondent to his idea of the Instructions, being sure in advance of Jefferson's consent. Therefore he wrote:

I have no illusions about the magnitude of the obstacles which could prevent the return of an order of things adapted to the general welfare

[10] Jefferson, *Writings*, Monticello ed., Vol. XI, pp. 103-106.

of all civilized nations, an order able to resist the efforts of ambition and greed. But this goal is so lofty and so dear to my heart that the difficulties it carries with it are unable to discourage me.[11]

It is not without sincerity—in view of the difficult situation of Russia during the smashing successes of Napoleon—that Alexander adds concerning the support which Jefferson rendered to his views on international relations: "I find in the justice you are showing toward my views the most powerful encouragement of my efforts." [12]

In 1812, as we have seen, Alexander's former friend and admirer Speranski was suddenly dismissed and banned as a result of reac- tionary blackmail accusing him of pro-Napoleonism. It was after 1812 that Alexander got more religious and began to read his Bible, as he confessed to his Quaker friend, Allan. Despite his growing mysticism he gave his signature to the Polish constitution of 1815, and appointed a new constitutional reformer of Russia proper, namely, Novosiltsev, to the passing of whose thorough project in 1819 only the signature and seal of the Czar were never given. In 1818, as the official head of the Orthodox Church, Alexander not only invited two leading Quakers to his palace but also, "bathed in tears," prayed with them and kissed them when parting. In 1822 he promised the Quaker Allan to oppose the slave trade and to out- law it as piracy at the congress of sovereigns in Verona; he also promised to introduce Lancaster schools in Russia and to promote a thorough reform of the penitentiary system. In conclusion he proposed that they should pray, and embraced and kissed the Quaker thrice over.[13] No action followed.

With the growing counterrevolutionary sentiment the friendship of Alexander toward America gradually diminished. The more in- fluential pietism became—in the person of the Baltic German baroness Juliana Krudener, who in reality behaved like a prophet of the idea of the Holy Alliance—the less friendly Alexander I be-

[11]Library of Congress, Jefferson Papers, Vol. 152, pp. 26550-26551, Aug. 20, 1805, Alexander to Thomas Jefferson.

[12] Library of Congress, Jefferson Papers, Vol. 160, pp. 28175-28176, Aug. 10, 1806, Alexander to Thomas Jefferson.

[13] John Cunningham, *The Quakers from Their Origin till the Present Time: An International History*, London, 1897, pp. 288-289, 301-305.

came toward America. Likewise, Jefferson's attitude to his august Russian friend grew more and more distrustful. Important doubts in connection with Alexander's leadership in the Holy Alliance were expressed by Jefferson as early as July 23, 1816, in a letter to Dr. Logan:

This conversation [of Alexander with Clarkson] too, taken with his late Christian league, seems to bespeak in him something like a sectarian piety. . . . I sincerely wish that the history of the secret proceedings at Vienna may become known, and may reconcile to our good opinion of him his participation in the demolition of ancient and independent States, transferring them and their inhabitants as farms and stocks of cattle at a market to other owners, and even taking a part of the spoil to himself.[14]

When, in the process of the reactionary policies of imperial Russia, Alexander's role became sufficiently clear, Jefferson wrote to Levett Harris, December 12, 1821:

I am afraid our quondam favorite Alexander has swerved from the true faith. His becoming an accomplice of the soi-disant Holy Alliance, the anti-national principles he has separately avowed, and his becoming the very leader of a combination to chain mankind down eternally to oppressions of the most barbarous ages, are clouds on his character not easily to be cleared away.[15]

It was not less a man than John Quincy Adams who formulated in the most convincing form the retreat of Alexander from his ideas of general pacification in 1804 to the creation of the Holy Alliance:

The memoir is a fresh exposition of the political system of Russia, founded upon the basis of the European alliance for the preservation of universal peace. It notices again the public comments and glosses upon the alliance, and the different charges which have been occasionally brought against it, as a league of great powers to oppress the smaller, or a combination of sovereigns against the liberties of the people. It defends the system against these and other objections, and holds it forth as a righteous and pure-hearted league of powerful sovereigns for the maintenance of justice, of good understanding, and of peace between

[14] Jefferson, *Writings*, ed. H. Washington, Vol. VII, p. 20.
[15] Jefferson, *Writings*, Monticello ed., Vol. XIX.

them and all of the world. . . . *It is Alexander's substitute for the armed neutrality.*[16]

The words which La Harpe wrote to his friend Stapfers on October 26, 1824, sound like a political knell:

I seduced myself by the hope that I had educated a Marcus Aurelius for fifty million people and during twelve of my best years of life I renounced all other kinds of work. True, I have had a momentary pleasure of high decency, but it disappeared irreversibly and a bottomless abyss swallowed up the fruits of all my works together with the hopes.[17]

This same crescendo of deterioration can be discovered also in the development of the foreign relations between Russia and the United States beginning with the period of John Quincy Adams as American minister at St. Petersburg (1809–1813) and finishing with the early 1830's. Alexander told him in formally receiving him on November 5, 1809:

With regard to the political relations of Europe . . . the system of the United States was wise and just . . . that the only obstacle to a general pacification was the obstinate adherence of England to a system of maritime pretensions which was neither liberal nor just; that the only object now to be attained by the war was to bring England to reasonable terms on this subject.

Indirectly defining before Adams the alliance between Russia and France, Alexander referred to it as conforming to his liberal views on neutral navigation and on English obstinacy, and added that these principles could be promoted only

by a state of peace and friendship between Russia and France, whose views, he believed, . . . were not at all directed to the conquest of England, but merely to make her recognize the only fair and equitable principles of neutral navigation in time of war.[18]

Chancellor Rumiantzev was even more open in his first interview with Adams. The chancellor admitted the usual Anglomania of the high Russian aristocrats but added

[16] J. Q. Adams, *Memoirs*, Vol. V, pp. 140-141, italics mine.
[17] K. M. Kozlovski, *op. cit.* Translated from the Russian text, which is a translation from the French original.
[18] Adams, *Memoirs*, Vol. II, pp. 51, 52.

that the English exclusive maritime pretensions, and views of usurpation upon the rights of other nations, made it essential to them, and especially to Russia, that some great commercial state should be supported as their rival; that the United States of America were such a state, and the highest interest of Russia was to support and favor them, as by their relative situation the two powers could never be in any manner dangerous to each other . . . that the Emperor had always manifested a favorable opinion of it.[19]

Despite the fact that Adams as American minister was in an incomparably better position than his predecessor Francis Dana, he repeated Dana's mistake by not trying to make friends with the people of the country in which he resided and with the liberal ruler with whom he was sometimes in informal contact. While Dana had never met Catherine, Adams often met the emperor in his capacity as diplomat and also unofficially upon the Fontanka River or at other places where they were accustomed to walk. The most important issue he pursued throughout the period of his residence was the continental system, which was the crux of Russian foreign policy and a detriment to American economic interests. It is therefore natural that most of his official conversations were connected with the Russian-American sea trade and the specific cases concerning the admittance of American vessels, decisions concerning the cargoes, and the exportation of Russian hemp, tallow, beeswax, iron and so on.

Neither political nor constitutional questions were raised by Adams in his conversations with the Emperor and Chancellor Rumiantzev, although he must have known about two things: constitutional reforms being prepared, and American sympathies being expressed by the Russian liberals. Even when meeting Count Speranski and Count Stroganov, actually interested in constitutional and administrative reforms—as we have seen—he never took occasion to learn about Russian public opinion upon impending measures. This political indifference was shown by Adams simultaneously with a vivid interest in all the ceremonial nuances, ritual and calendaric peculiarities of the Russian Church as compared with other churches, and a curiosity concerning the curricula and examinations in public and privileged schools. In his memoirs we dis-

[19] *Ibid.*, p. 65.

cover only one or two times when matters of public law or political reforms in Russia were directly discussed by the American minister.

One was the conversation with Count Rumiantzev about the provincial elections held every third year, in which the nobility had an election separate from that of the merchants. Rumiantzev mentioned that the elder Stroganov (father of the constitutional reformer) had been re-elected First Marshal of the nobility. Thus being almost provoked to switch over to constitutional reforms, Adams did not react.

Just once, Adams's later courageous and sincere antislavery stand throughout eight successive Congresses shines through. In a conversation in December, 1812, during the last weeks of the repulsion of Napoleon's invasion, with Russian Admiral Kutuzov, the nephew of the world-famous Field Marshal Michael Kutuzov, the discussion touched the abolition of serfdom in Russia in view of Napoleon's tendencies to liberate serfs in all European countries conquered by him. Backward and half-feudal Spain and Russia were the points in case. Many aristocrats in Russia were afraid the invasion of Napoleon would be immeasurably helped by his liberating tens of millions of Russian serf-peasants, and French agents sent to various provinces would incite the serf-peasants against their masters and the government. However, the Russian peasants, after the suppression of the Pugachov upheaval in 1775, did not rise in face of the invasion and Napoleon did not really act in this direction. The landed gentry were happy to witness this patriotism of their serfs, unshadowed by any clouds of social discontent. With this in the background Adams's description of this conversation becomes utterly picturesque:

I told him that I had witnessed with interest and admiration the spirit manifested by all classes of people in this nation under the struggle from which they are issuing with such triumphant glory; that I had never entertained a low idea of Russia, but that the conduct of the nation upon this severe trial had far exceeded my expectations. He said, *"Monsieur, la Russie, bien gouvernée, est faite pour commander l'Europe."*

I think she will not lose the opportunity. I observed, however, that the circumstance that appeared most to gratify the Admiral, in speaking of the conduct of the nation, was that the peasants had not shown the least disposition to avail themselves of the occasion to obtain their freedom. I see that this is what most touches the feelings of all the Russians with whom I have conversed on this subject. This was the point upon which their fears were the greatest, and that upon which they are most delighted to see the danger past. The admiral . . . professed to be pleased with my remarks.[20]

Adams was extremely reserved in his frequent conversations with Alexander and did not take any direct opportunity to be a political mentor of the Emperor or of his most outstanding subjects.

In May, 1811, Alexander met him and, in the course of the conversation, raised the question of the absorption of Florida. Adams hinted that the consent of the local population was a prerequisite in the annexation of new provinces, and the conversation went on:

"I hear you have lately made an acquisition."—I observed, I supposed his Majesty meant in Florida. He said that was what he meant. "But," said he, "it appears to have been a spontaneous movement of the people themselves, who were desirous of joining themselves to the United States." I said, so it appeared from the accounts which I had seen, but that I had received no communication from my Government upon this subject. I added that this was a part of the territory which had been ceded by France to the United States . . . that Spain, however, had entered into a controversy with us about it . . . that since then the people of that country had been left in a sort of abandonment by Spain, and must naturally be very desirous of being annexed to the United States. Under these circumstances the United States have taken possession of the country. The Emperor smiled and said, "On s'agrandit toujours en peu dans ce monde," and bowed; upon which I quitted him.[21]

This remarkable conversation must have left afterthoughts in the minds of both talkers. Alexander up to that time had taken possession of an ancient monarchy in the Caucasus, the orthodox Christian Georgia, of Bessarabia in the southwest, and of Finland in the northwest of Russia. In no case had the consent of the absorbed peoples been asked. The slight hint of the American diplomat had necessarily to be taken as a very soft reproach, but Alexander tried to coat the pill by remarking abstractly and universalistically: "On s'agrandit toujours en peu, dans ce monde." Adams too probably remembered this conversation in the later decades of his life, first when the treaty

[20] *Ibid.*, p. 425.
[21] *Ibid.*, p. 261. "In this world states always expand a bit."

for the cession of the Floridas by Spain (1818) was negotiated by him, after the conclusion of which his opponents called it a deliberate sacrifice of territory, and secondly when he opposed the annexation of Texas (from Mexico) in 1836 mainly out of antislavery considerations.

Adams, in general well inclined to the Emperor, was not at all embittered against him by the failure of his mediation in 1812 between England and the United States. True, this mediation was initiated by the latter. The American proposal, later strongly criticized in the Congress, had as its precedent the proposal by First Consul Bonaparte to Alexander I in the middle of 1803 that he assume the role of a mediator between France and England. Adams in his *Memoirs* describes the sincere attempts of Rumiantzev to activize the Emperor, wholly absorbed with French issues after Napoleon's retreat. But the endless procrastination of the negotiations and the helpless situation of the two American agents in St. Petersburg left a slight bitterness in the heart of the American minister.

Adams was much more critical and outspoken back in America in the position of Secretary of State. This was, of course, in the last years of Alexander and the first years of Nicholas I. In June, 1820, when the United States was suspected by the Holy Alliance and particularly by Russia of supporting the revolutionary Spaniards and the revolting colonies of Latin America, he had an official conference with the Russian ambassador Poletica. As to the revolutionary acts in Spain, Adams frankly stated

there was no country in the world where military mutiny would be more disapproved than in this. . . . Military interference with the organization or administration of our Governments had been unexampled throughout our Revolution, and ever since. On the other hand, there were many things in the recent transactions in Spain which were universally approved here . . . the moderation which had hitherto marked the revolutionary movement, the release of all prisoners for politics, and the abolition of the Inquisition, for example, not to mention the liberty of press, which we indeed approve also, but would not be so agreeable in Europe. I thought, however, that before the European Sovereigns should resolve upon any system for the treatment of the Spanish malady they would do well to consider the whole case.[22]

[22] *Ibid.*, Vol. V, pp. 142-143.

In connection with the American occupation of the Columbia River valley, the Senate nominated a commission to sound out this issue, and in January, 1821, the report of the commission was an object of public interest because of the suspicions regarding Russia's intentions. On September 4, 1821, in the middle of the discussion, Alexander issued a ukase simultaneously with the approval of new privileges for the Russian-American Company, closing all harbors of the Northwestern Russian Pacific coasts and the Aleutian and Kurile islands to all foreign ships, without any exception.

The immediate reaction was two protests: one from the United States and the other from Great Britain.

But here Russia's inability to defend the commercial interests of her subjects on the American continent as well as the arbitrariness of Russian autocracy in foreign policy became explicit in the most conspicuous way. In the broad plan of Alexander the Holy Alliance, with orthodox Russia on the top, was interested in an active interference in Greek affairs and the support of Ypsilanti's rebellion, supposedly the first steps for the partition of Turkey. Any complications or conflicts with the United States and England could have been only harmful for Russia; [23] hence Alexander's readiness to nullify the implementation of the ukase and to drop the interests of the Russian furriers, fisheries, and hunting trade.

This incident, no doubt, led to the final formulation of the Monroe Doctrine. The Russian autocrat, once an initiator of a scheme of real international peace, got an important lesson from the young American republic. A special convention was concluded in April, 1824, regulating the relations between the United States and Russia on the American continent, which actually was the first international instrument deriving from the new Monroe Doctrine. This was indeed a great moral victory of the forty-year-old "infant nation" over the thousand-year-old Russian monarchy.

Adams grew more and more critical of the reactionary policies of Nicholas I and his envoys. He did not conceal his negative attitude toward the Russian diplomat Poletica when speaking to Baron Paul Krudener in January, 1830, upon Russian affairs and the conference between three ministers mediating in the affairs of Greece:

[23] Semion Okun, *Rossiisko-Amerikanskaya Kompaniya* (The Russian-American Company) 1939, p. 78.

He [Krudener] said to me that the foundations of the friendly relations which subsisted so cordially between Russia and the United States
had been laid by my mission to the Emperor Alexander, that the policy
and the feelings of the present Emperor were entirely the same as those
of his brother had been; that he had taken great satisfaction in the
happy state of those relations, and that he regretted the disposition of
the Government of the United States was not now so friendly towards
Russia as it had been. He complained of a paragraph in the President's
messsage; of articles in the New York Enquirer, Mr. Van Buren's particular paper; and of many other incidents which he considers as manifestations of temper. He thinks the present Administration excessively
anxious to conciliate the favor of Great Britain, and is apprehensive that
in order to acquire a predominating influence here, to put down our
manufacturing interest, and to inflame the violent sectional passions of
the country, they will make great sacrifices—restore to us the intercourse
with their West Indian Colonies, and even yield to us the navigation
of the St. Lawrence.

I told him that I had no doubt the British Government would do all
they could, but that they would find it very difficult to manage their
own people . . .

The Baron told me that he asked leave of absence on account of his
health . . . But the relations between the two countries were growing
less cordial and more delicate. He was conscious that he had not the
talents necessary for the management of them.[24]

Baron Krudener was right in complaining that the disposition of
the United States toward Russia worsened very much in comparison
with the past. But how could that be otherwise in the times of the
growing Holy Alliance and Russia's intervention not only in European but also in American affairs after the declaration of the Monroe Doctrine?

Even the conclusion in 1832 of the commercial treaty between the
United States and Russia did not bring any actual rapprochement
between the most autocratic power in Europe and the most liberal
America. The sharp opposition in Russia itself against Czarism and
serfdom initiated by aristocratic Russian officers in the form of the
Decembrist movement strengthened greatly under the influence of
the democratic "American doctrine" without any direct political
support of this movement by the United States itself.

[24] Adams, *Memoirs*, Vol. VIII, pp. 168-170.

VII *Decembrism: Its American Leanings*

"There were no good governments but in America."
—Kondratii Ryleyev, a Decembrist who was hanged.

THE DECEMBRIST MOVEMENT IN RUSSIA WAS A REMARKABLE phenomenon. Here I shall deal only with those phases which bear the stamp of American political thought and institutions.

Whatever interpretation may be given to Decembrism, it stands alone, without any precedent in the political history of Europe. This liberation movement, which took definite form only in the upheaval of 1825, began after the defeat of Napoleon, especially after the European campaigns of the Russian army which was the leading force in his defeat. Led by the aristocracy it was primarily a reaction against the worsening of political conditions under Alexander I. We have seen that the official constitutional project of Speranski did not materialize, except in its least important and purely administrative aspect, the establishment of the State Council and the ministries. We have also seen that all attempts to solve the Russian agrarian problem were reduced to ridiculously petty ukases creating "free cultivators" doomed to remain the special beneficiaries of individual nobles or squires tired or repentant of the continued possession of peasants. There was no legislative "safety valve" for the growing dissatisfaction of the opposition. Alexander himself succumbed more and more to the most reactionary views of Arakcheyev with respect to internal conditions and domestic administration and to those of Metternich concerning foreign policy. Inwardly a covered kettle boiling with discontent, outwardly the reproachless sentry of the Holy Alliance, ready to jump against every foreign revolution—this was Alexander's Russia after the Vienna Congress.

The organizational patterns for the new movement, generally known after 1816 as the Union of Welfare—which later consisted of two large "Societies," the Northern and the Southern, which was more radical and closer to popular demands—were taken from the German romantic Tugendbund. However, the similarities between the two were more in external characteristics than in methods.

While the German Tugendbund was primarily a patriotic anti-French movement, the Russian Union, as it developed, became more and more a movement of opposition to the government. According to its statute, the Tugendbund was eager to enjoy the approval of every government; the Russian underground Union asked for a sacrificial and secret opposition to tyranny and autocracy.[1] Its aims were divided among the following fields: humanity; education; judicial equity; social economy.

The Decembrist movement had as its basis a program most naturally adapted to the typical bourgeois revolution. Alexander Muraviev defined the chief objectives of the Welfare Union, in addition to a representative constitutional government, as the abolition of serfdom, equality of all citizens before the law, publicity on all state affairs, and public judicial trials. As less important objectives, of temporary character, he listed: elimination of the military colonies (established by Arakcheyev); abolition of the state liquor and wine monopoly; improvement of the situation of the clergy; improvement of the welfare of the defenders of the fatherland; shortening of the term of compulsory military service; reduction of the army in peacetime. Subsequently, these planks crystallized politically, and full abolition of the monarchy or at least strong constitutional limitation of monarchic privileges was made the leading principle.

One important aspect of the Decembrist movement is of a sociological character. It would seem that such a movement should have been led by an aspiring bourgeoisie, by merchants and burgesses, with the participation of some splinters of the privileged aristocracy. But the fact is that the underground work—the organization and the upheaval itself—was carried on by both societies, the members of which were almost exclusively aristocrats. Some were noblemen in high military or civil posts; others came from the middle-class gentry. In any event, there was not one merchant member of the movement. This group of aristocrats, oddly enough, led the upheaval itself, pressing for the introduction of what is usually called a bourgeois democracy. This is a democracy of a republican or constitutionally limited monarchic type, calling for full equality before the

[1] A. N. Pypin, *Obshchestvennoye dvizheniye v Rossii pri Aleksandre II* (The Russian Social Movement Under Alexander I), 1900, p. 371.

law, abolition of feudal and estate privileges, and creation of legally
—and, as far as possible, socially—equal citizens instead of the
sharply defined social strata: gentry, clergy, burgesses and merchants,
and the serf-peasantry.

This aspect of the movement, which must be puzzling indeed to
the average Marxist, gives it its unique character. This phenomenon
—a sociological paradox—made the abolition of serfdom the most
vital common denominator of the whole movement. Aristocrats,
some of whom were "owners" of hundreds, and even thousands, of
enslaved Christian souls and white human bodies, fought an illegal
and dangerous fight against the established regime for the emancipation of peasants and for equality: a fight in which victory presupposed a curtailment of privileges with financial loss and a lowering
of social position, and the elevation of the present slaves to equal
citizenship.

Needless to say, there were many attempts to torture these facts,
to squeeze the picture into the frame of the obligatory class doctrine.
For instance, Michael Pokrovski, while he admitted that not one
merchant was a member of the underground "societies," nevertheless thought that the movement had to be recognized as bourgeois because the constitutional and certain economic views of the
Russian Decembrist aristocrats showed the influence of bourgeois
liberal ideas on their ideology. Pokrovski tries to reduce the very
sober and farsighted opposition of the Decembrists to the lamentations of some of the landed gentry who were dissatisfied with certain inconveniences or with the curtailment of aristocratic local government, or perhaps with the poor administration of the highways,
and so on.[2]

There is no doubt that the majority of the Decembrists were adherents of Adam Smith, and opponents of the official autocratic
fiscal policy with its taxes and duties which swelled the income of
the treasury but were an oppressive burden on the whole urban
population, particularly the prohibitive customs tariff of 1822. The
outstanding Decembrist Kakhovski, for instance, aptly differentiated

[2] See M. N. Pokrovski and K. N. Levin, "Dekabristy," in *Istoriya Rossii v
XIX vyeke*, Vol. I, pp. 98 ff.; Pokrovski, *Russkava Istoriya* (Russian History),
Vol. III, Moscow, 1924, pp. 268-279; and A. G. Mazour, *The First Russian
Revolution*, 1825, Berkeley, Calif., 1937, pp. 64 ff.

between the wealth of the nation and the wealth of the treasury or government. Other leading Decembrists like Paul Pestel and A. Bestuzhev tried to correct this situation, so unfair to Russian trade and to the merchants and owners of factories. They felt, too, that the burgesses were overburdened by duties and taxes, and that the time had come for them to be freed from the old guilds which only hampered industry. However, most of the arguments of the Decembrists were directed against the institution of serfdom. The only difference of opinion among the noble revolutionaries was on what kind of relations should exist between the landlords and the freed serfs. Should the emancipation follow the pattern of the Baltic emancipation in 1817–1819, in which the peasants had received personal freedom but no allotment of land, or should an allotment be made? This problem existed in all its sharpness down to the emancipation of 1861 and even after.

Despite the efforts to obscure the true nature of the movement, the salient fact remains that while the "progressive" issues were not elaborated into the revolutionary objectives of a third estate as in England in 1648–1688, or America in the last quarter of the eighteenth century, or even as in France in 1789–1793, the Decembrists nevertheless worked for the absentee bourgeoisie and, though aristocrats and landlords themselves, sacrificed their lives and their well established positions for goals outside, if not directly opposed to, their own interests.

A remotely similar, sociologically paradoxical situation occurred in Russia almost a hundred years later in November, 1917, when a radical ideological group with the backing of the urban proletarians, who numbered 3.5 per cent of the population, undertook a revolution against the tremendous bourgeois, nonproletarian majority.

Now let us analyze the American tendencies of Decembrism. There is no doubt that the French Revolution had its influence among the aristocratic rebels of the first, and more particularly the second, half of Alexander's reign. France was much closer to Russia than America, and its history and language incomparably better known; yet the majority of the Decembrists turned to the American Revolution for inspiration, because it had more substance than the French and was not distorted and confused by a sweep of counterrevolution. What the Americans had done, they had done thoroughly. They had pulled out some weak roots of transplanted quasi-feudal institutions; they had established a republic using elements snatched from monarchic England. They had created a new nation of equal citizens. In these circumstances, it was little wonder that America was preferred to France, General Washington to General Bonaparte, and Jeffersonian democracy to the restoration of the Bourbons. Let me quote from a letter of Kakhovski commenting on these developments:

We are witnesses of great events. The establishment of the New World and the introduction of the new regime of the United States of North America has stimulated Europe to emulation. The States will shine as a model to remote generations. The name of Washington, the friend and benefactor of the people, will go down from age to age; whenever his name is recalled, love for the fatherland's good will begin to stir in the breast of every citizen.

The Revolution of France, which began so virtuously, changed at the end from legal to criminal. The guilt was not the nation's; the fault lay rather in the intrigues of the courts and their policies, . . . the domination of Napoleon, the wars of 1813 and 1814 into which all the nations of Europe threw themselves, inflamed by the ideas of freedom and civil rights, later proclaimed even by the monarchs. . . . By what were the armies led on? Freedom was preached to us, manifestos, appeals, and orders! We were lured, and we, the good-hearted, believed and did not spare our lives and property. Napoleon is cast down! The Bourbons are reinvited to the French throne and, pressed by circumstances, they give a constitution to a courageous and generous people! Louis XVIII even swore to forget the past. The monarchs joined in a holy alliance, congresses convened and promised the peoples to establish political freedom and the balance of classes. But soon the aims of the congresses were unmasked; soon the people became aware that they had been deceived. . . . The kings violated their oaths; the constitution of France was broken at its very foundation. Freedom of the press came to an end; the French armies against their will attacked free Spain. . . . The Holy Alliance forgot that Spain was the first country to revolt against the violation of Napoleon; and Emperor Alexander defied the government, previously recognized by him, with the dubious justification that only under the pressure of circumstances had he recognized in 1812 the Spanish constitution. . . . The destiny of European peoples turned so gloomy that they longed for the past and began to bless the memory of Napoleon the conqueror. . . . We Russians are proud and glorify ourselves as the redeemers of Europe! The foreigners do not see us in this light; they regard us as the reserve army of the Holy Alliance's despotism. . . . To whom were we helpful? To what end has our blood soaked the plains of Europe? In all probability we aided autocracy and did not support the welfare of the people.[3]

Kakhovski's honest, if somewhat emotional, statement gives us the actual background of the romantic admiration for America which was felt by the most enlightened and noble minds among the Russian Decembrist revolutionaries. It was disappointment over Europe's progress, including the wrecked French Revolution.

Kakhovski's closest friend was Kondratii Ryleyev, who combined poetry with practical inclinations. At one time he was a member of the Criminal Court and became popular as a human and just judge. Later, following his pro-American sympathies, he entered the service of the Russian-American Company as the secretary of the firm established for the exploitation of Alaska. The company esteemed his services highly, and he was presented with a raccoon coat.

Although Ryleyev entered the movement relatively late, he was one of the most radical of the Decembrists. He believed it was necessary to assassinate the Emperor, and this objective brought him together with Kakhovski, who decided to sacrifice himself for the common good. Ryleyev often supported and spurred on Kakhovski in his role, which he called the role of a Russian Brutus, or Riego, or Sand, all of whom had murdered tyrants or their assistants.

Kakhovski considered the assassination of a tyrant as an act of the highest morality, whereas Ryleyev regarded it rather as an act of extreme necessity.

At the same time Ryleyev was actively spreading the ideas of the insurgents among the young officers and cadets of the army and navy. Official documents characterize his activities as follows:

Ryleyev acted upon the minds of some young officers of the Battalion of Marine Guards who were not members of the Society of the North

[3] P. E. Shchegolev, "Piotr Grigoryevitch Kakhovski," in *Byloye* (The Past), Vol. I, No. 1 (Jan., 1906), pp. 129-167.

nor of the South, and did not form a society of their own, but took pleasure in meeting for the purpose of censuring with bitterness the proceedings of the government, extolling the constitution of the United States of America, and delivering themselves up to the vain chimera of establishing a republic in Russia.[4]

In the same report Ryleyev is said to have stated "that there were no good governments but in America; that the whole of Europe, comprising even England, groaned under slavery, and that Russia would set the example of enfranchisement." [5]

Captain Lieutenant Torson, of English or Scandinavian descent, aide de camp of the Naval Staff, visited the United States as an officer. Neither Ryleyev nor Pestel could agree with the moderate views of this young Decembrist described as follows:

He saw, in fact, that the government of the United States of America was preferable to all others; but it was his intention to preserve for a time the monarchical forms, and to divide Russia into great provinces like the United States; moreover, he granted to society only the right of destroying things, not that of creating anew, without the concurrence of the representatives of the nation.[6]

Torson was also opposed to the extermination of the imperial family. Nevertheless, his moderateness and all his opposition to Ryleyev did not save him from being banished to Siberia together with his more radical companions.

Ryleyev, with all his sympathetic regard for America and his practical pro-Americanism, was the most important leader of the upheaval. At the time of his arrest he was subjected to long interrogation; but, though morally broken, he was still courageous enough to take upon himself the heaviest responsibility:

I own myself to have been the principal instigator of the events of the fourteenth of December. I could have stopped it all, yet I set for others the fatal example of criminal zeal. If anyone deserves exemplary punishment, which the welfare of Russia perhaps demands, it is I, notwithstanding my repentance.[7]

---

[4] *The Report of the Commission of Inquiry*, transl. from the French by G. Elliott, St. Petersburg, 1826, pp. 91-92.

[5] *Ibid.*, p. 103.   [6] *Ibid.*, p. 105.   [7] *Ibid.*, p. 109.

It is touching to note that this Russian Brutus, writing from the fortress before his death to his beloved wife Natalya and scraping revolutionary themes with a nail upon a leaden tray, was carried away by religious ecstasy and idealism, but not to the point of forgetting about such prosaic things as mortgages and his ten shares in the Russian-American Company.[8]

Less outstanding in revolutionary activity than Ryleyev or Kakhovski was Paul Pestel, colonel of the Guards, one of the four or five Germans among six hundred active Decembrists. Intellectually, Pestel was doubtless first among the Decembrists: not only did he have talents, he was also one of the best educated of the insurgents. He took a very important part in the establishment of the illegal Union. When the Union of Welfare was dissolved, after the Congress of 1821, he opposed the decision and immediately organized the members living in the South into the Southern Society as an affiliated branch of the Union, the dissolution of which he did not recognize.

Pestel, like his revolutionary predecessor Radishchev, had been graduated from the imperial Corps of Pages, in which he was first in the class of 1811. He was much interested in political science. His name was inscribed on a marble tablet in the imperial corps, but the tablet was removed after his execution.

That Pestel was ambitious and not free from vanity can be seen from a discussion between him and Poggio:

"Who," demanded Pestel of Poggio, "will be at the head of the provisional government?"

"Who, if it is not he who undertakes, and also doubtless will accomplish, the great design of a revolution; who, if it is not you?"

"That would be difficult, mine is not a Russian name."

"What does it matter? You will silence even calumny itself by renouncing, as Washington did, your power to re-enter the ranks of a private citizen. The provisional government will not continue long, a year or two at most."

"Oh no!" replied Pestel. "Not less than ten years. Ten years are necessary, if only for the preparatory measures." [9]

---

[8] Ten shares had a nominal value of 5,000 paper roubles. Emperor Alexander owned only twenty shares of this company.

[9] *The Report of the Commission of Inquiry*, p. 70.

As the ideologist of the movement, Pestel wrote a book entitled *Russkaya Pravda*[10] in which the basic principles of Decembrism were laid down. For conspiratory reasons, Pestel himself burned a part of this manuscript before December 14, 1825; but the leading principles and part of the contents of the book became well known. It is remarkable that the author of the *Pravda* was an admirer of the American constitutional doctrine despite his centralistic notions, which also differed decidedly from the federalist conception of Count Nikita Muraviev. Answering a question of the Secret Commission of Inquiry as to the sources from which he had drawn his liberal and subversive thoughts, Pestel stated:

I was turned from monarchic constitutional conceptions to republican mainly by the following issues and considerations:

The treatise of Destutt de Tracy written in French has had the greatest influence on me. Destutt teaches that the executive power should not be confided to a single person; he shows that wherever this was done, all the other powers were brought to submission, from which arises hereditary absolute monarchy or despotism.[11] All journals and political treatises hailed so frantically the growth of welfare in the United States of America, ascribing this to their constitutional structure, that it was for me a clear and sufficient proof of the superiority of a republican government. . . . Events in France, Spain, Portugal, and Naples also impressed me considerably. . . . All this was the cause of my becoming in my heart a republican and why I could not find any higher happiness and well-being for Russia than turning her into a Republican government.[12]

From the memoirs of his companions we know that Pestel studied Destutt de Tracy's volume with the younger members of the Union,

[10] The Justice of Russia. Parts of the manuscript—which actually was not only the text of a constitution, but an entire political treatise—were restored and published by P. Shchegolev in 1906. "Pravda Russkaya" was the title of a Russian code under Prince Yaroslav I in the eleventh century.

[11] A *Commentary and Review of Montesquieu's Spirit of Laws* (Philadelphia, 1811), pp. 125-132. The name of Destutt does not appear on the cover. In the preface to the signed French edition of 1819, *Commentaire sur L'Esprit de lois de Montesquieu*, Destutt revealed that his work had been completed twelve years before, and added: "It was written for Mr. Jefferson, a man of two worlds, whom I esteem very highly, and was published in 1811."

[12] N. Pavlov-Silvanski, *Dekabrist Pestel pered Verkhovnym Ugolovnyn Sudom* (The Decembrist Pestel Before the Supreme Criminal Court), Rostov, 1906, pp. 28-29.

trying to present it as a mathematically harmonized system. It became a kind of textbook for the members of the movement.[13]

Ryleyev could not measure up to Pestel in knowledge of political institutions and social problems, and reproached him for inconsistency; but Pestel's conception could not help being complex, for toward the end of the first quarter of the nineteenth century America was for him the political ideal of an actually democratic country, England the model of legalized balance, and Spain the only European country eager to solve its political problems in a revolutionary way. France, with her restoration of the Bourbons, had failed in his eyes, as in the eyes of all revolutionary Decembrists. Napoleon alone survived the disaster as the dictatorial liberator of Central Europe, including Germany from whence Pestel's father had come to Russia. It is against this background that we must judge the somewhat naïve reproaches of Ryleyev:

He showed himself by turns, says Ryleyev, a citizen of the United States of America, and a partisan of the fundamental laws of England; then of the constitution of the Spanish Cortes (1812), a terrorist and Napoleonist. . . . After having asserted that England owed her wealth, her power, and her glory to her laws . . . he agrees with Ryleyev that these laws presented a multitude of defects and that they could not have been passed but by merchants or by Lords. . . . As he extolled Buonaparte, Ryleyev observed that henceforth there could not be any more Napoleons, etc., that even the ambitious ought in their own interest rather to take Washington for a model. Pestel replied: "That is true, but even if we were to have a Napoleon, we should lose nothing by it." [14]

The Summary of the Inquiry Commission [15] twice mentions as a point of indictment the fact that Pestel created a constitution under the title of *Russkaya Pravda*, and worked out plans, statutes, and so on.

The republicanism of Pestel was a kind of American republi-

[13] V. I. Semevski, "Vopros o preobrazovannii gosudarstvennavo stroya Rossii, v XVII i pervoi, chetverti XIX vieka" (The Problem of Reforming the Russian State Order in the Eighteenth and the First Quarter of the Nineteenth Centuries), in *Byloye* (The Past), Mar., 1906, p. 158.

[14] *The Report of the Commission of Inquiry*, p. 72.

[15] *Donesseniye sledstvennoi Kommissii*, 1826 (?), p. 21 and the Index of State Criminals. In the Slavonic Department of the New York Public Library.

canism. There were some models of a republican regime in action—
the Netherlands, Switzerland, and, to a certain extent, Venice—
which were known to political thinkers, but they all differed widely
from the new American pattern. With regard to executive power,
also, Pestel was a follower of Destutt, who in his turn was very
critical of Montesquieu's "system of balances" and closer to Rousseau. In the separation and balance of powers the monarchic state
had a certain degree of justification precisely because here the monarch, as the head of the executive, was only one of the three pillars
of the secular trinity. Destutt was an outspoken opponent of this
system: "All systems which assume the name of balances are no
more than tricks; unless it may be said that they constitute an established civil war." In the same chapter Destutt emphasized that there
is an unbridgeable gap between the monarchic principle and the
principle of the supremacy of national will (*suprématie de la volonté
nationale*). "It is consequently essential to the security of an hereditary monarch that the principle of national sovereign will be destroyed." [16] Needless to say, for Pestel these ideas were maxims of
immediate application to Russia. They were also one of the reasons
why Pestel did not share the popular admiration for Montesquieu.
True, there was a great difference between the émigré Destutt who
wrote his volume for Jefferson in 1808–1811 and the Destutt who
published the book in the original French in 1819, when he was a
peer of France under the restored Louis XVIII. But to the credit of
Destutt it must be said that in general he did not change the quoted
"republican" chapter sanctioned by Jefferson. And Pestel, like most
of the Decembrists, could be led by the Jeffersonian Destutt, ignor-
ing his later membership in the French Upper House.[17]

Without taking into consideration the circumstances in Russia,
Pestel laid down the following supermodern principle of national
sovereignty: "All Russian citizens shall equally enjoy all private,
civil, and political rights throughout the entire territory of the

---

[16] Destutt de Tracy, *Commentary*, pp. 124, 132.

[17] For the sake of accuracy, however, it must be said that at the conclusion
of this chapter, where Destutt writes about the general will as the best means
of resisting oppression, he and the editor added a note and a footnote in which
the new French regime, as a constitutional representative monarchy, was justified, "despite its imperfections," as viable for a long time (*Commentaire*, pp.
210-211).

State." This principle was to become a rule of positive law—a sweeping denial of the ancient institution of serfdom and the affirmation of emancipation. All these citizens after reaching their majority (the age of twenty), regardless of their social and educational qualifications, were to have the right to vote. The people's assemblies were to be divided into two categories, the municipal (*zemskiye*) and the representative. The first were to be established in every volost (district comprising several villages) and were to be made up of all resident citizens. They were to elect the representative assemblies, with jurisdiction over all matters subject to the participation of the population. There were to be three levels of these assemblies: every volost was to have its volost representative assembly; every canton (*uyezd*), its cantonal assembly; and every province (*guberniya*) its provincial representative assembly. The provincial assemblies were to appoint national representatives for the national congress (*vyeche*), which was to be the supreme legislative body. In this aspect Pestel's constitutional scheme reminds one of Speranski's project.[18]

In his general conception of the Russian State, Pestel did not follow the American pattern as Nikita Muraviev did, but rather the French pattern of Napoleonic centralism. His leading idea was the complete Russification of the whole "multinational" subcontinent. This was to be done not only with all Slavonic tribes (the Great Russians, Ukrainians, and White Russians), who differed only in minor aspects, but with all the others—for instance, the Finns. Finland was to lose the autonomy granted by Alexander I, and only Poland was to be established as an independent state because it was too large to be simply absorbed and Russified. Besides, it had historical rights to national independence.[19] Even more drastic and brutal were Pestel's views on the Caucasians, including the highly civilized Georgians, who only recently had been absorbed under the

[18] Cf. Maxim Kovalevski, "Russkaya Pravda Pestelya" (Pestel's Justice of Russia) in *Minuvshiye Gody* (Past Years), Mar., 1908, p. 10.

[19] I can find no express utterances by Pestel on German home rule in the Baltic provinces. As for Poland, Pestel made a "deposition" before the Supreme Criminal Court that he, as the representative of the Southern Society, negotiated with the members of the Polish Secret Political Society. The Russian delegates promised to recognize the independence of Poland without going into details about the territory. N. Pavlov-Silvanski, *op. cit.*, pp. 101-107.

broken promise of Alexander I. Pestel proposed to divide all the Caucasians into two categories: the peaceful and the rebellious nationalities. The first were to be left in their homes and villages; the second were to be forcibly transferred to the interior of Russia proper, and Russian colonies were to be established in their old home in order to erase all vestiges of the previous inhabitants of the Caucasus.[20]

All the ethnical tribes of Russia must be fused into one nation in order that all inhabitants of the Russian State may be Russians. Different paths lead to this goal: first, the Russian language must predominate in the entire territory of the Russian state; second, even the various names for the component parts of Russia must disappear; third, the same law and the same political regime must be equally established in the whole of the country.[21] It must be said in all honesty that even the centralist autocracy of Czarism never went as far in its plans for unification as Paul Pestel, the Russificator and antifederalist.

This concept of the nationalities problem of Russia is connected with the antifederalism of Pestel. His arguments against federation date from the time of the American Confederation before 1787, and of the United Provinces of the Netherlands, and Switzerland before 1848. His criticisms, at the time they were written down, were already antiquated. For instance, when he stated that "in federation the supreme power does not legislate, but only advises, because federations cannot enact their own laws except by the mediation of the provincial powers, for they are deprived of all compulsory means," he had in mind confederations, and especially the American one based upon the Articles of Confederation. He feared that any kind of federation would be too weak to hold together such an immense country as Russia.

Although an antifederalist, Pestel was nevertheless an advocate of self-government in purely municipal or local affairs. Like the other Decembrists, he took as the lowest unit of self-government the volost. Here, however, he went farther than his more moderate colleague, Muraviev. The distribution of the land of the volost among the people had to be improved. Where there was need for land, the volost should consider the interests of the poorest. The lots were to

[20] *Russkaya Pravda*, Chap. II, Sec. 11.   [21] Cf. Kovalevski, *op. cit.*

be given each year to the members of volost, not in full ownership but merely for cultivation and consumption of the crops. Each year the parcels in actual use could be changed or left with the same landholders. In every volost a bank was to be established with an insurance institution, if possible, in order to develop agriculture and internal emigration to other lands and provinces. In general, this was a kind of cooperative collectivism which was to coexist side by side with private landownership.[22]

In other respects, Pestel's moderate agrarian socialism was coupled with a typical bill-of-rights Americanism. He proclaimed that "the right of property is a sacred and inviolable right which has to be strengthened and based on the most positive foundation in order that every citizen may be secure that no autocracy shall ever be able to deprive him of the smallest object he owns." And even more categorically than could have been said in any constitutional instrument in countries with fewer "injuries and usurpations" by a tyrant: "Personal freedom is the first and most important right of every citizen and the most sacred obligation of every government. On it is erected the entire structure of the state, and without it there cannot be either security or public weal." [23]

An entirely different structural approach was that of Count Nikita Muraviev. He worked out a completely new constitution of a federal character, following generally the pattern of the American Constitution of 1787.[24] It was a scheme as magnificent as it was audacious and visionary; it shines weirdly through a whole century, and its form, designed in the Western Hemisphere, casts a shadow across long decades of stupid, autocratic centralism until its final realization, around 1923, in a federal Russia of another social and political dimension.

As early as their illegal underground shadowy existence, Pestel's centralist constitution and Muraviev's federal constitution became two poles of vivid discussion; and they embodied the two concepts that were so important for the further political development of Russia.

[22] Kovalevski (*op. cit.*, pp. 12-13), considers these ideas of Pestel as a result of Robert Owen's social theories.

[23] *Russkaya Pravda*, Chap. V, Secs. 7, 10.

[24] Max M. Laserson, *Russia and the Western World*, New York, 1945, pp. 88-89.

As for rights usually included in bills of rights, there was no serious cleavage between the two Decembrist constitutions of Pestel and Muraviev. Both men were guided by the best traditions and constitutional enactments of the United States and France as well as by the specific needs of Russia, which, on the basis of the constitution, had to turn from unrestricted autocracy to a totally new state order. Although Pestel was a more radical adversary of serfdom than Muraviev, no difference is apparent in their constitutional formulae of civil liberties. Concerning this issue, the constitution of Muraviev contains three important articles. Article I and II take the place of the traditional preamble, in which very often —not only in the United States Constitution—general principles and some natural-law elements are introduced. The less solemn project of Muraviev contains no preamble; it lays down two main principles: freedom and the exclusive right of the people to initiate constituent functions. The two articles are as follows:

Article I.   The Russian people, who are free and independent, are not and cannot be the property of any person or family.

Article II.   The source of the supreme power is the people, who have the exclusive right to establish constitutional rules for themselves.

Article I, in a very general way, provides that serfdom and autocracy are completely abolished; it remains a splendid laconic formula of constitutional legislation. Article II is less original; it represents a certain mixture of continental European constitutions of the end of the eighteenth century and the beginning of the nineteenth. More curious and complex is Article XIII of the project:

The status of servitude and slavery is abolished. Any slave who touches Russian soil becomes free. The division into nobles and common people is herewith rejected, in so far as it is against Faith, according to which all men are *brothers*, all are born *noble* at God's will, all are born for *happiness*, and all are just people, because all are weak and imperfect.

Analysis reveals that this is a synthesis of American and Russian elements. Stating in Article X, "All Russians are equal before the law," the author adds considerations rooted in Russian soil. The remaining sentences are a short paraphrase of the American Declaration of Independence by a liberal Masonic Russian who wanted the statements to be popular and understandable by every simple Russian soldier and peasant. Consequently, the article does not speak in the rather abstract terms of the natural-law philosophy of the Declaration; it uses the closest and simplest form for the self-evident truth that "all men are created equal." Muraviev's almost biblical simplicity made easy to grasp for the listeners to his political Catechism,[25] the soldiers of the army under the command of their Decembrist generals, colonels, and lieutenants.

Chapter III regulates the rights and duties of the Russians. It goes into more detail about the rights of the farmers after the abolition of serfdom, their land properties as well as the lands of their previous masters. Article XXIII, granting the right of property, provides: "The right of property, which includes *only things*, is sacred and inviolable." The military colonies, established by Alexander I and Arakcheyev, were to be dissolved. The classification of all civil service employees into fourteen ranks, according to the Table of Ranks published by Peter I and following the German pattern, is likewise to be abolished, together with the older Muscovite differentiation. Says Article XXIX: "The division of people into fourteen classes is abolished. Various ranks, borrowed from the Germans, as well as ancient Russian ones, are terminated." This article

[25] The original text of the Catechism was written by Nikita Muraviev; later it was replaced by the wording of Count Serge Muraviev-Apostol, one of the five Decembrists who were hanged. The most curious point of this catechism is probably the following:

Q—What Government is most agreeable to God's religion?
A—That in which there are no Czars. God created all of us equal; when he descended to the earth, he chose his Apostles from the common people, not among the aristocracy and the Czars.
Q—Does not this mean that God does not like the Czars?
A—Certainly he does not like them. They are cursed as tyrants of the people, while God loves the people. Every one of you shall read Chapter 8 of I Samuel: "All the elders of Israel gathered themselves together . . . and said unto him: . . . now make us a king. But the thing displeased Samuel . . . And [he] prayed unto the Lord. And the Lord said unto Samuel, . . . they have rejected me, that I should not reign over them. . . . And Samuel told . . . the people, . . . ye shall cry out in that day because of your king which ye shall have chosen you; and the Lord will not hear you in that day." Thus the choosing of a Czar is against the will of God, because our only czar should be Jesus Christ.

Some of the rebellious officers were against political propaganda based on religion or the Bible.

remotely reminds us of Article I, Section 9, paragraph 7 of the American Constitution of 1787 with its rejection of all kinds of titles. The chapter also enumerates the usual guarantees of civil liberties (including religion, press, assembly, and association), the privilege of *habeas corpus*, and the right of the accused to a speedy and public trial; reform of the antiquated penal system is also introduced.

The structure of the legislative and representative machinery is modeled on and frequently enough copied directly from the American original. "All legislative power" is vested in a National Vyeche [26] which, like Congress, consists of an Upper Duma and a House of Representatives.

As for the composition and jurisdiction of both houses, Muraviev's project is frequently a mere translation, with slight change, of the first eight sections of Article I of the United States Constitution. Regarding the limitations on the legislative powers of the Vyeche, Article 98 of the project repeats the First Amendment of the American Constitution, with the slight variation that the Vyeche shall make no laws respecting a religion or a sect except where it is based on illegal or perverse practices.

Muraviev's constitution, in contradistinction to Pestel's establishes a monarchy. [27] The new Emperor is to be deprived of some of the traditional rights and specific privileges usually pertaining to a monarch; but he remains the supreme official of the Russian government, and his oath is identical with the oath of the American President (Art. XXIII). In some respects the Emperor's powers are more limited than those of the American President. Perhaps the most conspicuous instance of curtailment is the change made by Muraviev regarding the granting of amnesty. Article II, Section 2, of the American Constitution authorizes the President to grant reprieves and pardons for offenses, "except in cases of impeachment." In his enumeration of the powers of the Russian Emperor, Muraviev does not mention this right which is traditional for even the

[26] This term is taken from the ancient Russian nomenclature applied to the assemblies of the free democratic city-states of Novgorod and Pskov, and means an assembly or congress.

[27] Pavlov-Silvanski, *op. cit.*, however, mentions that in Pestel's project there was a specific version for a constitutionally limited monarchy, instead of a president.

most democratic kind of monarchy, but transfers it to the Vyeche which alone can enact bills or statutes of amnesty and pardon (Article 92, paragraph 3), with the intention of taking from the monarch a privilege through which he can gain popularity and influence among the people.

A special provision prohibits the emperor from inserting in treaties articles repugnant to the rights and the status of citizens within the Russian state. He may not, without the consent of the Vyeche, include in them clauses requiring aggression against another country, nor cede any part of the territory belonging to Russia.

Mindful of the numerous occasions on which Alexander I had confronted his country with *faits accomplis*, alliances or treaties entered into during his frequent and extended journeys abroad, and in an apparent effort to diminish the significance of the personal policies of the Emperor, particularly in foreign affairs, the constitution actually forbids the Emperor to leave Russia, even for the overseas dependencies—which practically could have meant only Alaska. In view of the Russian ukase of September 4, 1821, barring foreign vessels from ports of Alaska and the Aleutian Islands, and the protest by Washington in July, 1823, this prohibition may have had the practical purpose of preventing a clash between Russia and young America. Decembrists were certainly eager to avoid such clashes at a time when the Monroe Doctrine was in the making. The departure of the Emperor from Russia was to be considered as tantamount to his abdication, in which event the Vyeche was immediately to proclaim his heir Emperor.

Furthermore, the constitution undermined the very legal foundation of the court, and the privileges of the imperial family. Article 104 reads:

The so-called Court cannot have any existence legally recognized in a well-established country. The Emperor may have various chamberlains and similar servants, but all these foreign ranks do not give the persons who bear them any right to be regarded as belonging to the civil service. They devote themselves to the service of one person, and therefore they cannot receive any salaries nor any remuneration from the State Treasury. . . . Moreover, they are deprived, during the time of such private service, of all rights to vote or to be elected to state offices.

Needless to say, this attempt to lessen the arbitrariness of czarist autocracy remained in the written project. Czarism never ceded any of its specific privileges in the dynastic and diplomatic fields. The same is true for the Table of Ranks. The moderate Constitution of 1906 did not reform any of these rules. In February, 1917, czarism was buried in all its legally untouched dynastic magnificence and pomp.

We have seen that in questions of freedom and the construction of the state, including the executive, legislative, and judicial powers, Pestel's and Muraviev's projects have a number of common features, nevertheless the two diverge irreconcilably in Pestel's consistent republicanism and Muraviev's inconsistent monarchism. A second point of difference is federalism. American influence was felt in both areas: in general guarantees of freedom and the people's representation through elected legislatures and self-governing bodies, and in the crucial unitary or federal design of the state. With respect to federalism, the United States was of unique interest for young liberal Russia; and her constitutional model served as the pivotal point around which a hundred years of Russian underground federalism under the Czars revolved until the "revolt."

Muraviev's project dividing Russia into thirteen states, the number that originally constituted the United States of America, was at the outset the symbol of Americanism in Russian political thought. Political notions, after being introduced, have a lingering existence which may sometimes be only an incubative stage. Then, under favorable conditions, the virus becomes potent and new forces and new institutions spring up.

There is, however, one important difference between the formation of the federal United States in the 1780's and that of Russia. The United States Constitution of September, 1787, mentions in its preamble as the first reason for its establishment the strengthening of links between the various states: *"in order to form a more perfect union."* The same is true of other patterns: the United Netherlands, which did not survive the full modernization of the nineteenth century, but for which federalization was also a way to strengthen the whole of the commonwealth; and certainly Switzerland, whose unification into a Helvetic nation had been interrupted by Napoleon, and which took over the American Federal Constitution in the middle of the nineteenth century.

In Russia the unitary or "sole government"—to use the language of the *Federalist*—was in 1825 a long established fact. There was no need at that time to introduce the federal scheme for the amalgamation of the motley assortment of Russian dependencies. This centripetal procedure had begun in the fifteenth century, before Ivan the Terrible, and was completed by the time the Romanov dynasty came to the throne in 1613. The unification of Russia, from the half-confederation of the Middle Ages, is to the credit of czarism, if there are any political merits at all. A federalization newly established in an already centralized state could have meant only the dismemberment of the already united Russia. Federalization, therefore, was suspect of centrifugal danger for Russia.

The essential dividing line between Pestel's project and Muraviev's was the difference between the French concept of federalism and the American concept. This conflict, as it unfolded, became a fascinating struggle of ideas, which reached far beyond the territorial borders of France and the United States. In France federalism, since Rousseau, had been the most feared doctrine and practice; and in this field Napoleon showed himself to be a product of the Revolution of 1789 when he undertook the brutal checkerboard departmentalization of France, recklessly cutting across feudal frontiers of provinces of specific ethnic or linguistic character, of old duchies and princedoms, in order to achieve a really united France. In the language of the French Revolution, federalism was reminiscent of feudalism; in America, on the contrary, federalism was something to support national exigencies and to "give the Union energy and duration." [28]

It is not an accident that in America the federalist movement meant concentration and more or less obscured opposition to states' rights, while in Russia, after Muraviev, it meant the opposite, the subversive preservation of the various parts and their peculiarities against the nivellation of the center. It is therefore no exaggeration to say that in the history of Russian political thought and action America, to a very considerable extent, remained from the time of Decembrism down to 1917 a model for the formation of a new Russian body politic.

[28] *The Federalist*, No. 23.

Among the Decembrists the majority stood for the federalization of Russia. In the fragments of a constitution found, during an official search, among the papers of Prince Trubetskoi, federalization was motivated by the tremendous expanse of the empire, the diversity of its tribes and nationalities, the differences of economic interests, and the cultural niveau of various provinces.[29]

Let us look carefully at the thirteen states of federal Russia set up in the scheme of Muraviev.

State	Capital
Bothnic (Finland)	Helsingfors
Volkhov	City of St. Peter
Baltic	Riga
Western	Vilna
Dnieper	Smolensk
Black Sea	Kiev
Caucasian	Tiflis
Ukrainian	Kharkov
Transvolga	Yaroslavl
Kama	Kazan
Volga Valley	Saratov
Ob (Siberia)	Tobolsk
Lena (Eastern Siberia)	Irkutsk

We see that at least six—the first, third, fourth, fifth, seventh and eighth—have an ethnic basis connected with an old autonomous status and specific codes, while the others are mainly of a regional character. We know that the Ukraine, the Baltic provinces, the Western—previously Polish—regions, Finland, and the Caucasus enjoyed more or less undisturbed autonomy after their incorporation into czarist Russia. Muraviev's project was not at all a bad political prophecy if we consider that a hundred years later, in the federalization of Soviet Russia, the huge country was divided into eleven states which, after the conquest and annexation of 1940–1945, grew to sixteen republics. Of these the Baltic region alone has three republics, and thus, roughly speaking, the division envisaged by the project almost coincides with the present Soviet federal scheme. It should not be forgotten that Muraviev, with his feeling

[29] Kovalevski, *op. cit.*, p. 14.

for political equilibrium, added to the "American" scheme of the thirteen states the two federal districts of Moscow in the center and Don in the southeast.

This organic conception was in open conflict with Pestel's Napoleonism and Russification. Muraviev did not speak in plain terms about the guarantees for local self-determination in language and culture; but indirectly this is the prerequisite for the creation of half his states. Proof can be found in paragraph 9 of Article 92, in which the powers of the Vyeche are enumerated. He begins with the exact words of the American original (paragraph 8 of Section 8 of Article I of the United States Constitution), which grants to the Congress power "to promote the progress of science and useful arts, by securing for limited times to authors and inventors the exclusive right to their respective writings and discoveries." Then Muraviev adds that the Vyeche "has the power to propose to the several state legislatures the all-federal teaching of religion, the Russian language, the basic laws, and military science, *but is by no means authorized to limit in these areas the freedom of the states and the freedom of private education.*" This remarkable statement presupposes that the individual states will have educational systems of their own and in their own language with which nobody, including the central federal government and legislature, has the right to interfere. The Russian language is only *proposed* as a common denominator (together with Christian religion and basic civics) for all schools, it is not mandatory. This is certainly very distant and different from Pestel's obligatory Russification.

Let us turn now to the final difference between the two great Decembrists. Muraviev's project, in clear contradistinction to Pestel's, introduced a relatively high property qualification, particularly for persons elected to the Upper House of the whole federation and of each of the thirteen states. This project follows American constitutional qualifications for election to the Senate by requiring that the candidate for the Supreme Russian Duma be thirty years of age, a citizen for at least nine years, and domiciled in the state from which he seeks election. To these he adds ownership of land worth at least 1,500 pounds pure silver or personal property valued at not less than 3,000 pounds pure silver. Members of the state Upper Dumas must own land worth not less than 750 pounds pure silver or movable property of not less than 1,500 pounds. These property requirements reveal the aristocratic background of the moderate Decembrists. Pestel stigmatized them as the expression of "a horrible aristocracy of riches," adding that this was yet another reason why many Decembrists, including himself, rejected Muraviev's constitution, in addition, of course, to his plan for federalization.[30]

From the time of Muraviev and Pestel until 1917 there was a dichotomy between centralism and federalism. Federalism, supported mostly by the non-Russian intelligentsia of the Ukraine and the Caucasus, also had advocates among the Russian anticzarist opposition, ranging from moderate democrats and populists to anarchists like the famous Michael Bakunin.[31] This dichotomy sometimes penetrated Russian studies in history, political science, and constitutional law; but in all these works the United States was always the "King's evidence," for the vitality of federalism although the advocates themselves sometimes leaned on Calhoun against the more centralistic American statesmen.

Among the five hanged Decembrists three—Ryleyev, Kakhovski, and Pestel—were admirers and well known adherents of American political ideals. Count Nikita Muraviev, the American-minded Russian federalist, was in the first category of the condemned; but his death sentence was commuted to banishment to Siberia and forced labor.

The mass trial of the Decembrists in 1826—or rather their inquisition, as no public hearing or defense was granted—was a fatal blow to Russian peaceful political development. It was a delayed-action bomb. For three decades the teachings of the Western constitutional countries were wiped out. America became a forbidden country. Natural law was removed from the curricula of the universities. The best and bravest men, the real élite of a generation, were driven out by the despotic monarch as traitors, rebels, and rascals or barred from normal public activities. Nicholas I was powerful enough, externally and internally, to deprive Russian society of any further share in the government. No outlet remained for the energies of gifted statesmen and political writers—except, of course, the underground. All had to obey the will of the Czar or suffer the

[30] Cf. Pavlov-Silvanski, *op. cit.*, p. 137.
[31] Laserson, *op. cit.*, pp. 86-96.

consequences. The borders and the ports leading to the liberal West became unsurmountable walls, because passports were not extended for journeys abroad. Russia for thirty years was a sealed country.

The bolts were loosened only with the coming to the throne of Alexander II, especially through the abolition of serfdom and the other great reforms of the early 1860's.

VIII *From the 1830's to the 1860's*

E VER SINCE ITS POLITICAL EMERGENCE THE UNITED STATES HAS
been a model for Russia. As long as constitutional freedom
and the abolition of bondage were the two basic issues of political
and social thinking, as long as political democracy was paramount
to "the needs and wants," there existed in Russia an American
myth, a myth that was not associated with any intentions of emigration, as it was in the overpopulated and undernourished, relatively small countries of central and western Europe.

The reevaluation of America by the Russians resulted from a
slow change which preceded radical Bolshevism. The first sign of
this trend appeared as early as the 1840's; by the 1870's and 1880's
the symptoms were clearly discernible. Americanism, under the
guise of anticapitalism, began to sprout in radical and socialist circles. Stubborn obstructionism, by which basic political reforms
were continually withheld or endlessly postponed by the governments of Catherine II, Paul I, and Nicholas I while social problems were construed almost as illegal issues, produced as a reaction
which was called—superficially enough—nihilism. Russian social
philosophy, which was no longer confined to the aristocratic élite
but seeped slowly down to the petty bourgeois or half-proletarian
intelligentsia, was devoid of any spirit of conciliation. Not a branch
of administration or social activity could point to results of any
account that mght be said to have flowed from the good will of the
propertied classes or the readiness of state bodies to improve the
lot of serfs.

This social philosophy gradually became permeated with thinking in terms of extremes: black and white, good and bad, rich and
poor, power and helplessness, joy and sadness, servility and rebellion. The golden mean was despised. As in the days of primitive
early Christianity, the lukewarm became the most denounced and
therefore shunned. Before Russia even began to enjoy political
freedom, the ideologists of the left had set about "discussing" and

attacking democracy as a regime of *class parliamentarism;* before even a beginning was made at the introduction of a free press the "Western Hypocritical and/or bribed press" was smeared as the ugly image of bourgeois freedom. In the illegal underground Russian press of Geneva, London, Paris, and Berlin the Western press was excoriated as corrupt and rotten although the very fact that subversive pamphlets were permitted to be published was the best proof of the opposite, or at least that it was permitted to print in bourgeois capitalist Europe a huge literature dedicated to the undermining of the established order there.

Such a rigid, primitive, black-and-white social philosophy caused America to lose its attraction in the eyes of the Russian radicals, despite the fact that the first followers of the Decembrist ideals, who solemnly swore to carry out the ideals of that philosophy— Alexander Herzen, his friend Nicholas Ogarev, Nicholas Chernyshevski, and a host of others—still regarded America as much closer to Russia than petty bourgeois and prejudiced Western Europe. This pessimism of the Russian radical thinkers became particularly gloomy after the suppression of the 1848 revolution. But even earlier, in the middle of the 1830's and the beginning of the 1840's, partly under the influence of the utopian socialism of Cabet, Saint-Simon, Fourier, and Proudhon, radical circles formed which clandestinely began to propagate subversive libertarian ideas. Among such circles that of Herzen and Ogarev in Moscow in the middle of the 1830's and that of Petrashevski in St. Petersburg became most famous.

During the reign of Nicholas I (1825–1855)—despite, or perhaps because of, its extremely reactionary character—a third trend appeared and began to play an important role: the early socialist movement. An important diplomat, the Courland Baron Philip Brunnow, assistant to Minister Nesselrode, in his well known memorandum of 1838, considered the basic task of Russian diplomacy to be "the fight against revolutionary ideas"; but already these ideas were beginning to gain ground in Russia itself, mainly through clandestine circles in St. Petersburg and Moscow. One of the most important was the Petrashevski circle. Thus to the rightist, conservative and reactionary movement led for the most part by the Slavophiles, and the liberal movement centering on Westernism and explicit pro-

Americanism, represented by men like Nicholas Turgenev, a third camp was added: socialism. True, in the beginning socialism, propagated by the declassified intelligentsia and some aristocrats, was only an academic doctrine and did not embrace any practical measures to organize a mass onslaught on the existing order. It remained largely a politically radical anticzarist mental attitude. It cannot be denied that Russian Socialism as it developed, particularly after the abolishment of serfdom—which by no means solved the agrarian problem or satisfied the land hunger of the liberated peasants—grew more radical, passing from the romantic utopian stage to the ideas of a Marxian mass movement. In this chapter, we shall stay within the framework of the period that began after the upheaval of 1825 and ended with the great reforms of the 1860's and 1870's of Alexander II, the son of Nicholas I.

During that time two mutually opposed Russian movements achieved prominence and became almost equally hostile to republican federal America: reactionary conservatism and, later, young, idealistic, but radical socialism. In the middle was a third force: Russian liberalism which, after the blow of 1825, and down to February, 1917, tried to continue the Decembrist tradition of pro-Americanism.

Paul Svinyin

The first Russian political writer in the early nineteenth century to live and travel in America was Paul Svinyin (1787–1839), whose writings are freer from bias than those of his immediate followers, the early Slavophiles. One-sided patriotism is traceable in his negative attitude toward England and his diplomatically conditioned pro-Americanism.

Svinyin was an unusually versatile person, "diplomatic officer, artist, and author," as he is called on the title page of his *Picturesque United States of America*.[1] For one of his paintings he was elected to membership in the Imperial Academy of Arts. He was also a gifted journalist and publicist, and after he returned from

---

[1] Avrahm Yarmolinsky, *Picturesque United States of America, 1811–1813, Being a Memoir on Paul Svinyin, . . . Containing Copious Excerpts from His Account of His Travels* (New York, 1930).

his travels to Russia in 1818 he established the review *Otechestven-niya Zapiski* (Notes on the Fatherland), of which he was not only a permanent contributor but also one of the publishers. It continued to appear until 1830. Svinyin may be regarded as the initiator of Russian publicist writing on America. His little book on the United States did not discuss in detail the Constitution and the political regime of the country but limited itself to a short description of the Revolution and the first political steps of the new country, and the main organs of the state including the President and the Congress. Some of the statements are of such psychological immediacy and homespun freshness that they are worth quoting:

The American Revolution is not like any other, and there certainly must have been unusual causes to produce that magnificent common consent by which the Americans overcame all the insurmountable obstacles!

In 1776, on July 4, the colonies declared themselves free and independent. From this moment they began their existence as an independent political body, having laid down in twenty-three clauses all the injustices of the English government, all the persecutions directed against their independence, happiness, and commerce, and having sworn to sacrifice their fortunes and lives in defense of their rights.

Then a man appeared on the American scene, a man who attracted the eyes of the world, a man endowed with military talents and the highest virtues, the immortal Washington. Having given, after eight years of bloody war, peace and liberty to his compatriots, he prescribed wise laws, the execution of which he took upon himself. In vain did the grateful and adoring people ask him to take over the reins of government forever—Washington was not tempted by a crown and, like the ancient Cincinnatus, he turned back to his fields.[2]

To his somewhat stilted description of general American conditions, he added critical remarks to the effect that the Russian reader should not put too much confidence in some of the descriptions of the American Revolution by enthusiastic French or skeptical English authors. Regarding the first, "Dr. Franklin has said that if, in the work of Mr. Abertell on the American Revolution, the English General had been renamed Hector and the American General

---

[2] Svinyin, *Opyt zhivopisnavo puteshestviya po Severnoi Amerike* (A Description of a Picturesque Journey in North America), St. Petersburg, 1818, p. 8.

Achilles, we should have had a perfect description of the Trojan war." [3] As for the English authors on America, half of them wanted to sell profitably their lands in the United States and therefore present America as Eden; the other half either hated this new country or wrote according to the will of the English government in order to stop people from emigrating.[4]

Svinyin had a much better understanding of the commercial and economic prospects of America than his contemporaries or immediate followers, particularly the Slavophiles. In an article first published in a review and later reprinted as a chapter in his book he wrote:

The European [Napoleonic] war was of great benefit to the Americans. Under their neutral flag they took advantage of it to expand their fleet and their trade and enriched themselves at the expense of other nations. They were tremendously successful as regards the interest of their country, and because of it they jumped forward a whole century. On the other hand, the limitation on this same trade, the prohibition against the importation of products and commodities, including the *embargo*, created factories and manufacturers. . . . England thus lost every year a few million pounds sterling of exports of goods.[5]

He was interested in the prospects for introducing commercial steamboats into Russia and gave the following description of American achievements in this field:

The craftsmen who came from Europe added their knowledge and skill to the enterprising spirit of the Americans, and, inspired by protective legislation and by freedom, outdid themselves, so to speak. Unable to attract the capital necessary to organize large establishments or to find cheap labor, both of which the English enjoy, the Americans turned to perfecting various mechanical devices, simplifying them and making them easier to operate. In this field they showed creativeness of a high order, and, since necessity is the mother of invention, their accomplishments were extraordinary. Machines have completely replaced human hands in the United States. Everything there is done by machine. . . . In particular factories all kinds have been developed to the highest degree of perfection.[6-7]

[3] *Ibid.*, p. 32.
[4] *Syn Otechestva* (Son of the Fatherland), St. Petersburg, 1814, Nos. 36, 37.
[5] Svinyin, *op. cit.*, p. 63.　　[6-7] *Ibid.*, pp. 64-65.

He also mentioned trying to obtain from the Russian government a monopoly for the construction of steamboats, and finding that the American minister had obtained such a monopoly for Mr. Fulton, with an exclusive grant for fifteen years; and he wrote:

> If my labors have been in vain; if fate has deprived me of the happiness of rendering this service to my country, at least I rejoice that so great and useful an invention as this will be introduced among us, and that I was the first to suggest the idea to Mr. Fulton.[8]

In his general political impressions of America, he dwelt on the penitentiary system, a topic which interested all Russian political thinkers beginning with Radishchev:

> The American jails look rather like factories. Human beings do not suffer there, they are only under punishment; they are not humiliated, but deprived of freedom—the first public good.[9]

Svinyin also hailed the humanitarian approach and philanthropic activities of Americans and devoted a whole chapter to freedom of confession in the United States. But he insisted on the acquisitiveness of Americans. He proudly remarked that among the numerous emigrant farmers of America he could find no Russians:

> What pleasure for a Russian, what food for his complacency, what glory to his government, when, traveling through all these vast lands of America and seeing there inhabitants hailing from all the well ordered countries of Europe, priding themselves on their liberty and wealth, he does not come upon a single compatriot who has fled here, as did all the others, from the injustice of the laws of his country, from religious persecution, or to find freedom and a broader field for his industry.

The answer to this eruption of patriotic Russian self-satisfaction is that old Russia was a vast country embracing limitless regions in which there were no masters, no landlords, no serfs, and no serfdom. The more courageous and desperate peasants who were unwilling to submit to the injustices of the Russian agrarian order and to the religious persecution of the dominant Orthodox Church could flee to the northern parts of European Russia in Archangel province, all the territory east of the Ural Mountains—mainly Siberia and

---

[8] *Ibid.*, p. 67. (Cf. also Yarmolinsky, *op. cit.*, pp. 8, 9.)
[9] *Ibid.*, p. 29.

the southeastern provinces of Kuban and Don. These areas served as territorial safety valves for the release of peasant tensions which might otherwise have found an outlet in upheavals; in them it was possible for numberless fugitive peasants and tenants, landless vagrants, sectarians, dissenters, desperadoes, and other inflammable elements to find a place in the sun.[10] Verily Russia's dissatisfied masses did not need to cross oceans to find asylum. The opponents of the old established order had abundant recourse to internal migration.

Had Russian serfdom not been surrounded in the north, east, and southeast by a belt of non-manorial lands and provinces, the system might well have ceased to exist in Russia proper before the 1860's. As early as 1606 (the Bolotnikov movement) peasant riots were more or less usual in feudal Muscovy. After that there were recurrent upheavals at longer or shorter intervals under Peter the Great, Catherine II, Paul, Alexander I, and, in a less acute form, in the first years of the reign of Alexander II.

The statements of Svinyin, and later of Odoyevski and other conservatives, must therefore be appraised in the light of the Russian social and agrarian conditions from the 1830's to the 1860's. It was only in the last third of the nineteenth century that Russian peasants began to emigrate to the United States, and these were predominantly, if not exclusively, peasants and farm hands from the western regions of imperial Russia—mostly from Poland, the Ukraine, White Russia, and Lithuania—bordering on Germany and Austria-Hungary. The handful of Great Russians who settled in Alaska or on the Pacific coast as early as the time of Svinyin's trip need not be considered. The Dukhobors, and Stundists for decades persecuted as a religious sect in their native Russia, appeared in Canada and the United States in 1898 and the following years. The Dukhobors were supported morally and financially by Count Leo Tolstoy, who for years had been their spiritual mentor, and by his assistants V. G. Chertkov and Prince D. A. Khilkov.

[10] Cf. Max M. Laserson, *Die russische Rechtsphilosophie*, Berlin, 1933, pp. 4-6.

The Early Slavophiles

The Slavophiles, particularly Vladimir Odoyevski and Alexis Khomiakov, rejected America as a part of the Western world which had degenerated because it was tainted with mercantilism and utilitarianism.[11] "Having reached the heights of public and private wealth, the Americans do not know any other enjoyment than money." America was the country of slavery and mercantilism, while Russia was strong because based on a well established social order and popular psychology. "There is no economic slavery in Russia. Russian serfdom and Negro slavery are two entirely different things." [12]

Why was Russian serfdom, imposed for centuries on a well settled and rooted population, preferable to American slavery of recently imported foreign Negroes? No exact explanation of this thesis was given, but it lies in the innate blind nationalism of the author who refused to recognize that Russian serfdom was not one whit better than any other serfdom and much more unjust organically than Negro slavery in America.

A kind of excuse was given for the theory—not a genuinely Russian one—that the landlord, the owner of the serf, was not a private exploiter but a kind of public official entrusted with the care of "baptized living human property":

The rank of landlord belongs to state service. No service of any kind should be entrusted to a person except after having examined him intellectually and morally. A person to whom is given the hereditary right to be a landlord ought also to undergo such a test. This is a very important right which might be beneficial if it were entrusted to good brains and a

[11] A slight distinction must be made between official monarchists, who gave full support to the Czarist governments, and the more independent Slavophiles, who crystallized in the 1840's. Only when early Slavophilism developed into Pan-Slavism, in open opposition to Pan-Germanism, did the conservative liberalism of such early Slavophiles as Alexis Khomiakov, who sought judicial and administrative reforms and actually worked for the abolition of serfdom, turn into the aggressive jingo nationalism of the Katkovs, the Pogodins, and the Pobedonostsevs.

[12] P. N. Sakulin, *Iz istorii russkavo idealisma: Kniaz V. Th. Odoyevski* (On the History of Russian Idealism: Prince V. Th. Odoyevski), Moscow, 1913, Vol. I, Pt. I, pp. 586, 592.

powerful will but which might become harmful if handed over to a nonentity.[13]

This idea, added Odoyevski, might seem strange in 1840 but it would not be in the 1900's. This shows how sure he was about the endurance of serfdom in Russia.

Slavophile romanticism led its followers to very sharp anti-American criticism and sometimes to childish conclusions:

A private person as well as a nation will be able to enjoy real goods only if he previously has learned to sacrifice material goods in favor of spiritual and emotional ones. As an instance let us take the Americans. After reaching the highest levels of public and private wealth, up to now they do not know any enjoyment but money. Material interests and selfishness they appreciate as the highest values. In 1837, on the shores of the United States, two ships, the *Bristol* and the *Mexico*, were in the greatest danger of being destroyed in a shipwreck. They signaled for pilots, but the latter did not come to help because it was too cold. As a result sixty people were drowned on the *Bristol* and one hundred and eight on the *Mexico*.[14]

Among other criticisms we shall mention only the attacks on two American Presidents, Jackson and Van Buren. Odoyevski satirized Jackson's Farewell Address, which tried to show that the United States in order to secure its independence ought to use only silver and gold money, not paper bills:

This is almost something based on Lycurgus' views on political economy. And American democracy tolerates such ignoramuses at the head of the commonwealth. If this is so, how can you not agree with those who think that the majority of the votes is always on the side of the fools, because there are in the world more fools than reasonable men.[15]

Quoting Van Buren's Proclamation of March 4, 1837, Odoyevski added:

All that which, in Europe, people are afraid to speak openly and mention only euphemistically, Van Buren speaks very frankly. He defends the greatest absurdity ever defended by a politician. This absurdity consists in his complacent assurance that the American government is the embodiment of the one legal goal of political institutions, namely, the greatest happiness of the greatest number. After that, and having flat-

[13] *Ibid.*, p. 586. [14] *Ibid.*, p. 582. [15] *Ibid.*, p. 583.

tered the American people with a statement of their virtues and honesty Van Buren touches on the question of slavery and promises to follow here the path of conservatism laid out by the policies of the Fathers. How can this be brought in harmony with the pompous phraseology of the introductory parts of the proclamation? [16]

The attitude of the leading Slavophile Alexis Khomiakov (1804–1860) toward the United States and its bill-of-rights spirit is best suggested by his general legal philosophy and particular approach to individual rights. In his Address to the Serbs (1858) we find:

Don't speak much about law and rights and don't listen to those who speak about them . . . because duty is the only living source of law. Self-love implies rights, whereas brotherly love implies duties.

Khomiakov expressed his views on the United States in dealing directly with the problem of education. Under education in the broad sense he conceived activities by which one generation prepared the following generation for participation in the historic destiny of the nation.[17] Consequently education had to be social, because only so could the whole treasure of ideas and attitudes be hereditarily transferred to the future. Together with society the state had to participate in education. Here Khomiakov showed his connection with organic romanticism and with Hegel. Every great nation organically developed its own ideas and became a participant in the Absolute Idea of mankind. But this was true only for leading organic nations, of which America was not one:

There is no doubt that a state which considers itself as a simple or rather commercial aggregation of men and their natural interests, as, for instance, the United States of North America, has almost no right at all to intervene in the field of education, though they, too, would not allow any educational institution to continue that has manifest antimoral goals. That which, for a State like North America, is only a dubious right, becomes not only a right but an absolute duty in a state which, like the Russian state, considers it its own task to establish in human society the rules of highest morals and Christian truth. Such a body politic is obliged to reject everything that contradicts its basic maxims.[18]

[16] *Ibid.*, p. 583.
[17] A. Khomiakov, *Polnoye sobraniye sochinenii* (Complete Works), Moscow, 1900, Vol. I, pp. 406 and 351 ff.   [18] *Ibid.*, p. 353.

Khomiakov thus not only revealed his negative attitude toward the upstart American state, which was more or less characteristic of all conservative Hegelians, but also presented a curious ideological explanation for the absence of a department of people's education with its own cabinet officer in the administrative apparatus of the United States.

Nicholas Turgenev

Nicholas Ivanovitch Turgenev (1789–1871) was the link between the Decembrist movement and Alexander Herzen and later liberal and radical Russian thinkers. After graduation from the University of Moscow, he began a splendid career in civil service, which he left for a life in exile as a political thinker and writer. He was among the Decembrists sentenced *in absentia* to death by a Russian court. In *La Russie et les russes*,[19] written in the 1830's he developed his political credo, championing the abolition of serfdom and urging a basic change in the Russian political order. The famous Russian historian Paul Miliukov called him the best educated and most scholarly of the Decembrists.[20] During his residence in London from 1826 to 1833 before he left for France, Turgenev was in close contact with the English liberal aristocracy. This was one reason for the failure of Nicholas I's demand that he be extradited as a harmful revolutionary.

In an early diary we find an entry dated December, 1806:

I read and translated the dialogue in the *Kingdom of the Dead* between Penn and Cortez. Cortez is a warrior and at the same time a tyrant, Penn is the pure and honest founder of a colony in North America. What a difference! How much I would wish to travel and go to America! [21]

We occasionally find young Turgenev dreaming about a trip to America, and on May 30, 1810, he wrote: "Today I finished reading

[19] 3 vols., Paris, 1847.
[20] P. N. Miliukov, "N. I. Turgenev v Londone," in *Vremennik*, Paris, 1932, p. 61.
[21] *Dnevniki i pisma N. I. Turgeneva* (Diaries and Letters of N. I. Turgenev), St. Petersburg, 1911, p. 27. The sentence "What a difference!" is in English in the original Russian text of the young Turgenev.

the *Life of Pitt*. Particularly interested in his speech against the Stamp Act in America." [22]

In his basic work on Russia he touched, from time to time, on the issue of America. Needless to say, for him the new United States was a model of a just and admirable commonwealth. But there are other points that should be underlined.

First of all, it is noteworthy that Turgenev regarded the United States as "the magnificent creation of the English genius." [23] In general he attributed all the positive phenomena of American life to the tremendous influence England exerted on other nations.[24] He did not go so far as to ask for the most progressive American penitentiary reforms (Auburn and Philadelphia) in a future Russia; here he followed the footsteps of Radishchev.

Turgenev insisted that Russian serfdom, which held the whole country in the bonds of feudalism, was a more important issue than Negro slavery in America.[25] He exposed the hypocrisy of the once liberal Russian monarch, Alexander I, when, fulfilling the promise given to the venerable Quaker Allan, he supported the fight against slavery at the Congress of Aix-la-Chapelle:

How can we understand the great men of the world? A Russian autocrat plays the role of advocate of some thousands of Negro slaves before an all-European Congress, while he could by his sovereign word alone decide the same cause in favor of many millions of his own subjects! [26]

Turgenev's direct contacts with the United States are traceable through the American yearbook of radical abolitionists which appeared in Boston in the period 1839 to 1858. This annual review, in the first volume of which appears an article by William Lloyd Garrison, "The Cause of Emancipation," was initiated by the Friends of Freedom, among whom were such leading personalities

[22] *Ibid.*, p. 244.
[23] Turgenev, *La Russie et les russes*, Vol. III, p. 270.
[24] *Ibid.*, p. 269.
[25] *Ibid.*, Vol. I, p. 324, where Turgenev reproached La Harpe, the mentor of Alexander I, for failing to distinguish between Russian serfdom and Negro slavery in America. This he did after reading various memoranda and notes sent by La Harpe to Alexander I in the beginning of his reign. "All La Harpe said about serfdom was that it is harmful for universal education."
[26] *Ibid.*, Vol. II, p. 228.

as Garrison himself, Maria Weston Chapman, and Nathaniel P. Rogers. Its name was *Liberty Bell*.[27] To a certain extent this year-book represented an international front of fighters for political freedom and emancipation. Germany, Poland, Hungary, Greece, and even Russia were regarded as important countries for the *cause*. It carried *inter alia*, a sharp attack on Kossuth, the leader of the Hungarian freedom fighters in 1848–1849, for his reluctance to interfere in the American slavery issue, a reluctance motivated by a desire not to meddle in domestic concerns of the United States. Garrison, in a poem, asked him for such interference for the sake of freedom:

> . . . raise its voice
> In solemn protest, though in strange attire,
> Of foreign birth, in broken dialect,
> And boldly advocate "The Higher Law!"

It was understandable, of course, that the *Liberty Bell* should gladly open its pages to two letters from Turgenev. The first, written from Paris in French on October 30, 1852, appeared in 1853 preceded by some editorial remarks by Mrs. Chapman. The second letter was printed in 1856. Her remarks, which begin with a reference to his book *La Russie et les russes*, follow:

An admirable work bearing the above title on the condition and prospects of Russia was published in Paris in 1847 by Monsieur Tourgeneff. This accomplished gentleman is a Russian Noble, exiled and under sentence of death since 1825 for having cast in his lot with the Serfs by advocating their emancipation while Minister of Finance and member of the Imperial Council of State. He is one of those truly wise and good men whose opinions cannot fail to have great influence wherever they are known. With him Freedom is a question of fundamental right as well as of national policy. After reading certain copies of the *Liberator* and *Standard* and *Uncle Tom's Cabin*, which I had sent him, he addressed me the following letter, which I entreated permission to publish here. I am convinced that a body of good men, of all countries, who should be at the same time great enough to create for themselves a sphere of moral action higher than that of national policy and founded on the deepest principles of universal and absolute right, would soon be able to change the moral aspect of the world and abolish such institu-

---

[27] *Liberty Bell*, 1853, p. 299.

tions as Serfdom and Slavery. It is to make such men acquainted with each other for such a purpose, that the Liberty Bell is established.[28]

In Turgenev's first letter we find his credo of emancipation as applied to America and Russia:

When I come to speak of my work for Russia, particularly about the difficulties that the discussion on slavery and emancipation meets at every step because of the regime of this country, I cannot help casting an envious glance at the United States, where there is freedom of word and press and where in the South slavery is in full sway, while human liberty finds its advocates in the North. Legal crime triumphs in one part of the country, but in the rest of it eloquent voices, like that of Channing, are loud to brand this crime. Finally, sanctimonious missionaries too are found—real Christians, are they not?—who preach moderation to the masters and patience to the unfortunate slaves.

The reading of your journals, Madame, has compelled me to think over the usual justification of slavery by quotations from the Bible. With regard to the honor of the human race, if not for the sake of the success of the holy cause of emancipation, one wonders whether the silence imposed on Russia is not preferable to the horrible blasphemies mouthed by those men who, protected by the principle of free discussion, dare to make God Himself an accomplice of the abominable crime of slavery.[29]

But no,—freedom of discussion can never harm a just and holy cause. . . . All those who possess in their heart a spark of sentiment, of instinct for the good and the just, cannot but grow furious at such arguments, they necessarily finish with a condemnation both of the defenders and the cause which they defend.

There is no reason to doubt the benefits of free discussion at this time, when we witness the appearance of masterpieces in art, spirit, sentiment and eloquence, that do honor to your country and your sex, Madame. I mean the admirable volume *Uncle Tom's Cabin* which I read shedding tears not all of which were out of grief and sorrow.

God be gracious! Why is it that a country which has produced such women as the author of this immortal book and such men as Channing

[28] *Ibid.*, pp. 210-225.

[29] This argument reminds one of Charles K. Whipple's remark about the antislavery societies: "They are called into being by the delinquencies of the church, and they perform only their imperative duty in warning the community against a religion, falsely assuming the Christian name, which leads to sanction and perpetuate slavery" ("The Church and the Clergy," *Liberty Bell*, 1844, p. 199).

and many others should carry in its bosom not only whippers of men and women, who insult all that is sacred in Man, but also ministers, so-called protestants, who hide the most horrible infamies behind the screen of their theological science which is as false as it is hypocritical.

Well! Americans might have sufficiently just reasons to be proud of themselves if,—along with their *admirable political organization, which surpasses all mankind could have had and even dreamed of since the creation of the world,*[30]—they were not overshadowed by a very dark shadow, which—alas! must necessarily diminish, nay, lower its pride.

You may be surprised, Madame, together with many others to see me use the word "slavery" equally for Russia and the southern states of America. To tell the whole truth, in spite of all the difference between the Russian serf and the black slave of America, both are outside the law in their respective countries. I have said it and proved it repeatedly that the Russian serf is less protected by the Russian law than the animals in England are protected by Martin's law. I quote a description of a voyage, recently published in England, in which the author, narrating an instance of shocking cruelty committed by a master against his slave, made the following observation: "It is only a particular instance of cruelty which might, I have no doubt, be multiplied a dozen times, and which must continually take place when there is no law (not even a Martin's Act) to protect the Negro from the passion and spite of his owner."[31]

It is completely useless and superfluous to enter into endless discussions about the difference in the situation of the Russian slave and the American. The short remark, "not even a Martin's Act," can be applied to both and to the same degree. The Russian nobleman and the planter of the South can cordially shake hands, the one holding his whip and the other his knout.

Not even a Martin's Act! I should like to see these words engraved on the desk of the Russian Emperor, the sole legislator of his empire!

Despite Turgenev's political glorification of the United States, he considered the issue of Negro slavery as the most burning. In this respect he followed the radical American abolitionists who were ready to sacrifice the unity and indivisibility of the great Republic for the sake of emancipation.

This is clearly shown in the shorter second letter, written in English to Mrs. Henry Grafton Chapman.[32] Here he expressed admira-

[30] Italics added.

[31] The quotation is from Edward Sullivan, "Rambles and Scrambles in North and South America," *Junior Examiner*, Oct. 23, 1852.

[32] *Liberty Bell*, 1856, pp. 100 ff. It was dated from Paris, Sept. 29, 1855.

tion for William Lloyd Garrison and his address on the anniversary of British Colonial Emancipation, but above all lauded Garrison's "moral logic which leads him to prefer the separation [secession] of the States to the continuance of Slavery." This attitude also permeated the writings of Alexander Herzen, Nicholas Chernyshevski, and other leading fighters for Russian social and political emancipation. By Mrs. Chapman, who was leaving Paris for the United States, Turgenev sent to Garrison a copy of the book *La Russie et les russes*, which would prove to him "that a co-laborer in another hemisphere has long wrought in the same vineyard of the Lord." Farther along in the letter Turgenev wrote:

> Exile and proscription have compelled me to live far from my own land, and to plead the cause of human rights in a language which is neither theirs [the Russian serfs'] nor mine. I am thoroughly persuaded that all success obtained in America in the cause of the coloured race will be eminently serviceable to my poor countrymen in Russia. It is, then, first as a man, and secondly as a Russian, that I hail the efforts of Mr. Garrison and his fellow laborers for the deliverance of their country from the hideous plague-spot of slavery.

A major question passed by the liberal Turgenev in *La Russie*, which became a much varied and oft repeated *leitmotiv* in Russian political literature, was whether and to what extent Russia was destined to move along the paths already traversed by the Western nations. He stated positively:

> If Russia is destined to imitate Europe, she is not, on that account, condemned to pass in her turn through all the vicissitudes Europe has undergone in the development of its social and political order. She may freely choose between the results which time and experience have produced among the civilized peoples.[33]

This thesis became the shibboleth that distinguished in Russia between conservatives and progressives, between Slavophiles and Westerners, between Populists and Marxists, and later between moderate democratic socialists and the official doctrine of the Soviet Union, and outside Russia between the West led by America, and the East led by the USSR, in the years of ideological and political tension following World War II.

[33] Turgenev, *La Russie et les russes*, Vol. III, p. 294.

Ivan Golovin

While the defenders of Russian Czarism were represented by the enlightened diplomat and painter Paul Svinyin, the moderate conservatives by the early Slavophiles Odoyevski and Khomiakov, and the moderate radicals by the Decembrist Nicholas Turgenev, the moderate liberals were represented by the somewhat unique and lonely Ivan Golovin (1816–1883). A scion of ancient aristocratic stock, a confirmed liberal, a former army officer who embarked on a diplomatic career, he was an admirer of English freedom and constitutionalism. Despotic Russia of Nicholas I could offer him no broad prospects. After publishing *Russia Under Nicholas I* he freed his serfs, left his native country, and became a British citizen. He was "pardoned" by Alexander II but declined to return. He was therefore one of the earliest Russian political emigrants in the West and was the first to come to the United States to study this country.

Though he lived and studied in England, France, and Germany, and had a command of their languages, he never lost his passionate interest in Russian affairs, both political and social. He published a series of brochures and books written in a controversial, uneven, somewhat loose and unorganized manner. In doctrinal profoundness and splendor of style he cannot be compared with his somewhat older fellow emigrant Herzen. Among his English works the most noteworthy is his summary of his visit to the United States in 1853–1855, called *Stars and Stripes*.[34]

Golovin was in close contact with Nicholas Turgenev, whom he visited in Paris, and with Alexander Herzen. He already had completed five years of literary work in exile when Herzen arrived in Paris in 1848. During the July days the Paris police made a domiciliary visit to Herzen, whom they suspected of supporting the French rebels financially. Golovin successfully intervened in his behalf before General Cavaignac.

Golovin became president of the International Brotherhood Club. In November, 1848, at a meeting dedicated to the cause of

[34] Ivan Golovin, *Stars and Stripes, or American Impressions*, London, 1856. The book is in large part a collection of the author's letters written to friends about America and world events.

Poland, he voiced his sympathies to the Poles in the name of liberal Russians, for which Herzen expressed gratitude.

For a time relations between the two Russian émigrés continued to be friendly. Numerous letters and reminiscences of Herzen indicate that this lasted until late in 1853. Golovin was instrumental in translating Herzen's *Development of Revolutionary Ideas* into French. In March, 1853, Herzen, wholeheartedly, though ironically hailed *The Russian Tom's Cabin*, which Golovin had sold to an English publisher.[35] As late as August, 1853, they both signed a letter to the editor of the London *Morning Advertiser*, which had maliciously and stupidly accused Michael Bakunin of being an agent of the Russian government.[36] Yet there always remained a political gap between the moderate liberal Golovin and the radical Herzen, and relations between them deteriorated after the establishment by Herzen of the Russian Printing House in London to print various Russian periodicals and leaflets for smuggling into Russia.

Moreover tension in London increased with the Crimean War, and war hysteria placed even Russian émigrés under suspicion. Golovin wrote endless letters to newspaper editors concerning himself and Herzen. Some differences on the Polish question helped to widen the rift, and the final rupture between the two friends occurred in March, 1854.[37]

Golovin, after making several tactless insinuations against Herzen, tried to make peace with him in 1865; but Herzen rejected all overtures. However, even if Golovin had been more tactful and less jealous, a split between the two was almost inevitable. He did not take a firm stand as an émigré, nor did he have a political credo to defend against czarism. For Herzen, he always remained the slightly adventurous, badly educated, and morally unstable, disappointed, and embittered Russian "petty aristocrat."[38] On the other hand, Herzen was not objective enough to understand Golovin's unique

[35] Alexander Herzen (*Polnoye sobraniye sochineniy*), St. Petersburg, 1919-1925, Vol. VII, p. 196. This book of Golovin never was published.

[36] *Ibid.*, Vol. VII, p. 304.

[37] *Ibid.*, VIII, 74.

[38] This dividing line between the two is mentioned not only in Herzen's letters but also in Golovin's German book, *Der russische Nihilismus: Meine Beziehungen zu Herzen und zu Bakunin*, Leipzig, 1880, pp. 73, 74, 76.

position. He was certainly wrong when he accused Golovin of serving the Russian government;[39] besides, the accusation was a
senseless one, for it was made after Nicholas I had died and been
succeeded by Alexander II, who was generally regarded as the liberal
antipode of his father. Did not Herzen himself later hail the Emperor-liberator? Even if Golovin had accepted the "pardon" of the
new government and returned to Alexander's Russia, he would not
have betrayed his antidespotic and abolitionist principles. But he
did not go back to Russia. For a time America absorbed his interests.

Golovin's attitude toward America, expressed in his book of
American impressions, was much less abstract and colored than
the old Decembrist pro-Americanism, the remnants of which are
clearly discernible in Paul Svinyin, but especially in Nicholas Turgenev and Alexander Herzen. The Anglophile Golovin was certainly much more moderate than the radical émigrés of the older
generation; on the other hand, he was far from the later Russian
radical opposition, which went over to enmity toward America.
He took a middle-of-the-road position. An aristocratic neophite
subject of the English King, he was somewhat skeptical, though
tolerant, of Americans; at the same time he was Russian and liberal
enough not to compare the broadness and generosity of Americans
with the pettiness of Western Europeans. He also stressed his allegiance to republican democracy in the abolition of serfdom in
Russia as well as the emancipation of the Negro slaves in America.
There is no difference between him, Turgenev, and Herzen. On
the remark of a proslavery publicist, "We do not want Russian
slavery to be compared with our own," Golovin commented: "Yet
this comparison is in favor of American slavery, because the distinction of race does not exist in Russia as here."[40] On the other hand
he was straightforward, or cynical, enough to say what his friends
would not have said. Herzen, as we shall see in Chapter XI, regarded
future relations between Russia and America in the light of their
meeting in the Pacific as their common Mediterranean of the Far
East. For him, America and Russia were two antipodes that had to
find a *modus vivendi* because they were equally directed against rotten and senile Western Europe. Golovin was much more of a *Real-
politiker* than the rest of the Russian émigrés. To Richard Cobden

[39] Herzen, *op cit.*, VIII, 163.   [40] Golovin, *Stars and Stripes*, p. 101.

he wrote about the Americans in December, 1855, after the defeat of Russia in the Crimean War:

Hatred toward Great Britain is the main reason for their sympathy for the Russians, and to those who object to their friendly attitude toward the Czar, they answer that Napoleon III is as great a despot, and that Russia, at this stage of its development, is not expected to enjoy the blessing of American institutions.[41]

Of the Pacific he wrote:

Panama is nearer to Calcutta than London is, and the Americans can do great mischief in India, and the most important footnote: There is no trade possible on the Siberian shores of the Pacific. Therefore, the Russian fleet, which is to be built there, can have no other purpose than that of threatening Calcutta, in common with American squadrons. With some right the Americans say that they are not likely for centuries to come into hostile contact with the Russians, while the British are quarreling with their cousins on every point.[42]

The following excerpts from Golovin's book are of special interest:

The object of this book is to show that the United States are pursuing a wrong way in their politics and morals, falsely interpreting their destination, and losing sight of the principles which presided at their formation. While European thinkers, led into error by the panegyrists of American democracy, consider the institutions of the United States as a perfect model, deeper philosophers, already judging of the tree after its fruit, think that unlimited competition, unbounded love of material interests, are not fit to resolve the questions pending in our age.

The English, on their side, care too little about their cousins. I do not think that America is a better edition of Great Britain, but, certainly, it is a very much enlarged one, and a beautiful country, too, which every Englishman ought to visit.

Thiers said that the American republic is but an experiment, others say that it is but an accident. However, we do not think that any Yankee girl is soon to become the Queen, or any Southern gentleman the King of the United States.

Golovin's attitude toward the Crimean War represents a different issue of foreign policy. Needless to say, with Turgenev and Herzen,

---

[41] *Ibid.*, p. 147.   [42] *Ibid.*, pp. 151-152.

he regarded the defeat of autocratic Russia as something much to be desired. When this debacle took place, he and his friends were satisfied. In his German booklet we find an illuminating passage:

> When the Crimean War broke out and the dispatch from Sinop became known, I admit that I was joyful. Herzen told me that, should the Russians not be beaten in this war, we should never be in a position to lead a political fight [against czarism].[43]

In his English book, however, he was less outspoken than his friends were. He remarked:

> I also expect great improvements in Russia to take place in consequence of this one, which showed the necessity of railways and telegraphs, and of military reform. Neither can the intellectual capital remain asleep, it ought to be called to life, unless the Empire is to be humbled below every civilized country.[44]

There is a certain ironical skepticism in Golovin's judgment of America's exact attitude toward the Crimean War:

> The sympathies, however, of Americans for Russians are of a harmless nature; the Yankees sell gunpowder to both belligerent parties; the greatest part of their tonnage is employed in carrying munitions and the sick and wounded soldiers of the Allies to and from Crimea. To the Russians, who should complain of such a proceeding, they reply that they would be very happy indeed to lend their ships to the Czar but . . . they cannot neglect any opportunity of making money . . .
>
> American surgeons are engaged in great numbers in the Russian army, while the attempts of the British agents to recruit in the United States has created diplomatic difficulties of magnificent proportions.[45]

In some of his letters he goes into certain actual details of American everyday life, devoting pages to the financial side, including its less savory aspects. In the letters dated February 7 and March 1, 1856, he became very critical of America. The second bears the motto, "Rotted before maturity—Voltaire," and contains a description of the "corruptions of the United States" in which he is pitilessly critical of America and his native Russia:

[43] Golovin, *Der russische Nihilismus*, p. 74.
[44] Golovin, *Stars and Stripes*, p. 150.
[45] *Ibid.*, p. 149.

Suffice it to say, that the Americans themselves confess that corruption among them is so great that despotism alone can extirpate its root . . . that New York is a Sodom. As to the magistrates, they are nearly all of them indicted this very moment for misdemeanor; they must steal, having but this resource, for their situations are worth nothing, and take their whole time. The very reasoning you met with in Russia. Russia alone can match America upon this point; there they steal hay from horses, medicine from the sick, bread from the soldiers, fruits and wine from the Emperor.[46]

Not much more flattering is the earlier letter dealing with "American Business Transactions":

"Swindlers have free ways here," said a lawyer to me, who knew of the thing by practice, "one must be indeed either a swindler or a dupe here." "It is very difficult to be honest and make good business in this country," said my banker, certainly one of the most honest among Yankees.[47]

He was most friendly toward America when he said as a real republican:

The greatest service which the United States could render to the cause of European democracy, would be to purify their own institutions, to raise them above the sneers and criticisms of European monarchists, that they might be admired and imitated.[48]

Golovin was opposed to inviting America to intervene in European revolutions by helping nations to political progress. Denying any possibility for America to help France, he exclaimed:

For goodness' sake, no intervention at such a distance, unless unavoidably compelled. They find in Europe much difficulty in keeping up revolutions made by patriots, how could they save those made by foreigners, or helped by them? They have already crushed too many republics, let us save at least that one of the New World. Old Europe makes one despair of her fate, let us save at least the stars and stripes. Who would be free must strike the blow.[49]

On G. T. Curtis's *History of the Origin, Formation, and Adoption of the Constitution of the United States,* he remarked:

[46] *Ibid.,* pp. 170-171.   [47] *Ibid.,* p. 185.
[48] *Ibid.,* p. 222.   [49] *Ibid.,* p. 223.

Well, the Americans suffered greatly during the revolution, and their experience produced the Constitution of the United States. But since that time the happiness they have enjoyed has blinded them like children, and only new hardships can open their eyes as to the reforms they ought to introduce in their morals and legislature. No doubt there are men in the United States fit for the task, but every state being sovereign, no general code is possible; and then how can they settle morals as long as they keep up slavery? [50]

This is how Golovin, coming to America and shocked by some frivolity, "immature rottenness," and corruption of young America, tried to rescue the progressive, democratic, and antidespotic pattern which he had set for the world, lest it should become unworthy of its high vocation.

The Russian gentleman made his own "sentimental journey" to America to find some odd similarities between such remote symbols as Washington and Peter the Great, Martha the Ruler of ancient Russian republican Novgorod and Martha Washington, the first lady of emerging America; and a more justified comparison —the cracked bell of Novgorod that called to the town meetings, smashed by the Muscovite Czar, and the American Liberty Bell, "ten times" smaller than its Novgorod brother, but cracked too.

[50] *Ibid.*, p. 273 (in Chap. XXIX, "Manifest Destiny"). This is a letter from F. B. Goodrich (Dick Tinto of the New York *Daily Times*).

IX *American-Russian Relations*
After the Crimean War

I F WE LOOK BACK ON THE PERIOD IN RUSSIA THAT BEGINS APPROXI-
mately with the Crimean War and extends to the great reaction
of the early 1880's, we see that the diplomatic apparatus of both
imperial St. Petersburg and republican Washington did not, as
a rule, exactly reflect articulate opinion in either country. Only
sporadically, as during the high tide of enthusiastic cooperation in
the 1860's, was close contact established. On the Russian side, even
her most liberal monarch, Alexander II, was more independent
with respect to foreign policy than any American President, and
far freer than his Foreign Minister Gorchakov, once called by Earl
Granville the "immense talker." The Emperor was hampered, however, by the inertia of his diplomatic corps, recruited from the
nobility and the upper strata of the bureaucracy. To a large degree
this was also the case with Western European countries; but there
the control of constitutional bodies exerted sometimes a salutary
influence on the conduct of foreign policy.

As for Russo-American relations, the paralyzing influence of Russian aristocratic diplomacy was aggravated by the fact that America
was, in its very political essense, further removed from imperial
Russia than any other Western country. A second important factor
was the high proportion of Russian diplomats to the United States,
ministers plenipotentiary as well as attachés and secretaries, who
belonged to the most antidemocratic segment of Russian aristocracy,
the Baltic-German landed gentry. The traditional narrowness of
the Baltic diplomats was remarked by no less a personage than
Count Witte, himself of Baltic-German extraction.[1]

These polished aristocrats both of Russian and of non-Russian

---

[1] *The Memoirs of Count Witte*, transl. Abraham Yarmolinsky (New York,
1921), p. 136. Witte speaks of Baron Rosen, the second plenipotentiary in the
Portsmouth negotiations, as having the typical "mediocre intelligence of a Baltic
German and the manners of a perfect gentleman."

162

descent were *a priori* inclined to be unfriendly toward America, whose very origin they regarded as plebeian and revolutionary; the puritanic simplicity of the first American diplomats was too conspicuous a contrast to the stiff and solemn reserve of the old-regime conservative diplomatic corps of Europe, and especially of Russian-Baltic aristocracy. Men like Count Pahlen, a close relative of the courtier-assassin of Emperor Paul I (1801), and Baron Paul Krüdener, the nephew of Baroness Barbara Juliana, the mystic cofounder of the Holy Alliance, represented Russia in the first two or three decades of the nineteenth century when the United States was trying to establish the Monroe Doctrine, a political conception that was definitely inimical to the spirit of the Holy Alliance.

Golder's comment, that "no other two civilized countries were more unlike than Russia and the United States and there were many misstatements made about each other by their representatives," is apt, not only for the "middle of the nineteenth century," but for the 1820's and the 1830's as well. "It was but natural," he adds, "that a man trained in the philosophy of Nicholas I should judge American society by a different standard than one who had been brought up on the ideals of Lincoln." [2]

More than that. Even the old-fashioned diplomacy of the nineteenth century could not escape taking, from time to time, a definite position with respect to great international shifts or movements. And in such cases the different social and political backgrounds of the diplomats were of considerable importance. Russian aristocrat-diplomats in Washington, for example, were hardened landowners in mentality as well as, often, in practice. In the great clash between the North and the South, they were on the side of the southern slave-owning planters, as some of our diplomats discovered during their stay in St. Petersburg. The historian James R. Robertson states that Russo-American friendship during and after the Crimean War

was largely based on a belief of the South that Russia with her system of serfdom had interests in common with the South under its system

---

[2] Frank A. Golder, "The American Civil War Through the Eyes of a Russian Diplomat," *American Historical Review*, Vol. XXVI (1921), p. 454.

of slavery. Mr. Pickens, the American Minister to Russia, a South Carolinian, was very popular in Russia.[3]

These sympathetic inclinations, however, were always subordinated to considerations of foreign policy.

During the Crimean War, the United States was not on the side of the Anglo-French coalition, but was most friendly to Russia. Proof of this attitude may be found in the fact that local Russian authorities were warned by the American consul in Honolulu of preparations for an assault by an Anglo-French fleet off the coast of Siberia. This made possible the taking of adequate measures in Petropavlovsk, as a result of which a rather small Russian force brilliantly beat off the allied fleet, forcing the landing party into the sea.[4]

Particularly during the siege of Sebastopol, which in the spring of 1855 became very critical for the English and French, there was already an open split between the American friends of Russia and the Britons. A letter from London on April 29 of that year to the American clergyman Charles G. Finney illustrates this:

> I am afraid you proud Yankees care very little about us Old Country people. You have betrayed your wicked, worthless, and unfilial spirit in rejoicing at the supposed success of our great adversary, the Czar. For shame to you! In our turn should his successor cross to your continent, and fetter you all, we shall most heartily rejoice, and say, "You are simply reaping what you have sowed." [5]

As for the attitude of Americans toward Russia, immediately after the Russian defeat in the Crimean War many articles appeared in Russian newspapers showing that Americans often expressed their sympathy for Russia and their hostility for victorious England and France. The conservative monthly *Russkii Viestnik* (Russian Herald) carried a description of two events that had occurred in San Francisco. When the local English and French were

[3] James Rood Robertson, A *Kentuckian at the Court of the Tsars: The Ministry of Cassius Marcellus Clay to Russia, 1861-1862 and 1863-1869* (Berea, Ky., 1935), p. 17.

[4] Cf. E. A. Adamov, "Russia and the United States at the Time of the Civil War," *Journal of Modern History*, Vol. II (1930), p. 592.

[5] Written by John Campbell. See the Finney Papers in Oberlin College Library.

noisily celebrating the victory of the Allies over Russia with parades
and banquets a group of pro-Russian Americans asked the Russian
consul for the Russian national flag in order to stage a counter-
demonstration. He hesitated, fearing that it might be taken by the
more numerous opponents and dishonored. Nevertheless, he finally
gave the flag to the group, who marched against the Anglo-French
demonstrators. There was a fight, but the flag was returned to the
consulate.[6] Another symptom of the genuineness of American sympathy for Russia was the extraordinary influx of American physicians and surgeons into the Russian Crimean army mentioned by
Golovin and numerous Russian contemporary writers.

We shall not go into the details of the controversies and differences between the United States on the one side, and England and
France on the other. It is enough to mention Cuba, Central America, the Sandwich Islands (Hawaii), the Oregon question, and the
Caribbean. Napoleon "the Little" considered that his distinguished
predecessor had been wrong in ceding so much French territory to
the United States, and thought to compensate by scheming to place
Archduke Maximilian, brother of the Austrian Emperor, on the
throne of Mexico—an intrigue that was only a projection of a new
friendship well anchored in purely European matters. Previously in
a speech on January 31, 1854, Lord Clarendon declared that there
was "no portion of the two hemispheres with regard to which the
policy" of France and England, "however heretofore antagonistic,
is not now in entire harmony." His promise to interfere in American
affairs tended "to Russify us," as Secretary of State Marcy put it.[7]

Worth mentioning in this connection is the dismissal in May,
1856, of John F. Crampton, British Minister to the United States.
Marcy had protested as early as June, 1855, against British recruiting practices, and his charges rested partly on the "confession" of
a certain Henry Hertz to having been employed by Crampton as
a recruiting agent. There was no doubt that Crampton had fol-

[6] A. Kostromitinov, "Two Events in San Francisco in 1855 and 1856,"
Russkii Viestnik, Vol. LXIV (July, 1866). In the 1860's the Russian consul
in San Francisco was Peter Kostromitinov.

[7] The quotations from the speech and from Secretary Marcy's remark are
taken from F. A. Golder, "Russian-American Relations During the Crimean
War," *American Historical Review*, Vol. XXXI (1926), p. 464.

lowed Clarendon's instructions.[8] This controversy created hard feeling between the two countries and helped to bring America closer to Russia.

There were other factors in British and French foreign policy of the early 1850's that led to an increasing friendliness in official quarters not only in the United States toward Russia but in Russia toward the United States. Among them was the selfish attitude of aristocratic England which, in its foreign policy, was openly opposed to Cobden and other liberals, some of whom had struggled to avert the approaching war against Russia. One of these was John Bright, who stated in his famous letter to Absalom Watkin about the Crimean War:

We are not only at war with Russia but with all the Christian population of the Turkish Empire, and we are building up our Eastern policy on a false foundation, namely, on the perpetual maintenance of one of the most immoral and filthy of all despotisms over one of the fairest portions of the earth which it has desolated, and over a population it has degraded but has not been able to destroy.[9]

Lord Aberdeen, who opposed Nicholas's plan to crush Turkey on the Straits, was, on this score, in full agreement with Napoleon III. In general, he preferred peaceful means to push Russia away. Lord Palmerston, whose influence in the cabinet became greater than Aberdeen's, believed that war with Russia was not only inevitable but, under the diplomatic circumstances, even to be favored. Yet Aberdeen, and even Napoleon III, tried to deceive the Russian ambassadors in London (Baron Brunnow) and Paris (Nicholas Kisselev) by exaggerating the differences between Aberdeen and Palmerston and made a show of Aberdeen's disposition toward peaceful methods and solutions. About July, 1853, harmonious collaboration between Aberdeen and Palmerston was already established; and John Bright wrote on July 7:

Rumours of war, and of dissensions in the Cabinet, that Lord Aberdeen has resigned, overcome by Palmerston's intrigues, etc. Probably no

[8] The details are given by R. W. Van Alstyne in "John F. Crompton, Conspirator or Dupe?" *American Historical Review*, Vol. 41 (1936), pp. 492 ff.

[9] John Bright, *Diaries* (London, 1930), pp. 39, 386.

truth in rumours, only it is difficult to see how Aberdeen and Palmerston can act together on any foreign policy.[10]

Bright evidently did not know that peaceful cooperation and the division of functions between Aberdeen in the Treasury and Palmerston at the Foreign Office had been achieved. In fact, despite the difference in temper and political inclination of the two cabinet members, this cooperation went so far that as early as July 4, 1853, Palmerston proposed to Aberdeen that the British squadron be ordered to enter the Bosporus.[11]

Very interesting is Bright's diary entry under date of July 4:

This evening W. Brown introduced me to Governor Brown of the United States, just returned from St. Petersburg, where he has been Minister for three years. Had an interview on Thursday week with the Emperor Nicholas, who expressed his disbelief in war and his anxiety for peace, did not think hostilities would come out of the present disagreement between Russia and Turkey, etc.

This statement by Nicholas to the American Minister, on a date when war was practically certain, shows the extent to which he had been misled by the optimistic reports of his diplomats.

America was not, and possibly could not be, interested in the immediate causes, much less in the alleged religious reasons for the Crimean War, which centered around certain differences between the Orthodox Church of Russia and the Roman Catholic Church championed by France regarding rights to the Holy Places and particularly the Holy Sepulcher. Nicholas's despotism was so all-embracing and rotten that the interests of the Christian minorities of Russia were not even used as a convenient slogan for a war of liberation. The legitimism of Nicholas had been so conspicuously displayed on the fields of revolutionary Hungary in 1849 that the world would have been too much amazed to see the crowned actor play the opposite role of defender of revolutionaries fighting against their legitimate Turkish monarchic sovereign.

Chernyshevski in his Diaries from the end of 1840 through the

[10] *Ibid.*, p. 149.
[11] E. V. Tarle, *Krymskaya voina* (The Crimean War) (Moscow, 1944), pp. 252 ff.

early 1850's [12] reveals how exaggerated was the official description
of the religious enthusiasm of the Russian population concerning
Constantinople and the Holy Places before 1854:

> You open your mouth and are struck when you hear all this. You
> have lived all the time among Russian people; you remember that before
> the actual Russian battles for the Danube began, they did not know a
> thing about the preparations for war. When they were informed about
> the war on the Danube, they were scarcely interested in it. . . . But
> when they got the news of the tremendous sacrifices that the defense of
> Sebastopol had exacted from the Russians, they began to long for peace.

Here, quoting from Kinglake's *The Invasion of the Crimea*
(which he later partly translated into Russian with extensive additions of his own), he made caustic comments, ridiculing the Englishman's naïve belief in the unqualified devotion of the Russian
people to a religious war with Turkey. He quoted Kinglake's statement that every Russian Orthodox family had to put aside money
for a pilgrimage to Palestine, scarcely feeling that they were "truly
devout" if they did not visit Palestine, and his assertion that the
Russian Emperor, trying to acquire or hold for his church the Holy
Places of Palestine, spoke on behalf of fifty million honest and brave
pious subjects, many of whom "would joyfully risk their lives" for
this cause. On all this Chernyshevski remarked:

> Let us rub our eyes open; I have obviously dozed. —No, you did not
> dream! —But this is . . . —Please, don't contradict, be silent, this is
> history, and if you do not know these things, you are simply an igno-
> ramus.

In conclusion, Chernyshevski emphasized that Kinglake had
distorted history when he ascribed to modern Russians traits that
were characteristic only of people of medieval Western Europe.

Thus a reactionary legend and mystical claims to Constantinople,
to the re-Christianization of the Byzantine St. Sophia, and to the
Palestinian Holy Places and the keys to their various doors and gates
were made to appear as the main causes of the war. In all objectivity
it must be said that the politico-religious hypocrisy of Nicholas, the
ruler of an illiterate people in bondage, was less reprehensible than

[12] N. G. Chernyshevski, *Polnoye sobraniye sochinenii*, Vol. I, Moscow, 1939,
643-645. Cf. Chap. XII, following.

the similar comedy of polemics and arguments of the second party to the "case," Emperor Napoleon III, the ruler of a major European country that was a center of learning and culture.

But even if Russia had tried to play the role of liberator of the Orthodox Christian Balkan Slavs, which she did a score of years later, Seward lamented that he was sick and tired of adjusting American foreign policy to the standards of liberation, democracy, and independence or local autonomy of the various small nations of Europe, among which Poland was the most important.

The imperialistic policies of the Anglo-French Alliance were decisive; the interests of free maritime trade and exchange of goods, the defense of expansion and of the annexation of new territories were incomparably more important than the theoretical justification of American foreign policy.

Men like Edouard von Stoeckel, first attaché and later Russian Minister in Washington, knew this very well. Typical Continental aristocrat that he was, he was critical of American acquisitiveness, but at the same time unshaken in his policy of fanning the flames of hatred between the United States and England. Because both countries were engaged principally in commerce he assumed that England and the United States were fundamentally interested only in money. His peculiar analysis stemmed from the backward feudalistic views prevalent in Prussia and Russia, where foreign policy and diplomacy were in the hands of the landed nobility.

Stoeckel's master, Nicholas I, who was active in foreign policy and well versed in diplomacy, received direct reports from his ambassadors and often gave them orders or directives on how to present current issues of the Empire. Baron Stoeckel in Washington was as much under instructions from St. Petersburg as was Baron Brunnow in London. The views on the Neva of England's probable role in the impending Crimean War were expressed to Sir Hamilton Seymour, the British Ambassador to Russia, partly by Nicholas himself and partly by his main adviser, Count Nesselrode—a third non-Russian aristocrat—on the eve of the war. The Czar, although warned by Seymour of the dangers which he was running in his relations with England, tried also to play on the differences between the English dominating gentry and the bourgeois opposition.

My dear Sir Hamilton, Count Nesselrode seemed to say, Your Foreign Office speaks as if we did not know that England has her weak point. My dear sir, we have mastered the whole subject of the "School of Manchester" . . . we have now made out the difference between a "Meeting" on a Sunday morning, and a "Meeting" on a Monday night. Nothing escapes us. We comprehend the Society of Friends. Pardon me, Sir Hamilton, for saying so, but your country is notoriously engaged in commerce. With that we shall not interfere.[13]

Kinglake adds that the Czar's theory was that the foreign policy of the British Government was dictated by the people, that the people loved money, and for the sake of money they loved peace. In other words, the Czar thought that the English nation had undergone corruption.[14] If this was the attitude of imperial Russia toward aristocratically governed England, how much less respect must Russian diplomats have had for the unsophisticated Americans, and how much franker could they be in their American dealings!

The first bait held out to win America over to the Russian side in the Crimean conflict was the opening of commerce with the United States. Stoeckel was instructed by Nesselrode to tell the Americans that Russian commerce was theirs for the taking and to announce that on a number of articles tariffs had been greatly reduced.[15] The second bait was the promise not to view with disfavor the annexation by the United States of the Sandwich Islands (Hawaii). And finally, the Russians dangled before American eyes assurance of general support against England and orders for ships and materials during the Crimean War. The German-Russian aristocrat who was so critical of the acquisitiveness of the American burghers not only encouraged the Yankees to trade with Russia, but even tried to engineer a scheme for privateering as a weapon of war. In this he was halted by Nesselrode, who declined to act openly against international law and thus expose Russian Alaska to the danger of British reprisal and vengeance. Stoeckel later rendered purely commercial services to Russia by arranging for the sale of Alaska to the United States, for which he was very generously rewarded by Alexander II.

[13] A. W. Kinglake, *The Invasion of the Crimea*, Edinburgh, 1901, Vol. I, p. 200.   [14] *Ibid.*   [15] Golder, *op. cit.*, p. 465.

Stoeckel, minister to the United States from 1857 to 1868, never did become a real friend of the United States. Certain incidents, like the flight of the anarchist Michael Bakunin from Siberia via America to Western Europe, together with the refusal of the United States to extradite him, confirmed his conviction that the transatlantic Republic would never cease "to protect revolutionists." Elsewhere [16] he showed his fundamental hostility to American democracy chiefly as it was expressed in the North:

The events which we are here living through must necessarily have a tremendous influence on Europe. The revolutionaries and demagogues of the old continent have always found in American democracy moral support and frequently considerable material help. With the crumbling of the democratic system in the United States, they are losing one of their main supports. Finally, another and no less dangerous group of political dreamers—who, in their speeches as well as in their writings do not cease to preach limitless freedom and who are convinced that they have found in the American Republic the realization of their theory of free will—will necessarily become convinced that self-government, like all other human institutions, has its weak points even in the United States, where the ultrademocratic system, operating under uniquely favorable conditions, seemed to be absolutely secure. In this connection, the American revolution [Civil War] will, I hope, be a salutary lesson for European anarchists and visionaries.

On this eruption of counterrevolutionary frankness the Emperor Alexander II remarked ruefully: "I wish it were true, but I doubt whether it is really so."

At the end, however, where Stoeckel reverts to foreign policy considerations, he becomes completely pro-Unionist:

The deterioration of the United States as a power would present, from our point of view, a regrettable eventuality. The American federation is a counterbalance to English might, and in this sense an element of universal stability.

[16] The following excerpts are taken from Stoeckel's dispatch of Feb. 12/24, 1862, to Gorchakov in the Archives of the Russian Foreign Office, quoted in the Appendix to M. Malkin, "K istorii russko-amerikanskikh otnoshenii vo vremia grazhdanskoi voiny v S. Sh. A." (On the History of Russian-American Relations During the Civil War in the U.S.A.), *Krasny Arkhiv*, Vol. XCIV (1939), pp. 97-153. Some forty-odd documents, published in this Soviet review, consisting mostly of dispatches and letters, were not at the disposal of F. A. Golder and other American historians before the outbreak of the Second World War.

In any case, the American nation is too viable to be sucked down
into the revolutionary whirlpool. Only the ultraradical system has suffered a fiasco. Even assuming the conquest or submission of the South,
the civil war will necessitate, as a consequence, a new set-up of the whole
country . . . with a very powerful government. Only under such a
condition will the Americans be able to regain the position they have
held in the great family of nations.

Let us now turn to the two important events that, after the conclusion of the Crimean War, assumed the greatest significance with
respect to American influence on and international relations with
imperial Russia. One was the abolition of serfdom in Russia, officially proclaimed on February 19 (March 3), 1861, in the famous
manifesto of Alexander II. An interesting coincidence is worthy of
mention: on the very next day after freedom was proclaimed to
the Russian slaves, Abraham Lincoln took the oath of office as President of the United States.[17] The second event was the well prepared
revolt of Poland in 1863, kindled by the hope of restoration of her
independence from Russia, her mightiest oppressor in the triad of
Russia, Prussia, and Austria. The Emancipation Proclamation almost coincided with the initial demonstrations for Polish liberty
in Warsaw, which later developed into a war of independence and
eventually of brutal suppression that cast a shadow over the otherwise relatively liberal reign of Alexander II. The Polish situation
became not only an internal clash in local Russo-Polish relations,
but an important issue of diplomatic and international relations
with reverberations in France, England, and the United States.

These two developments will be treated *in extenso* when we
analyze the writings of certain Russian political thinkers, particularly Herzen and Chernyshevski. In this chapter we are dealing
with these matters chiefly in their relation to the international and
American scenes. Chronologically, the Polish issue preceded the two
emancipations and therefore it must be described first.

In the first half of the 1860's—and even earlier, after the Crimean
War—international relations began to revolve about the Polish
problem. Once having been dealt with internationally by the Congress of Vienna, it could not leave this forum in order to become
a domestic affair of Russia or of Poland's other destroyers, Prussia

[17] Stephen Graham, *Tsar of Freedom* (New Haven, 1935), p. 49.

and Austria. The two great powers, Britain and France, which, after their military alliance and victory of the 1850's, continued their friendship in peace, became sympathetic toward Poland in Europe and, at the same time, became commercial rivals of the United States.

A leading factor in pro-Polish sentiment was Napoleon III's determination—no secret even before the outbreak of the Crimean War—that in the event of the defeat of Nicholas I, Poland would be torn from Russia and made independent. These plans, about which Palmerston was well informed, were communicated to some of the Polish aristocratic émigrés in Paris [18] and doubtless helped to kindle the fires of revolt against Russia among the freedom-loving Poles.

This situation presented the United States with the necessity of making a choice. The pro-Mexicanism or rather pro-Maximilianism of Napoleon III was more important to it than his pro-Polishness, and the anti-Americanism of Palmerston of greater import than his anti-Russianism. The United States thus felt impelled to reorientate herself in the direction of unqualified friendship for Russia. Old friendships had to be revised, and even traditional sentiments. In spite of Kosciusko and Pulaski, the United States was forced to become anti-Polish; in spite of Lafayette, anti-French. In fact, for a time it was even to favor official Russia against the revolutionary Polonism of Alexander Herzen and certain other Russian friends of republican America.

The choice was not an easy one to make. Lincoln and especially Seward as his Secretary of State, were compelled to *faire une bonne mine au mauvais jeu*. The note of France, England, and Austria inviting the concurrence of the United States in mediating with Russia with regard to the insurrection in Poland had to be declined, and Russia had to be appeased. This was not so difficult. It was much more painful to have to shunt off the Poles, "the gallant nation whose wrongs, whose misfortunes, and whose valor have so deeply excited universal sympathy in Europe," [19] and to place by

[18] Tarle, *op cit.*, pp. 215, 289.
[19] See Seward's letter of Apr. 8, 1863, to Ambassador Dayton, in *Messages and Documents of the 38th Congress, 1st Session*, Washington,1864, Pt. II, p. 724.

connivance all hopes on the liberalism and magnanimity of Alexander II to concede their rights to the Poles. By thus winking at reality, Seward sought to bolster his position "that foreign intervention in behalf of the revolutionaries was unnecessary." [20] Very outspoken is his letter of April 24, 1863, to Ambassador Dayton:

The President has received with much interest Mr. Drouyn de l'Huys's exposition of the policy of the French Government in regard to the insurrection in Poland. The Emperor of Russia seems to us to have adopted a policy of beneficent reform in domestic administration. His known sagacity and his good dispositions encourage a hope that Poland will not be denied a just share of imperial consideration if, as seems now to be generally expected in Europe, the revolution attempted by her heroic people shall be suppressed.[21]

No less explicit is Seward's letter to Dayton on May 11, 1863, about the invitation from Napoleon to share in the mediation between the Russian government and the Poles:

This government is profoundly and agreeably impressed with the consideration which the Emperor has manifested towards the United States by inviting their concurrence in a proceeding having for its object the double interests of public order and humanity. Nor is it less favorably impressed with the sentiments and the prudential considerations which the Emperor has in so becoming a manner expressed to the court of St. Petersburg. They are such only as appeal to the just emotions and best sympathies of mankind. The enlightened and humane character of the Emperor of Russia, so recently illustrated by the enfranchisement of a large mass of the Russian people from inherited bondage . . . warrant a belief that the appeal will be received and responded by him with all the favor. . . .

Notwithstanding, however, the favor with which we thus regard the suggestion of the Emperor of the French, this government *finds an insurmountable difficulty in the way of any active coöperation with the governments of France, Austria and Great Britain*, to which it is thus invited.[22]

20 See H. Blinn, "Seward and the Polish Rebellion of 1863," *American Historical Review*, Vol. XLV (1940), p. 289.
21 U.S. Department of State, *Message of the President of the United States and Accompanying Documents*, Washington, 1864, Pt. II, p. 733.
22 William H. Seward, *Works*, Vol. V, *The Diplomatic History of the War for the Union* (Boston, 1884), pp. 382-383. Italics added.

If Seward, in full harmony with the liberal tradition, never gave up, at least officially, his sympathies for the gallant Polish nation, his agent in imperial Russia, the United States Minister C. M. Clay, played an entirely different tune. His attitude toward the notes of the three European powers asking, in behalf of Poland, for a new international congress like that of 1815, was an unnecessary, regrettable rejection because of "insurmountable difficulties," expressing a categorical and ideologically based unwillingness to support Poland. His report to Secretary Seward bluntly declared: "Our interests are on the side of Russia against reactionary, Catholic Poland." For his part, Clay, denying the liberating, antidespotic character of the Polish insurrection, described it as a fight for cultural and political independence or self-determination. Refusing to recognize it as a democratic revolution, he stigmatized it as an oligarchic and aristocratic uprising of nobles in the interest of the Roman Catholic Church.[23]

On this point Clay was, to a certain extent, influenced by the official Russian position. The Russian government and the rightist and Slavophile press, particularly Pogodin and Katkov, not only referred to the Polish revolt as reactionary, undemocratic, and narrowly aristocratic but acted cleverly to drive deeper the wedge between the Polish landed gentry and their peasants, both in Poland proper and in the Ukrainian and White Russian sections of Russia where the majority of the landlords were Polish. Special decrees of 1864 were more favorable to the Polish peasants than the statutes of 1861 had been to the Russian. Under the reform of 1864 the landed peasants received the full acreage they held from the landlord, and even some of the landless peasants received allotments. Similar arrangements were made at the expense of the Polish Catholic landlords of the western regions of Russia for the benefit of the non-Polish Greek Orthodox or Uniate peasants,[24] though there the expropriation was not complete. This was "the just share of imperial consideration" for Poland that Seward so optimistically hoped for.

The Russian opposition knew well the real value of the sudden

[23] Robertson, *op. cit.*, pp. 148, 150.
[24] Geroid T. Robinson, *Rural Russia Under the Old Regime* (New York, 1932), pp. 85-86.

agrarian democratism of autocratic St. Petersburg toward Poland. Herzen and Chernyshevski and the more moderate publicists and newspapers were not bribed or even deceived by the cheap redemption in the extreme west of the Empire. For Clay, however, the suspicions and considerations of Russian democrats were not obligatory, particularly where the strategic and diplomatic interests of the Union required the equation of the insurrection of the Poles with the rebellion of the Southern Confederacy. Under the sign of integrity—both of the American Union and of the Russian Empire —a consolidation of Russo-American friendship was much easier to achieve.

To return to the Polish insurrection, the first preparatory steps were taken in February, 1861, it must be said that it grew steadily despite certain timid half-reforms of the Czarist government supported only by the conservative Polish leader, the Marquis Wielepolski, and his circle. No clear constitutional changes were introduced in Poland. This Polish tension paralleled the increasing general radical opposition in Russia.

The matter became one of deep concern to the whole of Europe. Monarchic Austria, one of the three destroyers of Poland down to the end of the eighteenth century, rescued by Nicholas I in 1849, joined in ingratitude the enemies of Russia—England and France. These three great powers insisted on the international character of the Polish question.

Russia was aware of the military danger such a new—or partly renewed—coalition presented for her less than a decade after her defeat in the Crimea. She reckoned on the possibility of a naval and continental attack, in which her Baltic fleet would be the first victim in the interior waters along her northwestern seacoast. A second danger zone was the Pacific coast of Siberia. Certain movements of the Russian fleet toward the Atlantic and Pacific coasts of the United States, made at this time, became celebrated as movements directed, if not toward definite strategic support, then at least toward symbolic moral support of the Federal government of the United States during the Civil War. In reality, however, they were motivated by the sober and cautious consideration of avoiding the danger of a blockade of Russian harbors by the probable enemy and his superior fleet. In January, 1862, the "general admiral" of the Russian navy instructed Vice Admiral Popov to take command of the Pacific squadron and, in the event of war, to make for a safe port. In March the squadron anchored in San Francisco Bay. A similar step was taken by the acting Minister of the Navy, Admiral Nicholas Krabbe, after a report submitted to the Emperor in July, 1863, in the midst of the Polish insurrection. The Russian fleet, in his opinion, was too weak to put up an effective fight against the combined naval strength of England and France, but it was strong enough to prey upon their commerce. Toward the end of July a second Russian squadron, under Rear Admiral Lessovskii, left the Baltic Sea for New York. The arrival of the Russian fleets during the Civil War was a source of joy and satisfaction to the fighting North, though both squadrons, and particularly that of Popov, had received strict instructions not to interfere in the internal affairs or conflicts of any nation. Particularly enthusiastic was the American reception for the two men-of-war and three other ships which dropped anchor at New York in September. Their stay has been described as a long succession of banquets, balls, and receptions. Toasts were drunk to "the friendship of Russia and America, beginning with our national existence, in our darkest hour showing no abatement." The whole nation echoed Gideon Welles's fervent "God bless the Russians." [25] The open appearance of the Russian ships came as a shock and surprise to Great Britain. The Russian Ambassador in London, Baron Brunnow, an admirer of everything British, feared that the naval expedition would give England an excuse to start a war against Russia.

Golder was profoundly right when, notwithstanding exaggerated notions in both America and Russia, which had found their way even into the publicist literature of both countries, he concluded soberly:

It is, of course, true that the fleet was not ordered to America for our benefit, but this should not blind us to the fact that we did profit by the event as if this had been the case. If, as the Russians maintain, the presence of their ships in our waters saved them from a struggle in which they were not in a position to engage, we should be very proud that it was in our power to do so. It was a most extraordinary situation:

[25] B. P. Thomas, *Russo-American Relations*, 1815-1867, Baltimore, 1930, pp. 137-138.

Russia had not in mind to help us but did render us distinct service; the United States was not conscious that it was contributing in any way to Russia's welfare and yet seems to have saved her from humiliation and perhaps war. There is probably nothing to compare with it in diplomatic history.[26]

His conclusion later received full confirmation from Soviet Russia. This is particularly important, as the confirmation was given on the basis of new documents and letters that became available in 1939. Malkin stated:

> The appended published documents, supplementing previous American documentation, present Russian-American relations with sufficient clearness and put an end to all the tales that the Russian squadrons were sent in 1861 or 1863 to render help to the North, as well as those concerning a secret alliance between the United States and Russia. Established to be equally devoid of any basis is the contrary opinion that Russia did not show a friendly attitude toward the United States.[27]

During all these developments the United States received additional assurances of Russia's friendly attitude and diplomatic support. Among them the following event was of great importance. Late in 1862 a personal letter from President Lincoln was transmitted to the Russian Foreign Minister Gorchakov by Acting Minister Bayard Taylor. Taylor's conversation with Gorchakov was published by order of Congress, but Lincoln's letter was not made known. Said Gorchakov:

> Russia alone has stood by you from the first, and will continue to stand by you. Proposals will be made to Russia to join in some plan of interference. She will refuse any invitation of the kind. You may rely upon it, she will not change.

[26] Golder, "The Russian Fleet and the Civil War," *American Historical Review*, Vol. XX (1915), pp. 806-807, 811.

[27] Malkin, *op. cit.*, p. 107. The concluding sentence refers to Willis F. Johnson's book, *America's Foreign Relations*, New York, 1916, Vol. II. A question raised in Adamov's article, "Russia and the United States at the Time of the Civil War" (transl. from the Russian), *Journal of Modern History*, Dec., 1930, p. 602—whether the dispatch of the two Russian squadrons to America was undertaken merely to save them from an enemy attacking Russian ports or, as Adamov thinks, to put them in the most favorable position against the English and French fleets, or, lastly, whether both these purposes were pursued—is of minimal relevance.

From none of the great powers of Europe had the United States been able to win so positive a declaration. With this decision Russia aligned herself against England and France, who had fought her so recently in the Crimea. Also, Russia had no textile industries, as England and France did, that were suffering from a cotton famine.[28]

It was only natural that Russian reaction to the American attitude toward the Polonism of England and France should be enthusiastic. Humiliating notes from these two powers rained on St. Petersburg between April and July, 1863, in which Russian rejection of Polish independence was branded as an act that placed Russia outside the civilized world; *Punch* of London carried biting cartoons about America's friendship for the Russian bear and of the two liberators, Abraham Lincoln and Alexander II, standing united against Poland. In the face of all this, the appearance of the two Russian squadrons in American waters, together with America's refusal to join with the European West, produced a feeling of exhilaration in both America and Russia and cemented a close friendship that survived the treachery of England and France with respect to Poland and the insurrection. On September 26, 1863, when the revolt had been brutally crushed, Earl Russell made an unexpected statement: "Neither the obligations, nor the honor of England or her interests—nothing will press us to begin a war with Russia for the sake of Poland." This seems to anticipate Neville Chamberlain's classic statement in 1938 regarding a "small far-off country" that was not worth a war, viz., Czechoslovakia.

In Russia itself extreme patriotism and even chauvinism on the part of the conservative gentry and the awakening urban merchants became associated with pro-Americanism. This attitude is mirrored in a later work of the conservative Russian historian Tatishtchev, who regarded American refusal to join in Western intervention in Polish-Russian affairs as a gentleman's *quid pro quo* for the refusal of the Russian court (!) to participate in a similar demonstration against the unity of the transatlantic republic during the Civil War.[29]

[28] Carl Sandburg, *Abraham Lincoln: The War Years* (New York, 1939), Vol. II, p. 68.

[29] Sergei Tatishtchev, *Imperator Alexander II*, St. Petersburg, 1911, Vol. I, p. 487. He relies on Seward's letters to Dayton and Gorchakov's letter to Gen. Clay, both dated May 22, 1863.

An excerpt from an editorial by M. N. Katkov, the reactionary, anti-Polish editor of the Moscow *Viedomosti* (Gazette), will give vividness to the picture:

Under present circumstances the presence of Russian squadrons in the ports of the United States is an event of extraordinary importance. . . . The appearance of our three hundred cannons in the Atlantic Ocean and in the harbor of New York is worth almost as much as victory in a general engagement. It is scarcely possible to imagine a more effective demonstration than this, and the French press, on receiving this news, cannot conceal its anger.

Our rapprochement with the United States is useful for all purposes. Russia at present enjoys there a distinct popularity, and the United States can ally herself only with Russia. *In the event of a European war, the Americans are our natural and genuine allies.*

Thanks to recent events the system of political balance between states has ceased to be a European system only. Willy-nilly, America is drawn into its vortex. English policy has succeeded, with amazing skill, in entangling Napoleon III in a transatlantic affair and in linking the destiny of France to American issues. France is now not only in France, but in Mexico, too. Her European situation is, to a high degree, dependent on her American position. The Polish problem, which was exploited against us by France with so much enmity, has compelled us to send a part of our military forces into American waters. We anchored there without either aggressive or altruistic intentions. We don't wish to interfere in American affairs; we went there merely for our own convenience, while the Americans can appreciate these conveniences as well as ourselves. Now our presence in American waters will weaken France in Europe to the same degree that it will strengthen us. The government of Napoleon III cannot but see that in case of war Russia will not be satisfied just to defend herself and will strike a most painful blow at all of France's Mexican plans. The Civil War in North America is nearing its end. The South is obviously succumbing, and there is no doubt that our American friends will not let the opportunity go by to repay France for her generous attempts to recognize the South as a belligerent party, and for her adventure to improve American affairs in the best way and to load Mexico with benefits.

Our rapprochement with the United States would also be very useful for Russia in the sense that it would help her to gain more independence and freedom in her European alliance. This alignment, expanding the circumference of her political action, will move England to become more flexible and yielding in her relations with Russia. The nature of our international relations is such that friendliness toward France means enmity toward England, while every step of our rapprochement with the United States will be accompanied by a step on the part of England nearer to us, provided that we manage our relations with America so that, should she be in need of help, she would be reasonably sure to get it from us. The more profitable our alliance is to the United States, the more desirable will it become for England to bolster her good relations with us. We cannot repudiate our significance as a maritime power; we have a fleet, and we ought to have it. The Black Sea was taken away from us, but our fleet can be a real and useful force neither in the Black nor in the Baltic Sea, but only on the oceans. A few good frigates in the Pacific as well as in the Atlantic Ocean are worth an entire fleet in the Baltic or a Sebastopol on the Black Sea.[30]

No doubt the reactionary Katkov, in this trenchant editorial, perverted history, particularly concerning English policy toward Napoleon III and some American issues. But he at the same time revealed his intention of supporting and fomenting Anglo-American hostilities in order to benefit the interest of official Russia as he understood it.

Since the days of Katkov the rightist pan-Slavic wing has never found its way to a friendly and organic rapprochement with the United States.

---

[30] Katkov, *1863 God* (The Year 1863), 2 vols., Moscow, 1887, Vol. II, pp. 960-962 (italics added). The two volumes contain a collection of Katkov's editorials in the *Viedomosti* and the *Russkii Viestnik* in 1863, with diplomatic documentation.

X *Gustavus Fox's Naval Mission and Russian Public Opinion*

ANDREW DICKSON WHITE, THE STATESMAN AND FIRST PRESIDENT OF Cornell University, showed a genuine interest in Russian political as well as agrarian problems and in serfdom. He lived in Russia first as a secretary in the United States Legation in St. Petersburg for six months in 1855, when he witnessed the solemnities of the funeral of Nicholas I and received enduring impressions of the country at the opening of Alexander II's reign. From 1892 to 1894 he was minister plenipotentiary and envoy. After his first stay, he delivered a public lecture in 1857, which was published as a magazine article under the title, "The Development and Overthrow of the Russian Serf System," [1] to which he refers in his autobiography:

In this lecture I made no mention of American slavery, but into an account of the events of my stay at St. Petersburg and Moscow during the Crimean War, and of the death and funeral of the Emperor Nicholas, with the accession and first public address of Alexander II, I sketched, in broad strokes, the effects of the serf system,—effects not merely upon the serfs, but upon the serf owners, and upon the whole condition of the empire. I made it black indeed, as it deserved, and though not a word was said regarding things in America, every thoughtful man present must have felt that it was the strongest indictment against our own system of slavery which my powers enabled me to make.[2]

In his lecture-article White severely criticized the serf-holding caste which "made every effort to blast the good fruits of freedom." However, he did not mention the Decembrist movement, with a social program incorporating antislavery tenets and a political program endorsing American federalism. Although Nicholas began his reign by suppressing this movement, White merely says: "In

[1] *Atlantic Monthly*, Vol. X (1862), pp. 538-552.
[2] Andrew D. White, *Autobiography*, New York, 1922, Vol. I, p. 81.

MIANTONOMOH

The Monitor leading the American squadron across the Atlantic in 1866, anchored at Cronstadt, harbor of St. Petersburg

those first days of his reign when he enforced loyalty with grape-shot and halter, Nicholas dared much and stood firm."

Admitting that Nicholas had done a number of great things, White criticized him sharply, saying that each was "single, insu-lated,—not preceded logically, not followed objectively." As an example he mentioned the construction of the railway connecting the two capitals. "His own pride," wrote White, "and Russian in-terest demanded railways. He scanned the world with that keen eye of his,—saw that American energy was the best supplement to Russian capital; his will darted quickly, struck afar, and Americans came to build his road from St. Petersburg to Moscow." But Nicho-las did not continue the road to Odessa, the Black Sea port which could have had a tremendous economic and strategic importance for southern Russia.

In an entirely different tone White spoke of Nicholas's son, Alexander II, referring to him as Alexander the Earnest, the Chris-tian Patriot.[3] He described with evident satisfaction the fight in the ranks of the Russian aristocracy, particularly in the assemblies of local delegates, over emancipation, with which he was devoutly in sympathy. Later Russian historians have emphasized the hazards through which Alexander had to steer his plan, especially the scat-tered peasant riots, which were used as bugaboos to deter him from yielding to "subversive" elements. Correctly stating that Alexander insisted on "emancipation first, arrangement afterward," White added that the "arrangement" remained indefinite.

Significantly enough, White referred to foreign forces that had tried to dishearten the Emperor, not the least of which were the molders of public opinion in England:

Be it said here to the credit of France, that from her came constant encouragement in the great work. . . .

Not so England. Just as, in the French Revolution of 1789, while yet that Revolution was noble and good, while yet Lafayette and Bailly held it, leaders in English thought who had quickened the opinions which had caused the Revolution sent malignant prophecies and prompted foul blows,—just as, in this our own struggle, leaders in English thought who have helped create the opinion which has brought on this struggle now deal treacherously with us,—so, in this battle of

[3] *Atlantic Monthly*, Vol. X, p. 552.

Alexander against a foul wrong, they seized this time of all times to show all the wrongs and absurdities of which Russia ever had been or ever might be guilty,—criticized, carped, sent plentifully haughty advice, depressing sympathy, malignant prophecy.[4]

White, in full harmony with the Russian Populists (about whom he knew next to nothing), considered one of the most encouraging factors in Russian development to be the village community, which, by administering the partition of land among its inhabitants, played a routine role rather than one of economic improvement. As we shall see, Alexander Herzen and his friend Ogarev preached the same views in their underground London *Bell*. Without knowing that his views represented a fundamental slogan of Russian social reformers, White expressed the following remarkable thought:

And, to an American thinker, more hopeful still for Russia is the patriarchal democratic system,—spreading a primary political education through the whole mass. Leaders of their hamlets and communities are voted for; bodies of peasants settle the partition of land and assessments in public meetings; discussions are held; votes are taken; and though Tsar's right and nobles' right are considered far above people's right, yet this rude democratic schooling is sure to keep bright in the people some sparks of manliness and some glow of free thought.[5]

Local, or rather parochial, self-government also had been the pet idea of Russian constitutionalists, particularly in the 1870's and later, when they tried to create the small zemstvo unit (*melkaya zemskaya yedinitsa*) as the basic unit of the more extensive zemstvos of the gubernias and counties. White, anticipating a tenet of later Russian liberalism, also looked upon the small zemstvo as the basic unit of the future Russian constitutional monarchy.

The story of the development of Russian rural emancipation cannot and should not be retold here. Suffice it to say that the absence of direct resistance by the serf-owner group (*krepostniki*) to the act of emancipation in 1861 was more than repaid by a systematic legal and administrative implementation that aimed to mollify serf owners by postponement of the actual manumission. Here lay the tremendous difference between Russian and American emancipation. It was not in the fact of the racial identity of the Russian land-

[4] *Ibid.*, p. 550.   [5] *Ibid.*, p. 551.

lord and serf and the racial diversity of American master and slave, important as this may be from the psychological and ethical point of view; it lay in the mode of carrying out the emancipation. It was not only that there was no visible difference in the immediate environmental milieu between the "day before" and the "day after" the emancipation. The Russian liberation took on the character of a chronic condition in which payments by the free peasants to their former masters were repeatedly postponed until in 1905 they were finally canceled.

Not only Russian revolutionaries, but men like White who, for many years, had followed attentively developments in the Russian agrarian situation, were disillusioned. When White returned to St. Petersburg as United States Minister to Russia in the autumn of 1892, roughly thirty years after the statutory abolition of serfdom, he was intensely bitter over the sad results of a law that, at the time of its enactment in 1861, had been regarded by the whole world, including the United States, as an inspiring instance of unselfish social legislation. He points out:

> I do not deny the greatness and nobleness of Alexander II and the services of the men he then called to his aid; but I lived in Russia both before and since that reform and feel obliged to testify that, thus far, its main purpose has been so thwarted by reactionaries that there is, as yet, little, if any, practical difference between the condition of the Russian peasant before and since obtaining his freedom.[6]

While in the United States, too, changes were not felt immediately after the emancipation, and Negroes continued for a few years to live under scarcely altered conditions, nevertheless, the delay in upgrading in Russia was legally sanctioned for forty-four years, that is, until 1905. The Homestead Act failed to solve the problem of the American farmer, and therefore American radicals introduced in Congress two confiscation bills, which failed to pass; but even American radicals had to concede in a few years that American economy had changed basically and industrialization "in a climate of liberty" was beginning to develop on a large scale. Russian radicals could point to no such progress at the tragic end of Alex-

[6] White, *Autobiography*, II, 28-29. Cf. also Gerold T. Robinson, *Rural Russia Under the Old Regime*, pp. 94, III.

ander II's reign. The artificially created delay engendered profound bitterness and dissatisfaction among the radical Populists in the country, who were educated in the dogma of an agrarian messianism of Russia, supported in part even by the German expert Baron Haxthausen and the American economist and sociologist, Carey.

There was no thought, however, in the second half of the 1860's, of fighting what we would call today the legalistic sabotage of the czarist government by means of terrorism. Karakosov's attempt on the life of the Czar in April, 1866, was the act of an individual. Not only moderate liberals, but even the radical Alexander Herzen, condemned the act severely. Documents and historical research disclose that the plot later pieced together by the government and the political police never really existed. As a matter of fact, the members of the circle to which Karakosov belonged were opposed to the assassination, though this did not protect some of them from imprisonment and deportation.

It was the almost unanimous opinion of the Russian contemporary press that Karakosov's abortive attempt had very little effect on the carrying out of the reforms. Progress had been so slow that there could not be an appreciable slackening of pace.

In his report to the session of the Imperial State Council on March 8, 1881, following the "successful" assassination of Alexander II, Count Miliutin described the repercussions of Karakosov's shot in 1866:

> After his accession to the throne, Alexander II initiated a series of great reforms. . . . Unfortunately Karakosov's shot put a halt to the effectuation of many benevolent projects of this generous monarch. Except for the liberation of the peasants, all the other reforms materialized very slowly because of internal mistrust of their desirability. Measures were often taken that were opposed to the basic intentions of the newly published laws. Everyone lost confidence even in the best plans and projects. Indeed, all such undertakings were stopped, almost frozen in Russia, and everywhere dissatisfaction developed.

The reactionaries took the position that Karakosov's act resulted from the too broad liberties introduced at the beginning of the reign of Alexander II, which made it possible to undermine the existing state order.

The reaction of America to the attempted assassination remains outstanding in the annals of international relations. A joint resolution of Congress was adopted on May 8, 1866, and conveyed by Assistant Secretary of the Navy Gustavus V. Fox to St. Petersburg. It reads as follows:

Resolved, . . . That the Congress of the United States of America has learned with deep regret of the attempt made upon the life of the Emperor of Russia by an enemy of emancipation. The Congress send their greeting to His Imperial Majesty and to the Russian nation, and congratulate the twenty million serfs upon the providential escape from danger of the sovereign to whose head and heart they owe the blessings of their freedom;

And be it further resolved, That the President of the United States be requested to forward a copy of this resolution to the Emperor of Russia.[7-8]

The debate in the Senate was commenced by Charles Sumner, who extolled the Czar for his unwavering initiative in bringing about the emancipation of the serfs, securing for them an allotment of land, carrying out court reforms, and introducing the political rights of self-government. However, he was completely in error in stating that the assassination was attempted by an enemy of emancipation. He, like many other Americans, was disposed to see in Karakosov's act something akin to Booth's assassination of Abraham Lincoln. This is apparent in Sumner's assertion about Alexander that it was "this very thoroughness with which he has carried out his decree of emancipation that has aroused against him the ancient partisans of slavery, and I doubt not it was one of these who aimed at him that blow which was so happily arrested." Needless to say, no dissatisfied aristocrat-squire had any inclination toward acts of political terror.

Significantly enough a voice was raised in the Congress to strike out the words, "by an enemy of emancipation." This was supported by Saulsbury, but only on the consideration of "lack of evidence." The discussions gave no indication of any knowledge of Russian affairs; the Congressmen were wholly unaware of the existence of

---

[7-8] H.R. No. 133. For this and the following quotations see the *Congressional Globe*, 39th Cong., 1st Sess. (1866), pp. 2443, 2444, 2562.

a Russian revolutionary movement to which the emancipation of 1861, far from being a substantial achievement, was only a weak and dubious step toward full emancipation and the redistribution of land. Saulsbury was on the right track when he said of the attempt: "The statement that I have seen in the papers is that it was by a man in the humble walks of life, and I presume by a man who did not own many serfs." But his correct presumption was not supported by any knowledge of the facts of current Russian history. Sumner insisted on the original text of the resolution, and Howard supported that text with an additional consideration "that this resolution is but a fair, reasonable expression of the gratitude of the nation for the high, heroic stand which has been taken by that Emperor toward our own country." The proposed amendment was rejected, and the resolution passed.

What happened after this joint resolution by the Congress cannot be characterized as usual international courtesy or diplomatic routine; it was an extraordinary gesture. Fox's mission to Russia had as its official purpose the personal delivery to Alexander II of the resolution. In his address read to the Emperor during the audience in Peterhof, Fox referred to the Russian emancipation as an "edict of an enlightened sovereign [who] has consummated a triumph over an inherited barbarism, which our Western Republic has only reached through long years of bloodshed." In his reply the Emperor remarked that "the cordial reception which had been given to his squadron in the United States would never be effaced from his memory." [9]

Before further discussion of the main features of this mission, we must mention a speech by the Vice Chancellor, Prince A. M. Gorchakov, at a dinner on September 8, 1866, for the American mission that is important because it shows how eager the speaker was to impress his distinguished American guests. He said:

Our transatlantic friends are already acquainted with those feelings which their presence among us and the cause of their mission to Russia awaken in our country. . . . The unwonted fact, the unique example in history, of the Congress giving expression to feelings of profound esteem and sympathy toward our sovereign; the selection of the officer

[9] J. F. Loubat, *Narrative of the Mission to Russia in 1866*, ed. John D. Champlin, New York, 1873, pp. 88-90.

commissioned to convey hither the message of the Congress; the personal qualities of this envoy . . . the daring spirit of enterprise and the skill of those who conducted the expedition, and, by crossing the ocean, resolved a problem which until now was a question unanswered by the contemporary art of navigation; and lastly, the presence among us of the representative of the nation which, for many years and under all circumstances showed to us a constant readiness to continue the friendly intercourse between the two peoples—gentlemen, all this together composes something complete, undisturbed by any dissonance.[10]

Later in the speech he nevertheless felt it necessary to notice the error of the Congress as to Karakosov. However, his statements were definitely conditioned by his political inclinations; and he made an assertion regarding the personality of the culprit that is false and even preposterous:

An error slipped into the address of Congress—where enemies of emancipation are mentioned; an error, however, which is explained by distance and time. The madman alluded to does not belong to any nationality. He was not connected with the country by any personal interest, and represents but a blind hazard of birth.

As the speaker well knew, Dmitri Karakosov was by nationality a Russian, son of a Russian nobleman, the owner of a small estate in the Saratov gubernia. No "blind hazard of birth" can be said to mar the genealogy of this young revolutionary nobleman, a former student at the Kazan and Moscow universities.[11]

Equally unfounded is a second statement of the Vice Chancellor:

In Russia there is not a single enemy of emancipation, and those who are indebted to it for their freedom did not meet it with more joy than those to whom this measure was a duty attended by considerable sacrifices.

[10] "Russian Account of the Official Mission to Russia of the Hon. G. V. Fox in 1866," transl. for the Department of State, Washington, 1867, pp. 30-31. The French original of this speech can be found in Loubat, *op. cit.*, Appendices, pp. 936-939.

[11] The reactionary and chauvinistic press of those times insisted on the impossibility of this act having been committed by a Russian, and rumors were spread that it was done by one of the embittered Polish insurgents or even by some of the landlords who had been deprived of their property and serfs. Cf. the article, *Gorod Zhitomir v 1861 i 1866 godakh* (The Town Zhitomir in 1861 and 1866) in *Russkii Viestnik*, Vol. LXIV (Aug., 1866).

It is true that no one in Russia rose in arms against the abolition of serfdom, but neither before nor after March, 1861, did the Manifesto of Liberation have the unanimous approval of the Russian people. The slow realization of the emancipation was to a very large degree due to the stubborn unwillingness of the anti-abolition noblemen to understand that the greater the generosity in the earlier stages of the Emancipation, the less danger there would be of agrarian revolution. Eventually, two such revolutions took place, in 1905 and 1918. Stolypin's attempt to follow American homesteadism (1908–1911) was "too little and too late." [12]

The progress of Fox's mission through Russia is described in all its lavish hospitality and display by Loubat, who himself participated in it. There are only a few features worth mentioning. The delegation visited not only Kronstadt and St. Petersburg with some of its surrounding palaces, but also Moscow, the fair of Nizhni Novgorod (now called Gorki), and Kostroma, the cradle of the Romanov dynasty.

It is significant that in the receptions and banquets tendered the mission Russian merchants and municipalities took a prominent part; never had they participated to such an extent in such solemn diplomatic events. Indirectly this was a recognition of the need to let the urban bourgeoisie play a greater role in the public and economic life of the country, particularly after the emancipation of the peasantry. And inasmuch as the American mission did not consist of the usual stiff aristocratic diplomats but of undecorated and simply attired sons of burghers, even the czarist government could not help permitting this.

Most characteristic was the speech by a prominent merchant of Moscow named Shipov, hailing the leadership of the United States and stressing the need for further accord on protectionism and a sound attitude toward national wealth and labor:

Both countries are great in territory; both contain inexhaustible treasures; but these treasures require development, and this development can only be attained by means of adequately remunerated capital and labor. Of this the United States are fully convinced and consequently, in their commercial policy, maintain strictly the principle of protection,

[12] Cf. Georg Vernadsky, *A History of Russia*, new rev. ed., Philadelphia, 1944, pp. 160, 161.

not suffering themselves to be misled by the plausible theories of certain economists. Russia, too, is beginning to understand that in strict protection of national labor, in connection with the full development of the resources of a country, lies the secret of national wealth. And by no one has this truth been so clearly and so convincingly put as by that highly respected American political economist Carey and by our esteemed guest, now for the second time in Moscow, General Clay.[13]

Shipov was by no means the only holder of Carey's views. Another was Chetverikov, the president of the Merchants Exchange. At a reception for Clay and his secretary in January, 1866, by the mayor and the merchants of Moscow, he emphasized that the merchants and producers of Russia were in favor of the tariff mainly because the United States and Russia "possess similar means of development, and for that reason serve as an object of attack for the whole world." Clay, in responding to this speech, tried to find a way out by saying that "the true policy is not to declare absolutely for free trade or protection, but to subject both systems to a wise statesmanship." A manufacturer, Aksionov, in a toast to Henry Charles Carey, the American advocate of protection, said that the tariff should be "a mere temporary measure, as a means to develop home industry," that it should serve as a "barometer of the development of manufactures in a country." [14]

Here, too, there was a coincidence in American and Russian developments. America, after the defeat of the South, went over to protectionism, which found its full expression in the McKinley Tariff Act of 1890. Russia, after the emancipation and the emergence of free labor, lured the industrialists to fight for high tariffs in order to create its own broad industry. The tariff law of 1891 introduced higher customs duties than before. But in czarist Russia even moderate liberals were opposed to high tariffs and protectionism.[15]

[13] Loubat, *op. cit.*, pp. 259-260. Cf. Chap. XII, following.

[14] J. R. Robertson, *A Kentuckian at the Court of the Tsars*, pp. 256-257. The author gives Aksionov in a misleading Germanized transliteration, Axenhoff. A proof of Carey's popularity in Russia is the fact that his *Principles of Social Science*, containing a series of chapters (XXII–XXXVIII) on political economy, was translated into Russian by Prince L. N. Shakhovskoi and published in St. Petersburg in 1869.

[15] A. A. Golovatchov, "Svobodnaya torgovlia i protektsionism" (Free Trade and Protectionism) *Viestnik Yevropy*, Vol. V (1876), pp. 335-387.

We shall compare the positive appreciation of Carey by the foremost Russian merchants and industrialists with a rather negative one by Chernyshevski, the leader of radicalism and socialism, who dedicated some very bitter attacks to this topic of Carey and Russian protectionism.

Shipov, as president of the Nizhni Novgorod fair and as a man of commerce and industry, delivered a second speech in which he mentioned Lincoln and praised the financial ability of Secretary of the Treasury Chase. "He compared the status of the Russian paper currency with the American, greatly to the advantage of the latter. The reason why Russian paper money was below par was not that there was too much of it, and the cause of the rising of American currency to nearly what it should be was owing to the ability of our secretary's management." [16]

Another important merchant, later a rich banker, Basile Kokorev, a typical self-made man, devoted part of his address to what is an apotheosis of Lincoln, displaying a thorough acquaintance with all periods of his life.

The most theoretical and profound speech at the Moscow banquet was made by Michael Pogodin, a former professor of history at the Moscow University and later an academician. Except for the exaggerated complacent patriotism that led him to the false assertion that "the Russians, thanks to our gracious Emperor—who marks a new era in our history—may express their ideas and reason as freely as people do in New York," his speech had a distinct Slavophile flavor. Pogodin considered America as similar to Russia in so far as both countries denied old defunct Europe and, despite the differences in their regimes, were channels of real democracy. When he spoke of Russian democracy, he had in mind chiefly the old traditions of the Novgorod republican city-state, the medieval Estates Parliament (*Zemski Sobor*), and the most recent institutions of self-government introduced by Alexander II. Only in this light may we correctly understand the following conception of Pogodin:

I will add that this sympathy [for the United States] is increased by the resemblance of our institutions, by our connections with Europe, and history generally. I do not speak of the likeness as regards the extent

[16] Loubat, *op. cit.*, p. 297.

of our territory, our power and means; nor of the abundance of our natural productions. As regards institutions, the United States is a republic, and Russia an absolute monarchy; but here, as well as on the map, extremes meet. In the Russian absolute monarchy there is a democratic [17] stream that flows uninterruptedly throughout its history. . . .

I have but to speak, in conclusion, of the resemblance between Russia and the United States in reference to the Old World. It is impossible not to agree that Europe looks on the New World with some apprehension, some suspicion, some jealousy. I believe I make no mistake in asserting that the principal European governments, influenced severally by their own views and particularities . . . did not look at the American conflict so impartially . . . as we did. . . . They regard with the same eyes the other New World—I mean Russia. For fifty years . . . Russia was the chief supporter of peace in Europe; but, as soon as there was an opportunity, all this was forgotten, and Europe . . . leagued with Turkey against us . . . Where are we to look for the cause of such a disposition? Perhaps in the jealousy of her old age, in the general and involuntary conviction that America and Russia will have as much in their future as she has had in her past.[18]

By putting forth this notion of the decline of old Europe, Slavophiles attempted to get America on their side. Chernyshevski, as we shall see later, was the most ardent opponent of these views. He saw no reason to lament over the decline of a rotten Europe, which should be replaced by the "young" Slavonic peoples headed by Russia but excluding Poland. Pogodin was associated with the conception of the so-called reactionary "theory of the official nationality," a mixture of Russian patriarchalism and the German romantic philosophy of Schelling, a theory that served the throne and the altar. Even for these more or less reactionary conservatives America, pictured by them as an anti-Western growing power, was less objectionable than the "treacherous and ungrateful" European powers from England to Austria. Only if we bear this in mind can we understand why the Russian conservative review *Russkii Viestnik* never attacked the United States. At this point it would be well to recall Katkov's cynically frank editorial in the Moscow *Viedomosti*, quoted in Chapter IX. There the abstract Slavophile ideological

---

[17] Pogodin did not use the word *demokraticheskaya* ("democratic") but *zemskaya* ("local self-governing").

[18] Loubat, *op. cit.*, pp. 251 f.

premises were reduced to simple utilitarianism in questions pertaining to the general benefits of Russian foreign policy and particularly the policy against Poland. Only a few timid voices in the more liberal papers like *Golos* (The Voice) and *Den* (The Day) dared to contradict the blare of Katkov's paper.

In addition to all this we still have to recognize that the period which roughly begins with the accession of Alexander II and ends after Karakosov's attempt in 1866 is the high-water mark of Russo-American friendship. This era is mirrored in a poem written by Oliver Wendell Holmes, first recited by Fox in English at the dinner of the Good Birth Society in St. Petersburg and later read in Apollon Maikov's Russian version at the Moscow banquet to the mission and at other places:

> Though watery deserts hold apart
>   The worlds of East and West,
> Still beats the self-same human heart
>   In each proud nation's breast.
>
> .   .   .   .
>
> A nation's love in tears and smiles
>   We bear across the sea;
> O Neva of the hundred isles,
>   We moor our hearts in thee! [19]

The reply to the joint resolution of August 7, 1866, was addressed by Alexander II to the President of the United States, and reads as follows:

I have received from the hands of Mr. Fox the resolution of the Congress of the United States of America on the occasion of the providential grace of which I have been the object.

That mark of sympathy has moved me sensibly. It is not alone personal; it attests once more the sentiments that bind the American nation to that of Russia.

The two peoples have no injuries to remember, but only good relations. Under all circumstances new proofs of mutual benevolence are added.

These cordial relations are as conducive to their reciprocal interests as to the good of civilization and humanity, and answer the designs of

[19] Loubat, *op. cit.*, p. 180.

divine Providence, whose will is peace and concord among all nations.

It gives me a lively pleasure to see these ties constantly strengthening more and more. I have imparted my sentiments to Mr. Fox. I pray you to be my interpreter to Congress and the American people whom it represents. Tell them how much I appreciate, and with me the whole of Russia, the testimonies of friendship they have given me, and how happy I will be to see the American nation grow in strength and prosperity by the union and constant practice of the civic virtues that distinguish it.

Accept, etc.

Alexander [20]

The 1870's saw the first shift toward a cooler and more practical attitude between the United States and Russia. The purchase of Alaska, consummated through treaty by Seward and Baron Stoeckel, and the improvement of relations with Great Britain after the political eclipse of Lord Palmerston and Earl Russell—the living antipodes of Russo-American solidarity—helped to bring matters into sharper focus and accentuated differences. The industrialization of both countries—on different levels—tended to place their relations on a more matter-of-fact and less romantic footing.

It was a long process. During the period there still were recurrences of mutual closeness. On occasion, distant flashes recalled the past, and a sympathetic feeling for Russia lingered. Conspicuous evidence of this feeling is a small book on Russia by Captain Nathan Appleton, written in 1870 but not published until much later. It records vivid observations made during his stay and sets forth his carefully weighed conclusions on Russo-American relations. Russia, he thought,

will startle the world . . . and essentially change the features of the map of Europe. . . .
Although the spirit of the people is extremely democratic, the policy of the government is autocratic, and in the latter part of this century it is impossible for any but a government founded on popular principles and supported by the people themselves, to command the esteem and the envy of the masses in other portions of the civilized world, and thus to give them laws.[21]

[20] *Congressional Globe*, 39th Cong., 1st Session (1866), p. 143.
[21] Nathan Appleton, *Russian Life and Society*, Boston, 1904 (italics added).

Appleton, in his thought-provoking sketches, illuminates the need of the Russian state not only for several individual reforms, but for a secure foundation of order, above all, a separation of powers, and for roots in freedom. The second was achieved much later by the constitutional Manifesto of October 17, 1905, and the fundamental laws (constitution) of 1906; the third—freedom—was proclaimed in the same documents but, down to the February Revolution of 1917, had not been fully implemented.

Appleton was not, like Jonah, a prophet for a foreign country alone; he prophesied regarding his own country, too, and the two prophecies contain implications that are applicable even in our day, fourscore years after they were first made:

The mighty Republic of the United States, which sprang into existence less than a century ago, *will be the acknowledged law-giver and arbiter of the entire world.*

. . . Millions and millions of treasure seeking safe investment, would find its way to the United States.

America would become what England has been for many years, the strong box of the world. *England can be so no more.*

Telegraph communications and steam have put her so near the continent of Europe, that she can no longer be regarded as a sure land of refuge for men or money. Nay, it is doubtful if she could actually keep out of the conflict.[22]

Strange, in this atomic age, to read such comments hidden away in an unnoticed book written during the complacent and narrow isolationism of the 1870's.

Rare testimony to the awareness of the radical Populists of Russia of the attitude of the United States toward the political emancipation movement in Russia is the fact that this movement, represented by the much feared clandestine executive committee of the Narodnaya Volya (People's Will), sent to America in the late autumn of 1880 an illegal revolutionary "envoy" and established a permanent bureau to inform progressive America about the goals of the Russian movement and to appeal for moral and material support. The envoy was Leo Hartmann, a descendant of German colonist-farmers in inner Russia, and a terrorist who participated in one of the

22 *Ibid.*, p. 219 (italics added).

railroad minings intended to kill Alexander II. Arriving in New York at the end of 1880, a few months before the assassination of the Emperor-Liberator, he brought not only a power of attorney but a solemn "Address" by the Narodnaya Volya to the American people, the text of which follows:

It is difficult for contemporary American society even to conceive what the present situation in Russia actually represents. The unlimited monarchy, the almost contemptuous arbitrariness, and the state order itself which is based on the maxim, "The Emperor is everything, the people nothing," are utterly foreign to the whole spirit of American institutions.

The Russian people in their own country actually equal zero. The entire body of the people is no more than a taxpaying multitude which delivers to despotism the means of its shameful existence, a despotism, moreover, that is supported by forests of bayonets and mountains of bombs. Russian despotism draws its physical power from the people, extracting annually the flower of the youthful workers among the peasantry. Money and soldiers—these are the wellsprings of its very life. If the masses are unable to pay taxes, they are flogged in the markets.

No less sad is the situation of the intellectual class. To sympathize with the people, with their poverty and misfortune, is a heavy crime. . . . Talented publicists, scholars, litterateurs, and authors whose writings are dedicated to social problems are regarded as enemies of the government and traitors to their country. Many languish in exile, among them, for instance, such a luminary in the world of political economy as Chernyshevski.

Citizen-democrats! On which side are your sympathies? The reply to this question is for us a foregone conclusion. A country that, at the dawn of its history, has closed its ranks in defense of its independence, a country that has opened its arms to all the persecuted of the European continent, a country that has gone so far as to wage a fratricidal civil war for the sake of the emancipation of millions of slaves, such a country cannot but sympathize with us who have raised the banner of liberation of the Russian people from the chains of political and economic bondage. The abolitionists were your beloved and chosen sons. They really served mankind.

We are the Russian abolitionists! Your sympathies belong undividedly to us! Your indignation and contempt belong entirely to our enemies! Your sympathies as well as those of all peoples are cherished by us. We want to strengthen them.

That is why we intend to make you acquainted with the actual situation in Russia, with its political as well as its general aspects. For this purpose we send to your hospitable country our trusted representative, Leo Hartmann. He will report to you the history of our struggle, its bloody episodes, and the deeds of our martyrs. He intends to publish brochures and deliver lectures. People of America! We are confident that he will be received by you with friendliness and brotherliness.

The Executive Committee [23]

25 Oct. (6 Nov.) 1880

In 1887 Leo Hartmann established the Russian-American National League with branches in various cities of the United States. Being deprived of all support or salary from the Russian Populist movement, he soon became an electrician in New York. He never returned to Russia and died in 1913 a farmer and peaceful citizen of the United States.[24]

Among the flashes lighting the complicated relations was the assassination of Alexander II. His reign, which had begun so gloriously and so promisingly with a series of reforms, fell back into the inertia—somewhat polished and much humanized—of benevolent autocracy, the benevolence of which did not seem to convince the liberal Russians, let alone the radicals. These, coming from various strata of Russian society, were bitter because they could not fit into the administrative and economic apparatus of the state; and they leaned more and more toward subversive doctrines, including so-called nihilism. So much so, in fact, that they became blind to objective progress and minimized even the great reform, the long dreamed-of "crowning of the edifice," viz., the introduction of a constitution with legislative representation for the people. It is now an established fact that the assassination of Alexander II by Zheliabov, Kibalchitch, and Perovskaya, committed on orders of the executive committee of the Narodnaya Volya, was perpetrated when

[23] Taken from the Russian historical review *Byloye*, July, 1917, pp. 51-52.

[24] Victor Hugo, to his credit, insisted to the French government on Feb. 27, 1880, that Hartmann be not extradited to Russia: "Vous êtes un gouvernement loyal. Vous ne pouvez pas livrer cet homme. La loi est entre vous et lui. Et, au-dessus de la loi, il y a le droit. Le despotisme et le nihilisme sont deux aspects monstrueux du même fait, qui est un fait politique. Les lois d'extradition s'arrêtent devant les faits politiques. Ces lois toutes les nations les observent, la France les observera. Vous ne livrerez pas cet homme!"

the draft of the first Russian constitution was finished and only awaited final deliberation and the signature of the Czar.

The repercussions of this murder were tremendous both in Western Europe and in the United States, and, of course, in Russia itself. To those who did not appreciate the fact immediately after the event, it became clear in a few months that with the death of Alexander II an almost despotic autocracy would be established under his narrow-minded and terrified son and heir, Alexander III.

When the news of Alexander II's death reached the United States the Senate, then in special session, on March 14, 1881, unanimously adopted the following resolution:

WHEREAS, The Senate of the United States of America, convened in special session, has been informed of the death, by unlawful and inhuman violence, of His Majesty the Emperor Alexander II of Russia:

Resolved, That the Senate unites its voice with all civilized people in denouncing assassination as a means of redress for any grievances, either real or imaginary.

2. That, remembering and cherishing with satisfaction the relations of general friendship that have always existed between the people and the Governments of Russia and the United States, to the strengthening and maintenance of which the late Emperor has earnestly contributed his great influence, the Senate extends to the Government and people of Russia its sincere condolence in this sad national bereavement.

Resolved, That the Secretary of the Senate deliver a copy of these resolutions to the President of the United States, with the request that he communicate the same to the Russian Government.[25]

The resolution of the Assembly of the State of New York of the same day (March 14) was incomparably better formulated and, strangely enough, showed a much closer acquaintance with the more important features of the reign of Alexander II. It runs as follows:

Resolved, That the Assembly of the State of New York, representing more than five millions of the American people, and the moral, political and social sentiment of the State and country, have heard with profound sorrow of the death by assassination of Alexander the Second, since 1855 the Czar of Russia. He was the friend of the American Union when the

[25] *Congressional Record*, Senate, Special Session, 47th Congress, XII (1881), 20.

country was engaged in a fearful civil war; the emancipator of 23,000,000 of Russian serfs; the liberator of Bulgaria, and, at the time of his death, was engaged in the establishment of a constitutional form of government for the entire Russian people. Within the year past he had abolished an oppressive tax upon the poorest class of his people, and the despotic power of a secret police, which arrested citizens upon suspicion and banished them to Siberia without inquiry or any form of trial. The people of this State, while they everywhere sympathize with constitutional liberty and just equality, abhor assassins, whether under the rule of the Empire, as in Russia, or under the government of the People, as in the Republic of the United States. They recall the most brutal assassination of their own chosen chief magistrate, President Lincoln, and desire to put upon record their abhorrence of the crime of all official murders, regarding them as hostile to liberty, to civilization and to Christianity, and the worst possible foes of all reforms, whether in States or nations at home, or kingdoms and empires in the world abroad.[26]

A Russian conservative monthly stated with great satisfaction that the very mention of Lincoln's death in connection with that of the murdered Czar was, in the eyes of every American, a sign of the highest reverence for Alexander II: America, too, expressed its disgust and contempt for the theory of political murder.[27]

Most significant is the fact that the reaction of the United States had definite reverberations in the internal politics of Russia, viz., the trend toward constitutional liberty and even the change in the tactics of the radical Populists, who, for the most part, resorted to terrorism as a means to improve the social and political conditions of the country.

Naturally the neighboring empires, Austria and Germany, reacted to the violent death of the Czar with indignation and revulsion. England's attitude was equally characteristic. France, the only important European republic, was too much interested in Russia as a counterpoise to Prussian-dominated Germany to be an objective judge of Russian political terrorism. Thus America's verdict became in the eyes of the Russian people the most objective one,

---

[26] *Journal of the Assembly of the State of New York*, 104th Session, Albany, 1881, p. 387.

[27] "Zagranichnaya pechat' o tsaroubiistve 1. Marta" (The Foreign Press on the Czar's Assassination of March 1), *Istoricheskii Viestnik*, Vol. IV (1881), p. 910.

and its categorical repudiation of political terrorism, "whether under the rule of the Empire, as in Russia, or under the government of the People, as in the Republic of the United States," represented for the entire Russian intelligentsia—except the supporters of autocratic monarchism—a profoundly important dictum. This reaction was felt in the two camps of the czarist opposition; in the Populist Socialist wing led by the clandestine party of Narodnaya Volya and in the moderately bourgeois liberal movement.

Let us consider the first. On the day after the assassination a proclamation of the Narodnaya Volya explained the act as a reply to all the injustices perpetrated by the Emperor, including unbearable taxes, land restrictions, and exploitation of workers. But after nine days more, when the reactions of the West, including the United States, became known, the executive committee of the Narodnaya Volya published a letter to Alexander III. Revolutionary tradition has it that the letter was written by Nicholas K. Mikhailovski, who belonged to the right wing of the Populist movement.

The letter was a calm and sober one. Beginning with a general description of the numerous failures of the previous reign, which had brought frustration and embitterment, it stated that the existing government had no moral influence and no support among the people. "That is why Russia has so many revolutionaries, that is why even such an act as the murder of the Czar produces among the immense masses of the population satisfaction and even joy. Yes, Your Majesty, you should not be deceived by the opinions of your flatterers and servants. Regicide is very popular in Russia."

Continuing, the letter offered a well formulated political program: The two basic and immediate requisites for influencing the revolutionary movement toward moderation were a general amnesty for all previous political crimes and the calling of an elected body representative of the entire Russian people to revise the political and social order. Deputies must be elected by all classes and estates in proportion to the number of local inhabitants. The elections must be free, with guarantees of freedom of the press, of the spoken word, of assembly, and of the right of free formulation and publication of political programs.

Events suddenly put the Populists in direct contact with the United States. The attempt by Guiteau on the life of President

Garfield in July, 1881, resulting in his death on September 19, gave the Narodnaya Volya a chance to answer the official reproaches addressed to Russian revolutionaries by American legislative bodies and the daily press:

Extending to the American people our deep condolences on the occasion of the death of President James Abram Garfield, the Executive Committee considers it its duty to express in the name of Russian revolutionaries its protest against such violent deeds as the attempt of Guiteau on the life of the President. In a country in which freedom of the person guarantees full possibility of an honest struggle of ideas, where a free people's will not only makes the law but also elects the rulers—in such a country political murder as an instrument of political conflict is an expression of that very spirit of despotism from which it is our aim to extricate Russia. Personal despotism is as contemptible as party despotism, and violence can be justified only if it is directed against violence.

The Executive Committee

September 10, 1881 [28]

This brief document is not alone an attempt to justify to the West by implication a particular act, the assassination of Alexander II, by distinguishing it from a similar act committed in the United States; it also testifies to the lingering of the spirit justifying tyrannicide, a secular version of an old medieval doctrine based on the premise that a king preserves his royal prerogatives, sanctioned by God, only so long as he rules righteously. Otherwise, the old Roman principle, *Vim vi repellere licet* (It is lawful to repel force by force), has to be applied to the king, too. In this purely ideological sense, the Russian revolutionary declaration testifies to political backwardness.

Turning now to the moderate liberals, we can say that the terrorist activities of the radical Populists and the indignation they aroused abroad, even in the least immediately interested United States, brought about the first steps toward a new liberal movement of the constitutional type, which became an important factor in the early years of the twentieth century. The political platform and appeal

[28] The date is Old Style. The document, as quoted in the "illegal" political publication of Vladimir Burtzev, *Za sto let: 1800–1896* (A Century of Political Life), London, 1897, p. 180.

illegally published in 1883, giving the first evidence of Russian constitutionalism, stated:

A group of Russian constitutionalists deem it their duty to address themselves to the multitude who strive for—or at least sympathize with —the abolition of political serfdom in our country.

We do not approve the means used by the terrorist fraction of Russian socialist revolutionaries, and we are going to fight the government only by means of propaganda and persuasion. Nevertheless, we cannot conscientiously condemn a series of violations and crimes that have been provoked by a centuries-long brutality and mercilessness on the part of the government itself.

The Russian constitutionalists are striving to put an end to the police-state arbitrariness of our government.[29]

To this end the group included in its platform the calling of a body to be elected by the entire population of Russia. The modest platform ascribed to the elected assembly the character merely of an advisory body, in which all bills and annual budgets should be deliberated and publicly discussed. It asked for freedom of religion and the abolition of prior censorship,[30] and provided that offences committed through the press should be subject to trial by jury. Amnesty for political crimes and broad economic reforms, including those relating to the peasantry, were also demanded.[31]

This project of a Russian constitution, a very timid and limited attempt to liberalize Russian autocracy, was based on the unborn constitution of Loris-Melikov, Minister of the Interior under Alexander II. After 1881, however, constitutional projects began to appear which were carefully prepared, were based on a sound knowledge of political conditions in the country, and tended to erect a legal order of the state in which the monarch would be limited by the elected representative body (or bodies) of a full legislative character with the right of control over the administration.

The first such constitution was the one written by Michael Dragomanov and published in Geneva in 1885; another, more detailed constitution was published and commented on by S. Stepniak

[29] *Byloye* (The Past), Jan., 1906, p. 309.
[30] That is, censorship before publication, which was applied in Russia mainly to newspapers.
[31] *Ibid.*, p. 310.

in London in 1895 without mentioning the name of the author, who was later discovered to be Leo Kupernik, a famous Russian lawyer in Kiev. Both these projects, but especially the first, were constitutions for a United States of Russia, and some of their provisions and principles recall the Constitution of the United States of America. They called for a central parliament with two chambers, the upper chamber composed of an equal number of representatives from each of the provinces (or regions) of the whole country, while the lower one was constituted of representatives of the whole population. Somewhat in the American pattern, both projects provided that the Supreme Court (or the Russian Senate) should have the right to prohibit publication of a law it found to be unconstitutional. In Dragomanov's project the subordination of legislative power to the Supreme Court was even more complete than it is under the American Constitution. While the American Supreme Court cannot pass on the constitutionality of a statute until suit has been brought, this Russian project gave the highest tribunal the right, on its own initiative, to annul a law considered to be unconstitutional.

Kupernik's project provided that the upper (federal) chamber was to be elected, not directly by the people, but by the regional diets. The most significant phenomenon on the political scene was the appearance, about 1894, of a liberal, middle-of-the-road party called the Popular Rights (Partiya Narodnavo Prava), which made political freedom the core of an entire new order, together with improvement of social and material conditions. The manifesto of the party condemned czarism not only for its arbitrariness and its restriction of self-government, but also, naïvely enough, for "the systematic support offered to capitalistic production." These liberals tried to secure the material needs of the people "upon the basis of national production." Some of them paid tribute to the idea of federalization in the form of "political self-determination" for all the nationalities of the country.[32]

[32] The text of the manifesto is given in S. Stepniak and F. Volkhovsky, *Nihilism as It Is.* London, 1894, pp. 118 ff.

XI *Herzen on Russia and America*

> The French Revolution and German science are the Pillars of Hercules of the European world. Beyond them, on the other side, an ocean extends, and the new world of America becomes visible, a world that is something more than a second revised edition of Old Europe.
>
> —Herzen, *Epilogue 1849*

ALEXANDER HERZEN, THE GREAT RUSSIAN POLITICAL THINKER AND writer with a German family name and the pseudonym Iskander (Tartar form of Alexander), was the personal link between old Russian radicalism and its cousin to the left, moderate socialism.

He was born in Moscow in 1812, the loved illegitimate son of a wealthy Russian nobleman, Ivan Yakovlev, and a German girl, Louise Haag. Because of the bar sinister he could not bear his father's name, and consequently received from his father the German name of Herzen, symbolizing the relationship between the mother and the son. His pseudonym, Iskander, was a fine counterweight to the name Herzen, and emphasized his central Russian extraction. The circumstances of his birth have had a psychological influence on his later political views.

Herzen was a boy of fourteen at the time of the trial of the Decembrists in 1826. During a mass of thanksgiving in the Moscow Kremlin, celebrated at the coronation of Nicholas I on August 22, 1826, he solemnly swore to avenge the "five murdered men," pledging himself to fight against "that throne, that altar, and those cannons." In Russian literature this vow is called the "Hannibal's oath" of Herzen.[1]

For participating in a student organization at the University of Moscow he was arrested in 1835 and deported to northeastern Russia. He returned to Moscow in 1840. A second, shorter banishment was imposed in 1841. From 1842 on, he was a writer in the leading reviews. Early in 1847 he left Russia for Western Eu-

---

[1] Hannibal, the Carthaginian general, when a boy of nine, took an oath before his father, Hamilcar, always to hate and fight against the Romans.

rope in order to conduct from there the fight against the czarist regime and against serfdom; he remained the rest of his life in the West.

Herzen's attitude toward America was somewhat ambiguous. As the successor of the Decembrists, including the exiled Nicholas Turgenev, he appreciated the service the United States had rendered to human civilization and freedom. His admiration found expression in 1838 in a youthful drama, *William Penn*, that according to Herzen "was mercilessly slain by the critic Belinski." Whatever its literary merits, it shows that he was deeply influenced by America as the country of freedom. The ideological basis of the drama corresponds in general to the realities of Penn's life in England and in America, even if the author's lack of knowledge of English and American history exposes him to such errors as giving the name Charles Fox to a character easily identifiable as the peripatetic Quaker preacher George Fox, who spent six years in English prisons and visited the West Indies and America. Herzen depicts a lively meeting in which Penn blesses Fox for his generosity and bravery; and he somewhat ironically admits that he gave his drama a French-style finale. The last scene shows three pilgrim-travelers meeting at Penn's grave to pay him honor; they are Washington, Franklin, and Lafayette, the three most popular American heroes in Russia of the 1830's and 1840's.[2]

Up to 1848–1849 Herzen awaited a new revolution in "old official Europe," a revolution that would not only liquidate the legitimism of the Holy Alliance and the internal reaction of Russia and other European countries but also introduce definite social changes; and during this period he came to regard America as too moderate, and therefore unable to point the way for the Europe of the 1840's:

I agree that it is indeed high time to step out of our artificial and conventional life, but not by fleeing to America. What will you find there? The United States are only a fresh edition of the same feudal Christian text in a crude English translation.[3]

[2] A. Herzen, *Polnoye sobraniye sochinenii i pisem* (Complete Works and Letters), ed. M. Lemke, Petrograd, 1919, Vol. II, pp. 208-211.
[3] Herzen, *S togo berega* (From the Other Shore), London, 1855, p. 85. The essay was dated Dec. 1, 1848.

A year later he wrote: "Did not those who fled to America take with them old England?" [4] No less noteworthy is the closing dialogue in another essay: [5]

"Unfortunately there is not one single quiet and warm corner in the whole of present Europe."
"I will therefore go to America."
"It's very dull there!"
"That's right. . . ."

These and similar remarks were understandable immediately after the defeat of the 1848 revolution. But with increasing maturity and the growing need to understand the flux of events Herzen's attitude became more sober, and he regarded America with favor, reverting to the Decembrist pattern and realizing that she was not answerable for the failure of European democrats. Nevertheless, he always remained skeptical not only toward the petty bourgeoisie of Western Europe, but also toward America; he could never go back to the reverence of the Decembrists for the transatlantic antimonarchic Republic. Long after the debacle of 1848, in an essay on Robert Owen, he made the following sad observations on America, typical of a disillusioned anticzarist Westerner:

All that leads us, not to the question of whether R. Owen was right or wrong, but whether, in general, a critical attitude and moral independence are compatible with the existence of the state. . . .
There is one terrible instance before our eyes.
Within the memory of the human race there was never such a coincidence of happy circumstances favorable for a free and rational development of a state as existed in North America. All the obstacles usually encountered on exhausted or uncultivated historical soil were absent there. A foundation was laid for the teachings of the great thinkers and revolutionaries of the eighteenth century without any kind of French soldiery, and for English common law without the traditional castes. Could anything more be desired? Here was what old Europe had dreamed of: republic, democracy, federation, self-government, and self-legislation down to the smallest units, and a common governmental bond with a loose knot in the middle.
What became of all that?

[4] *Ibid.*, p. 164.
[5] "Consolatio," *ibid.*, p. 149. Dated, Paris, Mar. 1, 1849.

The society and the majority seized dictatorial police power; as for the nation, it executes itself the wishes of Nicholas I and of his secret police and his hangmen; a people which eighty years ago proclaimed "the rights of man" is divided now on "the right of whipping." Persecution and oppression in the southern states, which inscribed "Slavery" on their banners just as Nicholas I emblazoned "Autocracy" on his standard, were directed against freedom of thought and of the press and were by no means less perfidious than were the measures of the King of Naples against the Emperor of Vienna.

True, in the northern states slavery is not a religious dogma. But what can be the level of education and of free conscience in a country in which bookkeeping is abandoned only for the purpose of playing with little whirling tables and listening for ghostly raps, in a country which retains all the intolerance of Puritans and Quakers.[6]

Herzen was a fighter, not only against Russia's domestic policy, but also against her international position as a mighty reactionary power that could crush even foreign revolutions (Hungary) and revolutionary movements. Little wonder that in 1850 Nicholas I tried to get Herzen back to Russia, as well as Turgenev, his more moderate predecessor.

Herzen was eager to injure czarism in its foreign relations. He more than Turgenev, had the feeling that czarist foreign policy as well as domestic policy must be fought. From the end of the 1830's it became clear that one of the ways to battle internal tyranny was by undermining its prestige and weight abroad. This led to a split in the patriotism of the first great revolutionary: Czarist diplomacy ought not to be spared in the struggle; the czarist regime did not represent the interests of the Russian people in foreign relations, and therefore revolutionaries were not guilty of violating true patriotism. Despite his isolated position in London, Switzerland, and other places of refuge, Herzen was courageous enough to assume the burden of such a position, particularly in the early 1850's preceding the Crimean War and in 1862 at the insurrection of Poland under Alexander II.

Up to the end of the 1830's Russia was complacent and secure in its position in world politics. Between England and the United

[6] Herzen, *Polyarnaya Zvezda* (The Polestar), Vol. VI, London, 1861, pp. 295-296.

States, Nicholas I was anxious to stir up the old tensions and differences.

Except for the role played by Michael Speranski, George Mifflin Dallas made little reference to Russia's foreign and domestic policies in the diary of his period as United States Minister to Russia (1837–1839). He did record, however, an instance of the diplomatic subtlety of Nicholas I, who remarked at the end of an audience-of-leave with Dallas: "Not only are our interests alike but," with emphasis, "our enemies are the same." [7] Nicholas had in mind Great Britain and France, his two future enemies in the Crimean campaign. And it was said to the right man, too, for Dallas, concluding his diary at the Court of St. James's in 1861, characterized Great Britain as "this great country, which, while commanding my highest admiration, I find, after five years of trial, I do not and cannot like." [8]

Around this time America was in danger of attack from Great Britain in Canada, where Sir Francis Head was suppressing a rebellion. On the American side of the Niagara River the American steamer *Caroline*, in the insurgents' service, was attacked and captured by English forces, was set on fire and sent over Niagara Falls. President Van Buren made a formal protest to Great Britain against the breach of neutrality. This event and several frontier skirmishes made the attitude in the United States toward Great Britain more and more hostile. Emperor Nicholas, aware of the fact, took advantage of it to remind Minister Dallas that Great Britain was the common enemy of America and Russia; about the same time he tried to drive a wedge between England and France by sending Baron Brunnow to London. Needless to say, this attempt was not successful even after the failure of the Hungarian revolution brought about the intervention of Russian military forces. Nor were France and England split by the accession of Louis Napoleon to the French throne in December, 1851. On the contrary, the two countries drew even closer together, particularly in regard to the Middle East. To make matters worse, Nicholas I, in August, 1849, asked the Sultan to extradite a thousand participants in the Polish insur-

---

[7] G. M. Dallas, *Diary*, ed. Susan Dallas, Philadelphia, 1892, p. 209.
[8] *Ibid.*, p. 442.

rection of 1830–1831 and in the Hungarian upheaval, who had found asylum in Turkey.

For Herzen the gnawing anger at the reactionary role of Nicholas's Russia, which he was ready to fight with burning zeal, was mixed with disappointment in the revolution of 1848, around which all his hopes had centered. Napoleon III became for him the hateful symbol of the defeat of democracy not only in France, but in the whole of the West. His hatred for the monarch misled him to the conclusion that Napoleon was a nonentity. At the same time, however, his disappointment led him to attribute greater importance to foreign policy and international relations.

It is necessary here to clarify certain events in the relations between the United States and Russia from the revolutionary fiasco of 1848 through the period of preparation for the Crimean War, which coincides roughly with the Whig ascendancy (1849–1853).

About this time, as we have already shown, Russia entered on a close friendship with imperial Austria and Prussia. Hundreds of victims of the post-1848 reaction, among them many Germans, Hungarians, and Poles, fled to America. The sympathies of the Americans for European liberal and revolutionary movements were thus intensified, and it was only natural that Austria should become the object of American attack.

The Austrian government, through its chargé d'affaires Hülsemann, complained to the United States about its having sent an emissary to the rebellious province of Hungary to watch "in impatience for the downfall of the Austrian monarchy" in order to recognize Hungarian independence. Replying to Hülsemann's representations, Daniel Webster as secretary of state not only defended the Mann mission, but took occasion to expand on the proud position of the United States as a successful example of free government:

True, indeed, it is that the prevalence on the other continent of sentiments favorable to republican liberty is the result of the reaction of America upon Europe; and the source and centre of the reaction has doubtless been, and now is, in these United States.[9]

[9] Samuel F. Bemis, A *Diplomatic History of the United States* (New York, 1942), pp. 310 ff.

Later a joint resolution of Congress (March 3, 1851) was passed for the relief of Louis Kossuth and his associates, exiles from Hungary.[10] A banquet given to Kossuth by a large number of the congressmen and the speech by Webster extolling Hungarian liberty were only the climax of American libertarian policy of that time.[11]

Indirectly, the moral support extended to the Hungarian fighters against Austrian tyranny was also a demonstration against Russian tyranny and the suppression of the Hungarian uprising by the regiments of Nicholas I. Indirectly, too, the diplomatic defeat of Hülsemann of Austria was also a defeat for "Cossack" Russia, since Russia was regarded as the supporter of the reactionary Hapsburgs. In the eyes of Nicholas I, Kossuth was no less dangerous to Russia than Turgenev or Herzen. Nevertheless, the Russian Minister could not raise any questions about extradition. The "anomalous friendly relations" between the United States and Czarist Russia were not disturbed, externally at least.

The general international conditions briefly described here gave Alexander Herzen, as the "plenipotentiary" of the Russian revolutionary movement, the full right to proceed in open battle against the senseless policies of Nicholas, who was steering his silenced and hopelessly backward country toward the Crimean War.

In the years immediately preceding the Crimean War Herzen was greatly interested in the growing conflict between St. Petersburg and London, in which the United States, because its interests conflicted with those of the British, was on the side of Russia. He was glad, in 1852 and 1853, to support England as the mortal enemy of Russia. His pro-Americanism appeared clearly after the defeat of Russia and the death of her ruler in 1855.

Herzen's articles in the English *Leader* are worthy of note. He tried to unmask official Russia as the country of unrestrained autocracy, serfdom, and barbarity, precisely at the time the Crimean War against Russia was in the first stages of preparation, when all

[10] This comes up here because of the radical stand of the *Liberty Bell*, mentioned in Chap. VIII, regarding Kossuth and his evasiveness on the cause of slavery in America. Kossuth, after having found asylum in America, did not wish to create complications for the United States in its relations with his fatherland.

[11] *Select Speeches of Kossuth*, condensed and abridged by Francis W. Newman, N.Y., 1854, pp. 135 ff. The banquet took place on Jan. 5, 1852.

the Russian legation officials had left Constantinople and English and French ships were anchored in the Dardanelles and at the entrance to the Sea of Marmara.[12]

In an article entitled "Russian Serfdom," [13] Herzen tried to play on the similarities between Negro slavery in America and "White slavery" in Russia:

At the moment when all England was displaying profound and active sympathy for the slaves in the Southern States of North America, incited thereto by the great work of Mrs. Beecher Stowe, no one seemed to remember that nearer to England, across the Baltic, is an entire population not of 3,000,000 but of 20,000,000! A friend of mine proposed to publish a pamphlet to remind English charity of this fact. But his pamphlet was never published. I have taken it up and added a few general considerations which, however insufficient in themselves, may, I trust, contribute to throw some light on the melancholy subject.

He then related a story told by Nicholas Turgenev about the restoration of Empress Anne's duties and registration fees, which were to be paid on the sale of serfs. The Council of State after long debate acknowledged that the tariff was not a legal basis for the sales, and drew up a new law which it corrected and recorrected and finally sent to the minister of the interior. *"This took place at the time of the Congress of Vienna,"* Herzen added, hinting at the inconsistency of Russia's willingness to fight the international slave trade, while Russian serfs were bought, sold, and exchanged in the market and through advertisements in the newspapers.

In conclusion, he told that the president of the council, Count Kotshubey, had approached Turgenev at the end of the session and remarked with a half bitter, half mocking smile: "Only imagine, the Emperor is persuaded that for the last twenty years men have been no longer sold at retail."

An earlier article, "European Policy in America and American Policy in Europe," appeared on January 8, 1853, when a French naval force had taken possession of the peninsula of Samana on

[12] Cf. J. M. Callahan, *Russo-American Relations During the American Civil War*, Morgantown, W.Va., 1908.
[13] *Leader*, Nov. 5, 1853. A motto, taken from Gervinus, precedes the text: "The emancipation of all the oppressed and suffering is the vocation of the century."

Santo Domingo—outright interference in West Indian affairs. In it we find some lines designed by their flattery to win over America:

In fact, not only Louis Napoleon, but certain Northern prototypes of his, may be made to feel the weight of American influence in the world's politics. Non-intervention, in spite of all the cry about the failure of Kossuth, is almost an exploded doctrine in the United States. The *New York Herald*, edited by a practical man, and not a partisan of intervention, tells us that a sum of money will be set apart to be used in aiding nations struggling with despotic powers; and now we are told that a motion in the Senate has been made to the same effect. Even should it be untrue, it shows the set of the current. General Cass, in his place in the Senate, insisted that America was one of the family of nations, and that she could not remain isolated but must "keep on the line of political knowledge," share the general fortunes, protest against the defiance of the law of nations in the interest of despotism, and sympathize with, and morally assist, struggling nations. American policy in Europe will therefore be [as Mr. Ingersoll, the American minister, intimated at Liverpool] shoulder to shoulder with England in fighting the battle of constitutional liberty, if official England will be with America . . . knit together the two Anglo-Saxon peoples in a close alliance—the alliance of Freedom—and if need be, defy the world.

A third article appeared November 19, 1853, simultaneously with Count Nesselrode's cowardly circular on Russian prewar politics in Turkey ("We will await the attack of the Turks without taking the initiative of hostilities"). Herzen's last paragraph is an outburst against the foreign policy of his fatherland:

Shall these monstrosities, I ask, continue without an incessant, universal protest? . . . The mask must be torn from these slaveholders of the North, who go lounging and lisping over Europe, mingling with your affairs, assuming the rank of civilized beings,—nay, of liberal-minded men, who read *Uncle Tom's Cabin* with horror, and shudder when they read of sellers of *black* flesh. Why, these same brilliant spies of the *salons* are the very men who on their return to their domains, rob, flay, sell the *white* Slave, and are served at table by their living *property*.

Herzen's attitude toward the Crimean War was often called unpatriotic and defeatist because he hoped for the defeat of his fatherland, which, at that time, meant first of all the defeat of the rotten

Russian tyranny oppressing the country. Such an attitude later became characteristic of the entire revolutionary intelligentsia, especially during the Russo-Japanese War. In Herzen it can best be seen in his letter of October 27, 1854, to the editor of the London *Daily News*, "Conversations with the Russian Prisoners at Plymouth":

SIR:—It has repeatedly been said that the war of the Western Powers in favour of Turkey is not a war against a Nation, but a war against the turbulent and ill-regulated ambition of a single individual. My experience of Russia and a long study of the character of the Emperor Nicholas, carried on at St. Petersburg, have given me every reason to believe in the truth of this assertion. Nevertheless, liking to submit even my best founded convictions to such tests as may serve to strengthen or to weaken them, I thought that a visit to the Russian prisoners taken at Bomarsund might afford a curious opportunity of the kind. . . .

Will it be believed? The only fear which these unhappy men entertain, is to be obliged to return to their former life. Their captivity under the English flag they look upon as a deliverance. . . .

"I hope, my friends," said I to them, "that none of you will be obliged to resume your chains against your inclination. There is a question of sending you to Australia, should you desire it; there you will be free, as you have never been." This project, however, I am bound to confess it, did not at all seem to the taste of my auditors . . . "What should we do?" said one of the most intelligent among them to me. "What should we do in a strange and distant country, we who are unable to perform any kind of pacific work? Why do not the English and French rather enrol us among their troops?" "Is it possible," I observed, in reply, "You would fight against the Emperor Nicholas, your Sovereign?"

"He would no longer be our Sovereign, and his quarrel would no longer be ours."

These words, which I have repeated literally, proved to me what I have always thought, that we must not expect to find feelings of patriotism in the hearts of slaves. "Holy Russia"—this metaphor, which the cabinet of St. Petersburg holds out to Europe as a threat, falls like an empty sound on the ear of the enrolled Serf, and does not penetrate to the depths of his heart. To him Russia is not more "holy" than America is "free" to the plantation Negroes.[14]

[14] Herzen, *Polnoye sobraniye sochinenii*, Vol. VIII, Petrograd, 1919, pp. 106-111. The letter is included in its English original (from which we quote) with an accompanying translation into Russian. Some gaps have been filled by

During the raging war of Turkey, England, and France against the Russia of Nicholas I, Herzen recommended organized desertion by Russian soldiers to the armies of the anti-Russian allies:

Such a mode of recruiting would be as simple as it is easy, and would reduce the war in the Baltic and in the Black Sea to what in reality it ought to be: a struggle of mankind (without distinction of nations) against the arrogant disturber of the peace in Europe.

Only in the spirit of the motto from Gervinus, namely, "the emancipation of all the oppressed," can Herzen's defeatism be duly appreciated; it was justified by the struggle for Russia's liberation. On these preconceptions Herzen founded his London *Kolokol* (Bell) in 1857. Every number carried the motto: "Vivos voco!" (I call the living). This journal was interested largely in Russian problems, and most of its space was devoted to an analysis and sharp criticism of the czarist regime, questions of serfdom and its abolishment, administrative and judicial arbitrariness, persecution of minorities, and the defense of Poland and the Ukraine against Russification and national oppression. These constituted the main issues, together with criticism of the foreign policy of imperial Russia, including measures of reactionary intervention in the political life and liberation movement in the West.

Kolokol, though officially barred in Russia, nevertheless enjoyed a very wide circulation there, numbering among its readers members of the royal family, of the court, the highest aristocracy and bureaucracy, and all factions and shades of the opposition down to the clandestine revolutionary cells. A very moderate liberal, Konstantine Kavelin, a law professor at the Moscow University and later tutor of the heir apparent Nicholas, mentioned in his diary for 1857 that Prince Basile Dolgorukov, chief of the corps of gendarmes and director of the famous Third Division (secret police), had complained that "the highest personalities of the Empire coming home from abroad clandestinely import the publications of Iskander and even distribute them in Russia." What is even more revealing, immediately after being introduced to the Empress during her stay

comparison with the *Daily News* of Oct. 28, 1854, where the letter appeared anonymously with the signature, "A Cosmopolitan Traveller"—which the patriotic Herzen certainly was.

in Darmstadt, he saw her reading *Kolokol*. She voiced her indignation at Herzen's views expressed in the second issue (August 1, 1857).[15] It is known that the Emperor himself was an avid reader of the illegal *Bell*.

Kolokol was close to its American prototype, the *Liberty Bell*, mentioned in Chapter VIII. There are strong reasons for believing that Herzen deliberately chose the name *Kolokol*, following the pattern of the American journal, which was also strongly abolitionist and liberal and supported liberal movements throughout the world. *Kolokol* appeared about the time the *Liberty Bell* passed from the scene (July, 1857). Ten years later, in 1867, Herzen decided to publish a French edition, *La Cloche*, and in the first issue, addressing himself to all European peoples, he wrote that in order to find freedom we have to climb the Alps or cross the ocean: "Freedom is in the United States, and it feels no hatred toward Russia for the sake of her future."

This statement is important because it was written after an event in Russian political history in which America was a direct participant. In the December 1, 1858, issue of *Kolokol* is an article by Herzen entitled "America and Siberia," which was directly inspired by the article "Our Western Neighbor" in the Philadelphia *Evening Bulletin* of October 8 dealing with the foreign policy of the United States and Russia. The *Evening Bulletin* article was concerned with the conclusion of a treaty between Russia and China in May, 1858, on the expansion of Asiatic Russia to the Amur and Ussuri rivers with outlets to the Pacific Ocean, and stated:

The latest news from St. Petersburg announces that the treaty closed by Mouravieff had been the cause of great rejoicing in Siberia. . . . If the real influence which the Mouravieff treaty is eventually to have on the world and on American interests were duly appreciated, we should have good cause to celebrate it here, too, for that matter, as the history of the next half century must inevitably show. Russia is . . . devoting her mighty resources towards making a commercial and industrial

[15] K. D. Kavelin, *Sobraniye sochinenii* (Collected Works), Vol. II, St. Petersburg, 1898, pp. 1171, 1174. The Empress was obviously disturbed by the lengthy editorial "Revolution in Russia," in which the wavering of Alexander II with respect to necessary reforms was sharply criticized. Iskander asked that the Czar repudiate the reactionary St. Petersburg period with the same courage Peter I displayed in repudiating the Muscovite period.

country of East Siberia; and as the United States is her opposite neighbor, in fact her only really civilized one, it will be seen how nearly we are concerned in the matter. For it is our interest also to have neighbors with whom to trade, and the more rapidly California is developed, the more rapidly will our West be brought out, the more will the necessity of completing our Pacific Railroad be felt. . . .

When the Pacific Railroad is finished, and when Russia has an open sea coast, the American and the Muscovite can afford to look the one west, the other east over the Pacific—name of good omen—and turn their backs on Europe.[16] When flippant Master Sala, two years ago, sailed up into Cronstadt, he observed that "the stars and stripes of the great American Republic were very much to the fore . . . ; and as I found afterwards, the American element was what Americans would term almighty *strong in Russia.*" The Russians know the value of America and respect it; John Bull snubs us and France despises us. But the inevitable laws of industrial progress, as conditioned by geography and climate, will force their way. There is a manifest destiny for nations!

That the Americans meant business when they spoke of reaching hands across the Pacific to Russia may be gathered from a strange advertisement in English printed as a leaflet and inserted into *Kolokol*:

To the Directors of the Society for the Colonization of the Amoor in St. Petersburg

There is no doubt that the deal which you are at present undertaking will be in a few years recognized by the whole world as one of the greatest enterprises of our century. With the exploration of the region irrigated by the Amoor you will tremendously help the colonization of the western shores of America and in that way support the rapid development not only of the United States but also of Russia. Stating this we do not exaggerate at all. We have already seen in America that the peopling of California has pushed half a century forward all the regions lying between it and the eastern parts of the United States; this leads us to the conclusion that if the region pertaining to the Amoor will be colonized, Russia will immensely be pushed along the way she is already developing so well. We are sure that in your trying to protect Russian interests you will put a friendly glance at America and will discover in her population your natural ally from whom you may await

[16] Herzen in translating this part of the American article into Russian interpolated, "shaking hands with each other."

much use in the future. The sympathies of the United States toward Russia and the growing participation of our people in its development have no precedents in the past. We are two huge countries of the world peopled by nations destined to reach great power, by the last events of a few years we are turned to face each other—between us only the Pacific, this "Mediterranean of the Future," as one Russian said. . . .

From that follows that for us in America it is extremely important that your colonization of the Amoor region shall develop quickly, without wasting time. It certainly did not evade your attention that where there are gold-mines the most quick and lasting settlements spring up. California, Australia and the banks of Frazer [Fraser] are only the best cases in point. . . .

There are many causes to suppose that the Amoor and its arms irrigate a country as abundantly rich in gold as no other country in the world. Should that become finally established and gold-digging of Americans encouraged you have all reasons to be sure that in a few years Eastern Asiatic Russia will become much more important than California. The presupposition is, of course, that your far-sighted government will grant means and privileges to reach these goals. . . .

There is one outstanding fact, about which much was mentioned in our journals, viz. that American gold searchers which settled in English dependencies on the banks of the Frazer river have never indulged in hostilities with the Government or local administration neither in political nor in civil relations. Defending at home both kinds of rights, the American does not meddle in either of them on foreign soil. This is political tenet which he learned from childhood.

If you will get some information about the actual finding of gold in your soil and if you will think it fit to encourage American immigration there, I would sincerely ask you to let the inhabitants of the United States immediately get this information.

The letter was signed by Charles G. Leland for the publishers of the Philadelphia *Evening Bulletin.*

This constitutes a very rare phenomenon in Russian illegal *periodica,* a phenomenon that could have been produced only by the contact of *Kolokol* with America.

The somewhat more abstract reaction of Herzen to the article in the *Evening Bulletin* was less commercial and more political:

We are not pampered by the sympathy of other nations, neither do they understand us. There are many causes and explanations for this, chief among them the policies of St. Petersburg since 1825. But Russia is beginning to emerge from this period. Why is it that only America has realized it and is now the first to welcome us? It is because Russia meets America on the other side. Because there is a whole ocean of salt water between them but not a whole world of antiquated prejudices, petrified notions, jealous preferences and a paralyzed civilization.

It will soon be ten years since we expressed our views on the future partnership of these two countries in history. We pointed out that Russia had in the future only one comrade and fellow-traveller—the United States. We have repeated frequently: "It is only the empty, irritating diplomatic self-love, which we aped from the Germans, that presses Russia to intervene in all Western issues. In the coming clash toward which Europe is unwillingly marching, Russia should not have any part. We have no inheritance there, neither are we connected by memories or hopes to the destiny of the Western World. *If Russia will get rid of its St. Petersburg period, she will have only one ally—the United States of Northern America.*"

The wisest and most progressive men of our time, like Mazzini, smiled at our unhappy patriotism. . . . Down to the Crimean War nobody ever suggested that an internal process was going on in Russia; behind the inarticulate lips there were supposed to be hidden a dull mind and a stony heart. However, the ideas sown on December 14, 1825, grew, took root, and invisibly undermined the oaken gates of Nicholas I's jail. Before this process came to an end, the walls crumbled, demolished by the bombs of the allies.

All that we stated when we spoke of the inimical West, all that we predicted—from the secret fermentation of minds, through the inevitable emancipation of peasants accompanied with land grants to them, to our friendliness with the United States—all that has happened.

Incidentally, there was no need for the gift of prophecy. . . . We had only to look objectively at the whole world. America and Russia were the first to meet our eyes: Both countries abound in gifts, forces, flexibility, and a spirit of organization, and in persistence which knows no bounds; both are poor in their past; both began their march by breaking with tradition; both expanded across unbounded valleys seeking for frontiers; both countries advanced from opposite sides across immense spaces marking their way with cities, towns, villages, colonies, reaching the coasts of the Pacific Ocean, this "Mediterranean of the Future" as we once called it and as it was—to our great satisfaction—frequently referred to by American journals.

The contrast between the St. Petersburg military dictatorship, which, in the person of its autocrat, annihilates all persons, and the American autocracy [self-assertion] of every citizen is tremendous.

If you turn to the peculiarity of the American mind, you will be struck by two things: first, the federal democracy united by the legally established position of every community and every voter, which has become a solid form of civic life; second, the freshness and simplicity which the American mind introduces into the usual scholastic rubbish of political problems.

. . . When events following 1848 clearly showed that European peoples were unable to carry out the conclusions concerning the economic and political order reached by science, the Russian mind started to loose itself morally from the chains of authority.

The Crimean campaign has shown the inability of Russia to fight Europe. Our moral liberation from Europe is the beginning of the elimination of the St. Petersburg tradition based upon the subordination of everything Russian to everything foreign. . . . All this does not mean that we should cease to follow Western science or try to invent our own science.[17]

Disappointment in the European revolutions of 1848, particularly after the Crimean War, led Herzen to seek and to find something in common between Russia and America, two sprawling countries not hampered by the romanticism of a feudal past. We should not be wrong if we found in this statement of the vigorous political thinker some influence of Alexis de Tocqueville, no less pro-American, who also saw in Russia and America two great nations that had grown up until "the world learned their existence and their greatness at almost the same time." Tocqueville is also responsible for a classically concise expression of their diversity, which with certain slight changes would be appropriate in our time, more than a century after the publication of *Democracy in America*. The principal instrument of America, said Tocqueville, is freedom; that of Russia, serfdom. Slightly reformulating this antinomy and applying it to the years after 1945, we might say that the instrument or moving force of America is freedom, including freedom of competition, while that of Soviet Russia is the subordination of the individual under state authority and state economics. In Herzen's time, shortly after the abolition of white and black serfdom, Tocque-

17 *Kolokol*, Dec. 1, 1858. My italics.

ville's concluding sentence seemed incontrovertible. Russia's and America's starting points, he wrote, are "different, and their courses are not the same, yet each of them seems marked out by the will of Heaven to sway the destinies of half the globe." In the structure of the United Nations and in the whole political and social world arena, this great antinomy continues to hold even today, when these two almost elemental powers have finally met in the Pacific and overshadowed the others.

It is most significant that *Kolokol*, despite its moderate socialist coloration, set up the United States not only as a political but as an economic and agricultural pattern for Russia—a point of view that was not adopted by the liberal Russian press either in the 1870's or later. The only article by another writer that we shall consider here is one by Nicholas Ogarev, personal friend and collaborator of Herzen, dealing with the Russian village community.[18] He wrote that the Russian landlord, in his use of his serfs, was economically inefficient: He was not able even to bring his corn to the market, and almost never sold flour. It was only through the assistance of merchants that he sold his grain in other regions and abroad. In less than a decade Russia would be covered by railways; but if serfdom should remain the landlords, owing to their laziness and inertia, still would not improve their agriculture nor sell more grain than they were selling then. Like a typical bourgeois democrat, Ogarev tried to show that abolition of serfdom would be beneficial for both the landlord and the peasant and defended the agrarian reform. If, through Alexander II, it should soon take place the landlords would awake from their sluggishness and would themselves become good merchants, interested in the quantity and quality of their grain; they would actually invest money and labor in improving their agriculture. On the other hand, the peasant, freed from the dreadful tutelage of the past, would display just as much energy. The only socialist view to which Ogarev gave expression was his denial that the traditional Russian village community was a hindrance to the development of rural economics. This position was to become decisive in the fight of the Russian Populists (*Narodniki*) against the Marxists.

[18] *Ibid.*, Feb. 15, 1858.

Ogarev rejected any possibility of Russia's using the agricultural patterns of Western Europe, which rely on the importation of foreign grain. Only in America, he said, could Russia find resemblances to itself and things to emulate. Like Russia, the United States extended across vast areas with a relatively small population. The first circumstance that struck one with respect to agriculture was the foreign trade in grain. Russia, he continued, despite its relative successes after the Crimean campaign, exported about 2.5 per cent of its yearly harvest, while the United States exported 7.5 per cent. In the United States there remained for domestic consumption 23.2 bushels per capita, and in Russia only 21.5 bushels. The arable land of both countries was as 1.8 is to 1.4 in favor of the United States. Ogarev pointed out that the climate of the United States was more favorable than that of Russia, but admitted that even under equal climatic conditions, the productive forces of the United States were half again as great as those of Russia. The explanation for that, Ogarev found in the difference in the general level of civilization and particularly in the different types of administration in the two countries. In Russia the administration meddled with and hampered economic development. In the United States the administration was a product of the people; consequently, it helped them and did not hamper them. Both the Yankees and the Russians knew how to make the plains fruitful. Instead of Cossacks, the Americans sent out columns of men who struggled to take over the land, with the result that the natives and buffaloes disappeared before them. The newly acquired land became populated and organized in an American manner, that is, by social compact, with the establishment of schools, churches, and democratic courts, instead of by the Russian district police inspector. In the United States the government and the people were motivated by the same interests and went forward together, while in Russia the government was fenced off from the people by the bureaucracy and by officials who robbed the people and deceived the government.

In America itself Ogarev differentiated between the agriculture of the North, where science was applied to the tilling of the earth by free labor, and that of the South, which used slave labor. Ogarev gave an American professor of political economy, De Bow,[19] as authority on the stubborn resistance of the planters to change in the established order and to the setting up of parish agricultural societies. In this respect they were very like the Russian landlords, who were not eager to improve agricultural productivity.

*   *   *

Despite his radicalism, Herzen made political compromises. After the defeat of Russia in the Crimean War and the accession of Alexander II, he established as the program for the immediate future three basic demands: (1) emancipation of the peasants with allotments of land; (2) abolition of corporal punishment; (3) modern public court procedure and freedom of the press. It must be said that the first demand, though the most difficult because the Czar had to act against the interests of the slaveholding nobility, was carried out.

If one considers the backwardness of Russia in the 1850's, social and political, and the absence of an organized public opinion to push through the legislative measures of emancipation, then the eradication of an ancient and entrenched agrarian system from such an extensive territory in the short span of four years must be regarded as a great achievement. Beginning in numerous local preparatory commissions in 1858, it was finally accomplished on March 3 (February 19), 1861, with the promulgation of the famous Manifesto of Liberation, four years before emancipation was completed in the United States.

This achievement produced a wave of enthusiasm in all liberal circles in Russia. Herzen was carried along by the current and wrote a historic article on the crowned liberator, Alexander II, "Thou Hast Conquered, O Galilean!" [20] In it he evinced a deep appreciation of the liberating role of a monarch who, by his determination could play therein an outstanding part in emancipation and save

[19] James D. B. De Bow, *Encyclopaedia of the Trade and Commerce of the United States*, more particularly on the southern and western states, 2 vols., Washington, 1853, and London, 1854. Ogarev does not indicate where in the book he found his data.

[20] *Kolokol*, Feb. 15, 1858.

the cost in time and blood that a mass movement might involve. It is a fact that emancipation was achieved in Russia without civil war. Herzen therefore regarded Alexander not only as the legal heir of Nicholas I but as the heir of the Decembrists:

The name of Alexander II henceforth belongs to history; if his reign should be ended tomorrow, if he should be dethroned by the underhand attacks of certain oligarchs, believers in whipping and compulsory labor by serf-peasants, it would not matter. The beginning of the emancipation of the peasants has been accomplished by him; future generations will not forget it.

Here lies the significant difference between Alexander II and Abraham Lincoln, which the radical revolutionaries, beginning with Chernyshevski and ending with Lenin, never recognized. This specific appreciation—which has no relation to monarchism—constituted the great distinction between Russian liberalism and social radicalism. In the last analysis, here can be found the reason for the later rehabilitation by the Soviets of Ivan the Terrible and Peter the Great as progressive, antifeudal monarchs. On the other hand, the abolition of serfdom by Alexander II never led to an objective appraisal of his role in the emancipation of the serfs. These views of Herzen account for his indignation at the attempt of Karakosov to assassinate Alexander in April, 1866.

As we have already seen, there was a gap of several years in Russian emancipation between the first tentative steps and the final solemn proclamation of 1861. In this respect there is complete similarity between the emancipation processes in Russia and in the United States. In the United States, too, several steps were required: the early outcries for the abolition of slavery, Lincoln's initial doubts, the preliminary proclamation of September 22, 1862, the Emancipation Proclamation of January 1, 1863, and finally, permanent legislative implementation in 1865 in the Thirteenth Amendment to the Constitution.

Another strong and fundamental point of resemblance is the fact that in both countries pressure for emancipation was strengthened by the increasing need for free labor from industrialization. Finally, in both countries emancipation was achieved against the will of a vested interest: the Russian landlord class and the American planters.[21]

The processes in Russia and in the United States differed in the reverberations stirred up by the preliminary measures. In Russia there was no open military clash in civil war or regional localization of the problem as there was in America; in Russia the inevitability of emancipation led to the crystallization of the proponents of the reform into two groups, the moderates and the radicals, while the aristocratic opponents remained monolithic in their negative attitude.

Even before the Manifesto of Emancipation was published, Herzen was attacked by his more radical followers for his readiness to approve the acts of the Czar. They were suspicious of the trend of the first official discussions regarding abolition; namely, to smother the issue of granting land to the freed peasants by their former masters. The reactionary fellow travelers who, under Alexander's influence, were ready to carry out the emancipation, wished to do so along the lines followed in the earlier emancipation of peasants in Estonia, Livonia, and Courland in 1817 and 1819— personal emancipation of the peasant-serfs without any grant of land from their former masters, the Baltic-German barons.[22] The

21 That Herzen and Ogarev, his close friend and coeditor, were aware of the industrial necessity for emancipation can be seen in Ogarev's article "The Peasant Community" in *Kolokol* on Feb. 15, 1858: "In the United States, people who inherited from Western Europe capital and the adaptation of science to industry, free in their initiative, created wonders in manufacture. But here, too, when we turn to agriculture, we cannot but notice the great difference between the northern and southern states. Application of science to agriculture reached high levels in the North under free labor, while something different occurred in the southern states where slave labor prevails. We find in a book by De Bow, professor of political economy at the University of Louisiana: 'It is difficult even at present to convince the planters that something beyond the habitual routine could be done. In the entire State there is not one single parochial agricultural society.' Does not this remind you of the Russian landlords? Although De Bow is an advocate of Negro slavery in the southern states, he reluctantly finds it necessary to complain about the inertia of the planters, about the lack of a sufficient network of railroads, etc."

22 Arveds Shvabe, *Zemes attiecibu un zemes reformu vesture Latvija* (History of Land Relations and Agrarian Reforms in Latvia), Riga, 1930, p. 162: "After the publication of the acts of emancipation in Courland and Livonia, the noble landlords acquired full title to the private land of the peasants because

final acts of Russian emancipation, however, rejected the Baltic scheme; Russian peasants were granted parcels of land for which they paid over a long period.

Lenin was right in 1907 when, speaking of the 1861 emancipation, he remarked that there were for Russia in the 1860's only two paths for an objectively possible bourgeois development; namely, the "Prussian" and the "American." The remnants of serfdom could fall away either through the economic readjustment of the estates of the landed gentry or by a complete destruction of the aristocratic latifundia, that is, by reform or by revolution. The bourgeois economy could develop with large private estates at the top, estates that would become more and more bourgeois through the gradual replacement of serfdom with capitalist exploitation; or the small peasant holdings might be at the top, a revolutionary shift that would remove from the social organism the "excrescences" of the old serf latifundia and permit the development of full-fledged capitalist farming as in America. The struggle between peers and peasants revolved around the method of implementing the agrarian reform. Both groups advocated bourgeois development, the peasants being antilatifundian and favoring the expansion of the free peasants' land property.[23]

Regardless of which way of development was to be chosen, the reform viewpoint—or rather the objective task—was not represented by the peasants themselves, who were not members of the preparatory committees in 1858–1860. Their absence was somewhat compensated by the reform party among the aristocracy with Alexander II at the top and by the appearance of two radical trends, one moderate, the other revolutionary. In the 1860's Herzen belonged to the moderate wing; but, though appreciating the importance of freedom as such, he stanchly opposed the Prusso-Baltic approach, which in-

---

on private estates the boundaries between the manorial grounds and the peasants' lands were canceled. This meant that *by one stroke of the pen* approximately 900,000 peasants in Livonia and Courland *were made landless*, legally destitute of land."

[23] Lenin, *Agrarnaya programma sotsialdemokratii v pervoi russkoi revolutsii 1905–07* (The Agrarian Program of the Social Democracy in the First Russian Revolution of 1905–1907), in *Sochineniya* (Collected Works), Vol. XI, Moscow, 1929, pp. 348-349.

volved merely legal freedom; [24] and he proclaimed in a kind of political credo: "The liberty of Man is the most sublime issue; on it —*and only on it*—can develop the true will of the nation." [25]

In the meantime, the most radical Russian camp began to attack Herzen for his too moderate position. A letter to the editor signed "Russian Man," [26] apparently written by Chernyshevski, reminded Herzen that abolition could be realized only through struggle. The people are ready to accept their rights from anyone who will give them to them. Recently, when the English and the French landed in Crimea, the Russian people expected from them emancipation from land bondage; and the various sectarians, freedom of religion. The writer went on to say that a chasm was opening between the people and the liberals who thought that the peasant question could be resolved by peaceful means. He did not seem to be worried about the fact that the people would be deprived of the leadership of the liberals. "Why should we be sorry for the dandies in yellow gloves who are only able nicely to discuss the democracy of America without knowing what to do at home, and who basically despise the Russian people because they don't believe in Russia's future." The letter concluded with an exhortation to Herzen to change the tone of *Kolokol* not to ring for the church and prayer but to sound the alarm: "Call Russia to the ax!" It was not to be forgotten that throughout centuries belief in the good intentions of the Czars ruined Russia and Herzen should not support such a belief.

Herzen replied to the letter in a long editorial. We shall quote a few sentences because this exchange, taking place in 1860, is symbolic of the difference between Russian liberalism and radicalism

[24] As far back as 1856, five years before the emancipation, Herzen, in his "Russian Serfdom" wrote of the Baltic emancipation, which had granted the former Estonian and Latvian serfs personal freedom without land, and the possibility of its being extended into Russia proper: "Can you imagine a European rural establishment with the autocracy of St. Petersburg, with our officials [*chinovniki*] and our village police? Mind you, twenty million proletarians unemployed but seeking work on the seignorial lands, in a country where there is no legality, where the entire administration is corrupt and lies in the hands of the squires, where the individual is nothing, and where influence is all."

[25] Herzen, *Proshchayte!—S togo berega* (Goodbye!—from the Other Shore), in *Izbrannyye filosofskiye proizvedeniya* (Selected Philosophical Writings), Moscow, 1946, Vol. II, p. 11.

[26] *Kolokol*, Mar. 1, 1860.

through the entire span of modern Russian history. Later, during the revolution of 1905 and particularly that of 1917, the difference constituted the basic tension that decided to a large degree the destiny of democratic Russia. Herzen's reply reflected an amiable disagreement akin to that displayed by Paul Miliukov in 1917 when as leader of the cadets and minister of foreign affairs in the provisional government he insisted that the British government release Trotsky from arrest in Halifax and let him proceed to his native country. It is noteworthy that at this early date the letter from "Russian Man" already lumped together in one category all the Western countries—England, France, Germany, and the United States—placing the "dandies in yellow gloves" on one side and Russia on the other side.

Herzen regarded his more radical opponents as friends with whom he differed in opinion; to triumph over them would not be cause for exultation. He wrote:

> We differ not in the idea but in the means, not in the precepts but in the mode of acting. You represent one of the most radical expressions of our trend . . . but we shall not call to the ax, to this *ultima ratio* of the oppressed, *so long as there is the slightest reasonable hope of arriving at a decision without an ax*. The deeper we look into the Western world . . . the greater is our *disgust at bloody upheavals*.
> Who has done anything effective for Russia if not the Emperor? Let us here, too, render unto Caesar the things which are Caesar's! [27]

It was inevitable that the split between Herzen and the young untamed Russian revolutionaries should become wider and wider. His attitude toward the Karakosov attempt in 1866 was outspokenly negative and even indignant. He called it a "preposterous crime" and the attacker a lunatic. To Russian terrorists he remarked that "only among savage peoples does history develop by way of murder," and that "the responsibility which such a fanatic takes upon himself arouses my indignation."

Herzen's attitude differed little from that of the West in general and of the American Congress in particular, which could hardly remain a secret from him. This was very much resented by the radical wing of Russian political opinion, for even those who did not

[27] *Kolokol*, March 1, 1860. Italics added.

sympathize with terrorist acts regarded the attackers as misled martyrs rather than as political murderers.[28]

On the other hand, Herzen, while denying the existence of a plot and the participation of any organized group in the attempted assassination, was categorically opposed to the execution of Karakosov. At this point the unusual incident occurred which we have noted. Additional significance was given to the joint resolution of Congress condemning the attempt on the life of the Emperor by the decision to have Gustavus Vasa Fox personally convey it to the Emperor, traveling in the flagship of an American naval squadron.[29] Precisely on the day of Karakosov's execution, September 3 (Old Style), Fox left St. Petersburg after a farewell breakfast on the Russian yacht *Rurik*. Smolensky Field, where the execution was to take place, was near the harbor. As Herzen describes it:

The scaffold ominously escorted the Americans; this was the last thing they saw as they left Russia. . . . What chaos! Death, execution, an autocrat without power, the dreadful calumny of a non-existent plot, which burst, like a soap bubble, and the notes of "Yankee Doodle" mingling with those of the Russian "Kamarinskaya." [30]

Despite all the changes since 1858, including his own disappointment with the evasive attitude of the United States in the Russo-Polish conflict before and during the Polish upheaval of 1863, Herzen proudly emphasized on the occasion of the visit of American naval units to St. Petersburg in 1866 that he was definitely in favor of Russo-American friendship:

All Russian and non-Russian newspapers are full of news about the rapprochement between the United States and Russia. Western publicists are angry and look surly and, of course, they have reason. Russian journalists repeat in all its variations what I wrote on this issue eight years ago. It is what I suggested in *Kolokol* of December 1, 1858.[31]

[28] Cf. Stephen Graham, *Tsar of Freedom*, p. 107. Graham asserts that Herzen "was not indignant at acts of terrorism and destruction, never thought his cause was injured by these outrages." This view requires substantial revision. Compare also Nathan Appleton, *Russian Life and Society*, p. 136.

[29] Callahan, *op. cit.*

[30] Herzen, *Polnoye sobraniye sochinenii*, Vol. XIX, Petrograd, 1919–1925, p. 61.

[31] *Ibid.*, p. 63.

The swell of criticism from youthful nihilists combined with defiance against the old—and first—leader of an active anticzarist emigration annoyed Herzen but did not dampen his willingness to fight. The old revolutionary Iskander saw only too well how slowly real emancipation was working out. He realized at what a heavy price the legally liberated Russian peasantry had bought itself from lingering economic dependence on former noble masters. Yet as late as 1867, six years after the initiation of the reform, he tried to console himself with the political and administrative outlook for changed rural relations. In 1867 he wrote from Florence:

The village commune and the rural inhabitant have made great strides since 1861. The original ancient principle of *self-government*, so well appreciated by the Westphalian Baron Haxthausen and by the American sociologist Carey—a principle that was eliminated by the police and the noble landlord—begins gradually to free itself from its swaddling clothes; the institution of suffrage begins to take root. The bailiff, the communal judges, the rural police are elected.[32]

Another important difference between Russia and the United States in the aftermath of emancipation was that, while the fight for the homestead in the United States involved no great departure from the customary status of private landownership, the concept of the homestead in Russia remained within the frame of the mir with tenure subject to yearly partition and rotation of the plots.[33]

In this connection, Herzen, despite his cultural and political Westernism, retained strong traces of Slavophilism, for the social patterns of which the mir remained the common denominator. This belief in the village community, for which he was reproached by Marx,[34] led him to say: "The community, should it duly develop, *will make impossible the very existence of a proletariat*, if only the state order will not lie in the way of the community.

"The Russian peasant hates personal land property," asserted Herzen,[35] a statement later developed by the Populists to show that

[32] *Ibid.*, Vol. XX, Petrograd, 1923, p. 83.
[33] Geroid T. Robinson, *Rural Russia Under the Old Regime*, pp. 113, 119ff.
[34] *Das Kapital* (Hamburg, 1867), Vol. I, p. 763, quoted in Herzen, *Polnoye sobraniye sochinenii i pisem*, Vol. XX, p. 102.
[35] "Russkii narod i sotsialism" (The Russian People and Socialism—a letter to J. Michelet), in *Izbrannyye filosofskiye proizvedeniya*, Vol. II, p. 139.

Russia's trend toward socialism would not follow the lines of Western proletarian urban socialism. Of no less importance is his second postulate:

> The village community rescued the Russian people from Mongolian barbarism, from czarist civilization, from the landed gentry externally dressed and painted in the European manner, and lastly, from German bureaucracy. The whole organization of the commune, though badly shaken, still stood its ground against the invasion of the administrative power and lived to see *the unfolding of socialism in Europe*.[36]

This agrarian approach, first developed by Herzen and his friend Ogarev, later became the basic creed of all non-Marxian socialism in Russia. Chernyshevski, a more radical disciple of Herzen, and Russian Populists of all shades of political thought remained adamant in their support of the agrarian peculiarity of Russia.

The same peculiarity was later responsible for the popularity of the teachings of Henry George, which overemphasized agrarian relations as against urban industrialization and specifically correlated progress with the poverty of the laboring class embracing urban workers as well as rural workers and farmers. (See Chapter XIII.)

Herzen, as we have seen, admired America intensely as a country of promise that, along with Russia, would overcome bourgeois pettiness and the feudal infection with which Europe was afflicted. For him as for Goethe, America was the country of the future, unburdened with ruins or with barriers from the past. He quoted in the *Cloche* of January 1, 1868, Goethe's little poem "An die Vereinigten Staaten":

> Amerika, Du hast es besser
> Als unser Kontinent, das alte:
> Hast keine verfallenen Schlösser
> Und keine Basalte.
>
> Dich stört nicht im Innern,
> Zu lebendiger Zeit,
> Unnützes Erinnern,
> Vergeblicher Streit.

[36] *Ibid.*, p. 143. By "German bureaucracy" Herzen meant the disproportionately high percentage among Russian state officials of German-Balts, whom he regarded as particularly hostile to Russian democratic tendencies and extremely friendly to czarism, the throne, and the court. Cf. Chap. I. This is one of the most frequently repeated leitmotivs in Herzen's political writings.

However, Herzen did not see in America an entity that could begin *ab ovo*, from its own roots, a new history. For him America was only a continuation of Europe, though he did ascribe to it the capacity to overcome this connection. He wrote to Michelet on September 22, 1851, about the future of the Slavonic peoples should reaction and absolutism finally conquer Europe; and, asking whether the Slavonic world could disappear then, he answered that in such an event Europe, too, would perish, and then history would be transferred to America.[37] Two years later, on January 2, 1854, he came back to the same topic in his letter to W. J. Linton, editor of the *English Republic:*

Look at the two limitless valleys meeting with their backs on the fringe of Europe. What for are they so spacious, what are they looking for, what is at the bottom of their all-devouring passion for activity and expansion? These two worlds contrasting each other are the United States of Northern America and Russia.

Nobody doubts that America is the continuation of European development and *nothing else but* a continuance. Being deprived of any initiative or invention, America is ready to absorb those who flee from European reaction and to achieve socialism in a sense of her own, but she will never cross the Atlantic to demolish the old European structure and will never abandon her rich fields for that purpose.

This was a notion that almost a century later was repeated by modern American philosophers.[38] But for all that she lacked originality and was deprived of her own "genesis" in the field of philosophy and civilization, the United States manifested tremendous stability in the development of political and social institutions that were often rudimentary in the countries of their origin. Consequently, America shows a creative continuity in political and social relations. In the same letter Herzen wrote that the United States represented "the ultimate realization of all the republican and philosophical ideas of eighteenth century Europe." Elsewhere he remarked, in full harmony with his forerunners, the Decembrists, that

---

37 *Ibid.*, p. 153.

38 In the Preface to A *History of American Philosophy*, New York, 1946, Herbert W. Schneider wrote: "America was intellectually colonial long after it gained political independence and has been intellectually provincial long after it ceased being intellectually colonial. We still live intellectually on the fringe of European culture."

only America was able to introduce real democracy on a tremendous continent and make it the simple result of daily administrative routine. Russia of the Czars showed herself unable to harmonize Ivan the Terrible with Montesquieu but demonstrated that the Russian problem was also a social problem, while Europe trembled before the word "socialism." The European world had come to the end of its career. Of course, Russia did not have to go through all the phases of European history. Herzen denied the inevitability of such repetitions. Being basically an agrarian nation, Russia could not follow in the footsteps of Europe, whose revolutions liberated only the urban masses and not the peasants. The latter were legally emancipated, but were granted small allotments of land on the basis of landownership. In Russia such a distribution would kill the village commune.

Herzen conceived of America as the last Western country that could be considered to be as rich in promise for the future as his own Russia. This equality made it the duty of America, the country of revolutionary birth, to support revolutionary risings against reaction the whole world over. This view he had inherited from the Decembrists, and he handed down the torch of his conviction to rising generations of Russian revolutionaries. One can thus understand the conflict that must have torn him as he observed the friendship between official St. Petersburg, the outgrowth of Byzantino-German Russia, and modern America—a friendship that did not even touch the masses of the Russian people.[39] Particularly painful for him was the friendship shown by official and diplomatic America to the court of St. Petersburg during the early 1860's when Russian emancipation was followed by the suppression of the Polish uprising of 1863, which in its turn coincided with the Civil War in America. In an earlier chapter will be found the official correspondence between Washington and St. Petersburg, between Secretary of State Seward and Minister for Foreign Affairs Gorchakov. Under the circumstances the federal government in Washington was—in violation of its own feelings—compelled to support Alexander II

[39] In a letter to I. S. Aksakov, Herzen wrote from Geneva in 1867 that he considered it as one of his great merits that he was the first to show the necessity of a coalition between Russia and America. Cf. Herzen, *Polnoye sobraniye sochinenii*, Vol. XIX, p. 279.

against the Polish rebellion, paying only lip service to the heroism of the Polish people, while England, France, and—strange as it may seem even today—Austria were anxious, in genuine and feigned sympathy, to extend help to the Polish cause.

For Iskander, Poland's plight was overwhelming. He did not shrink, even in the face of the chauvinistic criticism of certain Russian liberals—let alone the government—from accusing Russia of barbarity. He urged Russian officers to refuse service in the punitive expeditionary forces sent to Poland, which he called "Poland, Mater dolorosa!" [40] And there were some Russian officers—courageous humanitarians—who supported the Polish uprising for independence.

It cannot be said that contemporary Americans were entirely unaware of the "unwritten obligation" of their country to support Poland against Russian despotism. In terms of foreign policy this was indeed a Gordian knot. George Washington's admonition against foreign entanglements and Monroe's doctrine found themselves in "insurmountable difficulties," if not in open conflict, with the theory of nonintervention and even more so with the vital diplomatic interests of the United States in wartime. It was not, therefore, a fortuitous happening that the ambivalence—traditional American libertarian antimonarchism and immediate tactical diplomacy—emerged sharply in a diplomatic document, a letter of Secretary Seward to the American Minister in France dated May 11, 1863.

After stating why mediation with Russia in regard to the Poles would be refused, the talented Secretary of State made a classically laconic statement regarding the situations in which America was inextricably involved whenever a liberation movement or resistance began:

> Founding our institutions upon the basis of the rights of man, the builders of our Republic came all at once to be regarded as political reformers, and it soon became manifest that revolutionists in every country hailed them in that character, and looked to the United States for effective sympathy, if not for active support and patronage.

This assumption—which actually was prevalent not only in Russia but also in a number of other countries in the nineteenth century

[40] *Kolokol*, May 1, 1861.

where a struggle for freedom was inevitable or actually in progress —may well have been the reason for the influence America exerted in Europe.

And here it must be said that Herzen, with all his burning enthusiasm, took on his shoulders the defense of Poland. Against him were hosts of antagonists among moderate liberal Russians; against him was a substantial part of the public opinion of the United States, including such responsible and important political figures as Secretary Seward and Minister Clay. He was ready to wage an open fight against the government of Alexander II, whose personal merits in the emancipation he frankly and even enthusiastically recognized. The suppression of Poland was for him an issue involving Russian reaction and fraught with danger for Russian humanism and liberty. He was well aware of the weaknesses of the insurrection above all, of its break with the Polish peasantry. He always insisted on the necessity that the movement have a popular and all-embracing character, with full emancipation as its basic slogan.

In *Kolokol* of October 1, 1862, Herzen published the manifesto of the leading organ of the insurrection, the Central Polish People's Committee in Warsaw, which contained the following most significant passage:

The basic idea of the Polish insurrection is the right of the peasants to the land they are tilling and the right of every people to dispose of its own destiny. . . . The common consent of all of us who stand at the head of this movement makes it possible for us to declare in our political program that the people's organization will, at the first moment of the uprising, allot to all rural inhabitants the ground they are at present tilling, and the People's Government will take it upon itself to compensate the landed gentry from the treasury of the state. . . . In Russia the social movement will create political freedom; as for Poland the reorganization of its society can only follow the emancipation and reconstruction of our own country.

An editorial comments on this manifesto: "That Russian who on these bases does not stretch out his hand in friendship to Poland, does not love freedom."

In the next issue of *Kolokol* (October 15), Herzen printed an appeal to "Russian officers in Poland"—those who had been sent with their troops to Poland to crush the rebellion—exhorting them to refuse "to raise arms against Poles" and, if necessary, to submit to being court-martialed and shot. The result was that certain liberal and radical Russian officers, who refused to have any part in suppressing the insurgents and serving as hangmen, were executed. On September 15, 1864, after the heroic and hopeless uprising was crushed, *Kolokol* had this to say: "The Polish insurrection was not defeated by executions; it was crushed because of the nonparticipation of the peasant element." And on December 1 Herzen printed an epitaph in which appear the following sentimental lines:

> With old Poland, the Polish Poland, the element of chivalry is disappearing from European life. . . . Rich with a fine youth and a decent old age, permeated with ideals, heroism, and Catholicism, she at the same time touched both the Middle Ages and the year 1789, the Crusades and the Grand Army of Napoleon.

A year and a half later, when the last sparks of the upheaval were extinguished, the revolutionary Iskander wrote another open letter to Alexander II on the occasion of the death of the heir apparent. After mentioning the mourning of countless numbers of Polish families and the atrocities of his leading hangman, Muraviev, it concluded in the most forthright terms:

> You, having once been the victorious Galilean, you were unable to hold the heights to which you were elevated by the Manifesto of 1861.
> Would it not be more honorable for you to convoke elected representatives from all strata of the people from all the corners of Russia, and sit down together with them to decide on necessary common efforts?
> Return from the funeral of your son to the old path you once began to tread.[41]

It was with a broken heart that Herzen had to make peace with the failure of the Polish insurrection and with the treachery of France and Napoleon the Little and with the broken pledges of England of Palmerston and Russell, the enemies of free America. He never ceased to be the revolutionist who, in the words of Secretary Seward, looked to the United States for "support and patronage." But after Fox and the American fleet, in September, 1866, left czarist St. Petersburg, flattered by the sympathy of republican America, his Bell rang out no more.

41 *Kolokol*, May 25, 1865.

XII *Chernyshevski's Study of Russia and America*

NICHOLAS CHERNYSHEVSKI WAS BORN IN 1828 IN SARATOV ON THE Volga. He belonged not to the nobility but to the clergy. His father, Gabriel, an Orthodox priest who became assistant to the director of the Saratov Theological Seminary, was a thoroughly educated man with a command of Greek and Latin as well as modern French. Nicholas, after preparatory work on the high-school level at the seminary and two years of intensive study at home, majored in philology in the Philosophy Department of St. Petersburg University and was graduated in 1851. All his life he devoted himself to social and economic disciplines and to the natural sciences. Besides Russian and other Slavic languages, he knew English, French, and German, and was well versed in classical philology.

There is a basic difficulty in presenting Chernyshevski's doctrines. Under pressure of czarist censorship, Chernyshevski avoided stating his socialist and radically democratic views directly, and developed an unusual faculty for leading the reader to a point or a comparison or even to a quotation from a popular poem or from classical prose, which would suddenly make the whole idea clear. The intelligent Russian reader, keenly perceptive and experienced in reading between the lines, was able to pick up the cues and interpret correctly allegories and ambiguities. This mode of expression, generally known in Russia as the Aesopic language (*Ezopovski yazik*), was employed by publicists of the antigovernment or liberal wing. Usually the only victims of the code were the censors, who either were not intelligent enough or were too lazy to fathom the circumlocutions and veiled expressions of the "subversive" writers. In this language, for instance, under Nicholas I the abolition of serfdom—an illegal goal—was camouflaged as "reasonable distribution of economic relations"; later, and until 1905, the establishment of constitutionalism—also an illegal cause—was deceptively termed "the crowning of the edifice." Herzen did not have to resort to Aesopics;

he lived in Western Europe and wrote all his articles in a daring, smashing, sharply clear style. The more radical but Russia-bound Chernyshevski was all his life condemned to an evasive mode of writing, a severe punishment not mentioned in the criminal code.

Unlike most Russian political and social thinkers of his time, Chernyshevski did not attend a German university; nor was he exposed to early German idealistic influences. Yet this descendant of clergymen and graduate of a theological seminary, a good-hearted idealist who later became a martyr of pitiless despotism, somehow managed to turn himself into a most outstanding utilitarian, a radical denier of German academic idealism and transcendental aestheticism. His dissertation, *Aesthetics and Its Relation to Reality*, denies "art for art's sake" and considers art to be a substitute for science, particularly for popular mass consumption. His later writings show a vague connection with Hegelianism and a much more definite relation to the aesthetic theory of Ludwig Feuerbach. But he always kept his mind open to Anglo-American and French influences and doctrines.

One is amazed to read the penetrating observation by the sage of Saratov dated January 25, 1848, when he was scarcely twenty, after reading Hegel's *Rechtsphilosophie*:

> I don't see anything remarkable in it. It seems to me that he is a slave of the established order and present social conditions, so much so that he does not even dare to reject capital punishment, etc. . . . Hegel's philosophy holds itself aloof from stormy changes and dreams of perfection; it prefers *die zarte Schonung des Bestehenden,* tender forbearance toward the existing.[1]

How different is this observation from what young Marx saw in Hegel! In this remark we find the explanation for Chernyshevski's dislike of German idealistic philosophy as exemplified by Kant, Fichte, and Hegel, and his predilection for Anglo-American and French thought.

To amplify Chernyshevski's philosophical and scientific preconceptions, we should mention another branch of his thinking. In

[1] The new and complete Soviet edition of N. G. Chernyshevski, *Polnoye sobraniye sochinenii* (Complete Works), Vol. I, Moscow, 1939, pp. 229, 231-232. The Diaries, which could not be published under the Czars, not even after 1906 under the monarchic constitution, fill most of Vol. I.

England it took a Herbert Spencer followed by others to apply Darwinism to social science. The survival of the fittest was translated from biology into sociology and political science. The state must not regulate industry or commerce, or introduce sanitary measures, or build harbors and waterways, for it must not interfere with selection, natural or social, or prevent "salutary sufferings" of the citizens. All this "social Darwinism" was preached by Spencer, Bagehot, and others, in notorious conflict with the views of Charles Darwin himself, who did not dream of applying his biological theory to human history or to the social conditions of nineteenth century capitalism.

In Russia, however, Chernyshevski went much further than Spencer and other Western social Darwinists. Though not a Marxist, but rather an economic materialist with some Russian Populist tendencies, he dared to insist that Darwin's whole biological theory, together with his extensive research, was motivated by a desire to find a justification for capitalism. Truly, this was more Marxian than Marx himself. In reality, said Chernyshevski, Thomas Robert Malthus with his theory of population was only trying to justify the political system, desirable to the Tories who ruled England. Darwin transferred Malthus's theory to botany and zoology.[2]

Chernyshevski's notions on biology were not confined to a theoretical fight against social Darwinism in the 1880's or 1890's. Today they constitute an ideological barrier between the West and the Soviet East. Sociologists have always been tempted to find a provocative similarity between the social struggle and the struggle for survival in nature as it is established and explained in biology. Certain Western thinkers, including Americans, who were far from the somewhat naïve Spencerian sociological Darwinism, nevertheless tried to find the driving factor in naturelike forces. The West did not care whether such a preconception came into conflict with orthodox Marxism. Did not Thorstein Veblen once say:

The forces which have shaped the development of human life and of social structure are no doubt ultimately reducible to terms of living tissue and material environment; but proximately . . . these forces may best be stated in terms of an environment.[3]

[2] Chernyshevski, "The Origin of the Theory Favorable to the Fight for Survival," in *Russkaya Mysl* (Russian Thoughts), 1888, No. 9.

[3] Veblen, *The Theory of the Leisure Class*, New York, 1899, p. 189.

Orthodox Marxism, while recognizing the importance of Darwinism, never attempted to change or even to water down ever so lightly historic and later dialectical materialism to something resembling the Darwinian struggle for existence. Nor did the Soviet regime in its early years move to bring its doctrine into harmony with that of the Russian Darwinists, such as the famous natural scientist, Professor Kliment Timiriazev.

It took Soviet Russia a long time to revise its relative neutrality toward the basic preconceptions of biology. In natural science there existed peacefully side by side adherents of heredity and of environment as the basic factors in biology and particularly in botany. With the increasing tendency to trace distinct lines of demarcation between the bourgeois West and the Soviet East even in natural science, this neutrality was ended. The Soviets took the position that to assign the decisive role to environment would be more in harmony with their new volitional Leninist-Stalinist Marxism than with the strongly neutral attitude of orthodox nonvolitional Marxism. The successes of the well known Soviet plant breeder, Ivan Michurin, were cited as an ideological justification and empirical basis for the newly proclaimed "environmental" Soviet biology as opposed to the "bourgeois" hereditarian genetics of the West. It was made a credo of Communist doctrine, and consequently textbooks and schools had to follow this line. Melnikov, a Soviet educator, formulated the new revision almost in Chernyshevski's very terms when he said:

> Pupils should be shown how the ideologists of modern imperialism try to use Darwin's Malthusian errors to justify the dying out of colonial populations or the poverty of the unemployed. [Teaching of evolution] should proceed from the basic thesis of Michurinite biology that no organism can be studied in isolation from the conditions of its life.[4]

Despite his Orthodox theological education, Chernyshevski was the first great Russian political thinker who had no part in the continuous ideological duel between Slavophiles and Westerners. Even the Westernism of Herzen, one of his teachers, was much colored by this duality. Herzen's Westernism was relative; he was an opponent of Slavophilism long before it became jingoistic Pan-Slav-

[4] *New York Times,* Sept. 5, 1948.

ism; but he nevertheless believed in certain specific values of the Slavonic world, untainted by the pettiness and political submissiveness of the West. His disillusion after his arrival in Europe, which almost coincided with the collapse of the 1848 revolution, had a decisive effect on his further political orientation. Chernyshevski, on the other hand, denied all positive premises of the Eastern or Russian world. He was free from the *a priori* Messianism of the Russian libertarian thinkers before and after him. Reviewing in 1861 the Russian translation of Guizot's famous work, *Histoire générale de la civilisation en France*, he stated with a good deal of irony and self-criticism:

It somehow reminds us of our usual landholding. There is nothing for Europe to borrow from us for any purpose whatsoever. Europe has her own mind, and a much more refined one than ours. There is nothing for her to learn from us, and she does not need our help. That which exists among us according to our customs and customary law is unsatisfactory for her more developed necessities and her more advanced technique.

Except for our communal landholdings it was impossible for the most eager dreamers to discover in our whole social and private land set-up one single institution or even the most minute embryo of such an institution for the rejuvenation of aged Europe with our youthfully vigorous help. . . .

Early, much too early, have we begun to speak about the moribundity of the Western nations: they are only beginning to live.[5]

This short but important statement hidden in the back of a thick Russian review was published in 1861, the year of the emancipation of the peasants. It became a kind of shibboleth of Russian social thought that retained its vigor down to, and even survived, the October revolution of 1917, to reappear in the great tension that existed in the late 1940's.

Chernyshevski, unlike the Slavophiles, stubbornly refused to ascribe to Russia any world-improving functions. He was well versed in economics and the social history of his motherland, and understood that Russia had its own peculiar features; at the same time he was sober and enlightened enough to realize that the peculiarities of the lagging development of his country could not be compared

[5] Reprinted in Chernyshevski, *op. cit.* (1906 ed.), Vol. VIII, p. 156.

with the rapid strides of the Western World.

That this insight, free of cheap patriotism, was deeply ingrained in Chernyshevski's thinking can be seen from another obscure source. In his Diaries, published over half a century after his death, his discussion of the destiny of mankind, comparing the political regimes of republican France and despotic Russia, concludes with the following contemptuous remark: "I esteem Russia very little; I almost do not consider her at all." [6]

Nor was he misled by certain external similarities between Russia and the United States in the 1860's. He knew very well that the social and juridical resemblance between Russian white serfdom and American Negro slavery, both of which were hindrances to a free capitalist society, did not lead the countries along similar lines. He must have understood, too, that the benevolent monarch, the first landlord of the country, who had effected the emancipation of the peasants, was surrounded by a group of the nobility, influential in all political and social affairs of the Empire and had to reckon with the passivity, if not the political absence, of a middle class, and that under such circumstances he could not have introduced radical innovations in agrarian relations.

The Russian peasant became a slowly convalescent serf for whom the mansion of the *barin* (landlord) ceased to be the seat of patriarchal control over his daily life. Rather, down to the 1905 revolution, it was the retreat of the intruding landed creditor, who was all the while getting poorer himself and therefore making more demands on the meager earnings of the peasants. For almost half a century more he continued to exploit his former serfs, and they were obliged to pay him endless indemnification. Under the lingering feudalism of 1861–1905 the Russian peasant had no chance to become anything like an American farmer, though in Russian liberal and revolutionary literature landlords were often called *plantatory* (planters), after their American prototypes in the South. In the United States the immense grants of land under the Homestead Act and other less spectacular confiscatory measures made slowly possible the creation of a farmer class whose dreams could be realized without revolution or rebellion. On the contrary, in the long run the progressive increase in land under cultivation reduced

[6] *Ibid.* (1939 ed.), Vol. I, p. 121.

American rebellion to political action, shutting off broad social issues from revolutionary interference. Shays' Rebellion and similar outbreaks were merely poor, faded daguerreotypes; agrarian socialism in the form of phalansteries and communes was a feeble transplant from Europe unable to take root in American soil.

The opposite is true for post-emancipation Russia, where the improvement of social—and primarily agrarian—relations became the main issue. There only pure liberals were politically minded; the further one went to the left, the less were constitutionalism and juridico-political forms emphasized and the more were social, positive, reconstructive policies of welfare demanded. The name of the first underground political party was Soil and Freedom (*Zemlya i Volya*). As has been pointed out, the similarity in the murder and attempted assassination of two liberators (Abraham Lincoln and Alexander II) was superficial; essentially there was a profound difference between them: Lincoln was killed because his most violent opponents thought he went *too far* in his social policies; Alexander II was attacked and finally killed by opponents who thought he did not go *far enough*, and thus betrayed the true social needs and policies. The United States Congress failed utterly to discern this fundamental distinction when it passed the joint resolution of 1866 ascribing the attempted assassination of Alexander to the expropriated landlords. That Alexander after 1861 did far too little on behalf of the freed peasants was tragically evidenced by the comparatively weak political resistance to rural collectivization in the 1930's. On the other hand, that Lincoln in 1863 had gone "too far" in the eyes of the expropriated Southerners is equally well manifested in the stubborn resistance of the anti-Negro South in 1933 to the Agricultural Adjustment Administration, and in 1948 to the practical application of the Bill of Rights in its own territory. Such are the delayed reactions to some reforms.

Against this background it is obvious that Chernyshevski's attempts first to have a republic set up—that is, to have an elected ruler or "bailiff" of Russia—place him essentially in the camp of the moderates.

In an illegal proclamation to manorial peasants he did not develop the need for the introduction of socialism. On the contrary, the democratic Western powers, particularly Switzerland, the

United States, and England, were held up as models of state order, and Switzerland and the United States were lauded as republican countries:

America and Switzerland have no czars at all: the Chief of State is not a hereditary ruler but is elected by the people for a certain time. That is why the people there have an easier life, and that is why people become richer there. There is real freedom. Without such order, there is no real freedom, but only deception.

Obviously, Chernyshevski was holding up the United States as the promised land of both political and social progress. With respect to the former, he did not need to exaggerate or even to color American realities. Politically the United States was so far ahead of backward Russia that in presenting the facts a slight retouching of evils, mismanagement, and omissions sufficed.

His current political survey of November, 1860, in the *Sovremennik* described the importance of Lincoln's election in that month. It should, however, not be forgotten that, writing under censorship, the learned but politically minded author always kept one eye on his own country. It was important for him to show that the social enemies on the banks of the Mississippi were identical with those on the banks of the Volga. And if the plowmen (*zemplepashtsy*) won out overseas against the planters they must win out here, too, against the landed nobility. That is why his survey of the United States was written in Russian agricultural terms:

On November 6, 1860, when the victory shifted to the party whose candidate was Lincoln—on that glorious day began a new epoch in the history of the United States; on that day the whole political development of the great North American nation turned. Until then American politics was dominated by the southern planters, the cavaliers who were proud of their distinction. Then the plowmen of the North and the West—literally, the tillers who cultivated the soil with their own hands —first became conscious of their ability to get along without the tutelage of the southern oligarchs and to rule the Union. On November 6, 1860, they shook off the yoke that had restrained them for many decades. Whatever vacillations and hesitations there may still be, the effort will reach its goal, the summit of American politics which it has not attained since Jefferson. The good repute of the North American nation is important for all nations, with the rapidly growing significance of the United States for the whole of mankind.[7]

Chernyshevski's optimistic faith in America in the early 1860's was largely explained by the dead calm which had followed the collapse of the 1848 revolution. Agrarian reforms and improvements remained pious desires; the triumphant reaction in the whole of Central and Eastern Europe was not favorable to any serious legislation in this field. Under such conditions the fight for abolition of slavery in the United States became an entirely new cause, sustained not by a courageous revolutionary minority against an established government, but by the elected head of a mighty and rich republic with more than 20,000,000 inhabitants. Besides, the putting into effect of this abolition in a possibly more radical and less compromising way was important for a similar reform introduced by Alexander II.

In America the leader in emancipation was not a monarch—the "first nobleman of the state," who sought to save his fellow landowners from the threat of financial sacrifices when implementing the reform. In America the introductory manifesto, the statutes and regulations were not worked out by committees of squires interested in making their effect relatively light on themselves. In the United States slavery was a huge and yet a sectional deviation which had to be set right, a calamity which undermined the Union because the planter regime became subversive. This was an ideal political situation for a Russian revolutionary abolitionist who did not believe any good thing could come out of an aristocratic Nazareth on the banks of Neva.

The great Russian publicist became an intransigent armorbearer for Lincoln, and the foe not only of the southerners but of any others who did not unconditionally follow Lincoln. All the political virtues were on the side of the Republican party, all the vices on the side of the southerners to whom he ascribed even the purely European desire to become courtiers. Every expansionism was also of purely southern character; "manifest destiny," as a general tendency, did not occur to our pro-American. His monthly political reviews of the Civil War, based on American and British sources,

[7] Chernyshevski, *Polnoye sobraniye sochinenii* (1906 ed.), Vol. VI, pp. 730-731.

are therefore sometimes to be taken with a grain of salt.

Even the social background of the United States was sometimes repainted by Chernyshevski. America was somewhat artificially beautified along the lines of Russian socialist idealism. The lineage of social revolutionism in America was traced back to Shays and his rebellion (loudly hailed even in the Soviet approach to old America), to Jefferson who was presented as the father of social justice, and especially to John Brown, "the leader of the martyrs for the Negro cause in the United States." John Brown was cheered for stirring up disorders in Kansas, for burning homes and fields in Missouri, for kidnaping slaves, and the like, which reminded the Russians of their own long history of agrarian riots and rebellions and their own fugitive serfs. John Brown's raid on Harpers Ferry was described not only as very significant, but as "the *first* of its kind." Chernyshevski admitted that this first attempt was unsuccessful, "as were almost all first attempts," but "there is no doubt at all that gradually the struggle will assume a new character." [8] There is no doubt at all that this was Russian revolutionary wishful thinking. Appended to the text is a document containing the statutes of Brown's military society for the emancipation of the slaves entitled "Provisional Constitution and Ordinances for the People of the United States." [9] This document was purposely included by Chernyshevski. First of all, it was a draft providentially called "constitution," itself a daring word to use in 1859, dangerous in the eyes of the censors; and secondly, its object was the abolition of slavery, an attractive purpose in a country where the abolition of serfdom was demanded. The preamble to this American "provisional constitution" was inflammatory yet could be quoted because it did not deal directly with Russia. It was such trickles of American influence that helped water the Russian political desert. The preamble, published two years prior to the famous manifesto of Alexander II, stated in Russian the old American original:

[8] Chernyshevski, in *Sovremennik* (Contemporary), Nov., 1859.

[9] The constitution is reprinted in Chernyshevski, *Polnoye sobraniye sochinenii* (1906 ed.), Vol. V, pp. 444-446. Cf. David Hecht, *Russian Radicals Look to America 1825-1894* (Cambridge, Mass., 1947), p. 112, who, quoting the same article, erroneously adds in the footnote that Chernyshevski reprinted two documents of the society. Actually, this is the second document; the first contains a letter from Napoleon III to the King of Sardinia.

Whereas, Slavery, throughout its entire existence in the United States is none other than a most barbarous, unprovoked, and unjustifiable War of one portion of its citizens upon another portion, the only conditions of which are perpetual imprisonment, and hopeless servitude or absolute extermination in utter disregard and violation of those eternal and self-evident truths set forth in our Declaration of Independence: Therefore, we *citizens* of the *United States*, and the *Oppressed People* who, by a recent decision of the Supreme Court are declared to have no rights which the White Man is bound to respect; together with all other people degraded by the laws thereof, do, for the time being, ordain and establish for ourselves the following Provisional Constitution and Ordinances, the better to protect our persons, property, lives, and liberties: and to Govern our Actions.[10]

Then came the body of the constitution, a natural law product accepted by a gathering in Chatham, in a country with Negro slavery, that influenced and inspired another country in its half-legal fight against serfdom abolished there before slavery in America by a later similar enactment.

This tendency to set America up as the model country for Russian "progressivism" and nihilism went beyond economics and politics. A further instance of coloring American social conditions and events in a manner favorable to Russian socialism is Chernyshevski's misrepresentation of social utopianism and rural phalanxes in the spirit of Fourier or that of his American disciple Albert Brisbane as a serious American phenomenon, sufficient to inspire faith in land communism.

In 1856 Chernyshevski wrote about Modern Times, a "community of reformists" in the State of New York.[11] "After Robert Owen and his New Lanark, America had a series of well established phalanxes and similar undertakings. Among them Modern Times was not the first and not the last. In America itself," cautiously continued the Russian publicist, "reformist views on land communities are not unusual, and nobody regards them as dangerous." Here Chernyshevski, in spite of his economic materialism, lent support to the persistent tendency of his Russian contemporaries to

[10] As quoted in Oswald Garrison Villard, *John Brown, 1800-1859,* Boston, 1910, p. 334.

[11] *Sovremennik,* VII (July), 1856, based upon an article in the *Fortnightly Review,* 1856.

exaggerate the economic importance of phalanxes and other manifestations of socialism within the framework of the capitalist
economic system. The peculiarities of American economy and agriculture were disregarded.

As has been said before, this was the fault not only of Chernyshevski, but of Bakunin, Chaikovski, Frey, and Count Tolstoy,
all of whom were permeated with the spirit of anarcho-communism.
If, however, the others (as well as the Russian Populists) could be
forgiven for their wishful, idealistic approach, devoid of all economic considerations, Chernyshevski, well informed about America,
should have known better. He should have known that utopian
rural communism had died out in the United States before the
1860's. True, during the forties and early fifties America had tried
to imitate European models. The Englishman Robert Owen and
Etienne Cabet came to America to establish such communities at
New Harmony, Indiana, and in Texas and Illinois. All failed,[12] but
this was long before the emancipation. Russian attempts to introduce in America agrarian communistic societies were made much
later and were—if we may say so—even more disastrous, particularly
those of Frey and Chaikovski.

Chernyshevski made much of the equality of the sexes, of the
fact that women were allowed to study in the universities, of religious tolerance in America. Most characteristic is his attitude
toward contemporary American literature, which he was always
eager to introduce to his Russian radical readers. He wrote a long
introduction to the translation of two works of Theodore Winthrop
"Washington as a Camp" and "Our March to Washington." [13]
Winthrop's most laudable qualities, to him, were a daring independence and disregard for European tastes. In Chernyshevski's
introduction we can see clearly his preference of America over
Europe:

American writers too often submitted to European tastes and ways;
they sometimes even assumed that American life with its strong and
firm republicanism, with its practical, businesslike customs, does not
yield to or have room for free fantasy. Not one single writer, says Haw-

[12] Cf. Louis M. Hacker, *The Shaping of the American Tradition*, New York,
1947, pp. 460-461.
[13] *Sovremennik*, Nos. 11 and 12 (Nov. and Dec., 1865).

thorne, who did not try it himself, can understand how difficult it is to write a novel out of the life of a country which does not have shadows, or antiquities, or mysteriousness. According to Nathaniel Hawthorne, for poetry as well as for flowers and plants there must be ruins about which to twine. But there is nothing more erroneous than this thought.[14]

In Winthrop one quality was significant: Social interest, the first goal of genuine citizens, created by American life, was not forgotten in his personal artistic activity. After working as a writer in behalf of Frémont for President, he participated in the election of Lincoln only in a small way, for he had become absorbed in literature. "But when the treachery which threatened the Union turned into an offensive, and he discovered how inevitable the struggle was, the protraction of the [Civil] war irritated him very much." [15] Although in the external structure of the American's stories and novels Chernyshevski traced the influence of the European novel and romanticism, the thinking was closely tied to the "American idea," in which Winthrop completely believed, and for which he saw a grand destiny. He consciously shook off all conventions and traditions, considering them entirely useless, after having had their day. The facts and systems of the past were now no more than fragments and scraps; only the present was precious. Such a spirit characterized all Winthrop's works, revealing in him a serious and realistic understanding of life, which was not always vouchsafed to a novelist.

Chernyshevski extended his hospitality to other American writers, including Bayard Taylor, who was secretary to the United States legation in St. Petersburg.

In 1858 *Sovremennik*, under Chernyshevski's direction, sent to all its readers as a free supplement Harriet Beecher Stowe's *Uncle Tom's Cabin*.[16] The acceptance of this story into Russian literature in the 1850's and 1860's is one of the most interesting features of American cultural and political influence on Russia.

Chernyshevski was very critical also of early racial theories attempting to prove the superiority of the white race over Negroes or other colored peoples. He called them "planters' theories of race"

[14] *Ibid.*, p. 49.   [15] *Ibid.*, p. 52.
[16] Cf. *Istoriya amerikanskoy literatury*, Academy of Sciences, Moscow-Leningrad, 1947, p. 334.

and denied such a theory when it was later defended by Louis Agassiz, an American professor who came from Switzerland. Scholars in the North were afraid to contradict the southerners who were threatening secession; and, strangely enough, the majority of European scholars quickly yielded on the racial question to the authority of Agassiz. Indeed, how could they reject the theory of profound differences between races? Mulattoes of both sexes were less fertile than the offspring of crossed wolves and dogs: this was asserted by northern scholars, who had studied and verified the facts on the spot. So they must be trusted! [17]

Needless to say, Chernyshevski rejected these theories, not for anthropological or other scientific reasons: he condemned them on ethical grounds as serving the cause of social oppression in America as well as in Russia.

With this went the cool objectivity of Chernyshevski on such issues as the liberation of the Balkan Slavs, which grew acute with the approach of the Russo-Turkish War in 1877 but had been in the columns of the dailies and the reviews since the 1850's. The very conservative Slavophiles who had approved the official anti-Polish attitude of the czarist government were the most enthusiastic champions of the liberation of the Bulgars and other Balkan Slavs. Chernyshevski was quick to unmask the Pan-Slavist Michael Katkov and even more liberal Slavophiles. He said: "The Turkish Slavs do not need the help of the Russian Czar for their liberation." Then, directing himself to the Slavophiles, he added:

You who are so kindly disposed toward the Turkish Slavs or at least incessantly speak about your feelings toward your Slavonic brothers, you actually only try to convince the Western powers that after the disappearance of the Turkish state in Europe Bulgaria and the Danubian principalities will not be annexed by Russia.[18]

[17] Chernyshevski, *Polnoye sobraniye sochinenii* (1906 ed.), Vol. X, pt. II, pp. 84 ff.

[18] Cf. N. Serno-Solovyevitch, *Unsere russische Angelegenheiten*, Leipzig, 1871. See also the Diary in Chernyshevski, *op. cit.* (1939 ed.), Vol. I, pp. 643-646, where he criticized Kinglake's *Invasion of the Crimea* and made a mockery of the English writer who claimed that all the fifty million devout Russians "would joyfully risk their lives" to conquer Constantinople and the Holy Places of Palestine and yearned to "extirpate the Turks." To this Chernyshevski remarked that nothing whatsoever of religious or patriotic enthusiasm was to be

In connection with this let us not forget that before and during the Russo-Turkish War (1877–1878), officially proclaimed as the war for the liberation of Balkan Slavs, Chernyshevski was as little jingoistic and nationalistic and fully as skeptical and defeatist as Nicholas Turgenev and Herzen had been in the Crimean War. The tremendous difference between them lay in the mere fact that while Turgenev and Herzen lived and worked freely in Western Europe, out of the reach of the agents of the czarist government, Chernyshevski, after completing his term at hard labor in Siberia, continued to live there as a political deportee under police surveillance, being allowed to return to European Russia only in 1883.

Chernyshevski certainly had more latitude in economic matters than in purely political or military issues. His criticism of the *laissez-faire* doctrine and Western political economy in general was rather complex. Space does not permit us to go into details; moreover, his views are dispersed through various writings, especially the long commentaries attached to his translation of John Stuart Mill's *Principles of Political Economy*,[19] and his reviews of various books on economic problems.

His attitude toward Adam Smith, Malthus, Bentham, Ricardo, and John Stuart Mill was in general positive. He was very critical of Bastiat and of most contemporary French economists, whom he considered incapable of a thorough theoretical approach; in this field they merely popularized English ideas and dealt largely with particular subjects or published well written pamphlets.

Michel Chevalier has given a very good description of the United States of America and has completely established that when, after the discovery of the gold deposits of California and Australia, ten times as much gold was extracted from them as had been mined before, and the quantity of silver mined did not increase, the price of gold had to shrink in comparison with silver. All this is correct but has no real scientific value. . . . Or take Bastiat, who wrote pamphlets against protectionists

---

seen or felt among the Russians, who were not in the least interested or informed about what had taken place on the Danube or in the Crimea. Only when they received the news of the tremendous losses and casualties in and around Sebastopol did they press for peace. Chernyshevski was not much more enthusiastic over the Russo-Turkish War of 1877-1878 than he was over the Crimean War.

[19] See Chernyshevski, *op. cit.* (1906 ed.), Vol. VII.

and communists. Once, when he learned through hearsay that the American Carey had written some objections to Ricardo's theory of rent, he himself drew up a refutation of that theory along the lines of Carey's ideas, themselves devoid of substantial basis. Such things do not serve to move science along.[20]

Chernyshevski's basic approach to Mill was socialistic. What he appreciated most highly was the Englishman's recognition of the inevitability of the decay of capitalism, expressed in his conception of a new civilization in which the privileges of the class to which he belonged would be gradually diminished.[21]

There is no doubt that in Chernyshevski's whole economic approach one basic feature became of great importance. In *Kritika filosofskikh predubezhdenii protiv obshchinnavo vladeniya* (Critique of Philosophic Prejudices Against Communal Land Property) he came to the conclusion that there was no necessity for a particular social phenomenon to manifest itself in the unfolding of every society in the world. This idea was connected with Hegelian dialectics. The question was formulated as follows: "In the life of every society, must a social phenomenon pass through all its logical phases, or is it perhaps possible to go from the first or second phase straight to the fifth or sixth, leaving out the intermediate phases, as occurs in some processes of natural life?" To this Chernyshevski gave a direct answer:

1. The highest degree of development coincides in form with the genesis of this development.
2. A social phenomenon, which has attained a high degree of development in advanced countries, can be developed among other peoples very quickly and leap from the lowest phase directly to the highest, omitting the logically intermediate stages.[22]

Chernyshevski's immediate task was to show that there was no logical necessity for Russia to go over from its primitive village communism first to the stage of private landownership (capitalism) and only after this to the higher forms of communal landownership. This was the maxim that allowed him to jump directly to specific Russian socialism, by-passing the usual capitalistic system of the

[20] *Ibid.*, Vol. VI, p. 17.   [21] *Ibid.*, p. 189.
[22] *Ibid.*, Vol. IV, pp. 331 and 329.

advanced nations. Essentially, it was an anti-Marxist approach especially adapted to the Populist view, which held that socialism could be attained through the development of the Russian rural communes. It proves, too, if additional proof be necessary, how deeply Populist-Russian-minded this economic materialist was.

Paradoxically enough, this approach became most popular under the Soviets. It actually effected a leap from rural precapitalism to what the Soviets labeled and established in 1917 as Soviet socialism in a vast country 3.5 per cent of whose population were urban proletariat. The skipping of logically necessary phases, in which the rural collectivization of the 1930's was merely the final act, made Chernyshevski an economic prophet, one of the greatest of economists.

For his theory Chernyshevski was highly regarded by Marx and by Lenin. Lenin compared him with the moderate petty bourgeois Populists who believed in the necessity of a democratic, nondictatorial course for Russian progress. Russian Socialist Revolutionaries, however, regarded him as one of their founding fathers and would never consider him the precursor of Russian Marxism. This was often repeated, but most conspicuously in 1905 in the leading left Populist *Revolutsionnaya Rossiya*.

Important among Chernyshevski's economic writings was his review of the Russian translation of Henry Charles Carey's *Letters to the President*, dealing with the foreign and domestic policies of the Union.[23] However, before we go into the essence of his criticism of Carey's protectionism, which he attacked chiefly because the Russian government had tried for decades to put this economic conception into practice, a few comments should be made on Russian financial policy.

The protection of industries proved to be one of the most important factors in the precipitation of the agricultural crisis, for it considerably increased the prices of commodities without creating a corresponding increase in the purchasing power of the consumer. For instance, high duties on imported pig iron and steel raised the price of all metal produced and consumed in Russia. The government, from the time of Peter I, had adhered to protectionism for

[23] *Ibid.*, Vol. VIII, pp. 26 ff., 38.

the sake of its fiscal policy, favorable trade balance, and large customs revenues, at the same time protecting the interests of the
manufacturers. From 1877, when the duties had to be paid in gold,
the effects of protectionism became unbearably oppressive for the
masses. In the special literature on protectionism the official Russian policy was compared with that of the United States, which was
found by Russian experts to be much less prohibitive than the Russian. Needless to say, Chernyshevski, as a Populist expert in social
and economic reform, was well informed on this matter. But what
irritated him was the fact that Russian protectionists tried to base
their views and demands on the American Carey. We have already
seen that as far back as the 1860's the American mission under
Fox heard speeches by Russian industrialists enthusiastically quoting Carey.

For Chernyshevski, the quotation of Western authorities should
have been exclusively in behalf of progressive ideas, which were incompatible with the pro-government views of the propertied classes.
This certainly applied to protectionism, a subordinate and insignificant problem of capitalism.

Little wonder that Chernyshevski reproached Carey for his
"monomania," which led him to insist on high tariffs in the United
States and make them a central factor of the whole social life. He
wondered how the American, belonging to the school of Adam
Smith, could become a protectionist. Even stranger was the fact
that precisely in Russia, where free trade was needed, Carey found
so many adherents, including Besobrasov, Nicholas Bunge (economist, and minister of finance from 1881 to 1886), and Vernadski.
Moreover, Russia had more urgent economic needs than low tariffs.
The only thing for which Chernyshevski commended him was his
attack on the United States government for its inability to fight
slavery, for the fact that the planters' party dominated the New
York Stock Exchange, and so on.

Unconsciously, Chernyshevski substituted another "monomania"
for Carey's, reducing all the difficulties, defects, and faults of the
United States to one single cause, slavery. He even condoned the
American "sin" of high tariffs, because they represented a source
of income needed to carry on a successful battle against slavery, the
fundamental evil of the United States. For this purpose, he was

ready to waive his principal objections and tolerate high tariffs for a time.

Chernyshevski was eager to fight the doctrine of *laissez faire, laissez passer* not only from the purely economic angle, but from the philosophical and sociological angles.[24] According to him this principle could not be made a general postulate of science. The essential characteristic of science was universality: it had to be right for every time and for every place and for any given case. If political economy's claim to be a science was to be sustained, it had to have as its basic principle an idea that could be applied to every epoch and to any given situation.

Chernyshevski tried to show that from the purely economic standpoint this principle was not universally applicable or adequate:

> We do not deny that in the remote past the maxim of *laissez faire* was very useful, that even now in many countries and many cases it is beneficial . . . we are only going to show that this postulate neither contains the complete and ready answer to all possible economic problems nor is the exclusive solution of the entire social issue.[25]

Sometimes this backward liberal conception turns into a utopia unattainable under contemporary conditions and mores, when the state must necessarily retain its power over private life. The main source of such power is the failure of private persons to display their initiative. Chernyshevski asserted that if state legislation would expand over a greater sector of life beyond security, private initiative would become more inspired and stimulated.

The same disposition to justify social legislation is displayed in Chernyshevski's interpretative remarks to Mill's *Principles*. Mill tried to distinguish between two kinds of governmental interference, toward which the attitude of economists should be different. The first—in which governmental interference should be understood in a broad sense—is characterized by the prohibition against doing or undertaking to do something; the second involves the creating of governmental institutions parallel to private ones.[26] Chernyshevski paid lip service to Mill's general conclusion, at the same time leaving the back door open to specific cases that had to be decided on their individual merits.[27]

[24] *Ibid.*, Vol. VI, pp. 9, 10.   [25] *Ibid.*, Vol. IV, p. 423.
[26] *Ibid.*, Vol. VII, pp. 596-597, 601.   [27] *Ibid.*, p. 599.

In concluding this section, we would say that Chernyshevski by interpreting Mill's *Principles,* omitting some chapters of the English original and adding his own, like the last chapter on Ownership, popularized the great English economist in the spirit of utopian socialism, Russian radicalism, and state intervention in economics.

One American scholar and social critic whose ideas accorded with those of our Russian scholar and martyr was Thorstein Veblen. Both were polyglot; both had many-sided intellects embracing philosophy and the social and natural sciences; both believed that the struggle of each man to possess more than his neighbor was inseparable from the institution of private property; for both of them poverty was the most important economic phenomenon to be overcome; both were equally against *laissez faire* and free competition, against the political economy of John Stuart Mill as well as social Darwinism. To a certain extent, and only if all the differences of time, space, and sociopolitical conditions are correctly evaluated and compared, Chernyshevski may be called a forerunner of Veblen. And that means due discrimination between shackled Russia from the 1860's to the 1890's and free America from the 1890's to the early 1920's. To be contrasted with Veblen's immense superiority in research and in the study of modern industry, business, and general economics, his antidogmatism, indeed, his pitiless defiance of orthodoxy, is Chernyshevski's strict conformity with obligatory progressivism, which frequently distorted his research, analysis, and predictions.

All that Chernyshevski thought and taught on economics and social welfare, all his enthusiasm for the phalanxes and other socialist utopian enterprises in America and the European West, the importance of which he exaggerated, all his criticism of English classical political economy, and all his closeness to Marx did not make him a fighter for socialism in the modern sense. Of course, all this appeared quite otherwise to the overanxious defenders of the unripe capitalism of the czarist regime about the middle of the 1860's. For the police agents, after the reign of Nicholas I, his monthly review was a dangerous instrument of subversion, which spread after 1859 more and more. Chernyshevski himself was sentenced to seven years at hard labor and lifelong exile.[28] The "bulky," substantial review *Sovremennik*, of which he was the regular political editor and contributor, was also persecuted for a long time and finally forced to discontinue. In November, 1865, the first official warning by the ministry of the interior was published in the journal. This admonition, ominous of a final ban, stated that "in one of its articles there is an indirect condemnation of the principles of private property as implemented by capitalists who allegedly have taken possession in an unjust way of the savings of the worker class," and that "hatred is being stirred up against the upper and propertied classes, which are pictured as being essentially immoral because of the very fact of their existence and as being detrimental to the national welfare." [29]

This was approximately the atmosphere in which Chernyshevski had to continue to work and to write. A country that appeared externally very liberal and even "almost close" to America, a country that had introduced emancipation and broad reforms in the judiciary and self-government, a country that was to all intents and purposes a close ally of the United States—that country made martyrs of democratically minded sociologists, economists, and publicists. Her conservative journalists and writers tried to camouflage this fact in their intercourse with Americans and other Westerners, emphasizing how liberal Russia actually was.

It was inevitable that Chernyshevski should introduce his economic materialism into an analysis of the American Civil War and the period preceding it. In his famous article The Split in the North American Union,[30] dealing with this topic so vital to Russia in the year of the promulgation of the Emancipation Manifesto, he was especially fearful of a compromise in the effectuation of American emancipation. After treating political and constitutional matters in detail, he turned to economic conditions. He wanted to em-

[28] *Kolokol*, June 15, 1864. In writing about this, Alexander Herzen bitterly added at the end: "And this is the reign we hailed ten years ago!"

[29] *Sovremennik*, No. 10, Oct., 1865. After the attempt of Karakosov on the life of Alexander II, the review was banned for good.

[30] The full Russian title in *Sovremennik*, Jan., 1861, is "Rastorzheniye Severo-Amerikanskavo Soyuza" (The Split in the North American Union). It was reprinted in Chernyshevski, *Polnoye sobraniye sochinenii* (1906 ed.), Vol. VIII, pp. 367-388.

phasize the economic superiority of the North over the South, the superiority of the mines and machine production of New York and Pennsylvania over the cotton of the entire South—a factor, by the way, that was not properly evaluated in the European literature and was rejected by the European friends of the South.

Chernyshevski expressed his typically Russian revolutionary horror of compromise in the following terms:

> It is quite possible that the secessionists will prevail. This would be the worst possible outcome, but we do not dare to hope that it will not happen. In that case the North will once more be appeased, and the whole affair will end with some "compromise," viz. with mutual concessions, which do not solve any question, with mutual promises to postpone the slavery problem, which will never be carried out by either of the two parties. A compromise would be incomparably worse than civil war, worse even than a peaceful split-up of the Union. These two possibilities would lead to a reestablishment of the Union with slavery eradicated or at least with legislative measures leading to its eradication. But a compromise would only postpone the issue.[31]

The same attitude was expressed in his American survey of April, 1861. Relying on John S. C. Abbott's *South and North*, he wrote:

> For the good of the United States we have to desire either a serious war between the North and the South or the recognition of the full independence of the southern states in which slavery would gradually disappear. But mutual concessions will not lead to any solution.[32]

The various repetitions of this point of view are crowned with an essentially Marxist thesis:

> The enmity of the South for the North is a class enmity, the hatred of patricians for ignorant plebeians, the hatred of a very high social class for a republican state order.[33]

Yet in Russia even Chernyshevski was a supporter of continuous redemption of the lands acquired by the liberated serfs from the former gentry-masters.

[31] *Ibid.*, p. 387.   [32] *Ibid.*, p. 436.

[33] *Ibid.*, p. 452. An error in Hecht's translation of this thesis into English distorts the meaning. Instead of "ignorant [unenlightened] plebeians," Hecht, *op. cit.*, p. 115, translates Chernyshevski's Russian phrase *tiomniye plebei* as "dark-skinned." Moreover, though the Russian original speaks of "estates" (*sosloviya*), "classes" is the correct modern translation.

All these compromise steps were taken in a period which shortly preceded, or coincided with, ardent Russo-American friendship— most conspicuously paraded, as we have seen, in naval demonstrations held in the United States for Russians and in Russia for Americans. It may be said that the social compromise was greater, more protracted, and less favorable to the masses in Russia than it was in America after the emancipation.

When we turn from general propositions and theoretical postulates to practical views, it becomes necessary to consider how American emancipation of the slaves was mirrored in the writing of Chernyshevski, the typical representative of Russian radicalism of the 1860's, and to compare it with the reaction of the more moderate liberals who only in 1866 established their own journal, *Viestnik Yevropy* (Herald of Europe).

We quote from and analyze Chernyshevski's surveys of Lincoln's policies. But before we do so, it would be well to give his general opinion on Lincoln:

Abraham Lincoln was not a hero in the sense in which this word is used by Napoleon III or Carlyle. "Old Uncle Abe" was simply an honest, humane, sensible, and conscientious citizen of the United States, who, thanks to his abilities, energy, and industry, grew out of the most modest milieu to become an outstanding man. His honesty and power of conviction attracted the attention of his fellow citizens, and thus the majority of the American people entrusted to him the carrying out of a difficult reform, the necessity for which was recognized by this majority.[34]

And now to the American emancipation.[35] In this field, too, Chernyshevski's views were based on abundant information and represented a thoroughgoing analysis of the time preceding the Emancipation Proclamation of January 1, 1863. He displayed accurate knowledge of the progress of the Civil War, with all its ups and downs, victories and defeats, with all its geographical data; the names and personalities in civil and military life in the North and in the South were familiar to him. In his review of the situation appearing in the double issue of January-February, 1863, he came

[34] *Sovremennik*, Apr., 1865. Chernyshevski used the phrase "Old Uncle Abe" in its English form, without translation.
[35] See *Sovremennik*, Nos. 1-2, Jan.-Feb., 1863, under "Politika."

to the conclusion, despite the military stalemate, that "things have improved." This positive conclusion, in view of the difficulties of the North and the helplessness of McClellan, can be explained only by the political viewpoint of the author. As a Russian "nihilist," he regarded the political structure, even the very existence of the United States as a federal state, to be irrelevant. The abolition of slavery was the only interest and final goal of the Civil War:

The question is not whether the American States will represent one united commonwealth; who will be President—Lincoln, McClellan, Seward, Jefferson Davis, or Frémont—is also not important. The question is whether or not slavery will be eliminated in North America.

Chernyshevski found that things had been going better because during the previous eight to nine months events clearly established that Lincoln's goal was the emancipation of the Negroes. The very fact that the strategic situation had entered a stage of equilibrium helped to clarify the political and social picture. He admitted that Lincoln undoubtedly also desired the restoration of the Union, but this merely for the sake of the Negro emancipation, in order to be more secure as President of both the northern and the southern states. Sixteen months of the Civil War had shown that the conquest of the seceded states would be a long drawn-out operation, and Lincoln therefore decided to act. On September 22, 1862, he issued a preliminary proclamation which contained an important declaration: "That on the first day of January, 1863, all persons held as slaves within any State or designated part of a State the people whereof shall then be in rebellion against the United States shall be then, thenceforward, and forever free." Thus was the Rubicon crossed. Of course, in the North, too, some citizens were not elated by Negro emancipation; it might have some negative effect on the election of governors and other officials in November in New York, Ohio, and Illinois. A united front of the antiabolitionist Democrats had had some success. In Europe these elections had been badly misunderstood; they did not mean that the North would be compelled to yield to the South and therefore stop the war against the slave-owning South. At first, France and England even tried to intervene in American affairs because they believed in the weakness of the Lincoln cause.

The Russian review quoted the notes that the French Minister Drouyn de Lhuys had sent to the London and St. Petersburg cabinets. Here Chernyshevski's irony bit into the hypocrisy of worrying about the unemployed workers of Lancashire and Rouen, the workers who were doomed to starvation if American cotton was not brought to Europe. Besides, Americans themselves were sick and tired of the prolonged war, a feeling that found expression in the results of various elections. However, reported Chernyshevski, these hypocrisies produced in America the opposite result from what was desired. In New York, Democrats and Republicans reacted jointly and indignantly against the intrusion of France and England in the internal affairs of the American Republic. He then went on to analyze the annual message of the President to the Congress on December 1, 1862.

This analysis, thorough as it is, is the best example of so-called Russian radical nihilism, which to a certain degree was more Maximalist than the later Populist movement of the 1880's and down through the first two decades of the present century.

Chernyshevski, following the message, touched on the condition of the finances and the vast expenditures for the suppression of the rebellion and the continuance of the war. He even went into Secretary Chase's report, giving the increased debt of the United States, which stood at $1,122,000,000. All this led to a very brief conclusion: What do all these tremendous figures of hundreds and thousands of millions of dollars mean? To spend money for the creation of millions of free men is not to squander it!

Perhaps even more peculiar was Chernyshevski's reaction to the paragraph of Lincoln's message dedicated to national authority and integrity and to the necessity for restoring them in the whole territory, which embodied the endurance of the nation. To this the Russian "nihilist," who placed social considerations above territory and the indivisibility of the nation, had only one answer: In comparison with emancipation, the integrity of the state was unimportant. He said it in plain words:

In general, we did not understand the necessity for the restoration of the Union before reading Lincoln's message and we do not perceive it now. In our opinion it is entirely immaterial whether the Union is restored or not; what matters is only the main problem of slavery.

How dull is this conclusion in comparison with the nobility of Lincoln's historic words, which pose so lucidly the tragic duality of the problem, *emancipation with the continuance of the Union,* both equally imperative for national cohesion!

> Fellow citizens, we can not escape history. We of this Congress and this Administration will be remembered in spite of ourselves. . . . We say we are for the Union. The world will not forget that we say this. We know how to save the Union. The world knows we do know how to save it. We, even we here, hold the power and bear the responsibility. In giving freedom to the slave, we assure freedom to the free —honorable alike in what we give and what we preserve.

Needless to say, Chernyshevski did not know that the question of the relation between slavery and Union appeared in William H. Seward's "Some Thoughts for the President's Consideration, April 1, 1861":

> We *must change* the question before the public *from one upon slavery,* or about slavery, for a question *upon union or disunion.* In other words, from what would be regarded as a party question, to one of patriotism or union.[36]

Equally detached was Chernyshevski's reaction to the serious consideration given by the message to the total inadequacy of disunion as a remedy for the differences between the American people of the two sections. Lincoln pointed out that there was no suitable line for a national boundary:

> Place it between the now free and slave country, or place it south of Kentucky or north of Ohio, and still the truth remains that none south of it can trade to any port or place south of it.

To this Chernyshevski had a simple "nihilist" reply. He was not swayed by the geographic difficulties of Lincoln's statement; geography, he thought, could not hinder the emergence of two separate states. Were there not plenty of states in the world whose boundaries existed only in the imagination, and were there not rivers that flowed through many countries?

[36] As quoted in *The Record of American Diplomacy,* ed. R. J. Bartlett, New York, 1947, p. 277. There certainly was a tremendous difference between Seward and Horace Greeley, who in his letter to President Lincoln insisted on the contrary, on emancipation as *the* issue of federal policy.

But let us not be too schematic in analyzing the great Russian social thinker. We cannot know, from the material we have, how well informed he was about the two schools of American abolitionism—the Freesoilers and other moderates, and the radical Abolitionists—the difference in whose attitude toward the whole problem of emancipation was very important. The radical wing, especially Wendell Phillips, took a position close to that of Chernyshevski, above all toward the dilemma of Union or abolition. Phillips criticized Lincoln sharply, particularly for what he regarded as tactics of Fabian protraction. To him and to Chernyshevski the success of emancipation was most important, and the great goal of the Civil War was not to save the Union but to free the slaves. The difference between them lay in the fact that the American still hoped patriotically that in the long run economic considerations would compel even a South that had seceded to return to the Union —slavery being doomed by technological, industrial, and agricultural advance [37]—while for the Russian a most important consideration was the value attached to the successful abolition of slavery in America as an "example" in the fight against European and Russian feudal reaction. Over the political destiny of the Union, Chernyshevski did not worry much.

Let us turn to one of the most conspicuous socialist features of Chernyshevski's exhaustive article. Reverting briefly to the antagonism in England and France toward American emancipation, he emphasized that those who held it belonged to the upper classes and official circles, and opposed liberty at home also. Americans understood well the bad situation of some manufacturing regions. Their government took all steps possible to send cotton to Europe; and private persons at the New York Stock Exchange collected more than $100,000 for the workers of Lancashire. Completely confuting the hypocrisy of those who supported the South for the sake of helping the hungry toilers of Europe, he showed that those toilers were of an entirely opposite mind and favorably disposed toward the North, particularly toward Lincoln. He took up the "address to President Lincoln by the workingmen of Manchester, England," of December 31, 1862. Being afraid, in view of Russian

[37] Cf. Richard Hofstadter, *The American Political Tradition and the Men Who Made It,* New York, 1948, pp. 148-150.

censorship, to quote this historic address in full, Chernyshevski nevertheless related that the Manchester meeting expressed its indignation at the continuance of slavery in the United States and at the attempt of the Confederate States to establish in the Western Hemisphere a commonwealth built on slavery. The assemblage, he continued, paid honor to the President for having liberated the slaves and expressed their admiration for him that under extraordinary circumstances he still was able to remain faithful to the Constitution. The meeting assumed that Lincoln would persist in his humane and righteous course and stated that he could not now stop short of a complete uprooting of slavery.

This, added Chernyshevski, was the voice of hungry Manchester workers about whom their reactionary benefactors of the upper classes in England and France were so much worried. The workingmen of Manchester made it clear that they did not want to achieve material welfare at the expense of somebody else's freedom or well-being. Similar meetings took place in Sheffield, Glasgow, Bradford, and other manufacturing centers.

Chernyshevski, despite his general skepticism, turned with vehemence on those who insisted that Lincoln's was not an unconditional fight for liberty but only an attempt to conquer the South, and that he would be ready to give up freedom if the rebels of the South would capitulate:

We do not see any reason to doubt Lincoln's sincerity, and we repeat it again and again. But if, hypothetically, such insincerity actually exists, the course of emancipation can no longer be stopped and no peace can be concluded with the South even if Lincoln should wish it.[38]

April 14, 1865, would remain one of the saddest days in history. The plight of the southern Negro evoked no special sympathy in the American people, and they never would have suffered all the burdens and ravages of war out of an altruistic urge to liberate the Carolina or Virginia Negro from the onerous condition of slavery. However, during the four years of war, added Chernyshevski somewhat illogically, the Yankees got the idea that all the disorder and other troubles that had occurred in the United States during the

[38] *Sovremennik*, Mar., 1865. See also the April issue, containing an article on Abraham Lincoln signed "W."

preceding twenty years were due to slavery. They were further convinced that without slavery there would have been no civil war and they would have been spared all its consequences. Finally, it became clear to them that if this "peculiar institution" should be allowed to remain untouched, America would suffer again the same misery that had already been imposed on her.

After the death of Lincoln, President Johnson was criticized by Chernyshevski chiefly for his inability to carry on the great work of his predecessor, for preferring the way of compromise:

It is only the consequence of the unforgivable weakness and lack of political sense of Johnson that the situation of Negroes in the former slave-owning states is at this time by no means better, and perhaps even worse, than before the Civil War. Democratic newspapers have begun to dwell on the laziness of Negroes, their unpreparedness for freedom, etc., while the Negroes of North Carolina have filed a petition to the President protesting against the propaganda of the Democrats. Johnson himself is guided by his unfortunate notion of the independence of the domestic legislation of each state as against federal legislation. . . .

We are far from being pessimistic about the entire present situation of the United States; it all may turn out for the best in that country.[39]

It is worth while to compare this appreciation by a radical of the Negro emancipation and his criticism of Johnson with the approach of a more moderate liberal periodical, Herald of Europe, which in its first volume [40] gave the following survey on Lincoln's America:

All recognize that recent events in the United States show magnificent achievements.

Why did Americans of the North sacrifice hundreds of thousands of lives and billions of dollars? Was all this destruction of actual productive forces carried out only for the sake of satisfying personal passions? Many in Europe answer this question in the affirmative. But those who assert this are measuring America with European yardsticks. Indeed, in Europe any state that expended over three to four years some four billion roubles in only one war would have undermined its finances not only for a long time but in all probability forever. However, in the United States this tremendous sacrifice does not have such deplorable consequences for the future welfare of the country as it would have in a European country.

[39] *Sovremennik*, June, 1865.
[40] *Viestnik Yevropy*, No. 1 (March, 1866), Historical Section.

True, in Europe nations are asked to make tremendous sacrifices for insignificant ends, to satisfy personal passions (Napoleonic Wars), to support an artificially created balance of power (the Crimean War of 1854), or even for no reason at all. Even in cases where the apparent aim was the liberation of nations (the Italian war), dynastic interests played an important part. However, the aims and results of the recent American war are of an entirely different nature from those of previous great European wars. There are, of course, some shortsighted politicians in America who are convinced—and have tried to prove it to others— that the American war was undertaken *only* in order to restore the Union, which was dissolved by the secession of the southern states. Such politicians, to whom, obviously, the present President of the United States, Mr. Johnson, belongs, see in the restoration of the integrity of the Union not a means toward a radical reorganization of the institutions of all states of the Union, including the southern ones, but a final goal in itself, on the achievement of which one can rest peacefully and not worry about more or less substantial changes and improvements in American institutions. However, in reality the true issues behind political improvement are the people's interests. This is how the great martyr of the American renaissance, Abraham Lincoln, and with him the majority of the people, looked at the causes and results of this internal war. Their broad view had nothing in common with the narrow viewpoint of honest but shortsighted people like McClellan, Stanton, Grant, and Johnson. The majority of the American people finally understand that an end has to be put to slavery, to the evil which has penetrated the institutions of the country because of the negligence of the first legislators, and which has paralyzed the further development of those states in which slavery has flourished. Certainly, the majority of the practical Yankees came to this conclusion not out of sentimental or altruistic impulses, but out of the conviction that slavery is utterly harmful to their country and to themselves.

In connection with Pogodin's speech, we have noticed that the rightist Russian press, specifically the journal *Russkii Viestnik*, was not inclined to attack the political institutions of the United States. This Slavophile periodical vehemently disputed Chernyshevski's appreciation [41] of Tocqueville's classical *Democracy in America*, the Russian edition of which was published in 1860; and his review

---

[41] "Nepochtitelnost k avtoritetam" (Disrespect to Authorities), in *Sovremennik*, No. 6, June 1861; reprinted in Chernyshevski, *Polnoye sobraniye sochinenii* (1906 ed.), Vol. VIII, pp. 189 ff.

of it became a center of controversy between him and the rightists. It must be said that in the early 1860's the old divergence between the rightists and the libertarians hinged on centralization. Democratic Russia from its very genesis was, to a certain extent, in favor of self-government, which limits the all-embracing, centralized arbitrariness of autocracy. As we have already seen, the Decembrists were even for federalization of Russia. Both Herzen and Chernyshevski believed in decentralization; and for Chernyshevski it was very important to show that America, a freedom-loving democracy, was decentralistic, as was evidenced by her federal state. He went even further and tried to demonstrate that, despite Tocqueville, the United States would remain decentralized. Here his political attitude of always applying Russian yardsticks distorted his evaluation of facts. For him centralization and democracy were mutually opposed notions. He even attempted to establish that the centralization of France was not the result of the French Revolution, which smashed the old domestic feudal frontiers and tollgates, but of the administrative measures of Napoleon I.

The Russian rightists, on the other hand, were inclined to regard centralization as most desirable. The *Russkii Viestnik* argued therefore that Chernyshevski was blinded by prejudice against every kind of centralization, which to him was always deplorable, bureaucratic, and inefficient, and it demonstrated that he had not read Tocqueville carefully, for he distinguished between two kinds of centralization, governmental and administrative:

Chernyshevski does not realize that the federal government does not represent the entire state called United States; he forgets that every state is in itself a commonwealth, with its own legislative and executive power, with its peculiar centralization. . . . Tocqueville discovers in every democracy a natural gravitation toward a strong centralized power. Notwithstanding all that, in America democracy prevails, and the principle of self-government is well established there. The young critic bursts with laughter, as he himself admits, but he does not even suspect that Tocqueville's main idea consists in the assertion that American democracy is an exclusive and peculiar situation. American democracy was founded by English emigrants, by Puritans, men of a strong belief. . . . They brought with them all the liberties and institutions from the other side of the ocean. . . . Thus democracy in America became something other than what Mr. Chernyshevski wants to find in it.[42]

We cannot refrain from quoting two short passages from Tocqueville showing that the *Russkii Viestnik* and not Chernyshevski was right:

At the present day the lower orders in England are striving with all their might to destroy local independence and to transfer the administration from all the points of the circumference to the center.

The lot of the Americans is singular: they have derived from the aristocracy of England the notion of private rights and the taste for local freedom; and they have been able to retain both because they have had no aristocracy to combat.[43]

The Russian rightists of the 1860's have proved to be correct in this respect, particularly as concerns centralist tendencies in the development of the American political order. Chernyshevski fell a victim to his own preconceptions and dogmatism, violating facts for the sake of a fictitious incompatibility between democracy and centralization.[44] He was beaten not only by the chain of events following the Civil War in America, which corroborated the old French master, but by the post-emancipation period in czarist Russia, which for over half a century combined autocracy with the zemstvo self-governmental institutions.

[42] *Russki Viestnik*, 1861, pp. 145-147.
[43] Tocqueville, *Democracy in America*, ed. Phillips Bradley, 2 vols., New York, 1945, Vol. II, p. 298.
[44] Hecht, *op. cit.*, pp. 124-125, correctly calls this approach of the Russian thinker a "ludicrous error."

XIII *Henry George in Russia*

EHIND THE DRAMATIC FAÇADE OF POLITICAL STRUGGLE AGAINST
Russian czarism, a struggle in which the West was on common ground with Russian liberals and radicals, there was a less
apparent issue which revealed itself in economic and social problems. In this field disintegrating effects appeared at an accelerated
tempo. Whereas political differences between Russia and the
United States could be—and often were—easily bridged, economic
differences were much less tractable. These began after the 1860's
and continued to increase, alienating the two immense subconti-
nents more and more. They affected the habits of thought of non-
Marxist moderate and Populist groups as well as Marxist groups.
True, for the Populists, American approaches to economics were
more understandable and American measures more acceptable. This
explains the sympathy with which Henry George's ideas were met
in Russian economic periodicals as well as lay writings.

Most of the works of Henry George had been translated, read,
and interpreted in Russia by 1910, and he exerted a marked influence there from about 1880, particularly upon non-Marxist circles.
His popularity was at its highest between 1900 and 1910, when the
agrarian problem was the center of concern in the press and in and
around the Duma, the newly created legislative body of remodeled
czarist Russia.

The theory of Henry George, independent of its worth as political economy, was written in the spirit and for the sake of strengthening American populist radicalism. His theory was certainly
perceived in the whole of Europe, not only in Russia, to be conditioned by the specific social conditions of the United States in the
1870's.

One of George's basic maxims was that wages, instead of being
drawn from capital, are in reality drawn from the product of the
labor for which they are paid. The root of the social problem lies,
he thought, in the fact that the landowner takes possession of the

extra products created by the increase of means of production and the progress of civilization and culture, and that the laborers and employers do not profit from the growth of the wealth of the nation because the fruits of their work are absorbed into private landed property belonging to a class which does not participate in the creation of the wealth.

The propositions of George included the following: not capital but landed property oppresses the laborer; the capitalist and the worker have common interests; both suffer from their common enemy the landowner; and industrial crises are basically caused by landownership, viz., by real estate speculation on the part of capitalists who have seized vast stretches of land. All the propositions were fundamentally reformist and ill adapted to the peculiar requirements of a fighting socialism.

Marx himself took a distinct anti-George position and wrote to his friend Friedrich Sorge on June 30, 1881, about George's *Progress and Poverty*, which had had a tremendous vogue in English-speaking countries:

Theoretically, this man is completely *arrière*. He does not understand the essence of what *surplus value* is and therefore is trifling, in an English manner, with conceptions lagging behind even the English concerning certain fragments of surplus value which grew comparatively independent; to wit, those concerning the relations between profit, rent, per cent, etc. His fundamental dogma runs thus: *all would be quite in order* if only the land rent would be paid to the state (you will find this payment in the enumeration of transitional measures mentioned in the *Communist Manifesto*). This view originally sprang from the bourgeois economists. Subsequently it was advanced by the first radical adherents of Ricardo after his death. In connection with this matter, I wrote in 1847, in my book against Proudhon:

"We understand economists like Mill (the elder) and others request that the rent be given to the state as payment of taxes. This is a candid expression of the hatred which is nourished by *industrial capitalists* against the *landowner* who appears as a useless and completely superfluous being in the whole structure of bourgeois production.

"But to make from this *desideratum* of radical English economists a *socialist panacea*, to interpret this procedure as a solution of the contradictions underlying the modern system of production occurred only to Colain. . . ."

All these "socialists," beginning with Colain, have this in common; namely, that they leave untouched hired labor and consequently the modes of *capitalist production,* thus fooling themselves and the whole world by arguing that thanks to the change of the land rent into a tax paid to the state, all the *disorders* of the capitalistic production will disappear by themselves. All in all this is only faintly socialistically oriented in its attempt to rescue the *rule of capitalists* and at the same time to *establish it on a broader basis* than the present rule.

This is a horse's hoof—or rather a donkey's hoof—that protrudes from the declamations of Henry George, all the less endurable since he should have put the question in just the opposite way: how did it happen in the United States, where in comparison with civilized Europe land has been relatively accessible, and to a certain degree remained so, to the great masses of people, that the capitalist economy and its enslavement of the working classes grew quicker and more shamelessly than in any other country?

On the other hand, George's book as well as the sensation caused by it in your country is significant in so far as this is the first, though unsuccessful, attempt to get rid of the orthodox political economy.

By the way, Mr. George obviously does not know anything of the history of the earlier *American adversaries of the rent*—the Antirentiers who exerted themselves in practice rather than in theory. Otherwise he is a talented writer (possessing, incidentally, the talent for advertising America) as is proven by his article on California in the *Atlantic Monthly.* He also possesses an unpleasant complacency and arrogance which is common to all inventors of panaceas.[1]

The negative attitude of Marx and his numerous disciples toward George must be regarded in the light of a deep disappointment over the failure of organized socialism to send roots into the United States deeper than the circles of German immigrant workers and other hyphenated Americans. There were many such disappointments connected with this phenomenon which obviously contradicted orthodox Marxist preconceptions. In 1884–1886 Friedrich Engels put great weight on the results of elections, on the development of the Knights of Trade into a regular socialist movement according to European patterns and among native Americans, at that.

[1] Friedrich A. Sorge, *Rabotcheye dvizheniye v Soyedinionykh Shtatakh* (The Labor Movement in the United States): Translated from the German; St. Petersburg, 1907, pp. 183, 184.

As late as 1906, a German non-Marxist economist, Werner Sombart, also expressed his astonishment at the absence of a socialist movement in the United States:

It is well known that the United States represents a country in which the program of the Marxist theory of social development has materialized to the extent that the concentration of capital has reached the heights described in the last but one chapter of *Capital* upon which the Götterdämmerung must inevitably descend.[2]

In the same book he remarked:

If, as I myself have always thought, modern socialism actually is nothing but a phenomenon of reaction against capitalism, the country of the most integrated capitalistic development—namely, the United States—must inevitably become the classical country of socialism and its working people the bearer of the most radical socialist movement.

The "inevitability" never has materialized; but it is one of the basic reproaches by socialist Europe of America.

In this light, Henry George appears as a representative of petty bourgeois radicalism or socialism; in such a context, the Russian Social Democrats were not original, they simply followed the clearly expressed opinion of their Western teachers, Marx and Engels.

Less critical of the single tax and the nationalization of land were the Russian Populists, who were much more radical than their American prototype.

Naturally Henry George's *Progress and Poverty* and all his other writings had a more friendly reception from the non-Marxist Russian socialists and idealists. The reason was not so much the soundness of his doctrines as his practical views on the nationalization of land, which became the basis of Russian Populism and the agrarian socialism of the Socialist Revolutionaries. While Russian urbanocentric Marxism was supported by patterns of industrial Western Europe, the Russian Populists were eager to find an analogy for their program in an American project that would also strive toward nationalization of land and, furthermore, would make the agrarian issue the main item of social progress. No Western economist fitted this pattern better than Henry George.

[2] Werner Sombart, *Warum gibt es in den Vereinigsten Staaten keinen Sozialismus?* Tübingen, 1906, p. 11.

One must bear in mind that the idealist pro-peasant Russian Populists did not perceive in George's propositions either a universal remedy against agrarian evils or an essentially irrefutable theory.

The famous economist Tugan-Baranovski, who shifted around 1900 from Marxism to idealistic Populism, was very critical of the theoretical part of Henry George's doctrine; [3] nevertheless he welcomed it as a serious and original attempt to fight poverty. Although he decidedly did not share George's view toward rent and wages, he found it essentially wrong to seek social reform in the past, because capitalism was firmly established in the United States. He fully recognized the merits of George's teachings in the municipal policies of the towns and their taxation on rent and the application of the concepts in Australia and New Zealand.

When Tugan-Baranovski wrote his learned article in the *Novoye Slovo,* he was favorably inclined toward Marxism. He recognized that George's basic volume "represented the first independent and original American answer to the old problem which worries the contemporary civilized world—namely, how to eliminate poverty," and that George transferred to the sphere of economics "liberty, equality, and brotherhood," which, according to the French revolutionary doctrines, "must be made the basis of the social order." Capitalism, however, had grown rapidly in the United States, which since the early 1880's had ceased to be a country of the petty bourgeoisie; that class had gradually been replaced by a well-to-do industrial and agrarian owner class on one hand and the proletariat on the other. The filling of the non-populated areas in the West, for him, was only an accompanying phenomenon of industrialization. Therefore, the very "remedy" of George was only a bourgeois utopia because it denied the modern antagonism between labor and capital. He evaluated George's theory about profit as a "fantastic" one, but did not deny the positive side of his teachings as significant reform movements, nor the "prophet of San Francisco" himself as a man of exclusive brilliance and charm.

[3] Michael Tugan-Baranovski, "Henry George i natsionalizatsiya zemli" (H. G. and Land Nationalization) in the review *Novoye Slovo* (*New World*), June, 1897, pp. 108-129. Also his book *Natsionalizatsiya zemli* (Land Nationalization), 2nd ed., St. Petersburg, 1906.

Not less important, however, is the fact that Henry George's views were fully shared by Leo Tolstoy. Of all economic concepts, those of the prophet of San Francisco were most acceptable to Tolstoy and his disciple S. Nikolayev, the principal translator and advocate of George in Russia, where the publishing houses of Posrednick and Panteleyev issued George's works in widely distributed popular editions.[4] Furthermore, in 1905 Tolstoy published an Open Letter to a Peasant on Land, which was simply a popular version of George's teaching.

An earlier discussion of Henry George's works occurred in 1883 when the Populist review *Russkoye Bogatstvo*[5] (Russian Wealth) reprinted his introductory lecture at the University of California, recommending him as a "rising star."

The same bulky review made the following statement in connection with the publication in Russian of a book of selected speeches and articles of Henry George at the beginning of this century:

> In Russia the agrarian problem has always been of the greatest signifi-
> cance. Land socialization has always been the traditional dream of the
> Russian people. George was an ardent advocate of this idea. With the
> zeal of deep conviction and with a rare eloquence and talent for popu-
> larization of his theories, he proceeded to combat the original sin of our

---

[4] *Progress and Poverty* was translated twice into Russian and issued in 1891, 1893, 1906, and 1907. All George's most important articles and speeches were translated and were indeed highly appreciated for their manner as well as matter. The censorship was rather gracious to the American writer, but it was inevitable that some sentences should be stricken out, such as "The other crowned heads of Europe sit, metaphorically speaking, upon barrels of nitroglycerine," which was a direct stab at the Russian monarch. The many revised editions of *Progress and Poverty*, published after the revolution of 1905 during a more tolerant censorship, omitted one direct reference to an attempt to kill a government agent and political spy, Col. Sudeikin, for which the famous revolutionary and nobleman Valerian Ossinski was sentenced in 1879, and two accomplices to hanging by a Kiev military court: "While writing I have picked up a newspaper. In it is a short account evidently translated from a semi-official report of the execution of three Nihilists at Kiev (including) the nobleman Ossinski. At the foot of the gallows they were permitted to kiss one another. 'Then the hangman cut the rope, the surgeons pronounced them dead . . . and the Nihilists were given up to eternal oblivion.' Thus reads the account. I do not believe it. No; not to oblivion!" This passage in the short concluding chapter of *Progress and Poverty* is an enthusiastic expression of George's sympathies for the Russian revolutionary Populists and their fight for "Truth and Justice."

[5] No. 3, p. 609.

civilization—private landed property. . . . Particularly in relation to Russia, George's concepts of speculative rent dealt with one of the most anomalous sides of our peasant economy: simultaneous with the growth of culture, the increase of rent rates, the artificial rise in land prices, etc.

Despite the generally positive attitude of the Russian Populists toward Henry George's ideas, *Russkoye Bogatstvo* was objective enough to criticize his purely theoretical propositions; and it repeated several reproaches by Russian Marxists of the apostle of the single tax.

An outstanding Russian economist, the pro-Marxian Nicholas Sieber, wrote a detailed essay on George describing and criticizing his concepts.[6] The first attack by Sieber was on the assertion that the wages of the worker are not taken from capital, as most economists assert, but are produced by the labor of the worker. According to Sieber, the German economist Rodbertus had very similar views, which is all the more remarkable in that George was not acquainted with German theories of political economy. Sieber contended that George blurred differences between economic phenomena on lower levels and those on higher ones and, because of this, mistakenly applied the notion of wages to the booty of an uncivilized hunter or fisherman. However, the mere fact that the modern laborer, hired by the employer, produces his wages in the same way a member of a primitive community produces his means of subsistence does not necessarily indicate that he does not draw his wages from capital. In order to understand the issue, said Sieber, we must consider the dual nature of a wage or labor contract, in which the economic features are not in harmony with the legal ones. Law considers that a vendor and a purchaser are wholly equal, like the two parties to other contracts of hire, regardless of the fact that the value produced by the worker for his employer is necessarily greater than that which the worker receives in the form of wages, because otherwise no one would hire workers. For Sieber, it was precisely this legal feature of the hire-contract that George lost sight of, and that based itself on a misapplication to industrial relations of the concept of self-augmentation of goods or property, such as cattle or crops,

[6] Sieber, "O vliyanii progressa na bednost" (On the Influence of Progress on Poverty), *Russkaya Mysl*, 1883, Nos. 9, 11, 12.

which grow without any effort on the part of the owner but to his profit.

Sieber reproached George for being confused when he described the laws of distribution of labor production among rent, wages, and interest, and asserted, moreover, that such a concept had nothing to do with profit.

To George's criticisms of speculation, particularly in land, and of all the other negative features of American economic life, Sieber was sympathetic; but the critic was vehemently opposed to his basic proposition of land nationalization, despite the tremendous following and recognition this concept received in England, Australia, and continental Europe. Such a reform, wrote the Russian, was one-sided and insufficiently based on fact:

It has not yet been proved that speculation for a rise of land values and rent is the cause of industrial crises and all the subsequent calamities and distresses of the working classes. George's bold attack on landed property alone, whereas the principles of the whole economy and the vices of its organization derive from the functions of commercial and industrial capitalism, including banks and stock exchanges, is extremely one-sided and, therefore, useless.

These lines, directed against George, were written in 1883 by one early Marxist, Sieber, which helps to explain the agrarian views of the Russian Social Democracy, dogmatically and stubbornly undervaluing the uniqueness of the economics of its own country.

But what was a weakness of Henry George in the eyes of Sieber and other early Marxists became a high merit in the eyes of Russian Populists, who could not overlook the 80-odd per cent peasant population or pin all their hopes on the urban proletariat representing about 3 per cent of the population.

Even some Populists, as we have already stated, were doubtful about the purely economic side of George's doctrine. They too denied the all-embracing importance of the land rent or the harmony between capital and labor; [7] but all this could not undermine the importance of George's doctrine for Russian Populism. An

[7] B. Efrussi, "Genri Dzhordzh kak Ekonomist," in *Russkoye Bogatstvo*, 1898, No. 1, pp. 179 ff.

editorial introduction to a very long article in the Russian Populist review emphasized the importance of George's doctrine for Russia:

Our internal policy, expressed in the abolition of serfdom and the allotment of lands to the peasants, namely, of those lands which are owned on principles of communal property entailing the redemption of these lands by the state, and, later, by the Peasants' Land Bank through which the state tries to prevent the formation of a breach between labor and the means of labor, as formulated by George—this internal policy can to a high degree preserve us from the consequences of national bankruptcy and from slavery to capital which we observe in America and the West.[8]

With all their admiration for Henry George and his "epoch-making" teachings, considering him as their own Karl Marx, the Russian Populists tried to see these teachings in the light of the specific environment in which *Progress and Poverty* and the other essays were written. The economist Yuzhakov wrote about George's views on poverty:

George recognizes as the cause of poverty the turning of land into private property, but he ignores the concentration of capital in the hands of the few. Little wonder how this fallacy originated. Observing mainly the economic life of America and England, George came across a harmonious rise and decline of per cents (on capital) and wages, and thus concluded there was no antagonism between them; in these instances (in England and the American Far West) he observed that the increase of rent accompanied the decrease of wages and profit. Ricardo's law of rent explained this phenomenon to him, and he derived from it the idea of an antagonism between rent on one hand and wages and profit on the other. . . . The realization that private landownership was the first cause which greatly preceded ownership of capital and that until now ownership of the soil has been a mighty factor of poverty and injustice finally led George to the establishment of his doctrine in which the basic cause of the whole economic disorder is landownership alone.[9]

To George's basic theory that "wealth in all its forms being the product of labor applied to land or the products of land, any in-

[8] M. M. Filipov, "Sotsialny vopros po Genri Dzhordzhu" (The Social Problem According to H. G.), *Russkoye Bogatstvo*, 1885, Nos. 5-6, pp. 316-365.

[9] S. Yuzhakov, "K voprosu o Cednosti; yeyo prichinakh i ustranenii" (The Problem of Poverty: Its Causes and Its Removal), in *Otechestvenniya Zapiski* (Fatherland Notes), Vol. CCLXVI (1883), pp. 95-134, 427-452.

crease in the [productive] power of labor, the demand for wealth being unsatisfied, will be utilized in procuring more wealth, and thus increase the demand for land," [10] Yuzhakov objected: First of all, an increase in the productive power of labor will not *always* increase the demand for land because a good half of the increase of productivity means that the same quantity of labor applied to the same acreage of land will yield more products. All this increase of productivity will not necessarily expand the acreage of cultivation. Secondly, even where the augmentation of productivity results in the ability to get the same quantity of product on the same acreage of land but with less application of the labor force, this would not lead to a duplication of the cultivation acreage but to a much smaller expansion, since, if the efficiency of labor in producing raw materials has increased, a part of the labor unemployed in producing raw materials will necessarily be applied to refinement of the new raw materials and only a part of this labor force could be used for the expansion of cultivation. And finally, the expansion of production, being the result of an increase of productivity, can only follow this increase by lagging somewhat behind it; and therefore not all the labor set free by the more efficient productivity will be applied to the augmented production; hence, pauperism.

The immanent adequacy of George's social philosophy—including his ideas about progress and the individual—and its affinity with the social philosophy of Russian idealistic Populists can be well understood only if we desert political economy for a valuation of the conceptual postulates of both schools. The similarities are truly amazing, beginning with philosophy and ending with sociology.

The social doctrines of Russian Populism grew from the roots of the repartitional tenure of allotment land before the emancipation, implemented periodically by the village community. Periodic distribution and redistribution by village communal assemblies (*mirskoi skhod*) with the intention that such redistributions should be made justly and equitably to each member households [11] became routine and self-understood. From this institutional custom the Social Revolutionaries later built up their idea of equal land use

---

[10] *Progress and Poverty*, Bk. IV, Chap. III.
[11] Cf. Geroid T. Robinson, *Rural Russia Under the Old Regime*, pp. 74, 112-113.

(*uravnitelnoye zemlepolsovaniye*). Thus Russian agrarian Populism created its own conception of a new peasant socialism permeated by the ideas of natural law and justice. This in itself was a repudiation of Western Marxism, which was not dependent upon any subjective ethical awareness of the equality of the individual and his producing family. But strangely enough, it was in this connection that such Populist sociologists as Nicholas K. Mikhailovsky (1842–1904) met the socialist philosophy of Henry George.[12]

George wrote: "This natural and inalienable right to the equal use and enjoyment of land is so apparent that it has been recognized by men wherever force or habit has not blunted first perceptions."

The idea of the injustice of private landed property was also common to George and the Populist thinkers of Russia. He coined the sentence: "Whatever may be said for the institution of private property in land, it is plain that it cannot be defended on the score of justice." [13] This sentence was sooner or later repeated a thousandfold in the Russian agrarian political pamphlets. Returning to ethical social philosophy, one need only juxtapose the following pair of maxims in which the reconciliation of objective truth and justice is postulated:

GEORGE: That alone is wise which is just, that alone is enduring which is right. Must not Truth and Justice have something to give that is their own by proper right—theirs in essence and not by accident?

MIKHAILOVSKY: I have never been able to believe it is impossible to find a view wherein abstract truth and concrete justice could go together, each supplementing the other.

It may be remarked that Mikhailovsky's equation Truth=Justice was based on a well known double sense in the Russian word *pravda*, which signifies truth (*istina*) and justice (*spravedlivost*). He wrote:

Every time the word *pravda* comes into my mind I am compelled to admire the amazing beauty of it. I think there is no such word in any

[12] Max M. Laserson, "Russian Sociology," in *Twentieth Century Sociology*, ed. G. D. Gurvitch and W. E. Moore, New York, 1945, pp. 678-680.
[13] *Progress and Poverty*, Bk. VII, Chap. I.

European language. It seems that only in Russian are truth and justice expressed in the same word, and thus flow together in one grand whole.[14]

There are also striking similarities in the conceptions of progress as developed in different writings of George on one side and Lavrov on the other, along with Mikhailovsky. This brings us to their common negation of social Darwinism, and particularly of Spencer's teachings and the theories of Bagehot; and lastly to their common insistence upon natural rights in the midst of the sober environment of the last score of years of the nineteenth century, a period when natural law had been discarded by every university of Europe and America. It should not be denied that both in George's and in the Russian Populist theories there was something of circumventing industrialism—in different ways—something of an identification of farmers and workers in the brackets of the laboring class, and some conception that progress and justice—as ethical standards and social remedies—had to be connected with the problem of poverty.

N. K. Mikhailovsky gave his theory of progress in an essay reviewing and criticizing Herbert Spencer's *Collected Works* with hostile ardor.[15] This essay, "What Is Progress?" was published first in 1869 and subsequently reprinted. Mikhailovsky was in full agreement with Henry George when he made the struggle for individuality a fundamental universal principle appearing in the inorganic and gradually penetrating the whole organic world.

He also applied the ideas of the American scientist and historian John William Draper. Particularly quoted were his *History of the American Civil War* and his *History of the Intellectual Development of Europe*, which was so popular in Russia that the Russian translation had four consecutive editions. According to Mikhailovsky, Draper's views on social progress were based on the following processes: the identical development of the society on one side and the individual on the other, every individual representing society in

---

[14] N. K. Mikhailovsky, *Polnoye sobraniye sochinenii*, 3rd ed., St. Petersburg, 1911, p. 5 (Preface), where he mentions an article of 1899 in which he first expressed his opinion.

[15] Compare John Maynard, *Russia in Flux*, London, 1946, pp. 199-200; pp. 257 f.; Thomas G. Masaryk, *The Spirit of Russia*, London, 1919; William E. Walling, *Russia's Message*, New York, 1917.

a microcosmic form. However, Mikhailovsky was sharply against any alignment between an individual organism and that of the society. Progress, for him, was a gradual approximation of the integrity of individuals, reaching to the possibly perfect and all-embracing division of labor among the bodily organs of a man, and to the division of labor among men. All that is hampering such a movement is immoral, unjust, harmful, and irrational. Only that is moral, just, rational, and useful which diminishes the heterogeneity of the society by augmenting the diversity of its particular parts.[16]

It was concerning the ideas of Henry George that the Russian Populists and revolutionaries fell in with the followers of Tolstoy and his doctrine of nonresistance to evil. From Victor Chernov, the ideologist of the Social Revolutionaries who considered fundamental the equal right of every Russian citizen to land, down to Count Tolstoy who, despite his legal nihilism, regarded the right of everyone to a part of his native land as an inevitable and natural law,[17] Henry George's views were a moral refuge and justification for these somewhat anarchic conceptions. To be exact, George's radical program of land reform first inspired the "hermit of Yasnaya Polyana" to come out in the open in defense of any kind of legislation and law, since he always had spoken, both in fiction and other publications, with disgust, bitterness, and mocking contempt of legal or constitutional thinkers, as well as of reformers and judges. For decades he had fanatically condemned law for distorting morals; however, Henry George conquered the soul and heart of Leo Tolstoy, as a conscience-stricken landlord worried about the fate of Russian peasantry. Under the influence of George's work, he wrote an article defending natural law—a heresy far removed from his general antilaw position.

Only with the liberation of the majority of people from land slavery, Tolstoy wrote, would political reforms cease to be mere tools in the hands of politicians and become the expression of the desires of the whole people. At the end of his article, having quoted from a series of George's essays, he remarked:

[16] Mikhailovsky, *op cit.*, 2nd ed., St. Petersburg, 1888, Vol. IV, pp. 54, 186-187. Also P. Lavrov, *Formula Progressa N. K. Mikhailovskovo*, St. Petersburg, 1906, pp. 7 ff. There is a French translation.

[17] Tolstoy, "Velikii Grekh" (The Great Sin), in *Russkaya Mysl*, Vol. VII (1905), p. 248.

The solution of the land question painstakingly made by George is a perfect one *under the existing state-order with its compulsory taxation;* there is no other answer thinkable which would be better or juster, more practical or peaceful. . . . I think that Henry George is right in asserting that redemption from the sin of land property is near, and I am sure that the travail of the ominous birth will soon be over.[18]

But the greatest significance which Leo Tolstoy ascribed to George's doctrine consisted in the indication given that the redemption of the agrarian sin would create a new historic epoch in which the Russian Slavonic people, according to its spiritual and economic entity, will be leading mankind. According to Tolstoy, because the Russian people was not doomed to proletarianization as the other peoples of Europe and America were, it would resolve the agrarian problem by abolishing land property and showing the other nations the path toward a free and happy life outside industrial or capitalist violation and slavery. This, for Tolstoy, was the great vocation of the Russian people, and he became more Slavophile in the conviction than in any other social issue. In a tone of rueful repentance he expressed the hope that "we Russian parasites, brought up and endowed with mental leisure by the sweat and labor of the people, will finally understand our sin and try to redeem it for the sake of truth and justice against our own personal benefit."

Precisely because young America differed, particularly in agrarian relations, from Western Europe, it held an outstanding attraction for Russia. The abundance of land in the transatlantic republic seemed to be the only basis of similarity with Russia. The vast western lands were in the hands of the state, essentially; and the ability of the latter to dispose of it freely was the dream of Russian radical Populists. Some of them strove for a "black redistribution" (*chiorny peredel*) of all lands belonging to landowners, the church, and the peasants, as well as the domains belonging to the Empire.

Between 1850 and the early 1880's, the expansion to the West and the homestead movement of America became, in the eyes of the Russian subversive socialist intelligentsia, a kind of American black redistribution.

In 1905 an article by Lenin entitled "Marx on the American

[18] *Ibid.*, p. 266.

Black Redistribution" reproduced Marx's criticism of a German emigrant, his follower Hermann Kriege, as far back as 1846. Kriege had written an enthusiastic article about the demand of American National Reformists that 1,400,000,000 acres of land which had escaped the hands of grasping speculators should be declared the inalienable property of mankind. Marx poured ice-water on his young friend's aspirations, soberly stating that the distribution of these huge plots to farmers was not a communist measure for mankind's benefit, but an American petty-bourgeois step which might end in the ruin of the newly established farms. Lenin drew the following conclusion from Marx's writings:

For us, Russian Social Democrats, the approach of Marx to Kriege's conception ought to serve as an example. The genuine petty-bourgeois character of the modern peasant movement in Russia does not leave any doubts. We have to explain it powerfully and pitilessly, and we must implacably fight the illusions persisting about it among "Socialist Revolutionaries" and primitive socialists in general . . . however, to turn away from the peasants' movement would be hopelessly pedantic and Philistine. The revolutionary nature of this movement is undeniable, and we must support it by all means, develop it, and make it politically conscious.[19]

Some thirteen or fourteen years later the same Lenin found, under Soviet conditions, a new solution to the problem of agrarian redistribution, accomplished first by dividing the peasantry into the well-to-do kulaks and the "middle peasantry" (*seredniak*), an entirely new rural class—a theoretical invention which helped to turn orthodox Marxism, for which the whole peasantry was petty-bourgeois, into Leninism; and secondly by collectivizing village farming.

But in 1905–1906, Russian Social Democrats did not even dream about Russia's becoming the first socialist country in the world; on the contrary, they were vehemently against it. The non-Marxist Populists had incomparably greater influence upon the Russia of the huts and cabins than the Marxists, whose program was elaborated in Western countries like England and Germany with prevailing urbanization and industrialization. This predominance of the Populists in Russia remained untouched even by the October

[19] Lenin, *Collected Works, Polnoye sobraniye sochinenii*, Moscow, 1928, Vol. VIII, p. 219.

Revolution, and therefore they had, in the Constitutional Assembly convoked in January, 1918, after the Bolshevik upheaval, a decisive peasants' majority. It is against this background that Henry George's influence must be measured.

But even in the non-Marxist camp the social and economic differences between the United States and Russia were decisive, despite the tacit sympathetic preconception that America and Russia were equally detached from the narrowness of the "senile political economy of Europe."

We will quote here from one of many surveys of American conditions in the second half of the 1880's, that by Vera MacGahan in a leading Populist bulky review, the Northern Herald.[20] She expressed the complaint common to both Marxists and non-Marxists —that America had not developed socialism; but, as we shall see, her conception differed greatly from the Marxist:

The European worker, who is excluded at birth from any contact with the so-called upper classes, has no chance to become a man of standing. He tries his best to reach the highest possible degree of welfare in the confines of his own sphere to which his father and grandfather belonged before him. The social system of caste, orders, and estates thus helps to a certain degree to satisfy the life needs of the common man.

The United States, on the contrary, represents another extreme. Here every boy grows up with the confidence that all ways are open to him, that it is up to him alone to get riches and achieve the highest honors of the country. . . . It should not, however, be forgotten that this liberty of ascending in society becomes every year more limited, although this limitation is not yet obvious. . . .

It is very seldom that the family of a farmer or artisan retains its children in their original social milieu. However low a family may be in its social level, you will always hear from its members that one or another relative became socially outstanding in the past, or that he at present occupies a most important place. We ourselves happened to hire a carriage at Niagara, where the coachman introduced himself as the nephew of Chief Justice Waite; in the coal mines of Ohio, I met a miner who was the cousin of the famous American General Sheridan; a porter of another railway station happened to be an uncle of Jay

[20] *Severny Viestnik*, 1886, Jan., pp. 1-17, Feb., p. 9. Mrs. MacGahan was a Russian aristocrat married to an American.

Gould. Little wonder that only very rarely will an American lad be satisfied with the occupation which presents itself to him when he begins his life!

. . . The general instance of a feverish activity is so exciting that even well-to-do men don't leave their business or dedicate themselves to rest or leisure; the Americans have developed an indefatigable passion for work.

Mrs. MacGahan did not deny that the trade unions supported workers during unemployment and strikes, but she emphasized the limited organization of workers into unions. This brought her to American socialism:

A famous American economist, Henry George, expressed his conviction that the proportion of unemployed workers in the whole country must be equal to that in New York. As to whether there is danger for the country in the amassing of colossal fortunes, George is of the following opinion: [21] "The amassing of these large fortunes by individuals is likely to cause bankruptcy of the country. This circumstance is a terrible peril: we cannot continue with impunity to march in the same direction of enriching the few while the working masses are doomed to misery."

The most important aspect of her article is that a review of Populist orientation appearing in Russia, which had not yet attained the lowest levels of a rule of law and social legislation, should criticize the United States as a country of capitalist wickedness mistakenly admired by emigrants-to-be. Without denying that American life had admirable features, she emphasized that America was not a paradise for workingmen, but a country of crying injustices.

Having made socialism its credo, the radical intelligentsia was always surprised that the United States did not show any tendencies toward socialism. Interviewing John Swinton, Mrs. MacGahan raised this point and got the following reply:

Socialism in the United States? But you would have to preach it here under diverse fictitious names. Don't you know that all our American workers would run away in all directions on no more than hearing the word "socialist"? No, no, you could not utter the word "socialism," even if it is only state socialism. Of course socialistic ideas have begun to penetrate into the working class, some laborers have become ac-

[21] Quoted from his article in the New York *World*, Feb. 18, 1885.

quainted with the idea that they will never improve their position unless relations between capital and labor are regulated by legislation. . . . But all this looms in a very nebulous form, and therefore the American Congress does not feel any pressure to proceed with such legislation. There are no purely American socialist organizations in the United States. Socialistic doctrines are spread only among Germans who recently came to these shores and who have had no time to settle down in a satisfactory way. And furthermore, you should see how native Americans try to avoid any circles established by European immigrants.

The interview continued, as follows:

MacGahan: What do you think, Mr. Swinton? Is not the real cause of the fact that socialism does not find followers among the American masses to be found in the spirit of traditional individualism and the instinct of self-help which are the specific features of the American nationality?

Swinton: Individualism, you say? The individualism of the native American was manifest at the time when we had not rooted state order, when everyone was compelled to cut his way by his own ax. As long as fortunes were acquired in our country by legal enterprise, by trade, and so on, workers did not grumble. But now something else happens. In the last score of years legendary fortunes appeared. . . . You want to know what is done by legislation in favor of farmers and workers in different eras of prosperity and depression. We may reply, Almost nothing.

MacGahan: But lastly, are there not newspapers in the country which defend the convictions and doctrines of your newspaper?

Swinton: No, there are not any in English like my small weekly. There are, however, such papers here printed in German. This proves how undeveloped socialism is among us. Even those papers which are published in the interests of Greenbackers do not dare to admit that they are socialistic, although their claims that money should be issued only by the federal government and not by bank corporations as it is today are doubtless of a socialistic character. All the same, the Greenbackers have their six members of Congress. Their candidate for the Presidency, B. F. Butler, raised the banner of the Populists, while not more than one-fortieth of the votes of all electors in the country were cast for him. No, indeed, socialism, as yet, has not taken root in American soil. . . . Americans, even those who are linking their hopes to only the federal government and Congress do not even dream about the introduction of a socialism like that which was enacted during the last few years in Germany by the Iron Chancellor.

In the excessive hospitality of the United States lies the main peril for the free institutions of the country. The United States Constitution is a document of superior political wisdom, but it is well adapted only to a country populated by sensible and calm inhabitants.

Mrs. MacGahan admitted that persevering tenacity, loyal orderliness, and enterprising spirit, after leading to the creation of the American nation, had become its basic features and had enabled it to survive many crises. Could not American inventiveness, she asked, find a way out of this crisis also?

Having inherited evil from Europe, having been contaminated by her social ulcers, could not this young nation with its organic new forces find a new way out of the dilemma which the senile political economy cannot cope with?

Among the theoreticians of the Socialist Revolutionaries, Victor Chernov must be singled out in his approach to George as the most politically active advocate of Russian Populism. Both George and Chernov were non-Marxists; both had the passionate conviction that the synthesis of Truth and Justice was a "standard to be raised as a basic social maxim in this world," and, what is more, both regarded the injustice of private landed property and the establishment of new rights to land as a basic social problem. The more moderate wing of Russian Populism represented in the *Russkoye Bogatstvo*, particularly the writers Yuzhakov, Peshekhonov, and Myrakotin, hailed George as the only Western supporter of their ideas, particularly because he defended genuinely Russian ideas in the new world, which had turned full speed to capitalism and had never before had village communities in its agrarian history. Chernov was most specific. Defending socialization of land, he could not regard George's nationalization of the soil, well hidden behind the single tax, as much more than agrarian reformism. But it should not be forgotten that for Chernov not only George but Wallace, Oppenheimer, and other German and Russian Social Democrats would be nothing more than half-hearted reformers.[22] Chernov gave

[22] Victor Chernov, "Zemlya i Pravo" (Land and Law), *Sobraniye sochinenii*, Vol. I, Petrograd, 1917, p. 26.

a sweeping characterization of George's theory, as well as of those authors who shared his general views. The spiritual essence of this approach could, according to Chernov, be reduced to such an optimistic diagnosis:

The modern civil-law structure with its freedom of competition is the normal order of human co-existence. It cannot be blamed for the economic calamities of the masses. The one and only adversity consists in the fact that this order, based upon full freedom of private enterprise, has never had the possibility to unfold in its entirety; its beneficent advantages are crippled by the influence of a factor which is entirely foreign to its bases; namely, the monopoly expressed in private ownership of land. Once this essentially monopolistic form of private property is eliminated, exploitation, too—being always produced, in the last analysis, by monopoly—will disappear. This is the land nationalization school that does not doubt the fundamental principles of the bourgeois order, but merely tries consistently to purge it from any distortions. Hence their whole conception of land nationalization as a positive system. Some of the nationalizers, mostly in Europe, try to hand over all landed property to the state, all tillers of the soil becoming in this way free tenants. Another view defended by the American Henry George is characterized by an even simpler approach: his measure consists in a confiscation of the entire land rent by way of a specific tax. Actually, this measure would abolish all economic privileges of the owner as a monopolist and exploiter. In the two ways mentioned above, a free play of competitive forces logically leads, according to the nationalizers, to an extermination of exploitation.[23]

Chernov's ideal went a significant step further than George's; he asked for *socialization of land*, which became a basic slogan of the agrarian program of the Socialist Revolutionaries. The socialization, to be established under Russian bourgeois czarism, presupposed first of all the exclusion of land from the list of commodities exchangeable and from the market; this would remove land from the sphere of modern civil law. Land would, in such a conception, no longer be the property of the village community or of the state or province; it would belong to the whole people and to no one person. Utopian as the idea was, it became a stumbling block even for some adherents of Chernov in the Social Revolutionary party,

[23] *Ibid.*, p. 134.

which emerged in 1902. At its first congress, in 1905, many tried to go back to nationalization or "socialization" as the kernel of any further land reform, and were then reproached for Georgism.[24]

Thus, the crucial Russian agrarian issue became more than an ideological theme; it turned into a practical concern of the First, the Second, and (in part) the Third Duma. The famous bill of the Socialist Revolutionaries was supported in the Second Duma (1907) by one hundred and four signatures, outnumbering by far the Populist deputies (among these, the more moderate Agrarian Labor faction, "Trudoviki"); moreover, peasant members of the cadet and other rightist factions signed the radical bill.

After all, the difference between George's views and Chernov's, representative of the most radical Russian Populists, was one of degree, not of social or economic perception. Henry George himself wrote, in his chief work:

Our boasted freedom necessarily involves slavery, so long as we recognize private property in land. Until that is abolished, Declarations of Independence and Acts of Emancipation are in vain. So long as one man can claim the exclusive ownership of the land from which other men must live, slavery will exist.[25]

The best testimony of George's relation to Russian Populism is that the ideas referred to above found their first legislative expression in a Russian bill entitled "The Basic Outlines of the Statute on Land" that was introduced on May 3, 1907.[26] The opening articles of the bill were:

Art. 1: Every kind of (private) property in land is from now on and forever abolished.
Art. 2: All the land with its waters and subsoil is proclaimed to be the possession of the whole population of the Russian State.

On the other hand, the czarist government, terrified by riots and disorders as well as by the radical agrarian resolutions of numerous conferences including the Duma speeches and proposals, decided to put an end to all kinds of nationalization and socialization by

[24] *Ibid.*, pp. 130, 131.   [25] *Progress and Poverty*, Bk. VII, Chap. II, end.
[26] *Gosudarstvennaya Duma, II Sozyv, Zakonodatelniya Zayavleniya* (State Duma, Second Duma, Legislative Bills and Proposals), St. Petersburg, 1907, pp. 203-208.

gradually extinguishing the village collectivism of the mir and sub-
stituting for it new private ownership. The initiative was taken by
Prime Minister Peter Stolypin who, by the introductory act of 1906
and the laws of June, 1910, and May, 1911, managed to induce the
Duma to pass a new western private land property act despite a
powerful opposition. Around 1911, some 2,478,224 farmers left the
old village communities as private owners of their homesteads. The
outbreak of the First World War interrupted this new trend. But
in all these events the ideas of Henry George became pivotal, and
it is therefore little wonder that his concepts of agrarian reform were
resuscitated in Russia, particularly after the 1905 revolution, during
a period when the "prophet of San Francisco" lost recognition in
his own United States.

It remains a matter of lasting interest that the cousins of the
Populist radicals in Russia, the Marxist Social Democrats, were
against the socialization of land, which they regarded as utopian
and therefore unfeasible. Toward Henry George, however, their
attitude was preconditioned by Marx's comments on the American
reformist.

For those who can perceive the climate of Russian and American
radicalism and Populism, it is clear that in the concepts of both
these movements homespun and earthy originality is discernible.
It is all the more remarkable that both theories—in the persons of
Henry George and Edward Bellamy on the American side and of
Mikhailovsky, Lavrow, Yuzhakov, Tugan-Baranovski, Chernov,
and others on the Russian side—developed similar approaches, preconceptions, conclusions, and structures, and found themselves thus
mobilized against the same hostile front of Marxist socialism.

An original attitude toward Henry George was taken by a Russian expert in finance, economics, and labor legislation, Professor
Ivan Yanzhul of the Moscow University. He, neither a Populist
nor a Marxist, was a moderate advocate of state interference in
economic and social issues. He also made a study of American trusts
and visited the United States in order to collect materials and data.

In discussing The Social Problem and the Single Tax in his book,
Yanzhul condemned George's attempts to deny any connection of
his theory or his party of "single-tax men" with socialism, but disapproved more aggressively George's reproaches of the Pope for at-

tacking the acquisitiveness of the rich factory owners.[27]

Of the single tax and nationalization Yanzhul wrote:

Plans of this kind usually try to provide an amicable solution of the problem for all classes, and they presuppose an equalized, even if faulty, lessening of the burden for the whole population. Whereas the essence of Henry George's single tax, or expropriation of rent, consists in depriving one class of its property in favor of all other classes, which is tantamount to robbery, no matter what it is called, the robbery can never become the basis of a sound national life or a source of general welfare.

Even in Great Britain, the realization of George's single tax would cause an annual loss of £61,000,000 sterling. If such a result is involved for the richest country of Europe with a developed agriculture, what good can come from the application of George's schemes to poor and undeveloped Russia? [28]

In a sense, Yanzhul was one of the first serious Russian economists to blow the trumpet of retreat from Henry George's ideas.

Edward Bellamy's echo in Russia was certainly much softer than George's perhaps because his influence lay in the no man's land between fiction and political writing.

It is remarkable that, in a symposium published in behalf of the victims of the famine of 1890–1891,[29] three articles were devoted to the United States. One was by Mrs. MacGahan, on the Stock Exchanges of New York and Chicago; the second was by Henry George (Equal Rights and Common Rights). This article, containing criticism of Herbert Spencer's agrarian views, was sent by George for the symposium before it was published in the United States, and the translation was personally supervised by Leo Tolstoy. The third American item was an article by Edward Bellamy, especially written for the symposium (The Social Movement in America Which Developed Under the Influence of *Looking Backward*). It should be added that Bellamy's famous novel *Looking Backward* was published under different titles (After a Century, A Wonderful Dream, etc.) in the journal *Nedelya* (Week) and in

---

[27] Ivan Yanzhul, V *poiskakh luchavo budushchevo* (Toward a Better Future), 2nd ed., St. Petersburg, 1908, pp. 329, 336. The chapter mentioned analyzes closely Henry George's *Open Letter to Pope Leo XIII.*

[28] *Ibid.,* pp. 354-355.   [29] *Pomotch* (Help), St. Petersburg, 1892.

book form in 1891 and 1893, and was republished before and after the revolution of 1905; *Equality* was published in Russian in 1907, but the earlier novel remained much more celebrated in radical circles and was read in all revolutionary groups—particularly, clandestine socialist circles—offering, although a legally published novel, good material for analysis and discussion.

Bellamy gives a very good description of his doctrine of nationalism and tries to underscore the differences between the usual (European) doctrines of socialism and the new American one.

The first principle, from which this nationalism derived its name, was that production belonged to the nation. The majority of contemporary socialists strive to make production the property of society, to which its administration should be handed over. Nationalism, however, asked for the nationalization of production. The second basic feature was the economic equality of all citizens, men and women, including the use of the goods of national production. It also was based on the principle of common productional service, something similar to obligatory military service, a feature which was not so conspicuously expressed in other socialist movements. A third decisive difference between nationalism and the previous doctrines was the conception that social reform should be propagated not within the proletariat alone; all classes of society should be united to fight class struggle and class barriers. In the concluding part of the article, Bellamy described the transformation of free farmers into tenants under the influence of free closures and explained why "nationalism" must grow not only in the United States but also in Canada and England itself.

It is unnecessary to remark that Bellamy was incomparably more moderate in his Russian article than in his leaflet "The Program of the Nationalists" (1894), in Philadelphia, or in his "Principles and Purposes of Nationalism" (a widely printed address at Tremont Temple in Boston, 1889) printed in America for Americans who were mobilized by him to enter a new socialist party. He did not, for instance, dare to say in his Russian article what he mentioned in his American leaflets, that "nationalization will simply substitute one sort of government for another."

However, Bellamy's influence in Russia cannot be compared with that of Henry George.

XIV *The Turn of the Century:*
Andrew White and George Kennan

> We should not make America our idol
> Nor see in her the incarnation of our goal;
> America is backward, satisfied and idle,
> For ownership and money strives her soul.
> —Count Alexis Tolstoy, in a forbidden satiric poem
>
> Mais les lutteurs russes contre l'absolutisme sont heureux de
> savoir qu'ils ont remontré des sympathies fraternelles en
> Angleterre et en Amérique. —Peter Lavrov, May 8, 1890

WITH THE CONCLUSION OF THE CIVIL WAR, THE PURCHASE OF
Alaska, and the changes in international policies, American-
Russian friendship began to ebb. This ebbing was gradual, but after
the United States Senate resolution of March 14, 1881, stirred by the
assassination of Alexander II, relations grew more and more hostile.
As this trend accelerated, the political differences between the
transatlantic republic and the Russian Empire became increasingly
acute. At the high tide of rapprochement not only the diplomats
but even private citizens were inclined to belittle the differences
in form of government. Let us remember Herzen's statement: "We
are not interested in the forms of governments as such. We have
seen them all in action and have become convinced that all of them
are good for nothing if they are reactionary, and, on the contrary,
all of them are good if they are modern and progressive." [1] That is
why the disillusioned Herzen dropped his early republican dreams.
But with the growth of economic and cultural relations, with Americans appearing as builders of the expanding Russian railway network and the advances of industry, the very few diplomatists and
occasional enlightened travelers were replaced by real contacts.
Industrialists, engineers, technicians, shipowners, captains, and
businessmen were not diplomats; but they began to get in touch
with Russian everyday life, including the practices of its judicial
organs and administrative as well as police agents. The inefficiency,

[1] *Kolokol*, July 1, 1857.

the extreme bureaucratic formalism, the dilatoriness of the judicial
and particularly of the administrative machinery, corruptible on
the lower, and sometimes on the higher, levels—were scarcely felt
by Russians; and the press of the opposition was keenly perceived
and detected by Americans resident in Russia, because they were
interested in a normal flow of affairs and in reasonably quick decision in conflicts, trials, negotiations, and deals. American consuls
were more and more burdened by lamentations and claims of
American citizens, often helpless in dealing with Russian government officials. Sometimes such claims called for diplomatic inter-
cession, as in the famous protracted suit of Winans, Harrison &
Winans against the Russian government over a breach of contract
by the Department of Railroads. In this case, the Emperor made
a ruling, followed by complicated correspondence through a dozen
years between the American envoy on one side and Russian agents
and administrative bodies, including the Committee of Ministers,
on the other. In 1863, a collection of all related documents, accounts, and explanations was published, in 583 folio pages.

Other cases arose in which Russian despotism and political arbitrariness led to the transgression of generally recognized maxims
of public international law. In addition to domestic developments,
international affairs slowly brought a new reorientation of the
United States toward England and, of course, toward France.

Anglo-American relations deserve particular mention. In 1881
in connection with its unparalleled development on the Pacific
coast the United States expressed its desire to revise the old Clayton-Bulwer Treaty of 1850, under which the neutrality of any
canal that might be constructed across Central America by either
nation should be maintained by both. In view of its changed position on the Pacific coast, the United States asked for a right to
control the Isthmus transit. In January, 1882, Great Britain courte-
ously but decisively declined to alter the Clayton-Bulwer pact and
rejected any analogy between a future Atlantic-Pacific canal and
the Suez Canal. This cold shoulder supported the traditional intransigeance between the two countries to the full satisfaction of
Russia.

But after the first Hague Convention, in which the Russo-American relations became less cordial, conditions changed. The Hay-

GEORGE KENNAN
(after his 1865 journey through Siberia)

Pauncefote Treaty, which was signed by Great Britain and the United States November 18, 1901, became a milestone of a new rapprochement with Britain, the former opponent of the canal, and therefore it became also a symbol of growing alienation with Russia. This period showed a growing maturity in Russian political thought. On the extreme right were the defenders of Russian autocracy with such leading thinkers as Constantine Pobiedonostsev, professor of civil law at the University of Moscow, a tutor of the young Alexander III, since 1880 the procurator general of the Most Holy Synod and a prolific writer on civil law, politics, and the history of legal institutions. A leading statesman close to and towering over Nicholas II, he died in 1907. According to his reactionary doctrine, the two fundamental pillars of Western culture were rationalism and the belief in the essential goodness of man. For him, both these maxims led to a complete confusion and destruction of Western life and contaminated several "crazy Russian heads."

The center of Russian political life was represented by Russian liberalism, which crystallized in the form of a constitutional movement, with a spectrum of opinions in itself. As early as the late 1880's and particularly in the 1890's, liberalism in Russia was the whole camp to the left of the defenders of autocracy and to the right of the adherents of socialism. A socialist, even of the mildest and most moderate type, would not belong to the liberal camp in Russia. This political classification remained in effect until the democratic revolution of March, 1917.

The Russian liberals were mostly university teachers and members of the liberal professions, with some enlightened representatives of the gentry in the local zemstvos, and of the bourgeoisie.

The decisive moment for the appearance of the (provisionally underground) constitutional liberalism was the early 1880's. The first manifestation of it was the liberal movement of the zemstvos, beginning with that of the Kharkov gubernia (1879); a series of other zemstvos followed. An illegal Zemstvo Union was established which asked for political and social reforms and demanded full-fledged political freedom and self-government.[2]

To the left of liberalism was the spectrum of socialism, which

[2] Burtzev, *Za sto let* (A Century of Political Struggle), London, 1897, p. 209. Cf. Chap. X, preceding.

began with its moderate Populist wing (Narodniki) and which later after 1905 and in the subsequent Dumas was divided into the moderate Laborites (Trudoviki), Popular Socialists, and the Socialist Revolutionaries (non-Marxian democrats), the moderate Marxist Social Democrats (Mensheviki), and the radical Marxist Social Democrats (Bolsheviki)—with the democratic revolution of 1917, to become the founding fathers of the Communist party and the Soviet regime.

In the 1890's, to the left of Marxists, there were more or less outspoken anarchists, who in the first stages were only radical terrorists and by violence tried to introduce popular agrarian justice, the "black redistribution" (*chiorny peredel*) of lands, and to destroy czarism or any moderate parliamentarian state. The most picturesque advocates of this view were Tkatchev, Netchayeff, and Bakunin—a radical group remotely related to the Populists. Count Leo Tolstoy and Prince Peter Kropotkin were on the extreme left, but their views were significantly modified by education. Kropotkin became patriotic during World War I.

Most important, however, was the fact that the radicalism of the left-to-center movement was maliciously exaggerated by the defenders of autocracy. Radicals were stigmatized by the misleading common denominator of nihilism, and this misnomer was later exported to the West as a pattern of Russian political barbarism. Autocratic despotism on one side and nihilism on the other were the spiritual pillars of Russophobia in the whole West, including America. The use of terror as a means to political action down to 1906, by groups which sociologically were as moderate as the Western socialists, was one of the most decisive reasons for the inability of the West to understand the Russian liberation movement. Out of Marxist considerations the only antiterrorist group, the Russian Social Democratic party, could not change the well entrenched status quo.

Few visitors from the West in the later 1880's and 1890's were curious enough to scratch the surface of nihilism and discover its true character. One who did this successfully, was the American George Kennan; and perhaps another, our diplomatic representative in imperial Russia of that time, the educator Andrew Dickson White.

Among the prominent Russians whom White met in St. Petersburg and Moscow, the two capitals, were the two giant extremes Pobiedonostsev and Count Leo Tolstoy. He saw none of the leaders of the center, who made the closest approach to modern America, who indeed admired America and often gave themselves to the study of conditions in the United States. In general, he had no illusions about the procurator general's reactionary and extremely chauvinistic views and his anti-Western inclinations, writing, "While he was very civil in his expressions regarding the United States, he clearly considered all Western civilization a failure." [3]

The anti-Jewish policy of Alexander III reached its height during White's term as minister to Russia. Although himself opposed to it, White naïvely remarks of this policy, "which Pobiedonostsev more than any other man is supposed to have inspired," that he "seemed to have no harsh feelings against Israelites as such." [4]

In St. Petersburg, White saw also Pobiedonostsev's friend and colleague Theodore Dmitriyev, a legal historian and a university professor of foreign constitutional law, with whom he talked not about current problems but about the assassination of Peter III, the crazy husband of Catherine II, through her clever machinations. He visited the home of the St. Petersburg University professor of meteorology and geography Alexander Voyeikov—who, at the instance of the Smithsonian Institution, had contributed to James Henry Coffin's *Winds of the Globe* (1875) after his trip to America—but without discussing political topics.[5] He did not meet such outstanding liberal figures of St. Petersburg as Nicholas Kareyev the historian of Western Europe, Ilarion Kaufman the economist, and Vladimir Solovyov the great religious philosopher. In Moscow, of course, he visited Leo Tolstoy and had walks and talks with him which he describes in the most vivid way. Tolstoy expressed sympathy with the Quakers "in everything save their belief in property." He spoke admiringly of Theodore Parker's writings and seemed interested in White's reminiscences of Parker and his acquaintance with Russian affairs. He also made a glowing reference to a sympathizer of his as the foremost figure in American

---

[3] Andrew Dickson White, *Autobiography*, 2 vols., New York, 1905, Vol. II, p. 60.

[4] *Ibid.*, p. 59.   [5] *Ibid.*, pp. 44-45.

literature. White comments: "That greatest of American writers was—Adin Ballou! Evidently, some of the philanthropic writings of that excellent Massachusetts country clergyman and religious communist had pleased him, and hence came the answer."

White mentions only once meeting Moscow professors, among them one philosopher who "encouraged" him by assurances that the movement of Russian philosophy was "back to Kant": "In the strange welter of whims and dreams which one finds in Russia, this was to me an unexpected evidence of a healthful thought." [6]

It was more than a healthful thought. White obviously did not even suspect that Russian philosophy of the 1890's was to a large degree politically, so to speak, conditioned. To be sure, there was no real "back to Kant" movement. Philosophers such as Leo Lopatin, the two princely brothers Serge and Eugen Trubetskoi, and Nicholas Berdyayev, all professors in Moscow, were non-Kantians. Lopatin was even in opposition to Kant, a moderate indeterminist who defended *creative causality.* All advocated idealism and partly metaphysics, and were devoted to ethics and the fight against Marxism. The most outspoken Neo-Kantian was A. Vvedenski, a professor at the St. Petersburg University, less "Muscovite" and more Western. The Moscow group led the fight against French and Anglo-Saxon positivism as well as experimentalism, which were most highly evaluated in the Populist doctrines. It also wrote against the founders and numerous Russian popularizers of historical materialism, both in the form of "legal" or revolutionary Marxism.[7] Thus essentially this philosophical idealism was nothing else than an ideological basis of moderate liberalism and at the same time critical of the official teachings of the Orthodox Church. No "strange welter of whims and dreams"—nothing of the kind. It was a sound philosophical school which gathered around itself thousands of disciples. All these philosophers were deeply liberal in the Russian and the American sense of the word.

However, White, like his early forerunners Francis Dana and John Quincy Adams, was not eager or curious enough to establish contacts with thinkers who could have been of some use to him.

[6] *Ibid.,* pp. 74-100, especially pp. 73, 83.

[7] Max M. Laserson, "Russian Sociology," in Gurvitch and Moore, eds., *Twentieth Century Sociology,* pp. 671-702.

He did not come into contact with the leaders of Moscow liberal constitutionalism. He did not see Boris Chicherin, who in his Course of Political Science wrote about America since the Civil War; nor Stepan Fortunatov, whose History of the Political Doctrines in the United States (1879) began with the *Federalist* and Calhoun's treaties. Fortunatov lectured at the Moscow University on the constitutional history of the United States and of Western European countries, and was also a permanent contributor to the liberal and "professorial" Moscow newspaper *Russkiya Viedomosti*. Nor did White meet a single member of the splendid galaxy of Moscow constitutionalists and historians who could have given him different opinions from those of the "Torquemada of the nineteenth century" (Pobiedonostsev) on one side and Leo Tolstoy the denier of state and law on the other. Was it from pure indifference, malicious negligence, or simple ignorance that our minister failed to come into contact with the representatives of pro-Americanism in czarist Russia? I do not think so. The probable reason is that he did not regard such contacts as a part of his duties as minister.

With the growing economic contact between America and Russia and the increasing emigration from Russia—almost exclusively of the oppressed "national minorities" in the western regions, Lithuanians, Jews, Poles, Ukrainians, White Russians, etc.—American diplomatic representatives became involved in what for men like White, who were intellectuals not interested in bureaucratic procedure, were nuisance cases. The signing of the Russo-American extradition convention in 1893 added to this calamity, which soon became a political factor in itself. White makes an evasive and rather unjust conclusion to this field of his activities:

That there are many meritorious refugees cannot be denied, but any one who has looked over extradition papers, as I have been obliged to do, and seen people posing as Russian martyrs who are comfortably carrying on in New York the business of counterfeiting bank-notes, and unctuously thanking God in their letters for their success in business, will be slow to join in the outcries of refugees of doubtful standing claiming to be suffering persecution on account of race, religion, or political opinion.[8]

[8] White, *op. cit.*, p. 105.

We shall see, in the description of George Kennan's activities, what such a treaty meant for the subterranean fight of the revolutionaries.

White's understanding was not such as to permit him to distinguish sharply among the various parties of the liberation movement attacking the autocratic government of Russia. His diaries contain no direct reference to the August 20, 1890, resolution of the Congress concerning the persecution of Jews, nor to the vehement protest against the conclusion of the Extradition Treaty with Russia under the most reactionary Alexander III. There is only one field in which White remains politically consistent; that is his hatred of Russian serfdom (shown already in his early manhood), which we discover in his great appreciation of Alexander II, the assassination of whom he calls "the most fearful crime ever committed against liberty and freedom," and in his frank recognition that the Russian emancipation was a complete failure:

I do not deny the greatness and nobleness of Alexander II and the services of the men he then called to his aid; but I lived in Russia both before and since that reform, and feel obliged to testify that, thus far, its main purpose has been so thwarted by reactionaries that there is, as yet, little, if any practical difference between the condition of the Russian peasant before and since obtaining his freedom.[9]

This statement is in full accord with the criticism of the reform in Russian liberal and radical circles and reviews, and with the opinion of the American friends of Russian freedom in the 1890's and 1900's. In prediction one important passage of White's *Autobiography* may be mentioned, equally flattering to him as a scholar in history and as a diplomatist. White had the record of having met four Russian emperors: Nicholas I majestically driving in his sledge in the late winter of 1855 after—and despite—his defeat in the Crimea and later not less majestic in his coffin; Alexander II, liberator and reformer, and his cowardly son the chauvinistic hermit Alexander III; and lastly Nicholas II. Summing up all the sins of the Romanov dynasty, White wrote the following prophetic words before the revolution of October, 1905 broke out: "I put on record here the prophecy that this dynasty, if not Nicholas himself, will be punished for it. The young monarch whose weakness has led to

[9] *Ibid.*, pp. 28-29.

this fearful result will bring retribution upon himself and those who follow him." [10] The retribution took place in two phases: the downfall of Nicholas II in the first days of the February revolution and in the murderous execution of the Czar and his family in the summer of 1918—the first year of the Soviet regime.

In the early 1890's a new social and political movement appeared in the United States which tried directly to influence, even to fight against, a regime and a dynasty which had become unbearable to the rest of the world. This movement grew partly under the impact of liberal and radical England and America, and partly under the direct challenge given by Russian political refugees and immigrants.

The new movement inevitably reflected the growing discrepancy between Russia and the West, a discrepancy which was formulated in 1890 by Professor J. E. Thorold Rogers almost in terms of 1950. Russia, he wrote, "is isolating itself from the rest of the civilized world by a policy prohibitive of trade, and by social and religious intolerance."

It is not incidental that this movement favoring the Russian opposition and hostile to official Russia was led by England and America. The remaining important country, France, out of military considerations and on the eve of a Russo-French alliance, could not appear conspicuously on the world forum in this role. To the great moral satisfaction of the Russian underground and over opposition, the public opinion of both these countries was inclined even to make diplomatic remonstrances to the Russia of Alexander III.

The London *Universal Review* printed a symposium on the czarist system of Siberian exile,[11] posing two questions:

1. Is not the present system of Siberian exile by "administrative order" a disgrace to a civilized nation, and have not the atrocities lately committed under that system been of such a nature as to demand the severe punishment of those officials who were directly responsible for them?

2. Do you consider that steps should be taken to call the attention of His Majesty's Government to these outrages in order that a diplomatic remonstrance should be addressed to the Czar through his accredited representative, praying him to punish those who have abused

[10] *Ibid.*, p. 31.
[11] "Siberian Exile: A Symposium and Protest," in *Universal Review*, Vol. III (1890), pp. 1-22.

the authority which has been entrusted to them, and to make such alteration in the administration of justice as to prevent the recurrence of further acts of a similar nature?

Of the 278 answers, from outstanding British parliamentarians, writers, judges, etc., 254 assented to the first question and 185 (nearly three-fourths of the entire number) assented to both questions. Only one answer was wholly negative. The very interesting answer of Sir Frederick Pollock, the world-famous jurist and friend of Oliver Wendell Holmes, may be quoted:

I. Yes, without qualification. Yes, assuming the facts to be substantially as stated, which assumption is at least provisionally justified by the refusal of the Russian government either to make or to allow impartial inquiry.

II. No. Diplomatic remonstrance not intended to be followed by action would be as useless now as it was found to be in the case of Poland in 1863. A remonstrance from the United States might possibly be treated with more respect.

The symposium also contains two letters of Russian Populist emigrants, the founding father of Russian "subjective" sociology, Peter Lavrov, and Hespere Serebriakov, both explaining Russian Populism and denying that it was anarchistic or nihilist in character.

This Anglo-American trend toward supporting the Russian revolutionaries was in itself a much delayed action. It coincided in time with the metamorphosis of the Russian liberation movement from an essentially political and social one into a socialist movement. The more definitely socialist, and particularly Marxist, this movement became, the less attention it paid to the United States. This natural and organic development, which cannot be closely traced on the calendar but had its beginning at the end of the 1870's, found its sad culmination in the February–March revolution of 1917, with the estrangement between the American republic, the old model for Russian republicanism and progress, and the struggling Russian people, who then finally overcame the overripe and defunct autocracy. The failure of Elihu Root's Mission to Russia was magnified beyond every prediction in the estrangement between the Soviet Union and this country, including a sixteen-year rupture of diplomatic relations. This is why the era of 1890's deserves specific attention both for the mutual impact and contact in politics and civilization and for the reciprocal international relations.

It might be contended that there was not much harmony between the almost purely political interest of Grover Cleveland's America in Russia and the chiefly economic internal development of Russia itself, a development that, before it led to a revolution, created two schools of thinking which simultaneously were also schools of subversive strategy. The socially more moderate Populists, recognizing terror as a seditious method, nevertheless functioned in behalf of the whole populace, without discrimination between classes, whereas the Marxist Social Democrats, rejecting terror without a shadow of ethical condemnation, preached the class dictatorship of the proletariat as the final stage of the overturn of capitalism and bourgeois democracy. However, the basic difference between the Russians and their western brethren in faith, the German Social Democrats, consisted in the fact that the latter enjoyed incomparably greater political freedom in the federal Reichstag and the more or less democratically elected Landtags of twenty-two monarchies and three republican councils of the city states, Hamburg, Bremen, and Lübeck. Legalized trade unions, social legislation, and a free press were additional means constantly moderating the initial radicalism preached by the founding fathers of German Marxism. Russia did not have such moderating or mollifying factors. Moreover, as has been shown in Chapter XIII, the Marxists regarded the United States as a country of triumphant capitalism which, despite its unheard-of industrialization, showed no signs of social revolution. For this reason, she lost her golden aura in the eyes of Russian Marxists.

Some Russian Populists understood very well that the cruel and arbitrary Russian autocracy was a more sharply defined object stirring foreign hatred and counteraction than the complicated social relations overshadowed by the crucial problem of agrarian reform. With the growth even among the radical Populists of sympathy for constitutional reforms and with increasing Western contacts, some outstanding men such as Sergius Kravtchinski, a former terrorist and fugitive who wrote under the pseudonym Stepniak, did their utmost to attract to the Russian cause English and American radicals, former abolitionists who admired the heroic idealism of the Russian anticzarists. The first American crusader for Russian freedom was George Kennan.

Stepniak in a programmatic article developed an idea which contradicted the old Populist revolutionism by positing the supremacy of the social cause over the political. He clearly proclaimed that political enfranchisement should precede the solution of social problems. This is how this argumentation runs:

But what is this dream of mine?

This dream is to see one day a new crusade started in the West against the great sinner of the East, the Russian Czardom, to see an army spring into existence—not a host, but a well selected army like that of Gideon —composed of the best men of all free nations, making common cause with the Russian patriots, fighting side by side with them . . . until that nightmare of modern times, the Russian autocracy, is conquered and compelled to accept the supremacy of the triumphant democracy. . . . A whole generation—the best that has ever been born to Russia —was sacrificed before we learned the simple truth . . . that the social order cannot be changed before people have the means to change it . . . we accepted for the present the great and modest mission which history has laid upon our generation—the political enfranchisement of the country, the obtaining for Russia of those elementary guarantees of civil freedom and constitutional government which all the nations of Europe already possess.[12-13]

In the eyes of Stepniak, two events were important to the cause of overcoming Russian autocracy. The first was the appearance of the novels of Turgenev, Tolstoy, and Dostoyevski, who familiarized the world with living Russia and prepared the ground for dividing the Russian people from official Russia. The second was the publication of George Kennan's articles in the *Century*, showing the destiny of the victims of Russian tyranny. Furthermore, a paper *Free Russia*, started in England in August 1890, was published simultaneously in London and New York and a Society of American Friends of Russian Freedom was founded in Boston by the initiative of Julia Ward Howe, Thomas Wentworth Higginson, Mark Twain, William Lloyd Garrison, and of course George Kennan.

From its inception *Free Russia* became the organ of the English

[12-13] Sergius Stepniak, "What Americans Can Do for Russia," *North American Review*, Vol. CLIII (1891), pp. 596 ff.

Society of Friends of Russian Freedom. During the four years in which it was published a series of important political and inter-national questions between Russia and the United States was broached.

An editorial in the first number, entitled "What the Russian Opposition Is Striving for," surveyed the different groups from the most moderate liberals to the Social Democrats. Of the "nihilists," it stated that the majority were Populists (or Popular Socialists), which emphatically disproved the general supposition that they had no positive and constructive program: "What these supposed negators of everything actually deny is the Autocracy."

The demand for a National Assembly, first made by Herzen, was adopted by the whole opposition. It came to reality twenty-eight years later in January, 1918—a reality that endured only twenty-four hours.

The new group of American pro-Russian radicals, headed by Kennan, was hostile to terrorism as a method of combating and eventually overwhelming czarism; but it refused to close its eyes to the essential reasons for a terrorism that was self-sacrificing even though despicable. Such an attitude toward the basic Russian love for freedom goes back to the 1840's and the *Liberty Bell*, and to Walt Whitman's enthusiastic letter of 1880 "To the Russian People." [14] Among the friends of Russian freedom there were even a few, mostly poets and writers, who justified regicide in Russia. The *Fortnightly Review* in 1890 published Swinburne's ode "Russia," written after reading the account of Russian prisons, with the lines:

> Love grows hate for love's sake; life takes death for guide.
> Night hath none but one red star—Tyrannicide.

> God or man, be swift; hope sickens with delay:
> Smite, and send him howling down his father's way!

> .   .   .   .

> Down the way of Czars, awhile in vain deferred,
> Bid the Second Alexander light the Third.
> How for shame shall men rebuke them? how may we
> Blame, whose fathers died, and slew, to leave us free?

[14] Reproduced in *Letters Issued by the American-Russian Institute for Cultural Relations with the Soviet Union*, Vol. I, No. 1 (Philadelphia, Jan., 1943).

And in America, after George Kennan's report before the Lowell Institute on the treatment of political offenders in the Kara mines of Siberia, Mark Twain rose from his seat and, in a voice choked with tears, exclaimed: "If such a government cannot be overthrown otherwise than by dynamite, then, thank God for dynamite!" [15]

It was only natural that the radical abolitionist Wendell Phillips should express similar ideas on nihilism some four months after the assassination of Alexander II:

> Then note the scorn and disgust with which we gather up our gar-ments about us and disown the Sam Adams and William Prescott, the George Washington and John Brown of St. Petersburg, the spiritual descendants, the living representatives of those who make our history worth anything in the world annals,—the Nihilists.
>
> Nihilism is the righteous and honorable resistance of a people crushed under an iron rule. Nihilism is evidence of life. . . . Nihilism is the last weapon of victims choked and manacled beyond all other resistance. It is crushed humanity's only means of making the oppressor tremble. God means that unjust power shall be insecure, and every move of the giant, prostrate in chains, whether it be to lift a single dagger, or stir a city's revolt, is a lesson in justice. . . . I honor Nihil-ism, since it redeems human nature from the suspicion of being utterly vile, made up only of heartless oppressors and contented slaves. . . . Chatham rejoiced when our fathers rebelled. For every single reason they alleged, Russia counts a hundred, each one ten times bitterer than any Hancock or Adams could give. . . . But of all the cants that are canted in this canting world, though the cant of piety may be the worst, the cant of Americans bewailing Russian Nihilism is the most dis-gusting.[16]

George Kennan's two-volume *Siberia and the Exile System* has a background which is significant. His first journey to Siberia was in 1865, when the Western Union Telegraph Company sent him with the expedition to survey the extension of the telegraph from America across Alaska and Siberia to Europe. However, the idea of a submarine cable prevailed, and the expedition broke up in 1867, the American experts going home by way of Moscow and

---

[15] *Free Russia*, No. 2 (Sept., 1890), p. 12.

[16] "The Scholar in a Republic," address at the centennial anniversary of the Phi Beta Kappa of Harvard College, June 30, 1881, as printed in Phillips, *Speeches, Lectures, and Letters*, 2nd Ser., Boston, 1891, pp. 356-357.

St. Petersburg, where a splendid reception was given to them by the Russian government. Shortly after the emancipation, and in the era of close Russo-American friendship after the Civil War, Russian official liberalism could express itself more or less honestly in speeches and toasts to Americans. Kennan left Russia in a mood of enthusiastic friendship, and after his return to the United States became a journalist, friendly toward Russia and, from time to time, defending its government. He also was on good terms with the Russian Legation. Needless to say, before his second journey to Russia, he was an outspoken adversary of the "nihilists." In the preface to *Siberia and the Exile System* he described his views in 1882 as follows:

I then believed that the Russian Government and the Exile system had been greatly misrepresented by such writers as Stepniak and Prince Kropotkin; that Siberia was not so terrible a country as Americans had always supposed it to be.

Meanwhile, an American commercial agent, William J. Armstrong, returned from Russia, where he had lived in both capitals and in the South and the Crimea. He was well educated, had mixed with the intelligentsia, and was acquainted with the basic political and economic conditions of contemporary Russia. In April, 1884, by invitation of about seventy members of Congress and citizens of Washington, he delivered a lecture on the "nihilists," or revolutionists. It was an indictment of czarism in general and Alexander III in particular and at the same time an emotional but intelligent defense of the nihilists. The term "nihilism" was traced to the novelist Ivan Turgenev who in *Fathers and Sons* had applied it to a fundamentally socialist and radical group that advocated the abolition of family and property. It had been seized upon as a convenient epithet for all opposition whatsoever to the Czar. "This misconception, that the Nihilists themselves have chosen their own name as expressive of their destructive attitude toward society, is the basis and key-note of the whole misunderstanding, concerning them, in England and the United States." [17]

Armstrong showed that any prospect of peaceable reforms was

[17] E. E. Lazarev, "George Kennan" in *Volya Rossii*, No. 8-9 (Prague, 1923), pp. 36-50. William J. Armstrong, *Siberia and the Nihilists*, 1890, pp. 25, 35.

excluded by the czarist regime. He quoted the well known decision of the Kharkov zemstvo (1879) as a vain attempt to apply reform in czarist Russia, and denied the right to use the term "assassination" for the murder of the Czar:

> I have to state that that which is termed assassination at the hands of the Nihilists is, in no correct sense of the word, that which it is called. An assassin is one who without warning strikes stealthily in the dark, with the expectation of preserving his own life. The Russian Nihilists have a thousand times given the Czar and his officials warnings of their purposes and the cause for which they act.[18]

He placed the nihilist on a par with the farmers of Lexington and Concord, who hid behind hedges and stone walls and shot down the redcoats that marched to enslave them. As these patriots had not been described in American schoolbooks as "assassins," there was no reason to apply the term to Russian nihilists.

A sharp exchange of opinion between Armstrong and Kennan followed the lecture. For instance, Armstrong insisted upon an exaggerated number of 150,000 exiles sent to Siberia in the last year of the reign of Alexander II, while Kennan, using Russian statistics, admitted only 20,000.[19] But Armstrong was essentially right in his appreciation of czarist Russia, while Kennan was wrong. Kennan himself was convinced of this in 1885, when he went with George A. Frost on an expedition to Siberia for the *Century Magazine*. There is no need to describe here his substantial work *Siberia and the Exile System*, which makes a detailed and meticulous presentation of the wicked Russian exile system, the jails, the regime in Siberia for the political offenders—both those who went through a normal court trial and those who had to suffer administrative punishment.

George Kennan became unexpectedly a non-official American ambassador to the subversive élite, who fought czarism under the most terrible conditions. Known before his second trip as a friend of official Russia, he received all the necessary introductions and recommendations to the central and local officials. After he had dived into the ocean of suffering to the east of the Urals and of Lake Baikal it became impossible for Russian diplomatic agents

---

[18] Armstrong, *op. cit.*, p. 79.   [19] *Ibid.*, p. 99.

and the government press to deny the exhaustive testimony he presented.

Traveling through Siberia, Kennan met more than five hundred revolutionaries, among them the most interesting and often highly intellectual leaders of the Russian resistance movement, such as Vladimir Korolenko the novelist, who was exiled first "by mistake" and later because of his refusal to take the oath of allegiance to Alexander III, and Prince Alexander Kropotkin, brother of the famous anarchist writer and himself a mathematician and astronomer. Most picturesque is his sketch of the "Grandmother of the Russian Revolution," Catherine Breshkovsky, a highly educated and musical aristocrat who commanded French, English, and German in addition to her native tongue. One of the most admired founders of the Russian Social Revolutionary party, she had twice served out penal terms at the mines of Kara, in a God-forsaken part of Siberia, and was therefore a good source of information for Kennan. He wrote of her:

The unshaken courage with which this unfortunate woman contemplated her dreary future, and the faith that she manifested in the ultimate triumph of liberty in her native country, were as touching as they were heroic. Almost the last words that she said to me were: "Mr. Kennan, we may die in exile, and our children may die in exile, and our children's children may die in exile, but something will come of it at last." . . . But I cannot recall her last words to me without feeling conscious that all my standards of courage, of fortitude, and of heroic self-sacrifice have been raised for all time, and raised by the hand of a woman. Interviews with such political exiles—and I met many in the Trans-Baikal—were to me a more bracing tonic than medicine.[20]

Kennan described three groups of political exiles: the liberals, the revolutionists, and the terrorists. In glowing terms he depicted the liberals around the *Russkiya Viedomosti* (Russian Gazette), ending:

Most of the Russian terrorists were nothing more, at first, than moderate liberals or, at worst, peaceful socialistic propagandists; and they were gradually transformed into revolutionists and then into terrorists by injustice, cruelty, illegality and contemptuous disregard by the government of all their rights and feelings. I have not a word to

[20] Kennan, *Siberia and the Exile System*, Vol. II, pp. 54, 119-122.

say in defense of their crimes. I do not believe in such methods of warfare as assassination . . . but I can fully understand, nevertheless, how an essentially good and noble natured man may become a terrorist when, as in Russia, he is subjected to absolutely intolerable outrages and indignities and has no peaceful or legal means of redress.[21]

Among the Russian revolutionists, Kennan wrote,

are some of the best, bravest, and most generous types of manhood and womanhood that I have ever known. I am linked to them only by the ties of sympathy, humanity, or friendship, but I wish that I were bound to them by the tie of kindred blood. I should be proud of them if they were my brothers and sisters, and so long as any of them live they may count upon me for any service that a brother can render.[22]

Kennan had already become converted in Siberia to wholehearted friendship toward revolutionary anticzarism, but this found its most conspicuous expression only with the publication of his book. In many things, but particularly in his appreciation of the nihilists, he adopted the views of his former opponent, Armstrong. Many years after meeting George Kennan in Siberia, E. E. Lazarev described the importance of his journey to the revolutionaries on the spot and to the American public opinion:

After their return from the Kara and other jails, Kennan and Frost stayed with us in Chita two weeks. They remained with us to finish their political education . . . and in order to send from there with all necessary caution their numerous treasures of printed and written material, of documents, memoranda, and the like, which we and our friends had collected and prepared particularly for the American travelers, including the entire history of revolutionary and social movements of Russia in the 1870's and 1880's.

Kennan told in Chita, wrote Lazarev, in detail with what feelings and intentions he had arrived in Russia to study the Siberian exile.

Bidding us farewell, Kennan, with tears in his eyes, solemnly swore that from now on he would dedicate all his life to expiation of his involuntary sin; namely, the wrong which he had inflicted upon the Russian democracy by defending the Russian government and casting a shadow upon the nobleness of the Russian "patriots" as he called them.[23]

[21] *Ibid.*, p. 455.　　[22] *Ibid.*, p. 451.
[23] *Volya Rossii*, No. 11 (June 15, 1923), pp. 32, 34.

Kennan's observations, as published in the *Century Magazine* after his return to the United States, brought a gale of bitter indignation from the Russian government. It could not contradict his revelations, because his journey had been made with the encouragement and help of the central and local authorities; and, besides, all the revelations were thoroughly confirmed by incontestable witnesses and documents. Nevertheless, Russian diplomats in the United States, as we shall see, undertook to invalidate his statements and to weaken the bad impression created in the United States and in the whole Western world.

Moreover, Kennan undertook a series of lectures, touring all the significant cities of the United States, inciting indignation against Russian despotism and the persecution of the political opposition. Many American intellectuals, particularly among the "social workers," became ardent adherents of his. This anticzarist movement in America, led by George Kennan, coincided with a certain radicalization in America and with the projected conclusion of the treaty of extradition.

In Siberia itself, among the exiled and jailed political offenders, the American Kennan became most popular. When the persecutions became more severe, a group of them decided to appeal to their fellows to give up the idea of passive resistance by suicide and to cooperate in organizing illegal escape to America, in order to establish direct contact with Kennan, to strengthen world public opinion against official Russia, and to prevent the signing of the extradition treaty with the Russian autocracy, as a blow to the Russian liberation movement inconsistent with the character of the American republic.[24]

In America, Kennan had to lead a very difficult fight. Here, the Haymarket Riot in Chicago had caused a blaze of hatred against anarchists and socialists, often of foreign extraction, who in the heat of the day were not clearly differentiated, and it was not easy to persuade audiences to a cool reevaluation of the Russian revolutionaries known under the dangerous name of nihilists. Kennan fought most vehemently against any identification of Russian revo-

[24] E. E. Lazarev, "George Kennan," in *Volya Rossii*, No. 13 (1923), p. 9. Lazarev himself came to the United States in 1891 and stayed three years, meeting Kennan in Milwaukee.

lutionists with anarchism.[25] The very assassination of Alexander II was also used as an argument against the Russian opposition movement; and, as is often the case in a mass evaluation of different opinions or movements, an oversimplification was inevitable. A part of the American public defended the czarist government attacked by anarchists, socialists, and nihilists; another part was eager to defend the Russian liberals and revolutionaries.

In this atmosphere the conclusion of the extradition treaty between the United States and Russia was eagerly requested even by such outstanding legal thinkers as John Bassett Moore. The six long years from the signing of the treaty in March, 1887, to the exchange of ratifications in 1893 were filled with struggle in which the President, the Congress, and American public opinion were directly or indirectly involved. There was a tremendous agitation in both camps over the forthcoming treaty and its final ratification. The sympathizers with the Russian liberation movement had formed a Society for the Abrogation of the Russian Extradition Treaty; the review *Free Russia* became its organ.[26] The champions of the society were Stepniak (Kravtchinski) and George Kennan. Stepniak even wrote an open letter to the President against the treaty.

The society published a sharp protest against the forthcoming convention. Its chief objection was that the treaty would practically, if not explicitly, annihilate the right of asylum political offenders had hitherto enjoyed in the United States, and would therefore compromise the moral attitude of the American people. While utterly opposed to assassination as a revolutionary measure, it strenuously objected to a treaty which would lay down, in advance of the decision of a court of the United States, the principle that an attempt to kill the Czar or a member of his family was of necessity a nonpolitical and therefore extraditable crime. It also considered that to make "accessoryship" in such an offense extraditable would dangerously widen its scope. The society found both legal and ethical warrant for opposition to the compact in the fact that the systems of jurisprudence which this attempted to harmonize were irreconcilably opposed to each other: For political offenses, trial by jury did not exist in Russia.

[25] *Free Russia*, Vol. IV, No. 7 (Feb., 1894).
[26] *Free Russia*, Vol. IV, No. 2 (Sept., 1893).

The protest ended in an appeal to all who read it "to join with us in opposing the compact and demanding its prompt abrogation." It was issued in Boston, June 12, 1893, and signed by Julia Ward Howe, Edwin D. Mead, Lillie B. Chace Wyman, Francis J. Garrison, Edmund Noble, Arthur Hobart, and Pitt Dillingham.[27]

John Bassett Moore, advocating ratification of the treaty in a magazine article, did not limit himself to arguments based on modern international law. He tried to consider the arguments of the opponents to the treaty as unbased apprehensions or imaginary evils. He denied the validity of the reference to the fact that the United States has negotiated extradition treaties only with constitutional governments or countries whose judicial systems were similar to our own. He found that judicial proceedings of Russia could not be regarded as barbarous. Against the considerations of Stepniak and other adversaries of czarist Russia, he argued that Russia could not carry out false requisitions on the basis of the treaty because the accused was permitted to make his own statement and was entitled to counsel, and for the correction of any errors of the examining magistrate resort might be had to a higher court, even to the Supreme Court of the United States.

But Moore did not limit himself to purely legal considerations. He showed aversion from the Russian radicals and terrorists and lauded the moderate liberals, who "instead of trying to assassinate the Emperor addressed to him a memorial." To him the Emperor was a human ruler who had granted a constitutional form of government; the next day, before the proclamation had been made public, he was assassinated. Of the "nihilists" Moore wrote: "The worst enemies of freedom are those who by their conduct justify or excuse restrictions on liberty. . . . Any government will be despotic when assailed by assassins. The dagger and the bomb are the international arguments of anarchy." [28]

Moore's position was attacked by the American radicals, particularly in *Free Russia*; but this whole polemic will not be described here. It must, however, be said that Kennan towered high over all

[27] *Ibid.*, June, 1893.
[28] John Bassett Moore, "The Russian Extradition Treaty," *Forum*, July, 1893 (reprinted in his *Collected Papers*, 7 vols., New Haven, 1945, Vol. I, pp. 256-273).

other American friends of liberal Russia. He became an indefatigable fighter, giving all his time to the anticzarist cause. He became so well versed in Russian issues that his writings were read even by Russians as if they had been written by a well informed compatriot.

Kennan's basic work and all his important articles in the *Century* were translated into Russian, printed in London, Berlin, and Geneva, and clandestinely imported to Russia, where they were read with admiration. The discovery of little illegal pamphlets of Kennan printed in the 1890's and the early 1900's was a sufficient reason for arrest of the possessor. The publication of *Siberia and the Exile System* became a political event of first importance for official Russia. The fact that it was translated and smuggled into Russia was only an additional incitation to the government to react. Official Russia undertook a wide publication of articles in English for export and in Russian for home consumption. The line of defense was built up not only against particular attacks of American and other Western liberals, but also in justification of autocracy as a political system. This last feature was new, in the reign of Alexander III. The earlier defenders of Russia tried always to emphasize the liberal concessions or isolated acts carried out by the Czar, the similarities between Lincoln and Alexander II, etc. Now the official defense went further. In this connection, most noteworthy was a magazine article by the secretary of the Russian Legation in Washington who took as his starting point the proud assertion:

Autocracy is as natural and satisfactory to Russia as is the republican form of government to the United States; and that our Government is not felt by the masses of the people to be a despotism is evident from the facts that they submit cheerfully to be ruled by it and that they prosper under it.

Going beyond an abstract defense of autocracy, Secretary Botkine justified the main lines of its foreign and home policy. He insisted upon the natural and nonacquisitive "bridge of sentiment" between Russia and America which foaming waves of anti-Russian public opinion threatened to damage. The internal administration was, he said, paternal and benevolent to the population. Kennan's descriptions of the persecution of political exiles in Siberia were fallacious. As witnesses against Kennan, "to whom our government hospitably opened the darkest corners where it must keep the evil and pernicious of its subjects," he brought forward the Englishman Julius M. Price and some unnamed members of the Fourth International Prison Congress at St. Petersburg, all of whom had "repeatedly expressed their astonishment at the extremely humane treatment of convicts." He tried also to whitewash the persecution of Jews and many religious Christian sects, hailing the toleration on the part of the Orthodox Church.[29]

Kennan answered Botkine's article with the pamphlet *A Voice for the Russian People* which was translated and smuggled into Russia.[30] His whole argument was based on a thorough knowledge of Russian political, economic, and even legal literature. He quoted articles of Russian criminologists such as N. Sergeyevski and I. Foinitski and statisticians in special legal and economic reviews, the daily press and books; he went into the legal analysis of the old Russian Penal Code and denied on this basis any possibility for freedom of religion or toleration. Here he attacked not only the secular regime, but also the entrenched Orthodox Church which supported the criminal code rules of 1845, according to which conversion of an Orthodox believer to another Christian or non-Christian confession was punishable with loss of citizenship and other rights or with exile or hard labor. Kennan demolished Botkine's "bridge of sentiment" by saying: "If we will investigate carefully the foundations of the sympathies of the Russian despotic government to the free United States, we will discover that this friendliness is not based on the similarity of institutions, not on mutual esteem or liking, but on the common hostility to Great Britain."

According to Kennan a spiritual bridge between the transatlantic Republic and the northern Empire could not be built upon the state power or the throne of the Czar. Russia would not remain forever a despotism. Sooner or later the privileges of the autocrat would yield to the power of the people. When this time came, American liberals would at least be able to say to the free citizens of Russia that they had not extended their moral support to the persecutors. "As to myself, all my sympathies are with the Russia

[29] Pierre Botkine, "A Voice for Russia," *Century*, new ser., Vol. XXIII, pp. 611-615 (Feb., 1893).
[30] *Golos za russkii narod*, Geneva, 1896.

of the people and not of the Czar, with the Russia of the zemstvos, and not with the Russia of the secret police, with the Russia of the future and not with that of the past." [31]

Another illegal pamphlet of Kennan which was published in Geneva and ran into two editions was *The Last Declarations of the Russian Liberals*. This discussed in detail the tactics of the liberals and Populists and asked for the immediate establishment of a constitution based upon a legislative representation as well as for social reforms to elevate the standards of living, and particularly agriculture.

It is important to know how Kennan's libertarian role was evaluated *after* the outbreak of the Russian revolution of autumn, 1905, and the following appreciation is significant:

The historian of the revolutionary movement in Russia will remember with thankfulness the name of George Kennan, whose brilliant and truthful book made a formidable impression on the entire civilized world in the early 1890's. It appeared in the era of our severest governmental reaction, when, as it seemed then, the Russian revolution and Russian opposition had disappeared completely, and were crushed for good. . . . From this book it became clear that in a country where conditions prevailed such as those described by Kennan, where genuine heroes and fighters for freedom lived, worked, and suffered, the spirit of freedom could not be annihilated. The official czarist lie about the general well-being in Russia received the first crushing blow, while subsequent events were to prepare a new era of a revolutionary renaissance.[32]

Kennan could have boasted that he was recognized by the czarist government as an undesirable, revolutionary-minded foreigner. On July 24, 1901, three weeks after his arrival, he was officially expelled by the authorities. And, no doubt, at the beginning of this century he deserved to be regarded as an active and open enemy of Russian autocracy. The *Outlook* noted his expulsion as follows:

Mr. George Kennan, who was recently requested to leave Russia . . . because his book on *Siberia and the Exile System* and other writings about Russia do not meet the approval of that government, last week reached this country. Mr. Kennan appears in no way disturbed by the action of the Russian police but is naturally sorry to be deprived of

[31] *Ibid.*, pp. 34-35.   [32] Cf. *Byloye*, No. 1, 1906.

expected opportunities to study the present condition of affairs in Russia, and particularly disappointed in not being able to visit Tolstoy.[33]

Kennan characterized with bitterness the anti-Finnish policies of the government and its hostility to Tolstoy and his followers. He also noted that he had been civilly treated by the administration but had taken no steps to protest his expulsion; nor had he invoked diplomatic aid from the United States.

Kennan's links with the Russian revolutionary movement were not loosened; on the contrary he made the Russian struggle for freedom a universal cause. The Russo-Japanese War was for him only a further stimulus to attack the czarist fortress. In the summer of 1904 he visited Japan, the young Asiatic adversary of the old Russian Empire. A decision ripened in his mind to use the concentration of Russian officers, soldiers, and sailors in the prison camps of Japan as a special opportunity to mobilize their minds against tyranny at home. He himself described it thus:

The idea then occurred to me that the concentration in Japan of large numbers of book-hungry soldiers would afford an excellent opportunity for a campaign of education and enlightenment in the Russian army. These men, at home, had never had a chance to read liberal literature, on account of the strict civil and military censorship. . . . To enlighten them, it seemed to me, was a moral duty, because, if the army could be won over to the liberal cause, there might be a chance of success for the Russian people in their struggle for liberal reforms.

He exerted all his energy to get cooperation from the Japanese military authorities; he visited Minister of War Terauchi and finally was allowed to distribute literature, books, and journals among Russian prisoners of war. The American Friends of Russian Freedom sent Dr. Nicholas Russell to help him in distributing the literature he requested. Russell had the assistance of a few political revolutionists condemned to confinement on Sakhalin, and the political education was well organized; even a weekly magazine, *Russia and Japan,* was circulated among the prisoners. Kennan concluded:

Of the seventy thousand prisoners in Japan at least fifty thousand went back to Russia with new ideas of government and a clearer under-

[33] *Outlook,* Vol. LXVIII, p. 987 (Aug. 31, 1901).

standing of the causes of the war. All of them had become liberals and three fourths of them revolutionists.[34]

Kennan's alertness on Russia was intensified during the Portsmouth peacemaking and after. He hailed the Russian democratic revolution, and its defeat in November, 1917, was a blow to him. And it must be said that he was eager to help the democratic opposition against Bolshevism from the first months of its rise to power. In the four boxes of correspondence and documents in the Kennan collection of the New York Public Library, among scores of letters reaching back to 1886, are letters of old Russian pre-Soviet revolutionaries and liberals between December, 1917, and 1919 urging the United States to stand by democratic Russia and to send American military support.

In August, 1923, Kennan made out a sharp criticism of the second Soviet constitution, which he regarded as only a camouflage for the suppression of the basic freedoms and the lack of free elections. He began with the following sentences:

On July 4, 1923, the anniversary of American independence, the executive committees of the Soviet government in Russia adopted a "constitution" which is ostensibly modeled on that of the United States. It provides for . . . the creation of a federal government, that would seem on its face to be as free, liberal and modern as ours. But let no one be deceived. The Russian leopard has not changed its spots.[35]

It was a strange career for a boy from a little Ohio town. Coming to Siberia at twenty as an explorer and engineer interested in mammoths and tent life, he wondered at the Russians from Europe who were scattered among the natives, and at the mistreatment he sometimes saw them receive from officials and guards. Learning Russian, he soon came to have a magnetic attraction for the exiles, who would express to him their secret thoughts, confident that these would remain concealed from the police because of his sympathy. Through Kennan isolated friends could establish contact. Sincere, simple, ardent, and emotional letters beginning with the intimate "Dear Yegor Ivanovitch" reached him from all parts of Siberia. He

[34] "How Russian Soldiers Were Enlightened in Japan," *Outlook*, Mar. 17, 1915, pp. 622 ff., 626.
[35] *National Republican*, Aug. 11, 1923.

actually became a liaison between far dispersed political prisoners in exile, and often would defend them as an unpaid attorney before the highest dignitaries of Siberia. From sympathy with the suffering victims of a cruel autocracy, this natural conservative was involved in revolutionary activities, and became a devoted friend of subversive writers, thinkers, and leaders.

To his last days—he died at seventy-nine in 1924—Kennan never lost his interest in Russia, and continued his warm support of her democratic movement.

XV The Russo-Japanese War
and Russo-American Relations

The overwhelming majority of the Russian nation does not ascribe to the clash in the Far East the importance attributed to it by Europe and America.—*Russkiya Viedomosti*, Moscow, July 22 (August 4), 1905

AT THE BEGINNING OF THE TWENTIETH CENTURY, TWO BASIC FACtors assumed major importance in the life of the Russian Empire. The first, a domestic development connected only remotely with the United States, was the growing tension between the autocratic power of the Emperor on the one hand, supported by hopeless reactionaries, and the two great camps of moderate constitutionalism as well as the specter of Populist non-Marxist agrarian socialists and Marxist Social Democrats on the other. The second factor, the Far Eastern policy of the Russian Empire, was of much greater concern to the United States which was also interested in China, Korea, and Japan. This community of interests found diplomatic expression in the signing of the peace treaty between Russia and Japan at Portsmouth, New Hampshire, with American help.

In the early 1900's, a serious discrepancy appeared between Russia's internal and foreign policies. The aristocracy, now considerably weakened by the emancipation of the serfs, and the powerful bureaucracy, an offshoot and semicompetitor of the landed gentry, still ruled. Both these classes tried to sponsor and control the interests of young Russian industrialism, finance, and trade. And although the diplomatic field was closed to the sons of the Russian upper bourgeoisie, the old guard of the Russian Imperial Service acted as if they were empowered or delegated by the (constitutionally) absent middle class. In diplomatic process and bellicose readiness there was no external difference between Russia and the West, at least none sufficient to be perceived in Peking, Seoul, or Tokyo. As for the Russian bourgeoisie, its "natural" development still was hampered; and its financial, industrial, and commercial interests were not represented in the formation of a new foreign policy. It existed under the earlier conditions of the nineteenth century and remained of necessity under the influence of the traditional diplomacy, aristocratically formulated and monarchically led. Only slowly and by degrees, through the reforming character of a growing constitutionalism, could the Russian middle class hope for entrance into diplomacy and the discussion of foreign policy.

What occurred before our eyes in Russia from the time of the Boxer Rebellion to the conclusion of the Russo-Japanese War was the sociological substitution for a regular bourgeoisie of a group of adventurers and gamblers from aristocratic and bureaucratic circles, supported by the courtiers and occasionally—unfortunately, in some decisive moments—by the Emperor himself. One has only to study the era immediately preceding the Russo-Japanese War—the concessions of the Yalu River in Korea, the squabble over the Chinese Eastern Railway, such parasitical figures as Bezobrazov and Abaza who were protected by Nicholas II and some grand dukes to the detriment of the national interest—to discover a coterie which even Count Witte called an "unofficial force" striving under the cloak of an Eastern Asiatic Industrial Corporation toward a political scheme which dared to insist upon the support of the army.[1] The helpless Nicholas II, particularly weak and indecisive in Far Eastern affairs, was an active though unintelligent guiding spirit. Secretly from his Ministers of War, Finance, and Foreign Affairs, he created in July, 1903, a new Viceroy in the Far East: Admiral Alexeyev, an inept man incapable of civil, military, or naval administration. In January, 1904, this very man was appointed commander-in-chief of the Far Eastern forces. The appointment, to such a post, of a man who had never belonged to the army was so absurd as to be incredible;[2] it nevertheless took place and was one of the factors in the defeat of Russian armies in the Far East.

Ridiculous as these activities aiming at a "sure" victory over Japan were, they continued nevertheless. Because Russia at that moment was suppressing a rapidly growing dissident trend danger-

---

[1] S. J., Count Witte, *Memoirs*, New York, 1921, pp. 116-119. Witte admits that he was instructed by the Czar to place 2,000,000 rubles at Bezobrazov's secret disposal.

[2] *Ibid.*, p. 127.

ously near to a revolution, war in the Far East was regarded as a very convenient mustard plaster that could transfer international deterioration to a nice little colonial campaign and thereby stimulate a new patriotism in the discontented population. Such considerations induced Home Minister Plehve to join Bezobrazov and the whole adventurous Russian coterie seeking easy profit in China, Korea, and Japan.

The results of the unfortunate war of the Russian colossus with Japan are well known; instead of acting as a counterirritant, the war directly stimulated the first Russian revolution, of October, 1905. The devastating destruction by the Japanese of Admiral Rozhdestvenski's fleet at Tsushima in the spring of 1905 gave the signal for a direct attack upon the autocratic régime. The explosion of popular indignation turned into a mass movement which demanded an early convocation of elected representatives and the creation of a full-fledged legislative body instead of the projected advisory council, the so-called Bulygin Duma of July 6, 1905. Zemstvo liberals, in a deputation to the Czar in May, 1905, demanded constitutional guarantees of freedom and the immediate meeting of a state parliament to be elected by the whole population. All the defeats of the army and navy in the disastrous war against Japan were ascribed to the hated autocratic régime and its inferior leaders and commanders; indeed, it was demanded that the very declaration of peace or the continuation of war be decided by the House of People's Representatives.[3]

Despite the completely unsuccessful war, despite an unbroken chain of retreats and naval defeats, the principal culprits were as helpless in the conclusion of the war as they were in its guidance. Until July, 1905, when the peace became a bitter necessity and America appeared on the horizon as a possible peacemaker and redeemer, Generals Kuropatkin and Linevitch continued to bombard St. Petersburg with telegrams imploring continuation of the war for six additional months, during which they dared to promise the final rout of the Japanese.

It is most significant that, although the idealization of America had been reduced by Marxist skepticism and reactionary monarch-

[3] I. P. Bielokonski, *Zemskoye dvizheniye* (The Zemstvo Movement), Moscow, 1910, pp. 167-168.

ism, there still was a difference between the entrepreneur jingoism and expansionism of the Russian upper-class landlords around the throne, on the one hand, and the normal capitalists striving toward industrial hegemony on the other. The former group was described not only among radical Marxists, but also among moderate liberals, as the typical manorial greed of irresponsible landlords and bureaucrats for any land or country which was or seemed to be insufficiently defended, whether in Asia Minor, Afghanistan, Chinese Turkestan, Korea, Port Arthur, or the Sea of Japan.[4] Everywhere intrigues were plotted, unnecessary concessions, semifictitious expansion companies demanding artificial industrialization were established, and tremendous amounts lavishly spent or stolen. Of an entirely different character was the imperialism of the United States. There, territorial conquest was not an aim in itself, but only a means toward the opening of markets and the basis for the establishment of industrial hegemony. Therefore, Carnegie's suggestion that the United States replace the previous hegemony of Great Britain was taken into consideration.[5]

This general conception of Pavlovitch and the Russian Marxists was only partially true. The American bourgeoisie, for instance in the Spanish-American War, was by no means an initiator of expansion. Moreover, American business had been either opposed or indifferent to expansionism since 1890. But Professor Pratt has shown that when the war began, and particularly after the fall of Manila, a large section of American business became favorable to the absorption of the Philippines. This does not mean that commercial opposition ended. There were senators who from the trade viewpoint alone rejected the possession of the islands, arguing that "nine tenths of American exports went to Western Europe," and that markets for the surplus products must be sought "among people who could consume them" and not among the poor Filipinos.[6]

The weakness and inefficiency of Russia as a competitor of America can be shown by statistical data: The export of Russian kerosene

---

[4] See M. Pavlovitch, in *Sovremennik* (Contemporary), Mar., 1912, pp. 250 ff.; M. Kovalevski, "Portsmouth" in *Viestnik Yevropy* (European Herald), Vol. CCLI (1908), pp. 450 ff.

[5] Pavlovitch, *op. cit.*, pp. 251-252.

[6] Julius W. Pratt, *Expansionists of 1898*, Baltimore, 1936, pp. 233, 350-351.

into China, which amounted to 25,000,000 gallons in 1899, went down to 3,000,000 in 1908—a decrease of 88 per cent in one decade. On the other hand, the export of American kerosene to China rose from 42,000,000 gallons in 1899 to 122,000,000 in 1908—an increase of 195 per cent. The same situation existed in the Chinese tobacco market. Thus, the Russian government with all its local and foreign agents failed in defending the real interests of Russian industry in the markets of the Far East.

With a degree of understanding, if not sympathy, Russian liberal writers have revealed the absurdness of the czarist foreign policy to establish dominion over the western shore of the Pacific, thereby irritating the United States.

Of all Russia's wars since Napoleon, the Russo-Japanese War was least popular. It is well known that almost the entire political opposition—not merely the socialist faction—was against the war from its inception and regarded the defeat of Russia as a defeat of the czarist régime. Even the moderate liberals and constitutionalists, throughout the war as well as during the prewar stages, understood the inefficiency of the Russian staff, the ineptitude of the commanding officers, and their desperate inadequacy before the Japanese armies. The poor supply of arms, the unreliable transportation and communication systems, the misuses and frauds of the army contractors were the main topics of the daily press. The defeat itself was used by the opposition as the best proof of the absurdity and backwardness of the czarist régime. This defeat was not the cause of national disgrace or loss of morale; on the contrary, it became the opposition's favorite weapon to prove that the more the Russian army was used as a police force against the liberty-loving population, the less effective it was in the national defense. Taken historically, such a reaction among the people can be considered as a delayed payment to the old régime.

Even the losses of territory that resulted from the decisive Russian defeats did not deter the opposition to any marked degree. The anticzarist feeling was so entrenched and prevalent that sorrow over such losses was regarded as a symptom of half-heartedness in the fight against the autocracy. The slogan "Down with the Autocracy" was incommensurably more important than the whole issue of the war or the territorial losses in the Far East.

Only the reactionary and official press tried to play on the grievances of the patriots. Occasionally the revolutionary movement
was accused of being financed by "Japanese millions"; but little
credence was granted this claim.

Men like P. N. Miliukov, the leader of the Constitutional Democrats, were open defeatists. Even such a moderate as Prince Ukhtom-
skii, director of the Russo-Chinese Bank, admitted in an interview
with a correspondent of the *Frankfurter Zeitung*: "The Russian
public is very apathetic to the war, which is natural, because there
cannot be any war less popular than the present one. We were
entangled in the whole East Asian adventure against the will of the
nation." [7]

As a kind of political demonstration, the Socialist International
Congress of August, 1904, convened in Amsterdam,[8] where two
leaders from the warring countries—George Plekhanov, representing the Russian-Social Democrats, and Sen Katayama, at the head
of the Japanese delegation—demonstrated their spiritual brotherhood before the whole congress by embracing each other.

In the light of these events the pro-Japanese sympathies of the
Americans, strengthened by a severely critical attitude toward the
Russian autocracy, could not become an apple of discord between
Russian and American liberals. On the contrary, the hostile American attitude toward official Russia, which diminished noticeably
with the signing of the Portsmouth treaty, was fully comprehensible
to the Russian pro-American factions.

For an American newspaper, the New York *World* made a very
good guess about Russian domestic policy just before the Portsmouth treaty:

The truest hearts, the ablest minds in the beaten nation itself, if
they could make themselves heard from out the darkness and the silence
of the living tomb which tyranny has built around them, would [say]
. . . "The greater the humiliation of Russian autocracy . . . the nearer

[7] Quoted in the Russian underground newspaper, *Revolutsionnaya Rossiya*,
Feb. 15, 1904, p. 13.

[8] *Sixième Congrès Socialiste International, tenu à Amsterdam du 14 en 20
août, 1904*, Brussels, 1904, pp. 20-22. "La fraternisation des délégués russes et
japonais' est un démenti à la guerre. Les ouvriers russes n'ont pas démérité des
ouvriers japonais."

chance will grow of relief and reform for the Russian people." . . . A "generous peace" which should leave Russian militarism strong for repression would be . . . making war upon human liberty.[9]

One of the most admirable of the Russian conservatives was Prince Ukhtomsky, who has already been mentioned. This expert on Chinese culture and policies and former diplomat tried throughout the war to overcome American pro-Japanese sympathy and consequent coolness toward Russia. He wrote in *Harper's Weekly*:

> Our people cannot understand the reported pro-Japanese sympathy of Americans. In the first place, it seems incredible that the Japanese attack upon the Russian empire should be considered as something heroic. The comparison has been made . . . of the collision of a brutal giant with a comparatively weak adversary. In fact, we see the contrary. . . .
> Every other civilized nation, in Russia's stead, and in our position, would long have ripped up China with her gigantic natural wealth, Manchuria, abounding in gold, and Korea, and would have conquered Japan regardless of politics *manu militari.* . . . The West will never derive anything from an eventual victory of Japan. The so-called "open door" under Japanese management would very quickly change into a strongly fenced wall, such as the Russians never intended.
> Russia is, so to speak, the *pendant* of America in the old world. . . . When the Americans are discussing the dark sides of the social life in Russia and criticise sharply, we Russians, who do not close our eyes to many of the cancerous infections of our own country, know better than a Westerner may be able to judge how correctly such a criticism very often sounds. On the other hand, we Europeans might at times point out very strongly negative aspects in the public life of America. . . . But if all of a sudden, without any consideration of the real value of conditions in Eastern Asia, pro-Japanese sympathy inimical to Russia is brought to light, that can only serve to loosen the bond of good relations between the two countries. *Cui prodest?* [10]

This faint cry was muffled by the roaring anger of a mighty though belated national movement against czarism. There was left no place for patriotism and permanent issues of foreign policy, particularly

[9] New York *World*, Aug. 3, 1905.
[10] Prince E. Ukhtomsky, "A Russian View of American Sympathy," *Harper's Weekly*, Vol. XLVIII, p. 826 (May 28, 1904), where the name is spelled Oukhtomsky.

as far as the Far East was concerned. Even moderate liberals were embittered toward the régime which dared to anticipate a possible victory over Japan while indicating every week of this unfortunate war all its unpreparedness and inadequacy. And in so far as the intelligentsia was the most vociferous stratum of the opposition, during the war it clearly indicated itself as unconditionally against this war and all its aims. The war became in the psychology of all levels of the intelligentsia a private colonial expedition of reactionaries against Japan, a country much more advanced than the helpless clay giant of Russian autocracy. There was also in the psychology of the Russian progressives an undeniable reverence for Japan, a country which had shown the whole world the instructive spectacle of an unprecedented leap from total feudalism to profitable modern capitalism. An excellent witness who belonged to the modern socialist faction at the beginning of this century wrote in 1949, "I remember very well the time of the Russo-Japanese War, when almost the entire Russian intelligentsia was defeatist." [11]

Contemporary printed comment in Russia as well as in forbidden foreign revolutionary publications proves that this was the predominant Russian attitude during the summer of 1905.

The most conservative and formally patriotic press was extremely hostile to the United States and to President Theodore Roosevelt, the proposed peacemaker. *Moskovskiya Viedomosti*, on the extreme right, stated on August 26 (Sept. 8), 1905:

Diplomacy has said its word, and the destiny of Russia is sealed on the Far Eastern question. Port Arthur, Dalny, Yinkou, Liaoyang, Mukden are given away to triumphant Japan. Our ships, fortresses, ports, docks, railways—all are theirs.

The whole tone of this editorial gives the impression that Russia herself was not to blame for the defeat.

Novoye Vremya, official organ of the bureaucracy, close to the government but not wholly sympathetic, was just as anti-American although more moderate. On August 4/17, A. Suvorin, the editor, wrote:

11 Yekaterina Kuskova, "Kakaya Tsel?" (Which Aim?), in the New York daily *Novoye Russkoye Slovo* (New Russian Word), Jan. 2, 1949. Cf. D. Dallin, *The Rise of Russia in Asia*, New Haven, 1949, pp. 80-81.

Only the blind and deaf can doubt that America unites with Japan to dominate in Asia. The Japanese islands, together with Formosa and the Philippines, which belong to America, are the bases for the expansion of their domination. Should Russia lose the Far East, she will lose the richest countries for her future. . . . The matter of the protectorate for Korea—one of the most important causes of this war—the Japanese consider as a foregone conclusion; and therefore they are anxious to remain silent about this item in the negotiations of Portsmouth.

On August 18/31, after the agreement at Portsmouth *Novoye Vremya* commented in an editorial:

Tertius Gaudens [the merry outsider]—namely, the recently emerged grand peacemaker Roosevelt—positively swooned with ecstasy and rapture at the news of the termination of war and the treaty of peace.

Suvorin was somewhat less critical in an article in the same issue:

There will not be many among us who will be enthusiastic about Mr. Roosevelt. If Sergius Witte thanked him in warmer terms than Komura, this is only a matter of courtesy. . . . The whole of Europe is for the Japs . . . not excluding France. . . .
I think that two men, Roosevelt and Witte, wrote the last chapter of the recently finished war. Roosevelt wanted peace but insisted upon the reparation because he found it well deserved [by Japan]. Yesterday, an American journalist told me, "Japan will not hold this half of Sakhalin for good; you will get it back."

The infamous Menshikov wrote frankly in that issue:

The first peace treaty we have received in the twentieth century is a diploma of the ineptitude and criminal indolence of those social circles whom our people hoped to see as the guard of our destiny.

On August 20 (September 2), under the heading "Roosevelt in the Role of an Honest Broker," *Novoye Vremya* grudgingly observed:

The intervention of Roosevelt directed toward the decrease of the monetary compensation to Japan led to an almost decisive failure. . . . The payment of 1,200,000,000 yen to Japan has proved to be much too heavy for our budget. Doubtless it was Roosevelt's idea to divide Sakhalin into two parts and to cede to Russia the right to retain the northernmost part for this solid redemption. However, this "happy idea" of his had no success; the Emperor did not find it possible to meet the proposal, which was tantamount to the payment of the national military contribution to Japan. The later events are known. Japan abandoned the demand for payment of a monetary compensation, but in so far as the problem of cutting Sakhalin into two halves had already risen, according to the frontiers of 1875, it became impossible to eliminate this problem entirely. Having conceded on payments, the Japanese cramped down so much the more on territory; and we had to concede on that item.

On August 25 (September 7), it admitted that Count Witte had helped to attract the sympathies of the whole press of the United States to Russia, and an editorial played a more pacific but melancholy theme:

If the political lot is cast, it is the duty of every citizen to bow to the inevitable. Russia has suffered a terrific blow in the Far East. Our political role in Eastern Asia is reduced to virtual non-existence. Our participation in the destiny of the Pacific, the ocean that will henceforth become the scene of world history, is limited by the narrowest confines.

A much more equable and objective tone was that of the entire opposition press. It contained no blustering official patriotism, no beating around the bush, and no helpless attacks on other countries. It also was much more objective, and occasionally even showed gratitude to America and to Roosevelt in particular for the abrupt conclusion of this unhappy and senseless war. The moderate liberal press illustrates the point. The most moderate organ of the opposition, the *St. Petersburgskiya Viedomosti*, remarked on August 19 (September 1):

If we will awake and understand that this year and last year we were beaten not so much by Japan as by our Russian disorderliness, unscrupulousness, nonchalance, and laziness, then the terrific lesson given to us by this war will not pass away traceless and fruitless, but will push us to order and improvement, and will lead us to new and better forms of life. Effervescent America with her hero-president has rendered us a great service. Her merits must be recognized, and it would be a sin to forget them. *Had it not been for the vociferous and outspoken social life of the United States, the plenipotentiaries of both hostile powers would scarcely have been able to come so quickly as was the case to a peaceful compromise.*[12]

In greater detail and with equal recognition of America the moderate liberal review *Viestnik Yevropy* (Herald of Europe) noted:

The Portsmouth peace conference, actually convoked on the insistence of the President of the United States, had only a small chance of success. It would never have led to any positive result had it not been for the energetic interference of Roosevelt. Occasionally, it was ready to dissolve, in view of the obvious inability to come to any agreement. In every case Roosevelt induced both parties to seek a compromise; he himself made different combinations, sent telegrams to the heads of the respective states, and, at the last moment, persuaded the Tokyo government to agree to peace in the form in which it was most feasible. In his personal addresses, arguments, and requests, he did not observe any diplomatic traditions. He directly intervened in the activities of the plenipotentiaries, and if they met with certain difficulties or hindrances, he gave advice and instruction without any inducement. He did not even shrink from writing to monarchs when this was not diplomatically *de rigueur*, and tried to use all means to effect the success of the peace negotiations. If this conference had sat somewhere in Europe . . . it would have ended its existence with the first attempt to discuss the disputable points. . . . This position as an elected president of a great and mighty power helped him to complete things which an autocratic head never could have accomplished, bound as he would have been by the etiquette of a monarchy. An exclusive energy was needed to prevent the conference from collapsing and to support faith in its final success. . . . *Roosevelt can be justly regarded as the main creator of the Russo-Japanese Peace* concluded in Portsmouth.[13]

How far could a liberal newspaper go in criticizing the military and diplomatic measures of the czarist government under the conditions of an unfinished war with a mighty winning enemy? We read in the *Novosti* of July 2/15:

Be it as it may, the bureaucracy, the only support of which against a revolution is the army, obviously cannot risk losing the devotion and the allegiance of the army by dooming it to what it would regard as a

[12] The italics are mine.

[13] *Viestnik Yevropy*, St. Petersburg, Sept., 1905, pp. 365 ff. The italics are mine.

voluntary humiliation. It is even more obvious that the proposal [of peace] made by Roosevelt was accepted mainly in order to crush the rebellious internal movement provoked by the unpopular war. Now the ruling classes became convinced that not the war, but a peace concluded against the will of the army might turn out to be a decisive stimulus to the complete success of the upheaval.[14]

Another more solid and liberal daily, the *Russkiya Viedomosti,* was aware of the pro-Japanese attitude of the United States and was afraid this might hinder peace negotiations in America by Russian diplomats: "The American government cannot help reckoning with the public opinion of the country directed against Russia." [15] This newspaper's correspondent eagerly quoted all the details of the negotiations at Portsmouth but showed small interest in the territorial and financial demands of Japan. Peace remained the center of gravity. In a matter-of-fact editorial of August 18/31, the "professorial paper" noted that peace had been secured since the receipt of the last dispatches. "The whole of Russia will answer with a sigh of relief." It hailed the end of the trials through which the country had passed during eighteen months of the war, the end of bloodshed. With the termination of war, the paper forecast that government and society would concentrate on domestic issues. Even more outspoken was the editorial of the 19th of August (1st of September), which sounds like an indictment of the whole régime:

The past year and a half will be etched in the memory of the Russian people as a period of shameful oppression by the police state [*prikazny stroi*]. For many long years, all that was independent, critical, and enlightened in the nation was oppressed, and there was a kind of artificial selection of fools. A systematic persecution of free thought and free utterance was felt even in military activities, which should have been the subject of specific care.

[14] As quoted in *Russkiya Viedomosti,* July 3/16. By "bureaucracy" is meant government.

[15] *Russkiya Viedomosti,* July 26 (Aug. 8), 1905. The paper could not be sufficiently informed, nor could it foresee the sudden shift in American public opinion on the war after eighteen months of Japanese victories. That certainly must have meant also another American approach to the terms of peace. See Winston B. Thorson, "American Public Opinion and the Portsmouth Conference," *Amer. Hist. Review,* Vol. LIII, pp. 440 ff. (Apr., 1948).

Let us hope that after the heavy blows we have suffered in this recently finished war there may be no question of a return to the past, that the path of repression and pressure which brought us to Mukden, Tsushima, and Portsmouth may be deserted forever, that Russia may enter a new phase of peaceful and free development.

As the reader sees, there were not many considerations of the territorial losses of provinces and their possible return after a war of revenge. Constitutional reform and the overcoming of a social backwardness became the only concern of the whole freedom-loving camp of Russia.

The courageous tone of the press might also be ascribed to the fact that reform was, in a way, officially introduced through the creation of the advisory Bulygin Duma, as a consequence of the August rescript of the Emperor in 1905. One might say that steps in constitutional reform were favored and accelerated by Russia's need to appear at Portsmouth as something else than an autocracy without a parliament, while Japan was a moderate, constitutionally limited monarchy with a national representative assembly. This is even more probable in that the first Russian constitution of April 1, 1906, contained several features resembling the Japanese.

What was true of the liberal press was much more emphatically true of the Populist radical and the Social Democratic (moderate Marxist) press.

The radical *Syn Otechestva* (Son of the Fatherland) commented after the conclusion of peace at Portsmouth:

The more dearly we have paid for the war at Portsmouth, and the more expensive it has become for us, the deeper will our unfortunate and harassed country breathe again because the shadow of a great yearning for a blissful peace has finally been cast over it.

More radical than the conventional press was the foreign Russian press illegally imported into czarist Russia. In the clandestine *Iskra*—central organ of the Social Democratic Labor party, published at Geneva—one finds complete indifference to possible territorial losses and purely military considerations.

On September 1, 1904, *Iskra* had an article by F. Dahn, who wrote, "The Japanese vanquished absolutism not only at Liaoyang but also at St. Petersburg." Thus, the clandestine Social Democratic party started in Russia a campaign of antiwar meetings and resolutions.

Not much different were the sentiments of the illegal radical Populist press. *Revolutsionnaya Rossiya*, the central organ of the Socialist Revolutionaries, was just as hostile as *Iskra* to czarism and the war with Japan; but defeatism seemed to it to be a kind of moral cowardice. On April 1, 1904, it noted:

The lack of faith in revolution and even the fear of it, as well as a slavish psychology in general, force many Russian liberals to place all their hopes in the present régime. . . . Such a psychology is entirely foreign to us revolutionaries and socialists. True, calamities might accelerate the fall of an anachronistic régime; but this only in so far as there are present new progressive forces which have grown inside the country.

As early as February it had proclaimed:

Our internal liberation would have taken place without the additional horrors of war, and that is why we declare war on this senseless, ruinous, and autocratic-capitalistic war. We do it for the sake of human welfare and our socialist ideals.[16]

At the end of the war it observed:

Certainly the Russian people should not regret the loss of the ceded territories. Our people could never have spoken about these regions as their "own" lands save, perhaps, the island Sakhalin. We could have called it "ours" as a man condemned to hanging could call the gallows erected for him "his." This productive island, upon which the Japanese will not hesitate to establish a fruitful civilization, we, "by the grace of God," were stupid enough to turn into a huge and dark jail.[17]

Iskra on May 1, 1905 (No. 99), stated:

Before January 28 [1904], when the war was only a threat for Russia, our party through this organ declared "War to war." "Peace and Freedom" was the slogan of our party from the very outset of the war. . . . Our task is not only to unleash the revolution, but also to prepare the conditions of its victory.

[16] *Revolutsionnaya Rossiya*, Feb. 15, 1904—editorial Fatherland in Peril!
[17] *Ibid.*, Aug. 15, 1905—editorial The External Peace and Domestic War (my italics). Sakhalin was actually made into a Russian "Devil's Island" for highly criminal offenders.

After the defeat of the Russian fleet at Tsushima, it invited the
people to rise against autocracy and compel their rulers to finish the
war under the threat of an inevitable destruction of the whole Russian Manchurian army.[18]

The radical Populist review *Russkoye Bogatstvo* showed no satisfaction over Count Witte's activities at Portsmouth and indicted
him as one of the culprits of the Manchurian aggression against
Japan. The Marxist *Mir Bozhii* quoted the London journal *Nature*
on "Why Japan Is Victorious" with the comment:

> Russia, which is backward in all relations and which is immersed in
> the mud of bureaucracy, has necessarily fallen victim to a progressive
> country which has proved that inertia and ignorance must bow to
> progress and a rational conception of national aims.[19]

The anarchist Prince Kropotkin, in a letter to the Belgian newspaper *Soir*, expressed the novel view:

> The misfortune of the Russian people consists in that in its move-
> ment toward the east it did not meet a civilized nation which would
> live on the Manchurian coast of the Pacific. The ill luck of the Russians
> consisted in the urgency of populating the deserts of Amur and build-
> ing railroads in the wastes of Manchuria. This country will never be-
> come Russian; the Chinese peasant occupied it, and if the United States
> had chosen to take possession of it tomorrow, all, including Russians,
> would gain by it.[20]

This survey of the Russian press of the time necessarily leads to
the conclusion that the estrangement between the people and the
government had reached its peak, and that public opinion, particularly among anticzarists in all their current shades and varieties, was
defeatist. Even in that part of the moderate opposition which ran
close to the official line of the régime, the attitude was one of faint
resentment at the bureaucratic stubbornness of the old apparatus.
There cannot be any doubt that the youthful Lenin accurately

[18] *Iskra*, June 1, 1905. Cf. the anonymous booklet *God voiny* (A Year of
War), Geneva, 1905. It was published by the Russian Social Democratic Workers' party and recommended considering the Russo-Japanese War as a measure
in the fight against autocracy (p. 27).

[19] *Mir Bozhii* (God's World), Sept., 1905.

[20] As quoted in *Revolutsionnaya Rossiya*, Apr. 1, 1904, p. 15.

expressed the common opinion of the opposition after the capture of Port Arthur by the Japanese when he wrote:

It is not the Russian people but the autocracy that has suffered shameful defeat. The Russian people gained by the defeat of the autocracy. The capitulation of Port Arthur is the prologue to the capitulation of czarism.[21]

In later years some moderate liberals who in their youth had been outspokenly defeatist made useful confessions of what they later regarded as a political sin. Most interesting in this connection is a statement about the Russo-Japanese War by Joseph Stalin in an official "Address to the People" in 1945, forty years after the Portsmouth treaty. Stalin, during his youth and early manhood a revolutionary underground worker of the Georgian Social Democracy in the Caucasus, must have been at least as defeatist in 1904–1905 as any Great Russian Social Democrat;[22] and party decisions and resolutions of that time give ample testimony to the gratification with which the radical Marxist opposition received the shameful defeat of the army—a defeat that was considered as a capitulation of the old semifeudal régime. Forty years later, however, when imperial Japan had become an important bourgeois enemy and Stalin had become the Generalissimo of the Soviet armies, he tried to repaint his former attitude, to distort the earlier attitude of the Russian revolutionaries toward the defeat of Russia into a slumbering sorrow, and—as is required by all the best patterns of genuine patriotism—a silent, persistent hope for "revenge" upon the enemy who must be beaten in the future in order to remove the stain:

When Japan began her aggression against our country, as is well known, Russia suffered then and there a defeat caused by Japan—but this defeat of the Russian armies of 1904–1905 left sad memories in the mind of the people. It laid upon our country a black spot. Our people believed and expected that there would come a day when Japan would

[21] Cf. David Shub, *Lenin: A Biography*, New York, 1948, p. 66.
[22] The czarist government was so conscious of the defeatist mood of the Georgians that it repeatedly postponed mobilization of its first drafts there. When the recruiting was finally initiated in Kutais and other towns, the populace demonstrated against it with the slogan "Down with War" on red banners. (See *Revolutsionnaya Rossiya*, Dec. 25, 1904).

be beaten and the spot wiped out. We, the members of the older generation, have nostalgically waited forty years for that day. And now the day has come. Today Japan recognizes herself defeated and has signed an unconditional surrender.[23]

The "old" Generalissimo forgot to mention that this defeat of Japan was not by the military effort of the Soviet Union but by the United States: Russia had been scarcely eight days the declared enemy of Japan. Forty years ago Japan had begun "her aggression against our country"—but only four years ago she had directed her aggression against America, the ally of the Soviets. The label of revenge "Made in U.S.A." escaped the attention of the orator.

A full concealment of old Russian revolutionary defeatism is in Romanov's recent book on the Russo-Japanese War. With a whole chapter on The State of Mind of the Ruling Classes,[24] it carefully avoids describing the frame of mind of the lower and oppressed classes, the peasantry, the poorer urban population, the workers, and the more or less radical intelligentsia. We do not find in Romanov any suggestion of the almost elemental joy over the defeat of the czarist armies and fleets, the sweeping indication at and contempt of the senseless Russo-Japanese War. Only by such a disregard of the frame of mind of the dissatisfied classes, which formed an overwhelming majority of the population, can the legend of war patriotism in 1904 and 1905 be supported. Lenin's collected works, printed in millions of copies, show his extreme defeatism at that time. But only this patriotic background fits the picture of an old Stalin who had "nostalgically waited forty years" for revenge and for the return of Port Arthur and Dalny to the fatherland.

The Soviet government is afraid to show the present young generation that the founding fathers strove during the war against Japan not for the victory of their own country but for its defeat. Thus the Soviet ideology denies its own genuine Russian origin and past.

An American-Chinese commercial treaty was concluded October 8, 1903. Romanov's assertion that this put an end to the monopo-

[23] *Pravda*, Sept. 3, 1945.
[24] B. A. Romanov, *Ocherki diplomaticheskoi istorii russko-yaponskoi voiny, 1895–1907* (Essays on the Diplomatic History of the Russo-Japanese War), Moscow, 1947, pp. 313 ff.

listic mismanagement of Manchuria by old Russia [25] can be doubted. The treaty was made public after long differences between America and Russia not only over the Open Door policy and the Russian evacuation of Manchuria, but over American trade in the territory. The treaty does not even name Manchuria. Its twelfth article mentions the opening of the ports of Mukden and Antung to foreign trade and international residence, which thwarted Russian attempts to close the territory to the world.[26] Strictly these two ports were in the province of Shen-king (Fengtien), whose capital was Mukden. But no doubt after the conclusion of this treaty Russia knew well where the United States stood, and that for it the integrity of China remained a fundamental tenet. The treaty considered China as an independent state enjoying the privileges of a most favored nation. However, its silence on Manchuria, notwithstanding Romanov, was an evasion of the issue as such. Probably this silence should be associated with the disposition of American policy, after 1901, to regard Manchuria as an "irretrievably lost" Chinese issue. Griswold even asserts of the Open Door policy that preceded the treaty: "To all intents and purposes Hay had abandoned the doctrine of the territorial integrity of China, at least to the extent of recognizing Manchuria as beyond the Chinese pale." [27]

The truth obviously lies somewhere between Romanov and Griswold.

Returning to the American scene in 1905, let us conclude with a characterization of President Theodore Roosevelt as he affected the Russian moderate liberals.

Theodore Roosevelt can scarcely be called a modest man; in many cases he was inclined to exaggerate his achievements or to describe his diplomatic measures with a flourish. However, he rather underestimated his role in the mediation that led to the signing of the Portsmouth treaty. One has only to compare the

[25] Romanov, *op. cit.*, p. 305.

[26] *Treaties, Conventions, International Acts, Protocols and Agreements Between the United States of America and Other Powers, 1776–1909*, compiled by W. M. Malloy, Washington, 1910, pp. 261-270. Cf. Samuel F. Bemis, A *Diplomatic History of the United States*, New York, 1936, pp. 488-489.

[27] A. Whitney Griswold, *The Far Eastern Policy of the United States*, New York, 1938, p. 84.

recognition of his merits by Russian publications already quoted with his own account of the reconciliation of the representatives of the two nations at Portsmouth. Not a word is said about his many successful measures to remove stumbling blocks and smooth over difficulties. Although he loyally mentions the help of the American Ambassador to Russia, George von Lengerke Meyer, Roosevelt does not even name Count Witte or Baron Rosen, and makes only a vague allusion to the fact that "the representatives of the Tsar were often at cross purposes with one another." [28]

Although the diplomatic rivalry of Russia and the United States is described in the next chapter, we have here to consider that the preparation and signing of the Portsmouth peace was in itself an important deviation from the worsening of Russo-American relations. Russia's bad faith was established in Far Eastern American policy, particularly in the struggle over Manchuria and Newchang (1898–1904). With the disclosure of a secret agreement between Admiral Alexeyev and the Tartar general at Mukden, by which Manchuria, a territory of China, was subordinated to Russia, the United States found itself aligned with England and Japan against Russia. In 1902, a few months after the disclosure and the American protest against the agreement, the Anglo-Japanese alliance was concluded; and the effect, according to Dennett, was "much the same as though there had been a triple alliance." [29] If "from the outset President Roosevelt's sympathies were with Japan," [30] his success in bringing about the tremendous change of a Russo-Japanese peace and his modesty about the achievement are so much more impressive.

[28] Theodore Roosevelt, *An Autobiography*, N.Y., 1913, p. 558. Winston B Thorson, *op. cit.*, quotes Roosevelt as saying a week after the conference, "The Japs impressed me most favorably, whereas the Russians all pulled against one another. . . . Witte . . . interested me, [although] I thought his bragging and bluster not only foolish but shockingly vulgar when compared with the gentlemanly self-respecting, self-restraining qualities of the Japanese. . . . I could not help feeling much contempt for the excellent Mr. Witte." The criticism was denied by Baron Rosen, who said that there were no disharmonies between Witte and himself: the negotiations were conducted by both of them "as if we had been one man with one mind, one will, and one heart beating for our country." See R.R., Baron Rosen, *Forty Years of Diplomacy*, 2 vols., New York, 1922, Vol. I, p. 264.

[29] Tyler Dennett, *Roosevelt and the Russo-Japanese War*, Garden City, N. Y., 1925, p. 131.   [30] *Ibid.*, p. 27.

Of this modesty of Roosevelt, who received the Nobel Peace Prize for his Portsmouth mediation, it must be said that he was wrong when he anticipated only ingratitude or dislike from the statesmen and politicians of both countries. He was quite wrong in writing:

In both Russia and Japan, I believe that the new result as regards myself was a feeling of injury and of dislike of me among the people at large. I had expected this, I regarded it as entirely natural; and I did not resent it in the least.[31]

The reaction of the Russian daily and periodical press during the Portsmouth Conference has already been discussed. But much more important was the recognition gratefully accorded to Roosevelt by Russia after the establishment of peace. Attention may be called to the Russian political scientist Maxim Kovalevski, a man well acquainted with America, who wrote three years after the Russo-Japanese War, in an article on America's role in the Portsmouth treaty:

But why, it may be asked, was the initiative of proposing peace negotiations taken by the United States? Such a question upon reflection may appear naïve, and we pose it only because our diplomats turned their eyes toward other powers which had infinitely less contact with the problems of Pacific policy than that powerful federation the United States, the only rival, in maritime domination, of the Empire of the Rising Sun. For this reason, the peace negotiations aiming at a redistribution of the spheres of influence in the Oriental Ocean deserved to be initiated not at Paris or The Hague, but in America. The latter was more interested in the outcome of the Russo-Japanese War because she contributed the means for its waging, at least in a significant amount. Without a new American credit, the fleet of Togo and the armies of Oyama would have been powerless to conclude successfully one of the greatest (until then) clashes between the yellow and white races. If American public opinion had remained on the side of Japan, and if all her interests had not focused in the quick declaration of peace on conditions which, while saving face for Japan and securing her solvency, would deprive her of any hegemony over the Pacific, the Russian plenipotentiaries, or more correctly, Count Witte, would never have succeeded in returning from Portsmouth with a ready worded agreement

[31] Roosevelt, *ibid.*, p. 557.

to grant, as we venture to hope, a lasting peace in the Far East. The great skill of Count Witte consisted in turning the pro-Japanese and anti-Russian public opinion of the United States in our favor, and this so decisively that President Roosevelt, despite his personal relations and friendship with one of the leading Japanese diplomats, could not help submitting to the growing wave of American sympathy with a nation of the white race and Christian religion.

Kovalevski concluded:

In Europe it is admitted that the Portsmouth Peace is the only success of the whole Russo-Japanese War, and, indeed, there is a grain of truth in such an epigram. Our continental and naval forces have proved to be weaker than those of Japan, but our diplomacy has beaten theirs, perhaps because at this given historical moment, it was led not by a career diplomat but by a genuine statesman, albeit of the old régime.[32]

It is quite clear, then, that the diplomatic victory of Russia over Japan was, in the opinion of this authoritative scholar and member of the Upper House of Imperial Russia, directly traceable to the daring and nonorthodox approach of President Theodore Roosevelt, and only in a secondary degree to that of Count Witte.

We have discussed the Russo-Japanese War only so far as it yields light upon the American impact on the Empire. No doubt it is the personality of Theodore Roosevelt that stands out. However, the relatively quick peace "made in U.S.A." enabled the first Russian revolution of November, 1905, to remain basically an internal "Grand Rebellion" and escape degenerating into an international calamity. Had the war been continued, it might have provoked realignments and complications among the great powers that would have resulted in a conflagration. Portsmouth probably saved Russia from an upheaval of the kind which a dozen years later convulsed her in a violent social revolution.

[32] Maxim Kovalevski, "Portsmouth," in *Viestnik Yevropy*, Vol. VI, pp. 480-483 (June, 1908).

XVI *Worsening of Relations*

1. General Background and Far Eastern Policies

TOWARD THE END OF THE NINETEENTH CENTURY THERE WAS A strange external accord between two major Russian trends in sentiment toward America; though arising from different causes, both became unfriendly, if not actually hostile to the United States. The left felt that happy and carefree America—as it appeared to the average cultured Russian—growing in significance as a rich and mighty capitalist country, with a relatively satisfied rural population and practically no urban socialism, could not be a friend to poor, unsettled Russia standing on the threshold of an unknown future. For the rightist nationalists, on the other hand, young America ceased to be an implement of Anglophobia. It gradually rose to the rank of a rival, with industrial qualities surpassing even those of old Russia and policies particularly in the Far East that threatened to undermine the hitherto unchallenged colonial monopolism of the czarist empire. The continuous czarist expansion necessarily clashed with the open-door policy of Washington. The Russian rightists were most disturbed by the growing danger of a rapprochement between Great Britain, the hereditary enemy of Imperial Russia, and the United States. The effects of such a change in political climate could be observed in secret instructions to Russian diplomats in Washington as well as in the open lamentations of the pro-government periodical press and, after 1906, in the vociferations of right-wing state Duma deputies.

Only the central democratic sector, including some left-of-center segments, remained potentially and sometimes actually pro-American. With growing constitutionalism foreign policy, the old uncontested domain of the Czar, gradually became a matter of popular discussion; therefore shades of difference in the various factions grew clearly visible.

Because the groups left of center had a greater interest in domestic policies, foreign relations were much more discussed by the rightists and the moderates. In Russia, as in many other countries, leftists were slow in developing an interest in foreign policy; it was not until matters reached a crisis—for example, with the threat of war—that they became aware of its significance.

The growing anti-Americanism was heralded by daily newspapers like the widely circulated *Novoye Vremya* in St. Petersburg, *Moskovskiya Viedomosti* in Moscow, and journals like *Istoricheski Viestnik*, all mouthpieces of reactionary circles.

As has already been emphasized in the preceding chapter, the Russian bourgeoisie was to a certain degree squeezed out of the field of foreign policy, particularly in its financial, industrial, and explorative aspects, by the aristocratic semifeudal strata, who became increasingly adventurous when their estates, after the abolition of serfdom, failed to yield sufficient return. Among the aristocrats who gathered about Nicholas II, the most prominent were Count Michael Muraviev (important equally in the Hague Conference of 1899 and in the Far East), I. Bezobrazov, Admiral A. Abaza, in whose name the Czar's shares in the Far Eastern Company were registered, and General Kuropatkin. They were most hostile toward England and America. They did not see how systematically Germany was trying to keep Russia busy in the Far East, to distract her from Europe, and thus to weaken the Russo-French alliance. In the absence of constitutional representation, these aristocratic fortune-hunters substituted for a regularly functioning parliamentary bourgeois representation. Sergei Witte, the gifted Finance Minister, himself not entirely free from aristocratic prejudices, and Dmitri Mendeleyev, the chemist, both tried to counteract the court coterie. The reactionary newspapers of St. Petersburg and Moscow were the tools of the old regime.

These reactionary circles defended their views in literature and the press. A book by Konstantin Skalkovski,[1] stressed American imperialism and regretted the sale of Alaska to the United States —a position that the liberal and radical press of Russia never took.

In the same vein a very significant article on dollar worship, written by Pravdin during the Spanish-American War, was extremely hostile to the United States, attacking the people more

---

[1] Skalkovski, *Vneshnaya politika Rossii i polozhenie inostrannykh gosudarstv* (The Foreign Policy of Russia and the Position of Other Powers), St. Petersburg, 2nd ed., 1901.

sharply than the government. Americans were regarded as pirates, robbers, freebooters, and good-for-nothings who "never had any ideals," being motivated only by the impulse to seize, conquer, and destroy, which had nothing in common with the founding fathers of the eighteenth century. Pravdin used and misused the New York *Journal*. He reduced the program of "this most widely read paper in the whole world" to the conquest of Cuba, Puerto Rico, and the Hawaiian Islands, the completion of the Nicaragua Canal, the creation of a mighty navy, and so on. In the name of American democracy, he wrote, warmongers demanded the annihilation of all the "cruel and bloodthirsty" Spaniards. Cuba was demanded. Pravdin was sure that Cuba, Puerto Rico, and parts of the Philippine Islands would be annexed by the United States.

In spite of such personalities as former President Cleveland and Alfred Henry Love, head of the Universal Peace Union, Pravdin insisted on the basically aggressive and malicious character of Americans, who worshipped only the almighty dollar. In conclusion he indicted Americans for hypocrisy. Having themselves exterminated the Indians, prohibited the Immigration of the Chinese, and limited the rights of Negroes, the American people preached liberty and self-determination of colonial peoples in other parts of the world as against their various white masters. For himself, Pravdin considered that a Filipino victory over the Spaniards (with the help of American arms) would be a bloody and humiliating victory of a lower race over a higher, of barbarity over civilization.[2]

When one recalls that all this was written on the eve of the twentieth century after reckless Russian conquests and depredations in Central Asiatic regions on the southeastern boundaries of the Empire, one wonders whether there are any limits to political hypocrisy.

There is no doubt, however, that the article reflected the ebbing of the old official friendship between America and Russia. The whole official and governmental press of Russia was inflamed against "American imperialism." In September, 1899, soon after the conclusion of the Spanish-American War when the United States

[2] Yevgenii Pravdin, "Novorozhdionny Messianism strany dollarov i Stary Sviet" (The Newborn Messianism of the Dollar Country and the Old World), *Istoricheski Viestnik*, Vol. LXXIV, pp. 704-721 (November, 1898).

directed to the great powers—Germany, Russia, England, Japan, Italy, and France—a note proposing an "open door" policy in China, all but one of these governments came to the support of this doctrine. The exception was imperial Russia. Count Muraviev made a vague and evasive reply to the American proposal, stating that the imperial government had "already demonstrated its firm intention to follow the policy of the 'open door' by creating Dalny a free port." If at some future time that port, although remaining free itself, should be separated by a customs barrier from other portions of the territory in question, duties would be levied on all foreign merchandise in the zone subject to the tariff without distinction as to nationality. The note became even more negative when it pointed out:

> As to the ports now opened or hereafter to be opened to foreign commerce by the Chinese Government, and which lie beyond the territory leased to Russia, the settlement of the question of custom duties belongs to China herself.[3]

This reply strengthened suspicion in America, and marked the beginning of an era of worsening relations between the two countries.

Actually the worsening of their relations in the Far East began with the defeat of China in the Sino-Japanese War. As a result Russia tried to become the protector of the Heavenly Empire. On June 3, 1896, the so-called Moscow treaty of alliance between China and Russia was concluded. It was aimed at Japan. Should the latter attack China, Korea, or one of the Eastern Asiatic dependencies of Russia, it bound both contracting parties to mutual military assistance. In order to ease the transport of troops in fulfillment of the treaty China authorized Russia to build a railroad from Chita through Manchuria to Vladivostok on the Pacific. The concession to build the railroad was awarded to the Russo-Chinese Bank, which was founded in 1895 at the initiative of Witte. An additional railway agreement between the Chinese government and the Russo-Chinese Bank was signed on September 8, 1896. In it the Chinese Eastern Railway Company was established, a Russian company

---

[3] *Papers Relating to the Foreign Relations of the United States,* 1899, pp. 136-142. Muraviev's answer to Ambassador Tower, dated Dec. 18 (30), 1899.

with broad rights of own railroad tariffs, full administration of the extensive areas ceded to the company "for exploitation and defense" and an armed police. This became something more than economic domination, closely resembling an enlarged and armed Russian settlement.[4]

Outwardly, this project appeared to be only a territorial aggrandizement at the expense of China aimed at Japan; but it was also directed against the United States and the other great powers.

Russia regarded the United States as a direct commercial competitor in the penetration of Manchuria, and it became particularly hostile toward the project of an American "trust company" to build a new trans-Chinese railroad joining Canton-Hankow-Peking. This project raised a storm in Russian official circles—as a line linking South and Central China with Manchuria. The storm was over the grant of a contract for the considerable Canton-Hankow railway later transferred to the American China Development Company, a corporation promoted by a syndicate of prominent American capitalists. It is true that this huge North-South line, as a means of extensive traffic-exchange, was meant to have a connection with Peking and even to reach, at or near Newchang, the Trans-Manchurian branch of the great Trans-Siberian Railway.[5] This American project was regarded as threatening Manchuria with a flood of commodities in which Russian industry would be unable to compete, and, what is more, as threatening the political domination by Russia of North China.[6] Conditions became even worse after the resignation of Witte in August, 1903, when the jingoist adventurous Bezobrazov group, supported by von Plehve, monopolized Far Eastern policy. This was the remote prelude to the Russo-Japanese War.

The estrangement between St. Petersburg and Washington was

[4] B. A. Romanov, *Rossiya v Mandzhurii, 1892–1906* (Russia in Manchuria), Leningrad, 1928, pp. 126-127. Dennett, *Roosevelt and the Russo-Japanese War*, New York, 1925, p. 121, goes further asserting that the Russian interpretation of this treaty "would make the railway agreement practically equivalent to a cession of sovereign territorial rights."

[5] Clarence Cary, *China's Present and Prospective Railways*, New York, 1899, pp. 14, 17.

[6] *Istoriya diplomatii* (History of Diplomacy), ed. V. Potiomkin, Moscow, 1945, Vol. II, pp. 117-118. (Cf. my detailed review, "Russia and the World," in *International Conciliation*, Mar., 1947.)

followed by a rapprochement between the United States and Japan. More important, the continuously fostered improvement in Anglo-American relations found its distinctive expression in a common policy in the Pacific, particularly in the Far East, precisely where Russia and Japan were to cross swords in 1904–1905.

In the hourglass of an almost century-long Russo-American friendship the grains of sand were fast running out. We have seen that the friendship was built on the formula: Two powers that equally hate a third are necessarily friendly to each other. However, Russian czarism and the transatlantic republic could not cooperate to the degree for which their peoples were ready. The negative force of hatred worked well enough in some areas, but the open door policy was too broad a concept for the old and narrow Russo-American diplomatic cooperation. In the first years of the twentieth century the last vestiges of tension between the two English-speaking nations wore off. In May, 1811, on the eve of the war with England, John Quincy Adams, one of the architects of Russo-American friendship, wrote these angry, confessionlike words:

> If our trial is now to come, God of Justice and Mercy! give us spirit to bear with fortitude and to derive ultimate power and virtue from all the evils that they can inflict, and spare us from that woe of woes, the compassion of Britons.

Within the span of a hundred years history transformed the relationship toward compassion between England and America. At the beginning of the Russo-Japanese War Britons and Americans were being pushed closer and closer together.

As early as the Spanish-American War it was essential for America to win the friendship of Great Britain. Secretary of State John Hay, enraged at Muraviev's policies in the Far East, was at the same time convinced that "the interests of civilization are bound up in the direction the relations of England and America are to take in the next few months." [7] Joseph Chamberlain, expressing the British point of view, had said publicly on May 13, 1898:

> I even go so far as to say that, terrible as war may be, even war itself would be cheaply purchased if, in a great and noble cause, the Stars

[7] W. R. Thayer, *The Life and Letters of John Hay*, 2 vols., Boston, 1915, Vol. II, p. 168 (Hay to Lodge, May 25, 1898).

and Stripes and the Union Jack should wave together over an Anglo-Saxon alliance.[8]

The Anglo-American treaty of 1901 providing for fortification of the Atlantic-Pacific canal (the original Hay-Pauncefote treaty of 1899) became the symbol of renewed solidarity between these two countries and to that extent a sign of American alienation from Russia.

The field in which Anglo-American solidarity developed was China. Hay may well be regarded as one of the initiators and builders of the open door policy. It is clear that the negative attitude of Russia toward this policy would have been sufficient to motivate Hay's anti-Russian feeling; and the acts of official Russia in the Far East only served to sharpen his attitude and that of official America. Such moves as the "lease" of Port Arthur and Dalny, already mentioned, and the pouring of Russian troops into the North China provinces aggravated the tension.

Russia's apprehension with respect to the United States is unmistakably revealed by Russian diplomacy in the 1890's and 1900's when Anglo-American rapprochement became inevitable with the Spanish-American War and the deterioration of Russo-British relations in the Far East—particularly accentuated by the conclusion of the Anglo-Japanese alliance of 1902.

Of outstanding significance are the late 1890's during which there was a display of rivalry, in itself avoidable, that became sharper as the result of overvaluation of the political factors by the Russian aristocratic diplomats. This applies especially to Count Arthur Cassini, former Russian ambassador to China, who in January, 1898 was sent as ambassador to the United States. The opening of the Archives of the imperial Foreign Ministry and the publication of various secret documents thus made available provide scholars a particularly rich source of information.[9]

[8] *The American Secretaries of State and Their Diplomacy*, ed. S. F. Bemis et al., Vol. IX, New York, 1929, p. 124.

[9] "Severo-Amerikanskiye Soyedionnye Shtaty i tsarskaya Rossiya v 90-kh godakh XIX veka" (The United States of America and Czarist Russia in the 1890's), in *Krassny Arkhiv* (The Red Archives), Vol. LII (Moscow, 1932), pp. 125-142, with an introduction by F. Kelyin. Here will be found the "instructions" to Count Cassini from Minister of Foreign Affairs Muraviev and Cassini's two secret letters to Count Lamsdorf and Count Muraviev.

In his instructions to Cassini, Muraviev mentioned the old bonds between the two countries:

Ties between Russia and the United States doubtless exist and are historically well rooted. They have not forgotten in America that the Imperial Government was helpful to the United States in the crucial years of the Civil War during the upheaval of the southern states. This feeling of gratitude also found its expression in 1891, during the year of our famine, when from all corners of the United States flour, bread, and money were sent to Russia. . . .

Our giving up Alaska [!] in 1867 for a paltry compensation bears witness to the fact that we looked favorably on the strengthening of the continental power of the United States in contrast to the aspirations of Great Britain. . . . Now the Imperial Government has found another occasion to render the Federal Government a service, by supporting its acquisition of the Hawaiian Islands, which is also in accord with our interests. . . . In view of their inability to remain independent, it is more desirable that these islands should become a part of the United States. In this way they will remain forever a friendly and reliable midway coaling station and will not become a hostile nest or dangerous trap for us.

Toward the end the instructions become much more cautious:

Of special interest in this connection are the increased tensions between the United States and Canada. . . . The secession of Canada from the Empire has extreme importance for us. You will therefore have to determine how advantageous the secession of Canada from Great Britain would be for us. . . .

Would the United States, having already assumed the status of a great power, preserve the same passive good will toward our policies after the dismemberment of England, or would it become a competitor with whom we would have to deal as we do now with Great Britain? [10]

10 Edward H. Zabriskie, *American-Russian Rivalry in the Far East*, Philadelphia, 1946, pp. 47-49, quotes an admonition to Cassini to make every effort to create conflict between the Federal Government (United States), England, and Japan. He translates, "While remaining in the aura of Russian-American friendship, you must make every endeavor to create conflicts between the Federal Government and England and Japan," giving as his source Kelyin's introduction cited in footnote 9; but no statement in such terms could be found there, and the nearest approach to it in the official instructions to Cassini reads as follows in a careful translation: "While proceeding on the basis of good will between the United States and Russia, you must pay particularly careful attention to all clashes between the Federal Government and England and Japan." *Krassny Arkhiv*, LII, 137. Considerably more temperate language!

In the economic area the instructions to Cassini strike a note of apprehension as to American industry in the Far East:

Because of your knowledge of China, you will doubtless be able to make a clear distinction between those enterprises which are favorable to us and those which impinge on our sphere of influence. While conducting yourself in harmony with the first, you will take energetic action against the second.[11]

Undue importance is ascribed to the sealing industry as the only concrete economic subject matter of Russo-Canadian-American relationships.

In view of the impotence of Russian industry and trade to fight for their immediate economic and financial interests, it became unmistakably clear that the acquisition of the Philippines by the United States in 1899 as a result of the Spanish-American War was considered by Russia as a direct blow to her economic and political expansion in the Far East, particularly in North China and the western shores of the Pacific.[12]

In the chapter preceding we discussed two important events that indicated a worsening of Russo-American relations in the Far East and moreover influenced the Russo-Japanese War through the Anglo-Japanese treaty of 1902, which led to solidarity between Japan and England and—indirectly—the United States. To that treaty was added the commercial treaty of October 8, 1903, between China and the United States, which sought to draw a definite line between the Far Eastern policies of Washington and those of St. Petersburg, particularly on Manchuria. The Russo-Japanese War created new facts and relations. And in this sense the high tide of Russo-American friendship at and immediately after Portsmouth failed to modify the general trend toward estrangement.

It remains only to be said that whereas in the first years after the defeat of 1905 the Russian bear could only lick his wounds and look on helplessly while Austria-Hungary, in an overt act of aggression,

[11] *Krassny Arkhiv*, Vol. LII, p. 133.

[12] Zabriskie, *op. cit.*, p. 52. Cf. also the article, "Perviye shagi russkovo imperialisma na Dal'nem Vostoke, 1888–1903" (The First Steps of Russian Imperialism in the Far East) in *Krassny Arkhiv*, Vol. LII, pp. 34-124, with appendices containing official documents. A detailed introduction is written by A. Popov.

annexed Bosnia and Herzegovina in 1908, the picture in the Far East had changed by 1909, and steps toward a rapprochement between Russia and Japan at the cost of China and the West (including America) were taken on the initiative of Japan. Whereupon the United States was impelled to take countermeasures in order to halt deterioration in Russo-American relations.

In the summer of 1909 Japan sent an ultimatum to China. As a result an agreement was reached under which Japan was to build railroads in Manchuria and obtain coal mines there. The Russian agent Somov in Seoul (Korea) on August 29, 1909, wired his government about these concessions to Japan, adding that "a storm of indignation" had broken in the United States, which "now has decided to come to terms with Russia in view of Japanese steps to undermine the independence of China guaranteed by treaties." Nicholas II expressed his satisfaction at the emergence of Japanese-American rivalry in a short marginal notation on Somov's telegram: "Finally." Russia thus shifted to the position of a "rejoicing third party" (*tertius gaudens*). This position was strengthened when, on November 8, 1909, Ambassador William Woodville Rockhill pressed on Minister Alexander Izvolski the "necessity for Russia to go hand-in-hand with the United States of America in Manchurian affairs" and offered him a plan for the commercial neutralization of the entire network of Manchurian railways, thereby "putting a final limit to further Japanese designs" for expansion.[13]

In January, 1910, Russia, with the active participation of the Emperor, and Japan, rejected the neutralization plan, thus giving free rein to the rivalry with the United States. Although America grew more and more conscious of the aggressive power of Japan, Russo-American tension in the Far East continued, contributing to the deterioration of Russo-American relations. These conditions prevailed practically without change down to March, 1913, when Woodrow Wilson announced the withdrawal of government support of American bankers interested in financial plans connected with Manchuria.

[13] Cf. B. Romanov, *Ocherki diplomaticheskoi istorii russko-yaponskoi voiny* (Essays on the Diplomatic History of the Russo-Japanese War), Moscow, 1947, pp. 404-406; Zabriskie, *op. cit.*, pp. 252-254.

2. Hague Conferences

As if to show the whole world that foreign policy was not necessarily connected with or the same as domestic policy, czarist Russia
became the formal initiator of the two Hague Peace Conferences
of 1899 and 1907. This idea had begun to develop in the 1880's in
the United States, Britain, and Holland (conference of 1894) and
was much advanced by the Interparliamentary Union and its conferences. Russia was the prime mover in the convocation of the
first Hague Peace Conference of 1899. The second conference
(1907) was another matter. In reality, it was called at the urgent
insistence of the United States expressed as early as 1904; but that
country did not care to make it a subject of competition, and Russia was recognized as the moving spirit of the 1907 conference
also.[14]

For Russia itself it was the third instance of changing and improving international law, the first two being the Act of Armed
Neutrality promulgated under Catherine II and the Holy Alliance
of Alexander I.

The Russian official press and literature burned with patriotic
fervor over the Emperor's magnanimous gesture. Count Muraviev's
note of August 12/24, 1898, sent to all foreign powers diplomatically accredited at St. Petersburg, was written in a solemn and eloquent style. Hypocritically enough, this note, formally directed
toward ensuring to all peoples the benefits of lasting peace and
limiting existing armaments, was sent to the whole world, including the United States, only a few months after the conclusion of
the Sino-Russian convention which ceded Port Arthur and Dalny
with their territory and waters to Russia under the form of a lease
for twenty-five years, which could be extended indefinitely by
mutual accord.

Russian universitarian doctrine had two approaches: full enthusiastic acceptance (Count L. Kamarovski, a world-famous
authority on international law, F. F. Martens, P. Bogayevski, and
Prince V. Tenishev) and a more skeptical attitude, particularly in

[14] James Brown Scott, ed., *Instructions to the American Delegates to the
Hague Peace Conferences and Their Reports*, Washington, 1916, pp. 63-64.

the ranks of the moderate opposition (Baron Boris Nolde, Vladimir Gessen, Serge Kotliarevskii). Said Gessen:

There was no need for any prophetic inspiration to predict before the convocation of the conference the complete failure of all its attempts to halt the permanent growth of armaments. Contemporary militarism is not an isolated illness susceptible to immediate cure. On the contrary, it is merely an external symptom of another serious internal affection which undermines the organism of the present-day world. Militarism is inevitable as long as war is possible. The Russian proposals were only palliatives.

Gessen did not hesitate to point out some hypocritical propositions of the conference favorable for Russia:

A basic point of the project to suspend armaments proposes a convention be concluded against the increase of ground forces for a certain number of years. Simultaneously, however, it is proposed that this convention cover only the forces of the parent state, leaving to the governments full freedom concerning their colonial troops. Accordingly, the Asiatic parts of Russia were also considered to be colonies.[15]

Actually, official doctrine—czarist as well as soviet—never regarded the Asiatic provinces of Russia as colonies or indeed as anything other than an integrated part of the Russian state.

It is perfectly obvious that Nicholas II was spurred to his noble effort by the Russian lack of modern armament and the financial difficulties created by expansionist moves in the Far East. The War Minister, General Alexis Kuropatkin, fearing that there would not be sufficient funds to rearm the infantry in accordance with the new standards, proposed in 1897 a special treaty with Austria-Hungary mutually renouncing the intention to rearm the artillery. Count Witte proposed, instead of this too frank and transparent measure, a broad plan for universal reduction of armament and an international peace conference.

Ironically enough, the Muraviev note of 1898 caught the United States in the midst of its war with Spain. The Russian involvement in the Far East, already described, must have caused it to meet with a cool reception in America. Other powers, too, were caught flat-

---

[15] Vladimir Gessen, "O znachenii Gaagskoi Konferentsii" (On the Significance of the Hague Conference) in *Zhurnal Ministerstva Yustitsii*, Mar., 1900.

footed: Britain in her clash with the Boer republics in South Africa
and in her colonial rivalry with France (Fashoda); Germany in
her Chinese expansion and the implementation of her ambitious
program of continental and naval armament. But Russia's real intentions were more or less known to the diplomatic world.

In a sense the Russian scholar Kotliarevski was right when he
said that Russia and the United States reversed their positions on
the disarmament issue at these conferences.[16] Whereas in 1899
Russia was the pioneer of peace ensured by complete or partial
disarmament and America was rather reluctant, in 1907 the czarist
government, mindful of the disastrous defeat of the army and navy
in 1905 and the need of both for reorganization and rehabilitation,
refrained from proposing actual measures to limit existing armaments while the United States and Great Britain backed a broad
program of disarmament.

The meager results of the conferences—unanimous acceptance
of the principle of obligatory arbitration, unanimous adoption of
the resolution of the Conference of 1899 on the limitation of military burdens, and recognition that a "serious study" of disarmament was necessary—were not hailed by the exponents of Russian
constitutional and political doctrine, and skepticism with respect
to the Hague conferences remained unshaken. Thus did the universities display a certain independence of spirit toward the imperial government, which tried to impress the domestic opposition
with its international successes.

3. The Abrogation of the Treaty of 1832

A matter which, to all intents and purposes, was purely domestic
—namely, the suppression of religious and ethnic minorities in Russia, especially the Jewish minority, with specific discrimination in
the rights of residence and free movement—was turned by the
United States into an international affair and a conflict of the first
magnitude.

This affair would have remained domestic had not the tremendous pressure on the Jews and other racial minorities in western

[16] Serge A. Kotliarevski, *Pravovoye gosudarstvo i vneshnaya politika* (The
Rule-of-Law State and Foreign Policy), Moscow, 1909, pp. 319-320.

Russia led to a vast emigration to America. Russia could not prevent some of the emigrants from returning on visits; and that is where the Treaty of Navigation and Commerce of December 18, 1832, between Russia and the United States comes in.

Article 1 of the treaty became a bone of contention between the two countries, and the Russian interpretation led in 1911 to its abrogation. It was as follows:

> There shall be, between the territories of the high contracting parties, a reciprocal liberty of commerce and navigation. The inhabitants of their respective states shall, mutually, have liberty to enter the ports, places, and rivers of the territories of each party, wherever foreign commerce is permitted. They shall be at liberty to sojourn and reside in all parts whatsoever of said territories, in order to attend to their affairs, and they shall enjoy, to that effect, the same security and protection as natives of the country wherein they reside, on condition of submitting to the laws and ordinances there prevailing, and particularly to the regulations in force concerning commerce.

Throughout long decades marked by light immigration to America the fact that the "natives of the country" wherein they resided were not all equally secured or protected and that foreigners were not all regarded as on the same footing, did not come up. Only in the last two decades of the nineteenth century did this question become important.

As a rule, "foreigners belonging to all nations" could visit and reside in Russia. Article 819 of the ninth volume of the Code of Statutes (*Swod Zakonov*) made Jews the only exception. However, this prohibition against foreign Jews visiting and residing in Russia did not apply to the non-Talmudic Jewish sect of Karaites (Art. 818) nor, which is even more remarkable, to Jews of Middle Asiatic countries (Art. 819, subsec. 1). Thus Jewish subjects of Persia, Khiva, Bokhara, and Afghanistan were allowed freedom of travel and residence in Russia.

By Russian passport regulations, Art. 230, applicable to all foreign Jews except Asiatic Jews, only bankers and representatives of important commercial houses had the right of free entry into and residence in any part of Russia on equal terms with other foreigners. Others could enter Russia only by special permission of the Minister of the Interior (Art. 289). And only on the basis of such permission were Russian consuls permitted to give visas to foreign Jews.

The exception in favor of Asiatic Jews created by Russian public law can be explained by the vital interest of czarist Russia in Asiatic trade [17] flowing to Russia proper mainly through the Caucasus and Turkestan. In this way imperial Russia, independently of any international treaties with particular countries, established a discrimination against Western Jews and in favor of Asiatic Jews. Similar restrictions were also imposed on Jesuits, on traveling Armeno-Gregorian priests who were subjects of Persia and Turkey, and on all foreign gypsies (Arts. 266 and 308).

As far as it is possible to ascertain from the literature and the press of that time, this substantive public law of the Empire was never referred to in the American argument against the Russian interpretation of the treaty of 1832.

In an important editorial entitled "The Passport Question Between the United States and Russia," the *American Journal of International Law* tried to differentiate between the political approach, on the one hand, and the purely legal approach on the other:

Overlooking the many extravagant statements that have been made in denunciation of the treaty of 1832, it seems reasonably clear that the treaty is inadequate. Whether rightfully or wrongfully, Russia has interpreted the treaty in such a way as formally to exclude from her territory an important class of American citizens. Diplomatic representations have thus far been unable to obtain from Russia a more liberal interpretation. The United States may well refuse to continue to be a party to a treaty in which it recognizes or acquiesces in doctrines which are contrary to its political principles of religious freedom and the right of expatriation. It is another question to assert that Russia has been guilty of violating the treaty, and as pointed out by Mr. Root in his address before the Senate, those who have been so ready to make the charge would do well to consider the policy of the United States in a closely analogous matter [exclusion of Russian Mongolians and Mohammedans as believers in polygamy].

As a point of law it may be observed that the right to exclude what-

[17] Cf. N. M. Korkunov, *Russkoye gosudarstvennoye pravo* (Russian Constitutional Law), 8th ed., St. Petersburg, 1914, Vol. I, p. 265.

ever persons it pleases from entrance into its territories is one of the
sovereign rights of a state, and that nothing less than an express renunciation of that right can be regarded as estopping the state from arresting it. Russia claims that by general terms of the Treaty of 1832 in
which she agreed that the inhabitants of the United States shall have
liberty to enter her territories, she did not surrender her fundamental
right to exclude any class of persons she might later consider dangerous
to her interests. . . . What will be the situation if the treaty is abrogated? Unless another treaty is made in the meantime, the relations
between the United States and Russia will fall back upon general rules
of international law, and American citizens will have only such privileges in Russia as that country may, in accordance with the comity of
nations, deem it to her interests to grant. . . . On December 17, 1911,
the President, presumably having regard to the almost unanimous expression of opinion in the House of Representatives in favour of termi-
nating the treaty, caused the Ambassador at St. Petersburg to hand to
the Russian Minister for Foreign Affairs on December 17 a communication giving the official notification contemplated by Article 12 of the
treaty, whereby its operation would terminate, in accordance with its
terms, on January 1, 1913. The note pointed out that the old treaty had
been recognized as "no longer fully responsive in various respects to the
needs of the political and material relations of the two countries" and
that it had from time to time given rise to certain regrettable controversies; and it expressed the desire of the American Government to
renew the efforts that had been made to negotiate a modern treaty of
friendship, commerce and navigation.[18]

On December 18, 1911, the Senate Committee on Foreign Relations presented to the Senate a substitute for the House Resolution.

Doubtless the issue reached beyond the legal one, for reasons
other than that public opinion is not motivated by legal technicali-
ties connected with clauses of international treaties. Actually, the

[18] *American Journal of International Law*, Vol. VI (1912), pp. 186-191.
It is noteworthy that President Taft suggested that the problem be brought
before the International Court at the Hague. But this suggestion met with
objections from the Senate. See the *Independent*, Dec. 28, 1911. Similarly,
former President Theodore Roosevelt proposed in the *Outlook*, of Oct. 14,
1911, that the whole issue be regarded as a "case for arbitration," and that Russia
be requested, before considering the question of the abrogation of the treaty,
to find out exactly what the treaty meant "by submitting to the Hague Court
of Arbitration the clause in question with a recital of all the attendant circumstances, and asking the judgment of the Court on the construction of the
clause."

political aspects were incomparably more significant. The immigration of tens of thousands of Russian Jews was an important problem, for the readiness of America to receive the immigrants helped to resolve an internal Russian problem.

American reaction to the Russian position expressed itself in counterpressure on czarist Russia to reform its backward legislation with respect to Jews and other suppressed minorities.

Russia, by differentiating between and/or discriminating against American citizens on the basis of their confession or race, touched a particularly sensitive spot in American prestige and old political tradition. Unwittingly she revived an attitude for which not even England had been forgiven and which had led to the War of 1812. The debates in the House of Representatives may be summed up as follows:

In the first place, the treaty, in the closing sentence of Article 10, recognized a right on the part of Russia to enforce the doctrine of indefeasible allegiance. Inasmuch as the United States had long repudiated that doctrine, it should not be a party to a treaty which recognized it. In the second place the United States could not constitutionally acquiesce in any treaty that would permit a foreign government to set up between American citizens religious and racial distinctions that the United States itself did not recognize.

Basically, that meant that Russia had to make peace—as Britain was compelled to do after 1812—with the idea that, once a man was recognized as an American citizen, he ceased to be a deserter from his country of origin; nor were his rights otherwise abridged because of his previous allegiance to another country.

Even the pseudo-equalitarian consideration of the Russian authorities that allowing free residence to Americans of Mosaic confession in Russia would put Russian nationals of that confession in a position inferior to their foreign coreligionists could not be regarded seriously by the United States. It was an argument that was nullified by the legal privileges granted to foreign Asiatic Jews in discrimination against American and Western European Jews —which were carefully concealed by the Russian government in its diplomatic correspondence with the United States.

The following were the main legal criticisms of the House:

The provisions of Article 1 of the treaty were general and admitted of no exception; hence the refusal by Russian consuls to visé passports of American Jews was a violation of that article. There was discrimination against American Jews in that a passport which the Russian consul at New York had refused to visé, was viséed by the Russian consul in London. Even though Russia could not be charged with having violated the treaty, the compact was no longer responsive to the political principles and the commercial needs of the two countries.[19]

On December 4, 1911, the following joint resolution was introduced in the House by Representative William Sulzer:

Resolved by the Senate and House of Representatives of the United States of America in Congress assembled, that the people of the United States assert as a fundamental principle that the rights of its citizens shall not be impaired at home or abroad because of race or religion; that the Government of the United States concluded its treaties for the equal protection of all classes of its citizens, without regard to race or religion; that the Government of the United States will not be a party to any treaty which discriminates, or which by one of the parties thereto is so construed as to discriminate between American citizens on the ground of race or religion; that the Government of Russia has violated the treaty between the United States and Russia, concluded at St. Petersburg December eighteenth, 1832, refusing to honor American passports duly issued to American citizens, on account of race and religion; that in the judgment of the Congress the said treaty, for the reasons aforesaid, ought to be terminated at the earliest possible time; that for the aforesaid reasons the said treaty is hereby declared to be terminated and of no further force and effect from the expiration of one year after the date of notification to the Government of Russia of the terms of this resolution, and that to this end the President is hereby charged with the duty of communicating such notice to the Government of Russia.[20]

This resolution was passed on December 13 by a vote of 300 to 1. The sole dissenting vote was cast by Representative George R. Malby, who declared that he did not think it would remedy the

19 Cf. *American Journal of International Law*, Vol. VI (1912), p. 188.
20 *Congressional Record*, Dec. 13, 1911 (62nd Cong., 2nd Sess., Vol. XLVIII, pt. 1), p. 311.

evil involved. He felt that more could be accomplished by diplomacy.[21]

Subsequent diplomatic communications between the State Department and the Ambassador to Russia, Curtis Guild, were not written in the same brusque tone and did not speak in terms of a violation of the treaty of 1832. Rather, there was manifested a willingness on the part of the United States to negotiate a new treaty "more responsive to the interests of both Governments." The Russian Minister of Foreign Affairs, Serge D. Sazonov, stubbornly insisted that Russia would not consider signing another treaty unless it were along the lines of the old one.[22]

Russia's real reaction to this radical step by the United States came only when the news of it spread to the capital, setting off a series of demonstrations, generating parliamentary discussion in the Duma, and inspiring drafts of proposed retaliatory legislation. The reaction to the American abrogation of the old treaty was, broadly speaking, the first manifestation of a new Russia that, in 1906, had become a constitutional monarchy. Never before in that country had public opinion, the parliament, and the press been involved in a problem which, in addition to its foreign policy aspects, embraced many issues of domestic concern including that of the equal rights of its citizens. When the treaty was concluded, Russia was a crass autocracy under Nicholas I; when it was abrogated eighty years later, Russia had a regime that sometimes, particularly vis-à-vis the West, preferred to call itself a constitutional or rule-of-law state. Nevertheless, the reaction of the rightist factions was aggressive and arrogant. As we have already seen, they had been anti-American since the beginning of the century.

The first bill directed against the abrogation was initiated and signed by a group of thirty-one members of the Duma consisting of the Octobrists, Russian nationalists, and radical monarchists like Count Bobrinski, Bishop Eulogius, and Gololobov. Another, almost identical bill, signed by rightists, was appended to it.

The introduction vehemently attacked the American government as being under the pressure of Jewish agitation, which was trying to

[21] Cyrus Adler and Aaron M. Margalith, *With Firmness in the Right* (New York, 1946), p. 286. (Cf. *Independent*, Dec. 28, 1911).

[22] *Ibid.*, pp. 288-289.

enforce a right of unrestricted residence of American Jews for unlimited periods of time:

This agitation has been stirred up as much by newspapers, almost all
of which in the United States are owned by Jews or are dependent upon
them, as by meetings and all kinds of public manifestations striving to
instill hatred against Russia in the masses by spreading lies about the
acts of her Government and church, by asserting that the high distinction of American citizenship is insulted and that specific legislative
restrictions are created against foreign Jews who are American citizens.

. . . .

Having taken into consideration the above-mentioned, we, the under-
signed members of the State Duma, first of all declare that it is out of
the question to allow American Jews certain legal preferences—as
against other foreign Jews—with respect to their entry into and residence in Russia, as is requested by the Government of the United
States of America.

As for the specifically commercial consequences of the abrogation of
the treaty of 1832, they are very favorable to Russia. Because of an excess
of American imports into Russia over Russian exports to the United
States, Russia, on the basis of her trade balance, annually overpays to
American about fifty million rubles in consequence of this treaty, by
which America enjoys the right of the most favored nation. Now, being
freed from this for us extremely disadvantageous treaty, . . . Russia
can import American commodities—mainly agricultural tools and machinery—according to her own judgment. Thus an exclusively favorable
condition in international relations is created for Russia by the reckless
abrogation of an old treaty which, for scores of years, linked that country
with Russia.

We therefore propose that:

1. Jews who are citizens of the United States are barred from entering Russia regardless of whether entry is in connection with their position or occupation or not.

2. On commodities that are the products of the soil or industry of
the United States of America shall be imposed (a) a double customs
duty as compared with the ordinary levy on articles of the same kind
liable to duty; (b) a duty of 100 per cent ad valorem if the article is
among those which in the ordinary tariff are classified as free of duty;
(c) a duty equal to that prescribed by the tariff of the United States in
all those cases where the duty fixed in (a) and (b) proves to be lower.

3. Dues per pood double those fixed by the law of June 8, 1901,

shall be exacted of goods imported or exported by vessels sailing under the flag of the United States of North America.[23]

The bill never became law, but it mirrors the spirit of the rightist and jingoistic circles of the Empire.

A flood of anti-American propaganda and agitation, which St. Petersburg had never before known, also followed the abrogation of the treaty. We shall not quote from the press or the literature. Suffice it to say that the regime published booklets in English denouncing the abrogation of the treaty in order to influence American and other foreign public opinion.

The English booklet of Basile von Egert, a Baltic German and a member of the St. Petersburg Bar Association, not only followed the typical pattern of conservative anti-Semitism, but defended the bill of the Duma rightists, adding intemperate disparagement of American domestic relations and ridiculous threats to deprive the United States forever of the position of a most favored nation in trade with Russia.[24]

The title page bore the pharisaical statement that the pamphlet was written "for the sake of a better mutual understanding between two great nations at a moment when their good relations are troubled by the hostile action of an element alien to both."

The rationale of this malicious "motto" was that of a typical proponent of autocracy who had no respect for the parliament of a republic, and who could regard a joint resolution of an American national legislative body as no more than a product of Jewish intrigue, taking no account of the fact that it resulted from a careful evaluation of the foreign policy interests of the country.

The booklet revealed the basic arguments of all the opponents of a new treaty that would grant equal rights of entrance and residence to all American citizens, regardless of race or religion: It is

[23] *Prilozhenia k stenograficheskim otchotam Gos. Dumy* (Appendices to the Stenographic Records of the State Duma), 3rd Duma, 5th Session (1911–1912), Vol. II, St. Petersburg, 1912, No. 232 III/5.

[24] B. P. Egert, *The Conflict Between the United States and Russia*, St. Petersburg, 1912, p. 40. Here it is worth mentioning that the extremely chauvinist and anti-Semitic deputies V. Purishkevich and E. Markov-Vtoroi, leaders of the Union of the Russian People, defended the Baltic Germans in the Duma against accusations made by the Russian democratic wing. (See Ernst Seraphim, *Aus der Arbeit eines baltischen Journalisten*, Riga, 1911, pp. 294-298.)

probable that the grant of equal rights to American Jews would have to be extended to Jews of other Western countries; the grant of equal rights to foreign Jews might undermine long-standing discriminatory legislation against Russian Jews. These arguments did not appear in the diplomatic correspondence between the two countries; they were not put forward in parliamentary discussions; nor did the rightist Russian press mention them. On equality of entrance into Russian territory, however, Egert naïvely let the cat out of the bag:

Once Russia conceded this to the United States, the question of equal rights for Jews in general in her domain might be regarded as settled: Russia would then have absolutely no grounds for refusing Jews of other countries, at the request of their governments, what had already been granted to the Jews of the United States. With the residence in Russia of Jewish subjects of Foreign Powers, *how would it then be possible to maintain the Pale of Settlement and those other limitations of rights among her own Russian Jews?* [25]

The entire argument was supported by threats. Decisive political influence in Russia's two legislative chambers was arrogated exclusively to Octobrists and Nationalists, the liberal and radical deputies being completely ignored:

That a law . . . in favor of American Jews could be enacted in Russia and thus would be subsequently included in a proposed new treaty with the United States is not to be thought of. . . . On the contrary, it is possible that a new regulation, much more severe, will be introduced into these laws, absolutely prohibiting, under any conditions, their entrance into and residence in Russia, regardless of their position or occupation. A bill has already been introduced into the Imperial Duma on this point. Russia will then become a country as absolutely closed to American Jews as the United States is, for example, to Mohammedans.[26]

Egert then reached the height of ridiculous complacency and ignorance of economics:

With regard to the other wish of the American Government—the preservation to the United States in the proposed new treaty of the rights of the most favored nation in trade—there is not the slightest probability of its being fulfilled. The United States had these rights.

[25] *Ibid.*, p. 11 (italics added).　　[26] *Ibid.*, pp. 39-40.

They sacrificed them and friendship with Russia for the sake of the Jews, by abrogating the treaty of 1832. The privileges of the United States were burdensome to Russia but she bore them for the sake of the . . . United States. However, once the United States refused Russia their amity . . . how could there be any ground for imagining that Russia would again afford them the rights of the most favored nation in trade, in direct detriment to her own interests?

Obviously he was blind to the economic and trade issues involved for Russia, which needed a commercial treaty much more than the United States. Nevertheless, he graciously refrained from carrying the matter to its ultimate conclusion. "This does not mean," he wrote, "that Russia absolutely desires to enter into a tariff war with the United States." [27]

For significant strata of the aristocracy, bureaucracy and some elements of the upper middle class of czarist Russia, old prejudices and chauvinist political slogans were paramount to national interests in trade in cotton, agricultural machinery, and industrialization.

These circles did not understand that the reaction of America against rightist Russia's hatred for Jews and all other non-Russian, "allogeneous" peoples and tribes began much earlier than 1911, at least as early as 1880, gaining momentum after the bloody pogroms in southern Russia. They did not know—or did not wish to know— that a series of American diplomats, including John Watson Foster, James G. Blaine, and Andrew D. White, troubled the Russian Ministry of Foreign Affairs with their constant notes, often based on joint resolutions of the Congress.

Foster was appointed minister to St. Petersburg in 1880, remaining a year. His friends described his position by saying, "He had little to do there except to plead for leniency in the treatment of American Jews." On May 17, 1880, Samuel Cox introduced in the House of Representatives the following resolution, which was referred to the Committee on Foreign Affairs:

Resolved, That the President be requested to communicate to this House all correspondence in reference to the proscription of Jews by the Russian Government.

[27] *Ibid.,* p. 40.

We do not quote here all the speeches delivered, and the memoranda sent from different parts of the United States between 1880 and 1911 expressing sympathy and indignation over the miseries inflicted upon the Jews in Russia, nor the many resolutions about the handling of American Jews visiting Russia.

We will quote here only part of one joint resolution "expressing sympathy with the Hebrews in Russia" which hit the Russian bull's-eye. Mentioning the abject events connected with the pogroms in Elizabethgrad, Kiev, Odessa, and Warsaw, the resolution concluded with what must have been a heavy blow to the complacent czarism of Alexander III:

Resolved . . . to request His Imperial Majesty to exercise his august power for the sake of humanity to protect the Jewish subjects from violence of their enemies and to extend to them his protection as the late lamented sovereign, his father, did over the Christians of Bulgaria at a time when said Christians had been the victims of a like persecution.[28]

The elements around the throne against whom this exhortatory resolution was directed did not react, they were protected by the proud, common negation of the West and especially the United States. The Moscow weekly *Russ* asserted that the Russian people was not a state-minded nation and did not strive for political rights in general, less so for constitutional rights of equality before the law. The Russian people placed the unlimited state power at the disposal of its government. What the Russians sought was moral freedom.[29] An eloquent answer to the degenerated West and to bill-of-rights-minded America!

But the cleverly formulated resolution dealt a direct blow to Alexander III, a narrow-minded autocrat and jingoist, who tried in his foreign policy to nullify his father's aid in the liberation of Bulgaria from Turkey, and to turn this new little constitutional country into something between a satellite and one more Russian province.

This resolution was enthusiastically echoed by the philosopher Vladimir Solovyov, author of three volumes on *La Russie et l'église universelle*, who blessed America for her courageous action against the often cruel intolerance of his own government. He regarded

[28] *Congressional Record*, 47th Congress (1882), H.R. Res. 151, p. 1647.
[29] *Russ*, May 9 and 23, 1881.

Russia's regime of the eighties and nineties as basically pagan. In his essays on The Sins of Russia and The Judaeo-Christian Problem, he repented "as a Christian and a Slav" the systematic persecution of Jews. And there is no doubt that Solovyov's moral appeal rang loudly enough to magnify the faint voice of America of that time in spite of his somewhat detached political position between the conservative and the liberal camp.

But arguments and ethical admonitions had no hearing from the believers in "genuine Russian" monarchism. In 1911 the rightists and nationalists were unable to conceive that America's abrogation of the treaty was a delayed eruption of stored-up aversion to czarism, an aversion which was strengthened by the arrival in the United States of an ever growing number of emigrants from the most oppressed groups and sects of the western belt of the Empire, and not by "malicious" propaganda of Russia's enemies, as the bureaucracy and the privileged reactionary upper strata argued.

Although Minister of Foreign Affairs Sazonov was ideologically close to rightist circles, his speech in the Imperial Duma on April 13/26, 1912, when the first gusts of indignation had begun to die down, and the liberal opposition rose to criticize the exaggerated jingoism, was delivered in more moderate terms:

In conclusion I have to mention the statement of the United States regarding its abrogation of the Russo-American commercial treaty of 1832 to be effective December 18/31, 1912. You are well informed about the conditions under which this cancellation of an old agreement has taken place. I therefore do not consider myself entitled to burden you with all the details. Suffice it only to remark that the unfounded statements in the transatlantic press that Russia did not adhere to certain parts of the treaty are not believed even by Americans, who are thoroughly acquainted with the essence of the question. The President of the United States has rightly rejected such an erroneous notion and has given to the abrogation a form that is entirely acceptable from the viewpoint of international relations.

Russia has always faithfully performed her treaty obligations, and all assertions to the contrary cannot withstand serious criticism. In the event of a proposal to conclude a new trade treaty with the United States, the Government will take into consideration the desires of the interested circles in Russia. But being filled with a consciousness of national decency and being in this respect closely united with all strata of the Russian people, the Government has the firm intention not to allow any infringements from abroad of the inalienable rights of Russia, as a sovereign state, to regulate its internal legislation exclusively from the standpoint of its own needs and conditions.

We hope that the common sense which Americans possess will make them see the justice of our views and that the age-long friendly relations between the Russian and American peoples will not be overshadowed by differences of opinion.[30]

The first responsible economic body to react to the overheated measures of the Octobrists and Nationalists was the Council of the Conferences of Representatives of Industry and Trade. This body was convoked as early as December 12/25, 1911. It was fully informed as to the steps taken by Ambassador Guild to negotiate a new agreement to replace the abrogated treaty—a new treaty "more responsive to the interests of both Governments and more adequate to the needs of their important relations." [31]

Almost all the members of the Council condemned the legislative steps of the Octobrists and Rightists. The main address was delivered by V. I. Timiriazev, a member of the Imperial State Council (upper chamber of constitutional Russia). He presented figures to show that the implementation of the proposed bill would inevitably have the most harmful consequences for the entire economic life of the country. America, he said, did not depend on Russia; on the contrary, Russia needed America. The commodities and products imported from America were of tremendous significance, and any application of the brake would lead to general confusion in the industrial life of Russia. Particularly vital in this respect was the import of cotton and agricultural machinery, which Russian manufacture, industry, and agriculture had to have. Russia imported from America annually eight million poods of cotton. Timiriazev found that the merchant-industrialist class could only oppose the bill of the Octobrists.

Similar views were expressed by P. Avdakov, another member of the Imperial State Council. A detailed report on the question was

[30] *Stenograficheskii Otchot Gos. Dumy* (Stenographic Minutes of the State Duma, 3rd Duma, 5th session, Apr. 13/26, 1912, pp. 2172-2173.
[31] *Papers Relating to the Foreign Relations of the United States*, 1911, p. 699.

given by M. M. Fiodorov, former Minister of Trade and Industry, who concluded by stating that the bill of the Octobrists was a mistake even from the viewpoint of nationalism, because it would deliver a crushing blow to the productive capacity of the country.

A St. Petersburg journal reporting this conference of the Council concluded: "The United States has set a precedent unheard of in reactionary countries of Europe. The country of the dollar has proved to be at the same time the country of freedom and civic decency." [32]

The leading liberal monthly commented on the abrogation of the treaty and the reaction of the nationalists:

From 1904 on, the demand for abolition of confessional discrimination against American citizens in Russia has appeared in the planks of both leading political parties [in the United States]. In 1908 during the elections William Taft promised in the name of the Republican party to take all measures to satisfy the just demands. . . . It is simply absurd and arbitrary to assert, as the *Novoye Vremya* does, that the decisions of the government and the Congress are entirely a product of Jewish agitation, that therefore they do not deserve any attention. . . . But even if the Congress or the President would lend an ear to certain unrevealed captains of finance, the United States still remains a great and mighty power with which we must maintain friendly and favorable relations, particularly in view of our interests in the Far East. Whatever the internal political relations or conditions in the United States may be, they do not give the Russian press the right to minimize the significant role of the transatlantic republic in international affairs. Besides, it is not for our nationalists to speak arrogantly about foreign internal affairs. What would these Russian patriots say should an influential American paper disdainfully begin to characterize the concealed manipulations of our Russian administration and parliament? Most likely the *Novoye Vremya* would regard this as an impertinent foreign encroachment on our internal affairs. . . .

Some of our short-witted nationalists found it necessary even to threaten the Americans with a tariff war; in other words, they would be ready, in order to display their patriotism, to reject the proposal of President Taft to negotiate a new commercial treaty.

It still remains incomprehensible exactly by what the patriotic feelings of our nationalists were so badly wounded. Is it a fact that the government of the United States protects the rights of a category of citizens

[32] *Razsviet* (Dawn), Dec. 16, 1911.

who, within our boundaries, would be subject to various limitations? Americans are entitled to interpret their political and international obligations in their own way. . . . The practical leading men of our industry certainly could not be misled by the childish bill of the Octobrist leaders, but it is bad enough that these leaders saw fit to consider such a bill. . . . Various branches of our industry depend on regular trade with America and would suffer incalculably from any rise in customs. . . . Common sense as well as reasonable patriotism dictate that we should strive to conclude in due time a new trade treaty with the United States on the basis of real reciprocity and mutual equality.[33]

Essentially the same stand was taken by the liberal dailies of St. Petersburg—like *Retch*, which insisted on the conclusion of a new treaty satisfactory to both countries—and of Moscow—like *Russkiya Viedomosti*.

Among the parliamentary declarations of the liberal opposition on this question, only the short speech of Paul Miliukov, the leader of the Constitutional Democrats (Cadets), will be quoted. His speech was very critical, and it was marred by incessant hostile remarks from the pro-government benches. He began by refuting the distortion in American papers of an interview he had granted—a distortion taken from rightist Russian papers, which reported him as condemning "Jewish agitation" in America against the Russian government:

In the first place, it is my duty to repudiate such quotations of my opinion.

I categorically declare that I could not have ascribed the agitation for the abrogation of the treaty exclusively to Jews. The first sentence of my interview, "I condemn Jewish agitation," is wrongly ascribed to me. I know quite well that the entire public opinion of America—and not only her Jews—is indignant at the violation of the basic principle enunciated in the amendments to the American Constitution. And this, gentlemen, is not just my own opinion. Here is what was said in Washington by a prominent member of Congress who introduced the resolution that was rejected by the intervention of the President. (Count Bobrinski, rightist-nationalist, rose from his seat: "What is his name?") His family name is Sulzer. (Laughter from the benches of the center and right sectors.) You, obviously, are interested in the descent of the man. Your laughter shows that you are sure Sulzer is a Jew. Allow me to

[33] *Viestnik Yevropy*, Jan., 1912, pp. 370-371, 372.

give you some biographical information about him. (Noise on the right-ist benches; ringing by the chairman.*) Mr. William Sulzer, the member of the Congress who is at present the Chairman of the Foreign Affairs Committee of the House, was born in New York of Irish parents and he took his family name Sulzer from his stepfather of German descent. (Voice from the right: "From his stepfather?") So you see, not even through his stepfather, let alone his parents, could he possibly be tied to the Jews. And now what does this Sulzer say? (Noise from the right. Shouts of "Enough!") "This is not a Jewish question; it is an American problem concerning a most important principle."

The Minister of Foreign Affairs said that this is an issue of our sovereignty. We are convinced that Russian sovereignty remains untouched; nobody is going to ask of us a special consular jurisdiction for foreigners or any kind of extraterritoriality. It is shameful that such proposals should be made, which are on the border line dividing civilized mankind from uncivilized. I disagree with the form in which the agitation developed, though I fully agree with its content. (An ironical voice from the right: "I should say so!") I am ashamed as a Russian (noise on the rightist benches) when Europe and America become entitled to classify us as Asiatics; in fact, even Asia is beginning to recognize the basic principles of universal culture. I do not wish that we alone should remain degenerate among humankind. (Exclamations on the right: "Oh, oh!") What we really must do I cannot tell you in the few minutes left to me. . . . I do not wish to formulate my conclusion as an indictment of the Minister. I shall say only that a sad destiny awaits a country that tolerates a situation in which the whims and caprices of irresponsible diplomats are servilely acquiesced in by the whole Ministry and are checked, not by national interest or the will of the people, but only by the technical impracticability of these caprices and whims and by the paraphernalia of international diplomacy. (Applause on the left, booing on the right.) [34]

The bill of the Octobrists was submitted to the Financial Committee of the Duma, which was to decide on its desirability. As far as can be ascertained, the Duma did not return to a general discussion of the topic. It should be borne in mind, however, that over the abrogation of the treaty of 1832 a definite differentiation developed between the pro-government bloc and the opposition.

Official Russia, despite the persistent resistance of the opposition

* The presiding officer of the Duma used a bell instead of a gavel.
[34] *Stenograficheskii Otchot, etc.*, Apr. 14/27, 1912, pp. 2240-2242.

in the Duma and in the press, instead of introducing reforms, particularly agrarian, social, and self-determination for ethnic minorities, occupied itself with empty nationalism. It was as if the régime was deliberately trying not only to incite social discontent among the main strata of the population, but also to stir up the numerous ethnic and religious minorities by humiliating and insulting the Jews, a dispersed, nonterritorial minority that offered the least resistance, and the well rooted territorial "minorities" as well, the Finns, Poles, Ukrainians, and the Baltic and Caucasian peoples—the whole western and southern belt of the huge empire.

The abrogation of the treaty of 1832, an unusually courageous step, dealt a painful blow to St. Petersburg that was wholly unintended by Washington. Though during her imperial period Russia suffered a series of military defeats, none of these hurt government circles and their followers quite as much as the unrequited diplomatic lesson in human rights delivered by the Yankees, under conditions of cloudless peace, to an old great power, a lesson wholly free of even the slightest taint of transgression of international law. Even economic reprisals against America in the form of prohibitive tariffs could not be effectively undertaken. The lesson had to be accepted, albeit unwillingly.

It was helpful and desirable for the opposition. We have seen how it reacted to the American measure. There was neither rage nor indignation toward the United States on the part of the opposition, ranging from the moderate liberal Cadets to the less and more radical left, with regard to the "diminution of Russian sovereignty," as the Ministry of Foreign Affairs and the rightist press stated the situation.

The fourth and last Duma, elected for five years in the autumn of 1912, was less nationalistic than its predecessor, the third. Under pressure of the grave events of the First World War it was compelled to concentrate—belatedly—on constitutional reforms.

Reluctantly it even attempted in 1915 and 1916 to step toward the enactment of a law granting equality of rights. However, the split between the nationalist rightists and the democratic opposition which organized itself into a progressive bloc was too deep for bridging. To the very end of the old regime the political forces and factions in and around the Duma could not escape the American impact and American patterns of valuation. As if to make this clear, in the last year of the Imperial Duma, the parliament had to think about American credit and a loan under the financial strain of war. Even the extreme monarchist wing could not neglect the issue. It went along with the bill discussed in the Duma in the early summer of 1916 for legal equality covering persons of all allogeneous nationalities in the huge Empire and the abolition of the last remnants of discrimination against persons previously registered with different orders (peasants, urban artisans, etc.).

The specter of America, which five years earlier had abrogated her treaty with Russia, continued to haunt the Duma; and now all were afraid America would reject a loan. The radical Petrograd paper *Den* warned in June, 1916, that the fact that the United States had not changed the views on equality had caused it to abrogate the 1832 treaty. It also reminded Markov-Vtoroi, the leader of the nationalist monarchists, that, not wishing to reject financial relations with the United States, he could not proudly insist on unlimited state sovereignty, which to him consisted of the full right of Russia to have rightless citizens. According to *Den*, what for America was a question of decency—the equality of all citizens— proved for Markov to be a humiliation to his patriotic pride. But Markov's pride cost Russia too much.

Birzheviya Viedomosti presented equality as a presupposition without which Russia could not be regarded as an equal partner in the Western alliance against the Central Powers. But most clearly *Russkiya Viedomosti* on June 22, 1916, emphasized that the ethnical inequality of Jews and other minorities was harmful for the overdue normalization of the international relations of Russia with the West, and particularly with the United States, "which cannot and will not make peace with our handling of minorities. Ethnic and religious nondiscrimination is the common denominator of modern culture." Russia had to reach equality in domestic policies in order to defend it in the world against the German idea of Teutonic hegemony.

In the last months of its existence after the czars the Duma participated in the first stages of the democratic régime under the Provisional Government, which in its first weeks sweepingly enacted full equality in constitutional and civil rights for all citizens.

XVII *Russian Constitutional Thought on the United States: Kovalevski and Ostrogorski*

Russia was known by those who knew it best to have been always democratic at heart, in all the vital habits of her thought.—Woodrow Wilson

THERE WAS ONLY ONE FIELD IN WHICH AMERICA CONTINUED strongly to impress its influence on Russian thought: political science and particularly constitutional law. And this influence lingered long after disappointment over social developments in America, particularly in the areas of social reform and socialism, had faded.

Although there was always censorship in Russia, *Moskovskiya Viedomosti* (Moscow Gazette) in 1784 could allow itself the luxury of printing A Short Description of the Life and Character of General Washington, which stated courageously: "George Washington has established a republic which in all probability will become a fortress of Freedom, of Freedom driven from Europe by her luxury and debauchery."

This first indication of the intense attraction of young America for the élite of Russian society, felt as early as the Enlightenment under the benevolent autocracy of Catherine II, foreshadowed future political doctrine concerning the transatlantic republic. Here was fruitful soil for moderate constitutionalism as developed in the United States. Strangely enough, the doctrine of constitutional law and politics in Russia was always far ahead of the actual régime and official ideology.

The imperial state universities—there were no private ones in czarist Russia—as a rule were not the handmaidens of the régime. From 1814 to 1855, during the second period of Alexander I and under Nicholas I, the most consciously reactionary among Russian monarchs, efforts were made to extirpate Western liberal influences in university education, but with little or no success. The academic chairs in history, philosophy, jurisprudence, and natural law, economics, and even public law were often centers of liberal, subversive doctrine opposed to the teachings advocated by the Crown. An interesting commentary on this situation is the fact that the courses in constitutional law, which usually covered Western foreign countries, and jurisprudence were the most popular not only among students of law but also in other departments. Under Nicholas I these courses were dropped from the curriculum.

Even the interpretation of Russian positive public law was influenced by liberalism. In the last third of the nineteenth century A. Gradovski and N. Korkunov of the University of St. Petersburg, Boris Chicherin and A. S. Alexeyev of the University of Moscow, and other leading professors of constitutional law tried to temper the arbitrarians of the czarist regime by special interpretation of the provisions of written law and of the decisions of the administrative departments of the Supreme Senate. The small group of defenders of the "unlimited autocratic power of the monarch" was always on the defensive, while the champions of liberalism felt themselves on the offensive as academic prophets of the fulfillment of the only just political ideal. In the very centers of Russian autocracy and after 1906 under the shaky constitutionalism, democracy was the regulative idea of the social élite and of broad strata of the urban lower classes, despite the fact that down to February, 1917, Russia had not achieved a democratic state order.[1]

Down to 1905–1906, when the October constitutional manifesto was published and the first constitution providing for a limited monarchy was enacted (April 23, 1906), few professors of constitutional law would publicly defend the three official tenets of Russian absolutism: autocracy, orthodoxy, and Russian nationalism. After 1905–1906 the constitutionalists were in a better position; the old autocratic fundamental law had been abolished, and they tried to interpret the new quasi-representative constitution, in the hands of a weak legislative Duma and ministers without any responsibility to the central legislature, as a real constitution limiting the absolute power of the monarch. From 1906 down to February, 1917, the champions of the prerogatives of the monarch were

[1] Max M. Laserson, "Democracy as a Regulative Idea and as an Established Regime," *Journal of the History of Ideas*, Vol. III, pp. 351-352 (June, 1947).

a negligible minority. The majority of the political science and history faculties in both capitals were for a more radical constitution, for the establishment at least of regular Western parliamentarism, including responsibility of the members of the Cabinet to the Duma as heads of their departments or ministries.[2]

One of the leading monarchists complained about constitutional law:

Our science has never gone ahead of the existing regime; it has never helped the state order to develop; it has never done anything in favor of the monarchical principle except to compile numerous statutory articles. This shows that our political science, being mainly imitative, has never attained the level of European creative scholarship.[3]

Years later N. A. Zakharov repeated these lamentations:

Our constitutional doctrine, which fed itself in the past and continues to do so in the present only on Western material without checking it and without proper comparison of Russian and Western European historical ways of life, adopted the conclusion of Western science as a general basis of constitutional law, rejecting the Russian state order as an unacceptable exception from the general rule. Throughout the entire nineteenth century our constitutionalists continually emphasized in their works the originality of the Russian monarchic principle, but they never tried to discover its own ways, nor did they consent to a common formulation of our state order.[4]

V. V. Rosanov, one of the nonacademic advocates of Russian absolutism and a contributor to *Novoye Vremia*, relates in a reminiscent passage on his university studies:

The late A. Gradovski in the early 1880's fumed with rage at the unwillingness [of Alexander III] to grant a constitution and insisted that the natural current of events would inevitably lead to constitution-

[2] That is why, after 1905, the increasing autonomy of universities, which became represented in the Upper Chamber, led in 1911 to a clash with the imperial Ministry of Education under Leo Kasso. It resulted in the resignation of a group of liberal and independent-minded professors of the Moscow and Petersburg universities. They were replaced by Minister Kasso with appointees more amenable to the government.

[3] Lev Tikhomirov, *Monarkhicheskaya gosudarstvennost* (The Monarchic Idea of the State), Moscow, 1905, Pt. III, pp. 54, 213-216.

[4] N. A. Zakharov, *Sistema russkoi gosudarstvennoi vlasti* (The System of the Russian State Power), Novocherkassk, 1912, p. 96.

alism. Another much revered professor of general history used to inter-rupt a student in an oral examination when the latter mentioned that Russia was not a constitutional country and ask in a mocking tone: "Tell me, please, what other European country besides Russia is deprived of a constitution?" To which the student would timidly reply, "Turkey." And in this answer was concealed by implication a biting irony arising precisely from the comparison of a backward Moslem country with the student's own fatherland.[5]

We shall here concentrate only on the Russian academic writers who were experts in political science and constitutional law. The sympathies of many Russian political thinkers in respect to certain features of the American government have already been mentioned in previous chapters. Among the more important Russian publi-cists who devoted much of their effort to research or interpretation of the United States, we shall deal principally with Stepan Fortu-natov, Boris Chicherin, Maxime Kovalevski, and Moissey Ostrogor-ski. But the Russian enlightened public was not wholly dependent on Russian writers in this field; it was also acquainted with the most important English and French books treating of American political ideas, history, and public law both in the original languages and in Russian translation, from the writings of the founding fathers of the American Republic, down through Tocqueville and the his-torians of the Civil War (Draper, Ingram, the Count of Paris, La-boulaye, etc.), to the popular volumes of James Bryce.

Stepan Fortunatov

Fortunatov, a liberal professor of constitutional law and political history at the University of Moscow, published in 1879 a work on the History of Political Doctrines in the United States,[6] the first volume of which dealt with *The Federalist* and John C. Calhoun's disquisitions. It appeared at a time when the current of reforms initiated by Alexander II during the early 1860's began to stagnate. Actually, the intention of the book was to put pressure on the czarist

[5] V. V. Rosanov, *O podrazumevayemom smysle nashei monarkhii* (On the Underlying Meaning of Our Monarchy), St. Petersburg, 1912, pp. 71-72.
[6] *Politicheskiya ucheniya v Soyedinionnykh Shtatakh*, Vol. I, especially pp. 60, 64, 104.

government to continue these reforms along the lines followed in the United States; namely, separation of powers, individual rights, and self-government. The book begins with a description of John Adams's *Defence of the Constitutions of Government of the United States of America.*

There can scarcely be any doubt that the description and analysis of *The Federalist* made it possible for Fortunatov to speak in support of self-government. A kind of modern local self-government had been introduced in 1864 under Alexander II, which was much attacked by the conservative elements. Fortunatov was delighted to rely on *The Federalist* to show that precisely a large country like Russia was destined to have a network of self-governing bodies. To this end he wrote:

> It is no less certain than it is important, notwithstanding the contrary opinions that have been entertained, that the larger the society, provided it lies within a practicable sphere, the more capable it will be of self-government.

Fortunatov elaborated in detail Calhoun's ideas on nullification and the concept of states' rights; but he was unoriginal and sterile in his analysis. He did not draw any parallel with the tremendous growth of Russia at the expense of such absorbed states as the Ukraine with its own "state rights." Calhoun's whole theory was for him no more than it was for his German teachers at Berlin and Heidelberg; the politically colored juridical difference between the federal *Bundesstaat* and the confederated *Staatenbund.* In general, he did not even wish to turn to Calhoun's social and broad political ideas except state rights and liberties. For the rest, he described at great length the changing galaxy of Anglo-Saxon doctrines, beginning with those of Hooker, Gibbon, Algernon Sydney, and even John Locke, without being able to show exactly how this splendid English political heritage was changed or institutionalized on American soil.

Obviously, Fortunatov's more modest aim was to acquaint the intelligent Russian reader with American political doctrines. However, he took Calhoun's constitutional arguments too seriously when the clever Southerner spoke of the derivation of the federal government from the people of the states, or the necessity of defending the representation of the minority from the tyranny of the majority, or even the harm of the protective tariff.

In contradistinction to most Russian constitutionalists Fortunatov was an adherent of American federalism.[7] He published a series of profound articles on American democracy in the review *Russkaya Mysl* and also in the liberal daily, *Russkiya Viedomosti*. With the emergence of the revolutionary movement he stressed American federalism and the possibility of an adaptation of some American institutions to a new Russia. He supported an upper chamber, but only on the lines of the United States Senate. Beginning with the summer of 1905 he openly propagated the doctrine of American federalism.

Boris Chicherin

Boris Chicherin (1830–1904), a landed nobleman, was one of the leading political thinkers of imperial Russia, a legal philosopher, and professor at the University of Moscow. He was the author of an important History of Political Doctrines in five volumes and a Course in Political Science in three volumes, the third containing a description and evaluation of American political life.

An uncle of the future People's Commissar for Foreign Affairs (George Chicherin), a conservative liberal, an ardent defender of private property and federalism, and a rightist Hegelian, Boris Chicherin was spiritually predestined to become the extoller of the classical period of young America and a reluctant critic of the United States after the Civil War with its complex economics which he failed to grasp and its political excrescences which he indignantly condemned. Ideologically, he stood between Tocqueville

[7] In a very interesting article, Some Reminiscences, printed in the *Arkhiv Russkoi Revolutsii*, Berlin, 1926, p. 189, Professor N. N. Alexeyev, a Moscow constitutionalist, remarked on the political orientation of the higher Russian intelligentsia during the Provisional Government and shortly after it: "We were particularly suspicious of the slightest remark regarding self-determination or federalism. Perhaps this was one of our fatal mistakes. Now I feel that the political consciousness of the various provinces of Russia with respect to their own political existence is an inevitable product of the revolution, a fact which may be regrettable, but with which we must reckon. . . . Every reasonable Russian policy consists in channeling the action of this force in the direction of Russian interests and not in suppressing it by aimless and senseless violence."

and Bryce. With the exception of a few Supreme Court cases, his bibliographical sources on America did not touch positive law; they consisted mainly of ideological literature pertaining to political theory.

Chicherin was a moderate conservative; though a major adversary of autocracy, he could not be a proponent of democracy. His attitude toward democracy in general and the United States in particular was to a high degree conditioned by his aristocratic origin, going back to the decline of Byzantium. It was his position that in political life the leading role did not necessarily fall to the most ethical or the most educated part of society. This fundamental fact of every democracy was particularly evident in the United States. Not only were the burdens of the state forced on the shoulders of the well-to-do classes, which became the chief source of state revenue, but the political power tended to become unlimited. Chicherin went so far as to assert that in this respect even an unlimited autocrat was less dangerous, because of his anxiety not to provoke dissatisfaction among the people lest they revolt and overthrow his authority. A dominant aristocracy was also afraid of the enmity of the people. A democracy, on the other hand, had nothing to fear because it had behind it the majority and the political power. That was why the democratic despotism was the most terrible of all despotisms. The French terror was ample proof of this. Such a despotism was inevitably against the freedom of the individual. All critical observers of democracy, even those who sympathized with it, principally Tocqueville and after him John Stuart Mill, Spencer, Maine, and Lecky, admitted that this was the weakest point in democracy. Democracy in its entirety was based on freedom, that was its whole meaning; nevertheless, if not checked, democracy inevitably led to suppression of liberty. Chicherin quoted Tocqueville:

In my opinion the main evil of the present democratic institutions of the United States does not arise . . . from their weakness, but from their irresistible strength. I am not so much alarmed at the excessive liberty which reigns in that country, as at the inadequate securities [of the individual or minority] which one finds there against tyranny.[8]

[8] A. de Tocqueville, *Democracy in America*, ed. F. Bowen, New York, 1898, I, 332.

Studying the United States in its best period, Tocqueville came to the conclusion that democracy represented the supremacy of mediocrity. Democracy lacked tradition, which produced stability and permanence in political life. It did not look backward but forward; it did not look for preservation of the status quo but for improvement. This was a natural striving of the lower classes which had attained a position of dominance.

That was why Chicherin concluded that democracy could by no means be regarded as ideal for human welfare. However, it could not be condemned out of hand. A moderate democracy that respected freedom and gave free play to the various currents in its society could become a very good form of political order. The United States was a case in point. There was no tradition of monarchism there; it was difficult even to imagine that the United States would under any conditions turn into a monarchy.

In a somewhat involved way Chicherin, obviously following the doctrine of Aristotle, tried to show that American democracy had degenerated into an ochlocracy. He regarded the United States as the main type of modern democracy. For him there was no doubt that in Washington's day America had represented a lofty pattern of both civic virtue and civil order:

Love of the common cause combined with the broadest development of liberty was the predominant feature of the North American commonwealth. The rational, cautious, and practical transformation of the federal order, after the original confederation had proved inadequate, was beyond all praise. It was one of the most splendid pages in the political history of nations.

However, subsequent development did not bring perfection but rather a distortion of the established order. In spite of tremendous economic prosperity, disintegration set in, in the foundations of the state order. The Presidency of Jackson was not on a level with Washington's.

None the less, the moral foundations of American life stand firm. Impartial observers like Tocqueville, admitting the defects of the democratic order, were able to dwell on its advantages with love and admiration. Its darkest stain was slavery in the southern states. No matter how indignant northern public opinion has been over it, political considerations of extraordinary importance, particularly fear of a civil war, compelled the toleration of this evil. . . . But particularly after the abolition of Negro slavery the elements of degeneration continued their dreadful work. Uncurbed private interests slipped into all branches of political life. The whole state order became the spoils of politicians for whom social activity meant nothing more than an instrument of gain and profit. The most sordid kind of reckless robbery is openly committed and gains force against which honest citizens futilely struggle. Money interests and undisguised bribery dominate in the highest circles of the Union. Comparing the description of political and social conditions in the United States as given by its most recent explorer, Bryce, with the picture given by Tocqueville in the 1830's, one is inevitably terrified by the speed with which the disintegration and the distortion of a sometimes very high body politic takes place. Bryce tries, but in vain, to soften this impression by remarking that very recently some slight improvement can be noticed. Such weak statements lose all significance for our times. A system of pensions for fictitious participants in the Civil War, pensions which just ruin the State, a law that forces the Treasury annually to buy silver at impossibly high prices only to enrich the owners of silver mines, the present agitation in favor of free coinage of silver in order to repay debts with fictitious money—all this demonstrates clearly the disappearance not only of a feeling for the social good but also of all moral restraint.[9]

Chicherin reproached Bryce for not mentioning the many social disadvantages and dark aspects of American life, including the exaggerated role of journalism without any juridical or moral limits, and the injustices to the southern states through the legal equalization of the Negroes with the whites, which led to horrible mismanagement by the Negro majority. His final criticism was directed at socialism, which he despised:

Up to now, thanks to economic conditions in North America, thanks to an abundance of land and capital combined with a small population, socialism has not taken root there. But in recent times socialism has grown and has threatened the democracy with endless conflicts and innumerable other difficulties. The main strength of the North American democracy consisted and still consists in a miraculous efficiency of the people, for which full freedom is the first and necessary condition; socialism, on the contrary, is based upon suppression of freedom and self-activity, which is replaced by state activities. Unquestionably, in American society socialism will meet a most powerful resistance, for

[9] *Kurs gosudarstvennoi nauki* (Course in Political Science), Vol. III, Moscow, 1898, p. 205.

there is no other movement that is more contrary to the spirit of the American people. However, in time of economic crisis, when there are masses of unemployed people who know no limits and who strive exclusively for material satisfaction, these could revolt. And what could prevent them from seizing power and becoming the chief managers of the state's destiny? [10]

Democracy, Chicherin went on, did not have at its disposal forces able to meet mob attacks. Even in peaceful times the mob committed arbitrary executions which were called lynch law. But, with all his skepticism toward American democracy, he concluded: "Be that as it may, if there is a people for whom democracy is well suited because of the natural conditions under which they live as well as their spirit, ideas, and mores, it is the North Americans." [11]

Maxime Kovalevski

Maxime Kovalevski (1851–1916) was born in Kharkov (Ukraine) into a wealthy and highly educated aristocratic family. From the very beginning of his studies at the University of Kharkov he was under the influence of French and British tradition and institutions. Both his dissertations for advanced degrees were on British topics: the first, for the degree of Magister of Constitutional Law, was on the History of County Police and Judiciary in England; the second, for the doctorate, dealt with the Social Structure of England to the End of the Middle Ages.

These dissertations were written in France and England. At the University of Berlin he attended the lectures of Rudolf von Gneist, the famous expert on English political and social institutions. In Paris he worked under Emile Boutmy of the Ecole Libre des Sciences Politiques, under whom his younger Russian colleague Ostrogorski also studied.

In London, Kovalevski was introduced to George Henry Lewes and made the acquaintance of Karl Marx. With the help of Lewes and his wife, the famous writer George Eliot, he was elected a member of the Athenaeum Club. It was a great honor for a young foreigner and provided an opportunity for him to be introduced to Herbert Spencer.

[10] *Ibid.*, p. 206.   [11] *Ibid.*, p. 207.

As professor of Western European constitutional law, very popular among the students for his liberal views and his hostility toward czarism, Kovalevski fell under the suspicion of the reactionary regime of Alexander III; and in 1887 it was suggested to him that he leave the University of Moscow. From that year until 1905 he worked as a writer and teacher, mainly in England and France. At Oxford University he gave a course in the history of Russian law. From 1889 his chief residence was in France.

Kovalevski was a lifelong friend of another Russian Anglophile, (Sir) Paul Vinogradov who, in a solemn session of the Russian Society of the English Banner following Kovalevski's death in 1916, described his friend, the former president of the society, as belonging to that school of Russian liberals who, after the 1880's, by-passed neighboring Germany and turned to England and its libertarian tradition. The same tendencies in Kovalevski's education and orientation were described by the famous Russian historian N. Kareyev.[12]

It must be said that for Kovalevski interest in the United States was subordinated to his all-embracing knowledge of English history and public law. The list of his writings on the United States is comparatively short: an essay on American Constitutional Law;[13] The Agrarian Policy of North America;[14] Local Self-Government in the United States;[15] a mimeographed course on the History of the American Constitution (214 typed pages);[16] and a few prefaces, among them one to the Russian edition of Woodrow Wilson's *State*[17] and another to Wilson's *Constitutional Government in the United States*.[18] But he also touched on American political doctrines and institutions in other works, particularly in his voluminous Genesis of Modern Democracy.[19]

Kovalevski visited America first in 1881, a second time in 1901.

[12] See the symposium, *M. M. Kovalevski, Uchiony, Gosudarstvenny i Obshchestvenni Deyatel i Grazhdanin* (Kovalevski, Scholar, Statesman, Social Worker, and Citizen), Petrograd, 1917, pp. 62, 176.

[13] In the symposium *Politicheskii stroi Sovremennykh Gosudarstv*.

[14] In *Russkaya Misl*, Vol. IV (1883).

[15] In *Viestnik Yevropy*, Vol. II (1885).

[16] This material was used in a course taught by Kovalevski at the St. Petersburg Polytechnical Institute. There seems to be no copy of it in the United States.

[17] Moscow, 1905.

[18] St. Petersburg, 1909.

[19] Moscow, 1897; 2nd ed., 1901.

In his preface in 1905 to the Russian translation of *The State* he mentioned the first trip:

> Wilson belongs to that school of American publicists who, on the initiative of Herbert Adams, turned Johns Hopkins University at Baltimore into a nursery of political science for the entire Union. During my first trip to America I visited this university and was present at the very emergence of that scholarly library with the help of which Herbert Adams and his closest co-workers, including Wilson, intended to stimulate in America an urge for a juridico-historical investigation of local institutions and habits, in which the comparative method would be used. . . . Herbert Adams went through the school of Bentham, Austin, and Mills, a school well known to American and English learned jurists. This school educated the Americans in a spirit of sobriety and wholesome restraint by positive facts, customs, judicial decisions, and statutes. Adams learned something in Germany, too, particularly from Bluntschli, but he remained free of any kind of German metaphysics. This is also the way that Woodrow Wilson looked at the State.

There is no need to emphasize that Kovalevski was unqualifiedly pro-American on a series of problems and issues. America was for him a more democratic and pleasant, less formal and stiff body politic than her mother country. Even in the relations between person and person, group and group, in everyday life, in dress, manners, folkways, he preferred Americans. More than that, he admired the boundless energy, the brilliant and many-sided creativeness, the independence, the friendliness, and the tolerance of Americans.[20] In his speeches both in the Duma and after 1907 in the imperial State Council, Kovalevski often cited the United States on matters of freedom of association and assembly, on the bill of rights, as well as on economic matters, and on the building and development of railroad traffic.

One of the most spectacular discussions in the first Duma was opened by Kovalevski who, though belonging to the party of Democratic Reform—a more conservative group than the Constitutional Democrats—suddenly appeared on the rostrum to speak for a bill on freedom of public meetings introduced by the Social Democrats. The bill was rather loosely drawn. Kovalevski used this occasion to

[20] Pitirim Sorokin, professor of sociology at Harvard University and former secretary to Maxime Kovalevski, in a letter to the author dated July 9, 1949.

develop before the first Russian parliament the Anglo-American conception of freedom "which has already prevailed for two hundred years in these two countries," and presented the views of Albert Venn Dicey and other English and American constitutionalists on the right of public assembly.[21] He defended the old rule of English constitutional law that any given person A can meet another given person B or an indefinite number of persons at any appointed place as long as the law is not thereby broken. True, he did not dwell on meetings of a mischievous character or on "engagements to embark on any seditious or mutinous purpose" through the public meeting. The Russian and Caucasian Social Democrats, unversed in the niceties of Anglo-American constitutional law, vociferously hailed Kovalevski as an undreamed-of savior of their draft.

Aligned against Kovalevski, for all his simple goodness and charm, was a phalanx of Russian constitutionalists and legal scholars, including Shershenewitch, Petrazhitski, and Kokoshkin, who supported the continental European view built on an exact statutory formulation of the rights of the citizen as against the state or its police agents and requiring precise laws on public meetings. They argued that Anglomania or Americanism could not be applied to continental Europe, where an old tradition of the all-embracing tutelage of the state over its living subjects flourished under the police state and had been introduced from Germany into Russia by Peter the Great—a state order "which even now continues partially to exist with us." It may be noted that the majority of the Duma, particularly the peasant representatives, did not appreciate or even understand the discussion.

From March, 1907, Kovalevski's career was in the State Council, the Russian equivalent of the House of Lords, as one of the few representatives of the Academy of Sciences and the universities. In the Duma he had belonged to the moderate center; in the State Council, ironically enough, he stood at the extreme left.

The number of speeches in the State Council in which Kovalevski referred to the United States as a model, a necessary precedent, or a source of important information is astonishing. A careful sifting of the stenographic minutes of the Council from March, 1907, to

[21] *Stenographic Minutes of the First Duma,* 1st session, 29th meeting, June 19, 1906, pp. 1458 ff.

March, 1916, when he died, reveals mention of the United States on the most diverse fields imaginable: constitutional law; self-government, including zemstvos; constitutional rights and autonomy of Finland; criminal procedure; suspended sentences; local judiciary; agrarian reform and the defense of the Russian village community; the expansion of Russia in the Maritime Provinces, the Amur region, and on the borders of Manchuria; the income tax; contracts concerning petroleum and oil fields; reform of the economy; technology of the Russian railroad system; *porto franco* and customs duties; the program of the university extensions; and even such abstract subjects as academic freedom and freedom of religion. When we read his speeches on the extension of the zemstvo self-government to Siberia, as we follow the correlation between political consciousness and local culture and the density of population illustrated by colonial America and the United States, we feel that we are attending a wonderfully rich lecture built on a comparative excursion into the past of America and Russia, wherein all the differences between the northern and southern states are taken into consideration. When Finland's right to autonomy was mentioned and the chauvinist Russian anti-Finnish proposals were discussed, Kovalevski cleverly described how America—from the early days of Franklin to the English offer to include a few Americans in Parliament, exactly like the proposal made by Russian nationalists to include three or four Finnish deputies in the 500-member Duma—progressed by way of confederation to full independence from England; and then it became clear why all the "genuinely Russian" jingoists outrageously attacked this "extreme leftist" of the Russian upper chamber.

When Kovalevski dealt with the necessity for an expanded, efficient, and well administered railroad network to serve the huge empire including Siberia, he felt compelled to mention specifically Prince Michael Khilkov, a pioneer in the Americanization of railroad technique in Russia. Khilkov had undertaken two trips to America, the first in 1860 and a much more extended one in 1864 when he entered the service of the Anglo-American interests constructing the Union Pacific Railroad. In order thoroughly to study the American system of railroad building from the ground up, the prince and former royal page became a simple American worker.

Later he was promoted to the traffic department. After years of American apprenticeship Khilkov returned to Russia, where he had a splendid career as a railroad engineer, became in the middle of the 1890's Minister of Communications and Roads, and died in 1909 as a member of the State Council.

In conclusion it should be said that this great Russian political thinker did not confine his interests and creative abilities to the political ideas and constitutional bodies of Russia and other countries. Between 1901 and 1914 he wrote seven volumes on the Economic Development of Europe Before Capitalism, which were translated into German, and lesser essays in the field of economic history. By some writers he was compared with the outstanding American political scientist John William Burgess; but the comparison should not be carried too far. Their common source of inspiration was the Ecole Libre des Sciences Politiques in Paris, on which Burgess patterned the School of Political Science at Columbia College which led to the latter's conversion into Columbia University. Kovalevski, too, used the Ecole Libre as a model for the Second Private University of St. Petersburg, including in its broad scope public law, sociology, and economics. Others compared him to Henry Maine, but he was much more scholarly than the brilliant Englishman, who avoided original investigation and travel. Kovalevski's scholarly activities included also travel and local research, ethnography and sociology. His classic two volumes on Law and Custom in the Caucasus (1890), based on an expedition to the Caucasian peoples, particularly the Ossetines, still have importance. In 1891, a course delivered at Oxford on Modern Custom and Ancient Law in Russia grew into an English book under that title.

The indefatigable and encyclopedic scholar produced a volume in Russian on Contemporary Sociologists (1905), two volumes on Sociology (1910), and a series of articles in that field. There is no doubt that his life in France and England and his two trips to the United States brought him in contact with the leading spirits of Western social science and greatly widened his horizon.

Most interesting is the fact that Kovalevski was under the influence of such American sociologists as Franklin Henry Giddings, pioneer of American sociology, and Lewis Henry Morgan, the world-famous ethnographer. Of Giddings's *The Principles of Sociology,* he wrote:

> This book deserves attention in many senses; in no other book have I found such abundant material on gregariousness and other social phenomena, particularly those connected with the life of animals, which can serve as an explanation of the nature and emergence of human society.[22]

Moissey Ostrogorski

> Mill could write, in 1861, a work, *Representative Government,* in which he paid not the slightest attention to the party system. There was no systematic study devoted to the subject until Ostrogorski published in 1902 a fine analysis of parties in the United States.—R. M. MacIver, *The Web of Government.*

Moissey Ostrogorski (1854–1920) was born in Grodno, the son of a Jewish merchant. He surpassed all his Russian predecessors— and, thus far, his successors—as a writer on constitutional and extraconstitutional problems of the United States. No other foreign author, except perhaps Sir James Bryce, has become so deeply rooted in the American scene of political science as this Russian whose *Democracy and the Organization of Political Parties* is a classic in English and American political literature.

After graduation from the Law Faculty of the University of St. Petersburg, Ostrogorski entered the civil service in the Ministry of Justice. However, with the growth of reaction under Alexander III he gave up this career. With all his love for the broad humanitarian study of law, the tenuous subtleties of Russian law and procedure bored him; and his profound interest in political history and political science led him to enter on the career of an independent scholar. His textbooks on Russian history for public schools were a tremendous success, long providing him with a substantial income; but they exercised only a small part of his capacity. More

[22] See M. Wagner on Kovalevski as a Sociologist, M. M. Kovalevski, *Uchiony,* etc. On Giddings see Kovalevski's *Sovremennye Sociologi* (Contemporary Sociologists), St. Petersburg, 1905, chap II. Cf. P. Sorokin, *Contemporary Sociological Theories* (New York, 1928), p. 727; Max M. Laserson, "Russian Sociology," in *Twentieth Century Sociology,* New York, 1945.

and more he was attracted by the general problems of the West. His first French book, on the rights of women, was an outgrowth of his training in France.

Young Ostrogorski was ambitious enough to dream greater dreams. Being deeply disappointed with the political conditions of his native country, he gave more and more thought to general political problems of lasting value for mankind. He was uncomfortable in the atmosphere of dogmatic admiration of the West which surrounded the deniers of Russian autocracy. He was also strongly opposed to the naïve tendency of some Russian publicists to idealize Russia's next-door neighbor, imperial Germany, as a model democratic national regime—a tendency of which even the professorial daily *Russkiya Viedomosti* was not entirely free.

Being spiritually frustrated in Russia, Ostrogorski directed his attention not toward Germany but first toward France, where he studied political science, and later toward what was then called in Russia the Anglo-Saxon world—embracing England, the British Dominions, and last but not least, the United States of America.

The study of English and American history and politics became his vocation. He plunged into it with all enthusiasm. But he would never have composed his work on democracy without having gone through a complete metamorphosis of methodology. He doubtless was impressed by the works of Tocqueville, Bryce, Green, and a line of English and American writers. He stopped writing on political problems on the basis of a knowledge of juridical sources: constitutions, laws, decrees, by-laws, ordinances, and the like. He became an empiricist and pragmatist; after that he courageously decided to deal with the complex and massive material of British and American politics, which, somewhat *a piori*, he regarded as basic to a general conception of the political problems of the world.

I met Ostrogorski during the troubled years of 1918 and 1919. The Russian intelligentsia was at a most depressing crisis: A choice had to be made between resistance and adaptation to the crystallizing Soviet regime. At that time his great successes in France and America, stemming from the appearance of his two volumes on Anglo-American democracy (in French and in English), were behind him. So was the publication of the abridged English edition of his great work in 1912. Further back was his election to the first

Russian Duma (1906), in which he participated together with Maxime Kovalevski, and which the two represented in the Inter-parliamentary Union. Appointment to a professorship in political science at Cleveland was another of Ostrogorski memories.

In spite of all the tremendous political shifts, Ostrogorski's attitude continued to be nonconformist. With many of his previous sources of income drying up and the limits of academic freedom shrinking daily, he made no change in his ways. As though nothing had happened, in Ostrogorski's spacious study lined with books in Russian, English, French, and German, a prominent place continued to be occupied by reproductions of two fundamental documents: the Magna Carta of England and the American Declaration of Independence.

Long before Ostrogorski produced his work on democracy and political parties, his conception of "extraconstitutional government" had ripened. He loved to recall his two sojourns in the United States, particularly the first when he interviewed a number of statesmen, high officials, and political bosses in order to get first-hand information on the functioning of American political institutions and parties. One of the more important was Theodore Roosevelt, then President of the Board of Police in New York City. Delightedly he recalled that Roosevelt had been reluctant at first to receive him but later had granted him a long interview in Hoffman's Vienna Café.

Here was something of a miracle. Ostrogorski was a Russian scholar, educated along the traditional lines of European jurisprudence—Russian and French—and with a knowledge of political, constitutional, and legal facts and sources of the remote liberalized autocracy of Alexander II which had almost nothing in common with the Anglo-American background. Yet he became the author of two volumes, in which, with his brilliant insight into political sociology, he made an entirely new construction of the evolution of Great Britain and America.

Ostrogorski's fundamental work, which appeared first in French in 1903 and later in English, was not published in Russian during his lifetime. It must be said that before and after 1905 this work was hailed in the special and general literature of Russia. Experts frequently called for its publication in Russian, particularly after the October Manifesto of 1905 marking the revolutionary transition to quasi-constitutionalism. But down to the Soviet period this did not take place. Indeed, in the 1900's, the opinion was prevalent that liberal Russian political scientists and constitutionalists, while admitting the outstanding qualities of this work, preferred not to see it printed in Russian. They did not wish to stir up criticism of Western democracy and the Anglo-American state order at a time when the old autocratic Russian regime was challenged by world opinion and the country was on the verge of establishing a Western type of administration based on a large parliamentary representation.

Ostrogorski himself, close to the Cadets without belonging to their faction in the Duma, was eager to publish his work in Russian; but before 1914 he did not have time to translate it, for he was occupied with the preparation of the English text. This task was of much more interest to him—in the distressing position of having written a book on Anglo-American constitutional government which could not reach Britons and Americans because it was in French—than publishing a Russian edition which could never become a textbook for Russian universities that did not have full-fledged political science departments.

Ostrogorski, like all the other representatives of Russian democratic thought, admired the American Constitution. However, he rejected a dogmatic and purely legalistic approach to it, differentiating between the text of the instrument of 1776 and the U.S.A. constitution which represented the high-water mark of political ideology at the time and a guide for the main course of future development, and the actual lines the legal rules of the Constitution would follow in adapting themselves to, if they were not to retreat from, the social and political impacts, needs, and factors. Ostrogorski was right when he said in the preface to the abridged edition of his *Democracy and the Party System in the United States* that the fathers of the American Constitution "did not anticipate a flood of Democracy rising above the gates erected, nor the all-pervading development of Party, nor the coming of conquering Plutocracy."

A modern legal sociologist, however, who knows the difference between normativism or the prescriptive force of legal rules, on the one hand, and on the other the necessity for law to deal with and regulate social and political factors and needs that ask for recognition and satisfaction, would not entirely agree with Ostrogorski's thesis: "These factors—Democracy, Party, and Plutocracy—taken together completely altered the direction of government and went far to reduce the Constitution of the United States to a paper constitution." [23]

With all its changes, particularly the Amendments and basic court decisions, even important economic and social shifts did not reduce the Constitution of the United States to a paper constitution. After Charles A. Beard and other writers, this may now be regarded as the general view of American constitutional and political doctrine.

But it should not be forgotten that the views which Ostrogorski defended in 1902 in his standard work, views on the caucus in general and the legislative caucus in particular, on the relation between business and political parties, on political bosses, on the President's obligations to his party, on the necessity of nonpartisan primaries—all these views not only are discussed in modern textbooks on American politics but also remain in their most important features subject to reform half a century after their initial formulation by the Russian interviewer of Theodore Roosevelt.

Most intriguing, however, is the fact that the first volume of a substantially shortened Russian edition of the great work appeared much later, in 1927, as a textbook under the auspices of the Communist Academy of the U.S.S.R.[24] The second volume, dedicated to the United States, appeared three years later. The author of the prefaces, Professor E. Pashukanis, after 1932 rejected for deviations from the official Stalinist line, wrote of Ostrogorski's work:

The author, according to his views, unquestionably stood on the average platform of the liberal Russian society of that time. Yet notwithstanding all this, that is, despite the fact that the representatives

[23] M. Ostrogorski, *Democracy and the Party System in the United States*, New York, 1912, Preface. The author calls the factors mentioned extraconstitutional.

[24] Ostrogorski, *Demokratiya i politicheskiye partii* (Democracy and Political Parties), 2 vols., Moscow, 1927, 1930, transl. from the French with a preface by E. Pashukanis (Vol. I, on England, and Vol. II, on the United States).

of this society exercised an almost complete monopoly in literature and science and despite their enthusiastic propagandizing of the ideas of constitutionalism and democracy, the work of Ostrogorski, brilliantly and skillfully describing the political regime of the two most outstanding bourgeois democracies, never appeared in Russian translation. It would not be correct to say that it remained unknown in Russia; it was quoted and cited, it was described as a work "most extraordinary in the abundance and originality of its underlying material," the author was recognized as an equal of Bryce . . . and still the book was not published in Russian although many less valuable and less interesting foreign books were translated.

It may be that a fortuitous coincidence of circumstances prevented the translation of this work of Ostrogorski's into Russian. But behind this fortuitousness there is undoubtedly a more general hidden cause: The work of Ostrogorski contains a pitiless revelation of the real core of bourgeois democracy; it unmasks the true mechanism of the parliamentarian state ruled by bourgeois political pressure groups, and shows the ugliness behind this mechanism which tries to put on the deceptive face of "national sovereignty," the "will of the majority," etc.

Professor Pashukanis did not shrink from admitting that the Soviet publication of Ostrogorski, whom he regarded as dull, stupid, and miserable in his positive conclusions and proposals, was done precisely to demonstrate that even a serious bourgeois writer shows up the meanness and hypocrisy of bourgeois democracy.

In the preface to the second volume Pashukanis added a few observations of his own on the United States, for America as a democracy was—and still is—of greater actual interest in Soviet Russia than England, and furthermore, in this second volume, Ostrogorski developed a positive program in his conclusions.

As for his positive proposals for the improvement of the American party system and the institution of nonpartisan primaries and free leagues—to mention only the most important—it must be said that Ostrogorski placed too great faith in the abilities of the critically and ethically "thinking individual"—a concept deeply rooted in Russian Populism and critical idealism. Even the unsophisticated must realize that, no matter how one may idealize other factors in the American political scene, the significance of the American party system with all its evils could not be minimized. That is why in the eyes not only of orthodox Marxists but also of educated American utilitarians and modern positivists Ostrogorski's views appear naïve, foreign to the economic and political life of America. Arthur Macmahon wrote of him:

> Despite the apparent sophistication involved in his method of observation, . . . the core of his thinking was a vast naïveté, which indeed was the ardent spirit of the man himself. He believed in spiritually emancipated individuals, who, in keeping with the principle of "union without unity," . . . would act politically through flexible and impermanent associations. . . . Ostrogorski's slogan, "Down with party, up with league," was in large degree realized in a period of flaccid politics and active, piecemeal reform. Fundamentally, however, the limitations of this faith caused him to miss the trend of events.[25]

If such an evaluation of this great thinker was made in the United States, it is little wonder that his positive proposals for reform were ridiculed in the Soviet edition of his monumental work. Pashukanis wrote in the preface to the second volume that while it ended about the time Taft became President (1908) all the negative traits of American democracy had become sharply defined, particularly the tyranny of the party bosses, bribery, corruption, and open trade in votes; and he cited the numerous election campaigns with their enormous expenditures and abuses, and the oil scandal of 1923–1925 in which even a member of the Cabinet was involved. According to Pashukanis, Ostrogorski himself admitted that the main power of his writings lay in their critical description and not in their positive suggestions for the reform of bourgeois democracy. In calling for the rejection of permanent parties and their replacement by looser *ad hoc* organizations united around specific political demands, Ostrogorski did not even try to show that the objective tendencies of development followed the lines of his proposed reforms.

> All these reforms [wrote Pashukanis] represent a petty-mindedness in so far as Ostrogorski evades the fundamental fact that turns the bourgeois democracy into a deceitful, partial, and purely formal one; namely, the domination of capital. . . . Ostrogorski imagines that powerful parties, fighting for domination, become obsolete because even the

[25] Arthur W. Macmahon, "Ostrogorsky," in *Encyclopaedia of the Social Sciences*, Vol. XI, New York, 1933, p. 503.

sharpest contrasts tend more and more to fade. What actually happens is the contrary. . . . The era of imperialism brings an unprecedented sharpening of conflicts. . . . If the volume contained only his positive conclusions, it would not be worth while to publish it in Russian. But it is valuable because of its rich concrete material and because it contains a critique of bourgeois democracy, a critique that still retains its full significance and force.

Ironically enough, Ostrogorski's impact on his native Russia was more direct and telling after his death than under the St. Petersburg monarchism, when his French and English books were read only by a small élite. Under the Soviets the circle of his Russian readers widened tremendously. At least, his main work not only was published in Russian, but was even made a required textbook for Soviet universities and other schools of higher learning. In the new Soviet environment Ostrogorski's somewhat naïve criticism of the defects of the American party system, accompanied by glowing admiration for America's democracy, must have had anti-Soviet repercussions. In a country where party despotism is at its worst, the incomparably lesser shortcomings of the United States system must necessarily appear not so significant, for they are tempered by freedom of the press and of association. Back in the 1920's and 1930's the awakened minds and feelings of young Russian students must have reacted much more against the party system of the Soviet Union than against that of the United States.

When Ostrogorski depicted the physical liberty implicit in *habeas corpus* as an established freedom enforced by Anglo-American law, while what remained to be fought for was moral and spiritual freedom, *habeas animum*, then the intelligent Soviet student must have been compelled to realize that he was deprived of both kinds of freedom—in other words, that he had no political liberty whatsoever. Under such conditions how these words of Ostrogorski must have rung in his ears when given to him in plain Russian!

The greatness and the poverty of contemporary democracy turn on this distinction between the two formulas [*habeas corpus* and *habeas animum*]. Through the mere fact of having realized material liberty, democracy has given more happiness to the nations than the other regimes had ever afforded them. . . . The critics and detractors of democracy forget this fact as well as the condition in which mankind

lived under the former regimes. . . . The disorders of which democratic government has presented or continues to present the spectacle
in certain countries are paralleled or equaled by the experience of the
antecedent regimes; but the latter had no political liberty to compensate them and to cure their ills, and they have passed away. Democracy
has brought with it liberty, and it has renewed the life of societies. This
liberty has been realized in its highest degree, other circumstances contributing thereto, in the United States, and never has the earth re-
sounded with so mighty a song of triumph as that endless paean chanted
by American life with a joyousness and a fervor which inanimate objects
themselves to share. But nowhere also has it appeared more clearly than
in the United States that political freedom, which alone can build up
external liberty, is not complete without the citizen's independence of
mind, and without the spontaneous and vigilant energy of his will. In
the absence of this independence and this vigilance, demagogism and
corruption have entered the house in broad day as a thief enters in the
night.[26]

This passage and other parts of the two volumes, with all their
sharp criticism of Anglo-American democracy, could not lower
bourgeois democracy in the eyes of young Soviet students; in fact,
the criticism must sometimes have sounded to them like a song in
praise of the West.

The guess may be ventured that the sudden disfavor into which
Pashukanis, an outstanding Soviet scholar, fell and his later removal
from his university professorship were due not only to his popu-
larization of Ostrogorski's teachings and writings but to his defense
of the "withering away of state and law," which gradually became
an anti-Soviet conception.

As far as I can discover Ostrogorski's last important treatment of
English and American political ideas was in four brilliant essays
printed between September and December, 1913, in the monthly
Viestnik Yevropy, under the general title, The Constitutional Evolution of England. In the last essay, on the Apotheosis of Monarchy
and the Triumph of Democracy, he quoted President Taft's address
to the Congress in 1912 to show that America's newest concept of
the essence of a constitution was the establishment of political guarantees for minorities against the majority. It remains to be seen

[26] Ostrogorski, *op. cit.*, Vol II, pp. 356-357.

whether Ostrogorski was right in attributing to this "new" American idea of a constitution the power to curb the ruling majority. However, his analysis bears witness to the optimistic view of America, her Constitution, and her political wisdom held by one of the last of old Russia's liberal thinkers and political idealists.

Ostrogorski was the third of the magnificent trio of non-Americans who wrote treatises on the transatlantic republic. Tocqueville, Bryce, and he, all were born and educated in countries geographically and politically distant from the United States. Each of the three dealt with a specific stage of development and a particular aspect of the subject in his own way, but the conclusions of all substantially influenced American political science and doctrine. Each of them came to America to observe and to absorb, and each produced his own individual reflection of the same body politic.

Bryce, who graciously wrote a preface to the English edition of Ostrogorski's work, was, as a Briton, somewhat shocked at the similarities the Russian writer revealed in the development and the outgrowths of the party system and competition in the two English-speaking countries. He even argued that "party organization is a totally different thing in England from what it is in the United States," England, in his view, not having fallen so far below the level of genuine democracy. Nevertheless, he wrote of his younger Russian colleague's work: "Few books of our time show equal appreciation of the problems democracy has to solve, or bring more useful materials and more acute criticism to their discussion."

And it was living America that inspired Ostrogorski in his work of lasting value.

XVIII *The Brief Stage of Russo-American Democratic Identity*

> I have been more than once in your country and may bear witness that the ideals which are represented by the Provisional Government are the same as underlie the existence of your own country. I hope that this great change which has come to Russia will do much to bring us closer together than we have ever been before.—Foreign Minister Paul Miliukov replying to American recognition of the new democratic Russian government.

THE PERIOD BETWEEN THE ESTABLISHMENT OF A LIMITED CONSTI-tutional monarchy in 1906 and February, 1917, was one of relative political stability and economic progress. The *coup d'état* of Prime Minister Peter Stolypin, attempted in conjunction with the abortive dissolution of the second Duma in 1907, was accompanied by an open breach of the constitution of 1906 aimed at bringing about a more moderate and rightist representation in the Duma that would favor the substitution of a new landowning farmer class for the old mir,[1] and a basic reduction in the number of deputies from the national minorities in order to make the Duma "purely Russian." The opposition refused to be extinguished. It began with the Constitutional Democrats and progressives and ended with the Populists and moderate and radical Social Democrats, the latter eventually growing into the Bolshevik party.

Far from impeding the rapid industrialization of the country, these new political developments accompanied a trend toward increased trade and financial dealings. Down to the First World War, the role of foreign capital continued to broaden. In this field the activities of the United States were insignificant. Germany was influential in Russian trade and industry. France was particularly so in finance, and imports of machinery and textiles from Great Britain were enormously significant to the economic life of the country.

[1] The commune, whose land was periodically redistributed.

After 1906–1907, industrialization became a slogan of the times. The years 1910–1914 especially brought a very significant expansion of railroads and of heavy metal industries, coal mining, and residential construction. Even the bad harvest of 1911 in eastern European Russia had no serious effect on the trend.

In the drive toward industrialization the United States was held up as a model. It is interesting to note that, later, the Soviet regime set, as one of its objectives, "to match and surpass America."

Ivan Ozerov, professor of finance and financial law at the Universities of Moscow and St. Petersburg and member of the State Council, was one who looked to America. In a book entitled *What America Teaches Us*, he argued against the competitive protective tariffs of national sovereign states and called for an All-European Federation of nations based on community of interest. Some European countries, particularly the Russian Empire, had rich natural resources—minerals, coal, oil—while others had capital, knowledge, and technological know-how; but "Europe does not have the industrial genius which the United States has developed in its own country." One reason for the uninventiveness of Europe was its system of education, which was entirely different from that in America. American schools strove to develop initiative, energy, alertness, and an enterprising spirit in the young, while the European schools worked to instill obedience and humility:

> In Europe there are even now illiterate countries. Russia, Italy, Spain —they must follow the American pattern. Illiteracy must be proclaimed a pestilence. Look at the United States, how much it spends on schools and education. . . . We have to "fight" the United States not by mechanical but by organic means; we have to improve our productive forces. . . . We have to learn from America how to support a high culture, meaning a democratized culture that seeps into every pore of the people's life, including the lower strata.[2]

Ozerov defended these views enthusiastically in budgetary discussions in the upper chamber in 1910, contrasting Russian backwardness in production with American efficiency. He pointed out that Russian production of iron ore had been closer to that of the United States in the 1870's than in 1906. In 1871 the difference in produc-

[2] *Chemu uchit nas Amerika*, Moscow, 1908, pp. 181, 184-185.

tion in favor of America had been 2,649,000 tons, but in 1906 it had reached 5,000,000 tons. Concluding his remarks, he said: "I am a Russian, and I become sad when I see where we are heading." [3]

For liberal Russia the victory of Woodrow Wilson over William Howard Taft in the presidential election of 1912 was a great relief. For the entire Russian democratic opposition this victory signified a break by the United States with the imperialism of Theodore Roosevelt and Taft. The Russian liberal press quoted President Wilson's first inaugural address on March 4, 1913, and his special address to Congress, April 8, and hailed their "high ethical" character. The switch from Taft's definition of American diplomacy as a "handmaid of commercial intercourse" to the new broad anti-imperialist approach of Wilson was well received. Wilson's speeches and acts restored America as an ideal in the eyes of the whole anti-autocratic camp of the old Empire. When he remarked in his inaugural address that the nation had been deeply stirred "by the knowledge of wrong, of ideals lost, of government too often debauched and made an instrument of evil," liberal Russians were stirred too. These vices were more than familiar to them; but they could not be eliminated by an election of the Chief Executive. And when Wilson told the Congress on April 8: "We long ago passed beyond the modest notion of 'protecting' the industries of the country and moved boldly forward to the idea that they were entitled to the direct patronage of the Government," these words might well have been repeated in the Duma against the old Russian protectionism of the St. Petersburg government and its finance ministry.

The leading organs of the press stressed that Wilson's policies implied rejection of the annexation of Cuba and the evacuation of the Philippine Islands. No less characteristic was his unwillingness to intervene in Mexican affairs.[4] The strengthening of progressive democracy, flowing from the struggle against Tammany Hall, and the general eradication of corruption throughout the country, was

---

[3] *Stenographic Reports of the Council of State* (Stenograficheskiye Ochoty—Gosudarstvennyi Soviet), Session V, meeting 33, March 22, 1910, pp. 1747-1763.

[4] See the article by N. S-n and V. Moravskii on the internal politics of the United States in the *Riech* annual for the year 1914, *Yezhegodnik gazety Riech na 1914 god*, St. Petersburg, 1914, pp. 489-490.

hailed by Russian democrats of all shades.

As we shall see, Wilson's influence deepened during the democratic revolution of March–November, 1917, and in the last stages of Russian participation in World War I.

The outbreak of the World War in August, 1914, sharply interrupted the belated industrial improvement of Russia. But this war brought America closer to Russia; more, it made America a factor in Russian political and economic life, discernible not alone by the highest strata of society and the state machinery.

Earlier chapters have shown to what a high degree American ideas vitalized Russian political and socioeconomic philosophies. However, this took place only on the higher cultural and political levels. Even the active role of America in the liquidation of the Russo-Japanese War was regarded as solely a matter of international friendship.

The appearance of America first as a friendly neutral and later as an ally of Russia offered the intelligentsia the strongest challenge to revise thoroughly its previous views on this distant country. Unfortunately, the prolonged indoctrination of the radicals after the 1870's with the ideas that the United States was a country "striving for ownership and money," had an enduring effect on the chief leaders and advocates of the democratic revolution. The notions that had permeated political ideology and writing for decades settled on Russian soil like a sediment, giving off its noxious vapor during all the eight months of 1917 that Russia remained in the war. The moderates were most inclined to favor America; the more radical the movement, the more skeptical it was of the United States and the less disposed to distinguish between it and the old bourgeois countries, England and France. There were, as we shall see, some important shifts; certain Marxist groups, of a more compromising and patriotic character, revised their old attitudes toward the West in general and America in particular. Even more important were certain new approaches of the social-revolutionary Populists. But the time was too short and too hectic for calm reflection on the importance of the United States. In the heat of the fight it was simpler to regard all the Western powers as a selfish pack eager to use for their own ends the human and material resources of gigantic but temporarily exhausted Russia.

The very fact that America had entered the war when Russia was near exhaustion was used against it. German propaganda hammered home the slogan that the Western powers were determined to fight to the last drop of the Russian soldier's blood. A crucial question of that time was whether the Embassy of the United States and its *spiritus rector* could dramatize effectively the difference in America's approach to the war from that of France and England, for which political freedom and progress were not articles of export; and it is questionable whether this was done.

In periods like the hectic March to November, 1917, domestic and foreign policies approach each other most closely. This was true of the American Revolution and the French in the eighteenth century; and it was demonstrated again in the Russian democratic revolution of 1917. If for America severance of all the old ties with England was fundamental, it was as much a matter of domestic as it was of foreign policy. If the new revolutionary Russia rejected its predecessor, imperial Russia, it rejected it completely, domestically as well as in international relations. It was impossible to take over old lines, old issues, or old purposes into the new Russia. Paul Miliukov—the Russian Mirabeau who began to storm the stronghold of czarism in the fourth Duma, and whose speech on "treason or folly," directed against the German-born and German-inspired Czarina and her clique, gave a battle cry to the March revolution —stumbled badly as the democratic Minister of Foreign Affairs when he adopted the old slogan of Russian domination over Constantinople and the Dardanelles for the new Russia, a republican Russia closer to the Fourteen Points of Woodrow Wilson, with their emphasis on the self-determination of nations, than to the most modern Slavophilism traditionally built on domination over the Turks. Nicknamed Paul Dardanelovitch,[5] he became subject to political mockery and was compelled to resign.

From the first year of the World War Russian liberal newspapers and leading reviews displayed an interest in the American attitude toward the war in general and Germany in particular. From the moderate *Russkaya Mysl* and *Viestnik Yevropy* to the radical *Letopis* (Chronicle), the reviews became increasingly aware of the significance of the United States in the titanic clash.

[5] The ironic reference to Miliukov's policy toward the Dardanelles is apparent.

The moderate *Russkoye Bogatstvo* (Russian Wealth) began by being dissatisfied with Wilson's neutrality and with some of his utterances which could be interpreted as containing pro-Germanism, and Russanov's articles in it were in full harmony with similar criticism in the United States.[5a] More important is the fact that from April, 1917, this review, representing the Socialist Revolutionaries, the most numerous party in the revolution, stressed the unconditionally positive attitude of the United States toward the March revolution, in contrast to England and even France, which continued stubbornly and selfishly to be interested only in the pivotal question: Would the revolution strengthen or weaken the military energy of the former Empire?[6]

It must be said here that the integrity of democratic Russia in her foreign policy has gone unnoted and perhaps even unremembered since the fall of the provisional government in November, 1917. The world has shown scant appreciation of the far-reaching consequences for the outcome of World War I had this democratic Russian government, in the interest of self-preservation, cynically decided to conclude a separate peace with Germany and Austria-Hungary.

The temptation to make peace must have been great during the eight months of the democratic interlude. The majority of the soldiers were sons of peasants who had been mobilized and put into uniform by the old regime. Mobilization had been for them tantamount to war and discipline; but revolution was going to be the opposite, a kind of demobilization. This was the prime motivation of the peasant soldiers homesick for their villages and drawn there

[5a] Wilson's note of May 13, 1915, to the German Government after the sinking of the *Lusitania*, was severely and justly criticized. It contained the following misleading expression of the President's motivation: "recalling the human and enlightened attitude hitherto assumed by the Imperial German Government in matters of international right [law]." W. R. Thayer, in his biography of Theodore Roosevelt (1919), observed incisively: "That President Wilson, by profession a historian, should laud, as being always engaged in justice and humanity, the nation which, under Frederick the Great, had stolen Silesia and dismembered Poland, and which in his own lifetime had garroted Denmark, had forced a wicked war on Austria, had trapped France by lies into another war and robbed her of Alsace-Lorraine, and had only recently wiped its hands, dripping with blood drawn from the Chinese, was amazing!" Cf. Harold Garnet Black, *The True Woodrow Wilson* (New York, 1946), p. 153.

[6] *Russkoye Bogatstvo*, Jan. and Apr.-May, 1917.

by thoughts of the wonderful things that awaited them. There is a good deal of tragic truth in some words ascribed to Lenin. When he was reminded that the decision whether or not to make peace had first to be voted on by the army, he replied, "The soldiers have already voted against the war with their feet"—that is, by deserting in the thousands to go home. In such a situation it must have taken heroic will and eloquent persuasion to hold the men in the trenches and later, in July, 1917—after considerable diplomatic pressure from the Allies who sought the reassurance of a demonstration of solidarity—to lead the exhausted armies in a successful offensive. Credit for this offensive against the Austrian and German armies —quite apart from its strategic importance—is due not only to Kerensky, the Minister of War, but also to the rousing appeal of the All-Russian Congress of the Workmen's, Soldiers' and Peasants' Delegates.[7] It was a clear act by the "Russian Revolutionary Democracy" of solidarity with the "cause of international democracy" which had to be preserved from defeat by the double Kaiserism of Germany and Austria.

It is only in terms of this deep feeling of responsibility toward the Allies and a burning will to defend the unpopular "ought"— meaning the continuation of the war—that we can understand why it was morally and politically impossible for the first free Russian government in history to betray the West in a "shameful peace" with Hohenzollern Germany, the hereditary friend of official czarist Russia. We have already seen that the old dynastic and political contacts between Russia and Germany (Prussia), so long and carefully fostered, had begun to be undermined in the early 1890's. Yet they had lingered even after the Franco-Prussian rapprochement. They burst into a last flash of life when the Czarina Alexandra, the Russian Marie Antoinette, set up a short-lived pro-German regime—during the war with Germany, in the presence of the Duma, and under the very nose of Allied diplomats—thereby hastening the end of czarism. Reaction against pro-Germanism in the imperial court had begun during the revolution of 1905 and led broad social strata as well as Russian diplomats to a much closer rapprochement with the distant French and Anglo-American West.

[7] Cf. A. J. Sack, *The Birth of the Russian Democracy*, New York, 1918, pp. 405-406.

The effects of this rapprochement and of three years of military association were stronger than practical considerations of survival. During these hectic eight months socialists became imbued with a fight-to-the-end patriotism.[8] For the first time, after long decades of obligatory defeatism, a Social Democratic newspaper, *Yedinstvo* (Unity), edited by George Plekhanov, the father of Russian orthodox Marxism, could appear in which Russia and her national interests were plainly defended against Germany, the vehicle of reaction and the mortal enemy of Russia's independence as a growing democracy. And last but not least, there was a long educational period during which, as we have seen, a galaxy of courageous thinkers created an antiautocratic political doctrine with a Western democratic orientation.

Moreover, during the life of the provisional government the freedom of the press remained untouched, forming a stout bulwark of patriotism and pro-Ally sentiment against which cowardly considerations could not prevail. It stood firm, too, in the face of all attempts by agents of the Central Powers to spread demoralization by instigating desertions from the front.

The best proof of Russia's Westernism at the time may be found in what happened in the first months after the Bolshevik November revolution. The numerous and courageous anti-Soviet press was not suppressed until the summer of 1918. It is now an established fact that the separate peace with Germany and Austria-Hungary and the conclusion of the "forgotten peace" of Brest-Litovsk in 1918 were the result of a protracted procedure (lasting from December 22, 1917, to March, 1918, with the additional conventions of August, 1918), in which a calamitous split in the Soviet government became well recognized. The period of "no peace, no power," initiated and defended by Trotsky, finally had to be terminated by Lenin, caught in the heavy fire of the bourgeois-liberal and moderate socialist press.

This conflict over Russia's orientation toward the West not only drove a wedge into the Bolshevik party, but eventually led to the ousting of the only coalition group of post-November Bolshe-

[8] Very much in this vein is an article by G. Alexinski on The Contrasts of the Russian Revolution in *Sovremennyi Mir* (Contemporary World), July-Sept., 1917.

vism—the left Socialist Revolutionaries. The rift between Bolshe-
vists and their non-Marxist coalitionists began to appear in 1918
when the diplomats of the Allied countries refused to reside in
Moscow, where the German Embassy headed by Count Mirbach,
became a stronghold of German influence on the Soviet government. The Allied diplomats withdrew to the northern provincial
capital of Vologda, where the American Ambassador David R.
Francis acted as the dean of the diplomatic corps. They were repeatedly invited by Boris Chicherin, the Commissar for Foreign
Affairs, to return to Moscow but finally left Russia through Archangel. The tremendous tension between arrogant, victorious Germany and embittered, downtrodden Russia came to a sudden and
violent end with the shooting of Mirbach by the left Socialist Revolutionary Blumkin on July 6, 1918. This shot also destroyed the
last vestige of Prusso-German and German-Baltic dominance over
Russia.[9]

To return to the period with which we are dealing, did the Allies
really understand the difficult position of the Russian democratic
government throughout the eight months of its ordeal, and did
they exercise the political responsibility and foresightedness the
situation demanded? The position of the new Russian regime was
indescribably difficult. It could not rest content with victory over
czarism and holding the positions achieved. Having determined to
continue the war in support of its allies, it had to change the very
character of the war. The new Russia had to reject the old war aims
based on its own and its allies' selfish national interests and adopt
entirely new ones.

Partly under pressure from the Petrograd Soviet of Workers' and
Soldiers' Deputies and partly under the influence of Woodrow Wilson's famous address to the Congress on April 2, the Provisional
Government published on April 9 (March 27) a declaration on
foreign policy containing the following Wilsonian remarks:

While leaving it to the nation to decide, together with our Allies, all
questions concerning the World War and its termination, the Provi-

[9] Count Wilhelm Mirbach was a representative of an old aristocratic family
one branch of which lived in Prussia and the other in Russia—Courland or
Livonia. Other such families were the Bismarcks, Brunnows, Keyserling(k)s,
and Manteuffels.

sional Government regards it as its obligation and its right to declare now that the aims of free Russia are not to dominate other peoples nor to deprive them of their national wealth, nor to seize foreign territories, but only to establish a secure peace on the basis of the self-determination of nations. The Russian people does not strive to strengthen its external power at the expense of other peoples; it does not aim at the enslavement or humiliation of any nation. In accordance with the higher principles of justice, our people have struck off the shackles from the Polish people. But the Russian people will not permit its fatherland to retire from the great struggle humiliated or undermined in its vital forces.

These principles are laid down as the foundation of the Foreign Policy of the Provisional Government.[10]

This declaration was actually a renunciation of all secret conventions concluded by czarist Russia with its allies. This revolutionary gesture of generosity was received rather skeptically by Great Britain and France. From the very beginning of the February revolution, they had been alarmed over the effect the revolution and the weakening of discipline might have on the Russian armies in the field; and they worried about guarantees and other assurances that democratic Russia would not "desert the Allies."

Foreign Minister Miliukov also was influenced or rather reversely impressed by Wilsonian doctrine. In stating Russia's war aims on May 3, he tried to reconcile Wilson's conception of World War aims with two factors in his government's foreign policy: the new popular slogan created by the left-of-center groups and parties— "Peace without annexation and contribution"—behind which stood all the most moderate labor and socialist, urban, and rural movements, and the demand by some liberal and all conservative groups for Russian control of Constantinople and the Straits, which he tried to show was not incompatible with the right of the Turks to political independence and self-determination. He wrote:

I never doubted that the United States could join only the powers of the Entente. In the definition of the objects of the war by President Wilson and the statesmen of the Continent, there never appeared any diversity of opinion. . . . The best pledge of America's entering the

[10] *Viestnik Vremennovo Pravitelstva* (Monitor of the Provisional Government), No. 18(64), Mar. 28 (Apr. 10), 1917. This declaration of the Provisional Government to the citizens of Russia was signed by Prime Minister Prince P. E. Lvov.

ranks of the Allied Powers was undoubtedly this accord of views in the domain of the conception of the war. Assuredly the formula "peace without victory" proposed by President Wilson is inadmissible for the Allies. . . . Only victory is able to give the powers of the Entente the possibility of solving [those] broad international questions. . . .The only obstacle to the development of normal international relations has always been found in German presentations [sic] to world domination, to the enslavement of peoples. . . . Without victory over Germany the establishment of the ideal international order of which President Wilson dreams is an utopia impossible of realization. . . . The program of the Entente Powers consists in the realization of the leading idea of President Wilson concerning the satisfaction of all national aspirations, the restoration of crushed nations and trampled rights. . . . Under these circumstances it is possible to speak of "peace without annexations" only under the condition that by the word "annexation" is meant a conquest. . . .

Starting from the principle of the liberation of nations . . . the fundamental task of the Allies tends toward the liquidation of Turkish rule over oppressed nations. . . . The same concurrence of views is also noticeable in the Russian endeavors to command the Straits. As it is known, President Wilson on the question of the Straits did not only take the position of their possible neutralization, but also of their transfer to Russian control." [11]

The United States always maintained "hands off" toward the new Russian regime as compared with that of Russia's old Allies. The difference in attitude is well illustrated by an incident that followed the suppression of the Kornilov revolt in September and the incidental significant moral strengthening of the Bolsheviks. The British, French, and Italian ambassadors grew particularly insistent on full restoration of military discipline, and most disquieting was the German offensive on the Baltic front, with the threat to the capital, Petrograd, to which the fall of Riga gave emphasis. In this perilous situation the Minister for Foreign Affairs sent the following "secret" cable to the Russian Ambassador in Washington on October 9 (September 26), 1917:

The British, French, and Italian Ambassadors were today received by the Prime Minister and they presented to him in the name of their

[11] As quoted in David R. Francis, *Russia from the American Embassy*, New York, 1921, pp. 107-108.

Governments an urgent memorandum on the necessity for taking measures to restore the military readiness of our Armies. This step naturally
made a painfully discouraging impression on the Provisional Government, particularly in view of the fact that it is known to all our Allies
that the Government is doing its best to continue unfalteringly our struggle with the common enemy. I ask you most confidentially to communicate to Mr. Lansing how highly the Provisional Government appreciates
the abstention of the American Ambassador from any participation in
the mentioned collective action.

Tereshchenko.[12]

This fundamental divergence in attitude was natural, and the
advantage gained by the incident could have borne better fruit if it
had been cleverly exploited in the negotiations with revolutionary
Russia, torn by two opposing points of view. One, espoused by
moderate socialists of Marxist and non-Marxist (Menshevik and
Populist) coloration who tended toward an informal coalition with
the liberal progressive bourgeois elements, was friendly to the
United States; the other, represented by the radical camp, was in-
herently hostile and indoctrinated against the "dollar country."
Between these two basic groups was a considerable segment of the
intelligentsia, more favorable toward America than toward France
or England. An act of purely political interference having taken
place, the way was opened for a well considered and expertly prepared policy of the United States to strengthen this middle group
which constituted the majority in the Petrograd Council of Workers' and Soldiers' Deputies. But those to whom the execution of
such a policy would have been entrusted were so badly informed
on Russian political thinking and movements and parties that the
intervention would have been doomed at the outset.

David R. Francis's book reveals, though only partially, the political disorientation of the American Ambassador to Russia. It gives
a good account of his tactics and shows his blindness to various
factors in Russian political life. This diplomatic representative of
the United States left a sad memory behind him and has received

---

[12] Cf. *Sbornik Sekretnykh Dokumentov iz Arkhiva byvshevo ministerstva
inostrannykh del* (Collection of Secret Documents from the Archives of the
People's Commissariat for Foreign Affairs), No. 1, Dec., 1917. This collection
is part of the series of secret documents of the czarist period published by the
Soviet government.

rather rough treatment at the hands of analysts of the international scene. Philip C. Jessup characterizes him as "a charming old gentleman with no appreciation of what was going on in Russia and without any other particular qualification for his difficult post," and quotes official documents and cables to bear this out. One of the cables, dated April 21, 1917, notes: "Extreme socialist or anarchist named Lenin making violent speeches and thereby strengthening government; designedly giving him leeway and will deport opportunely." [13] Foster Rhea Dulles has written of his attitude toward Lenin and Trotsky: "To his conservative mind, the doctrines they preached were so fantastic as to be nothing but the veneer of treachery." [14] Francis saw the Bolshevik leaders as German agents who would reap their well merited reward in arrest and execution. What he did not and perhaps could not see was that their activities constituted a serious threat to the stability of the provisional government. Characteristically, he wrote: "Lenin on arriving in Petrograd immediately began to disburse money which was supposedly furnished by Germany." [15]

This utterly irresponsible evaluation of Lenin is of a piece with Francis's total ignorance of the political "map" of Russia. He did not know the difference between "radical socialist," "anarchist," "maximalist," and "Bolshevik"; used the term "social revolutionist" only in connection with Kerenski, and "Menshevik" (moderate Marxist social democrat) scarcely at all. He did not know exactly who was fighting whom during the March–November period. His description of the crucial November 7 decision of the Petrograd Council of Workers' Deputies to introduce the new Soviet regime is a model of illiterate political reporting. In his account Dahn, an old Menshevik social democrat, appears as a leader of the populist Social Revolutionists. Francis's attitude toward the Kornilov antirevolutionary movement vacillated; at one point he hailed Kornilov, at another he could say, "It may be that the Kornilov fiasco was a blessing in disguise."[16]

[13] Philip C. Jessup, *Elihu Root*, 2 vols., New York, 1938, Vol. II, pp. 354-355.
[14] Foster Rhea Dulles, *The Road to Teheran*, Princeton, 1944, pp. 104-105.
[15] Francis, *op. cit.*, p. 135. On pp. 112-113 he wrote, "Lenin preaches anarchistic doctrines" and "is in the pay of the German Government."
[16] *Ibid.*, p. 163.

Francis greatly overrated the effect of American recognition of the provisional government in a remark that shows how little he appreciated the fierceness of the inner struggle of democratic forces in the months from March to November and the difficulties created by the arrival in April of Lenin and his followers:

> The Ministry of the Provisional Government frequently called upon Kerensky to exert his influence at this time, and had it not been for his efforts and the recognition by America of the Provisional Government, it would have been deposed and the [Bolshevik] revolution which took place the following November, eight months later, would have occurred in March, 1917.[17]

Despite his ineptness, it must be said that certain practical steps taken by Ambassador Francis on his own initiative or on instructions from Washington were expedient and sound. At the time, America had entered the war but was unable immediately to land troops in France or Belgium. The maintenance of the Eastern front was an urgent necessity, and on the recommendation of Francis a credit of $100,000,000 was extended to the provisional government; later an additional credit was made available.[18]

Francis also recommended that a railway commission be sent to Russia.[19] Its main task was to improve the facilities of the Trans-Siberian Railway between Vladivostok and the industrial and trade centers of European Russia, and after the November revolution it continued to operate under the young Soviet regime. In June, 1917, the provisional government sent a railroad commission to the United States headed by Professor J. V. Lomonosov, as part of the Russian extraordinary mission of which Boris Bakhmetev was the chief. The task of Lomonosov's commission was to acquire in the United States railway supplies, locomotives, and rolling stock that Russia needed very badly. This commission, too, survived the November revolution, and it maintained steady contact with the American commission.

The insistence of the United States, in concert with France and England, that the revolutionary armies launch an offensive in the summer of 1917 against the Austrians and Germans drew a rather bitter comment from a young American writer named Malcolm

---

[17] *Ibid.*, p. 103.   [18] *Ibid.*, p. 124.   [19] *Ibid.*, pp. 130-131.

Davis. The soundness of the criticism is enhanced by the fact that it was made almost at the time that pressure was being exerted on Russia, and the person who made it could speak Russian well and had had numerous conversations with Russians from the diplomatic and governmental levels down to the peasant in the village and the man on the street in and out of uniform. He wrote:

> Enthusiasm over the liberation of the Russian people undoubtedly had much to do with American ardor for the war against the imperialism of Prussia. . . . Then when Russia began to stagger and stumble under her burden of difficulties in reorganization, America groaned. . . . She apparently expected that Russian peasants . . . would immediately spring into action as enlightened citizens of a republic and conduct themselves as Americans accustomed to freedom would conduct themselves. . . .[20]

Davis pointed out that before the offensive, in early June, some farsighted people predicted the disintegration of the Russian front in the winter. The advance itself he regarded as an unnecessary "demonstration of unity." Many Russians, loyal to the cause of their country and of the Allies, told Davis they rejected the suspicion that Russia was ready to "desert the Allies," particularly in view of her splendid war record and the fact that she had the longest roll of honor of war dead. In the last analysis he found that Allied insistence on the offensive only added fuel to the spreading flames of Bolshevism; and he thought that a restatement of war aims by the old Allies and the United States and a period of reorganization and rest were indispensable for restoring the failing Russian morale. The offensive, which was very successful in the beginning, broke when the "regiments of death," composed of the best young officers, "the hope of the army of the revolution," failed to stand up under the German counterattacks. Moreover, "it robbed Kerensky and the Provisional Government of the best young blood which might have given vitality in the critical period of Russia's illness," [21] that is, in the final clashes of October–November, 1917, that ended in the fall of the Winter Palace and in Bolshevist victory.

A person who had represented the United States before a mon-

[20] Malcolm W. Davis, *Open Gates to Russia*, New York, 1920, pp. 8-9.
[21] *Ibid.*, pp. 24-29.

arch of a country could not continue to serve in that capacity before the people of that country who had removed the monarch by a violent revolution, and expect successfully "to continue inter-course," much less to influence the current of revolutionary events. True, there was the transitional international act of recognition of the new democratic regime. However, in the short text of this recog-nition as formulated by Francis there was, amazingly enough, no reference at all to the crushing of the monarchy in Russia. He had nothing to say about this first bloodless success of a democratic revolution dreamt about and fought for through long decades by the libertarian movement and enthusiastically greeted in the United States.[22] Instead he announced in his dry manner the "formal rec-ognition of the Provisional Government of all the Russias" [!] and added only that "it gives me pleasure officially and personally to continue intercourse with Russia through the medium of the new Government." [23]

Unquestionably, a new ambassador, a kind of minister extraordi-nary from the transatlantic republic to the new Russian republic, would have had much more of an effect on the public opinion of a revolutionary country. He could have worked on a certain republi-can romanticism of the past, the ideas of Radishchev and Herzen. A special mission headed by an American like George Kennan, who had fought in Russia against czarism, who had a command of the Russian language, and who was intimately acquainted with many exiled revolutionaries in Siberia, some of whom became important figures in the March revolution, would have made a tremendous moral impression. Such a person's statements and declarations would have carried much weight and could have motivated action, for his sympathies for liberated Russia would have been above all suspicion.

[22] Cf. the *Literary Digest*, Mar. 24 and 31, 1917, quoting a long series of articles in the American daily press.

[23] Ambassador Francis' use of the phrase "all the Russias" with the title "Provisional Government" was a senseless, amateurish mistake. The phrase had been used in the first of the former Emperor's titles, "autocrat of all the Rus-sias," and the democratic provisional government had deliberately discarded it as imparting too much of an aura of conquest, hostile to freedom and a free Russian union of states. It was therefore most disconcerting to have it sud-denly appear in a declaration of recognition of the Russian democracy by the equally antimonarchic and democratic United States.

President Wilson's idea to dispatch such a special mission to Russia was a sound one. The routine activities of the Petrograd Embassy had to be partly augmented and partly taken over by a special group more suited to the task of establishing new bridges between the peoples of Russia and the United States. However, his choice of Elihu Root to head the mission seriously impaired the prestige of the mission and consequently the prestige of the United States, and completely nullified what effectiveness the group might have had. The following comment by Philip C. Jessup indicates that a worse choice could hardly have been made:

What induced Wilson to select Root is not clear, but Secretary Mc-Adoo had suggested and urgently pressed Root's name. Organized labor was opposed to his appointment. The American socialists scoffed at the idea of sending a hidebound conservative Wall Street lawyer to a country where the socialists had control of the government. Morris Hillquit and Victor Berger announced that the socialists in Russia would be fully informed about Mr. Root before he arrived. . . . The American socialists were not appeased when Charles Edward Russell was added to the Mission as a representative of their point of view; Russell had split with the regular members of the party in endorsing American participation in the war . . . The Federation [of Labor] under Samuel Gompers was as far removed from socialism as was Root himself.[24]

Greater dissatisfaction with this mission is voiced by another American writer,[25] who called it "blatantly bourgeois in its composition":

The most ambitious attempt to bolster up Russian morale and aid the Provisional Government was the dispatch of a special mission, headed by Elihu Root. . . . But the whole project reflected the blindness of our government to the realities of the situation in Russia. . . . The personnel of the Root mission was poorly chosen for the purpose of strengthening the ties between capitalist America and what was rapidly becoming socialistic Russia. As an elder statesman Root was an impor-

[24] Jessup, *op. cit.*, p. 356.
[25] Dulles, *op. cit.*, pp. 105, 104. For the sake of accuracy it must be stated that Wilson himself insisted on omitting American Socialists from Root's mission. He wrote to Secretary Lansing in April, 1917, "And yet we shall have to be careful, if we are to send a real representative of American Labor, not to send a Socialist." See Ray Stannard Baker, *Woodrow Wilson, Life and Letters*, Vol. VII, New York, 1939, p. 29.

tant figure in American public life, but his background and associations were thoroughly conservative. . . . There was no one on the commission who was really acceptable to the social democrats in the Russian government, let alone able to talk the language of the Petrograd Soviet. "Root in revolutionary Russia," Raymond Robins, who was in Petrograd that same summer with the American Red Cross, later wrote Theodore Roosevelt, "was as welcome as the smallpox, and occasioned as much enthusiasm as would be aroused by an Orangeman leading a popular parade in Dublin."

Jessup, in general, is inclined to defend Root against the strictures of various statesmen. However, we cannot agree with his attempt at exculpation: "It is true that the Root Mission was foredoomed to failure, but it could not have succeeded even with another chief or a different personnel." [26] A mission that was more familiar with conditions and more sympathetic with the philosophy of the provisional government could have produced more constructive results. It might also have contributed certain imponderables that are sometimes immeasurably significant in the causational chain of a revolution as closely tied to foreign policy as this Russian revolution was. A French mission representing a mortally bleeding country on the verge of collapse, or an English mission representing a maritime power that insisted on Russian soldiers remaining for the fourth year in the trenches, would have been regarded as too strongly self-interested to be accepted with complete trust. Huge and powerful America, only then preparing to enter the battle, could have been far more readily received by liberated Russia on the basis of a contributing partner. This difference among the Western Allies was more or less understandable and could have been exploited successfully.

Jessup's final criticism, that among all the personnel of Root's mission "there was no one who could be called a real expert on Russia and no one but an interpreter who could speak or understand Russian," is crushing. At about the same time that the American mission was in Russia, a Russian extraordinary mission, headed by Ambassador Bakhmetev, was in the United States, all of whose members could understand English and some of whom could speak it. Bakhmetev spoke to the House of Representatives on June 23

[26] Jessup, *op. cit.*, p. 358.

Elihu Root in the suite of Catherine the Great
in the Winter Palace, June, 1917

Elihu Root greeted by General Alexis Brusilov
at the Railroad Station, Mogilev

and to the Senate on June 26 in English. Both addresses were based on Wilsonian precepts and rejected all idea of a separate peace.

The more radical elements in Russia were quick to make political capital out of this piece of misjudgment. Dulles certainly was not correct when he said that the socialists "were paying practically no attention whatsoever to the United States," at least in this connection. In the radical socialist review *Lietopis* (Chronicle), edited by Maxim Gorki, an article by the well known journalist V. Kerzhentsev attacked Root bitterly and castigated the United States for its anti-revolutionary tactics:

The name of Root was enough to eliminate all doubts about the nature and purposes of the delegation. This former Secretary of State has acquired the reputation of being the most reactionary statesman of the United States. His name became known in all Russia in connection with his attempts to help the Russian autocracy close the doors of the United States to Russian political emigrants and extradite to Russian authorities those persons who had found asylum in the United States. Moreover, the name of Senator Root filled the American newspapers in connection with his constitutional draft for the State of New York, which was so reactionary that even members of his own party felt compelled to vote against him.

It just so happens that every reactionary movement has found in him a defender and apologist. Little wonder, then, that the reactionary mission of the United States to Russia was entrusted to this particular statesman. Throughout all the successive stages of the Russian revolution the United States, with its sharply defined instinct of ownership, unflinchingly resisted the movement of the revolutionary underprivileged of Russia united under the banner of socialism. And if these lower strata were defeated on the entire front, the American bourgeoisie would be able, not without reason, to claim the credit for the "victory over anarchy." [27]

There were two forgotten men at that time who would have been the right men in the right place, in a mission to revolutionary Russia. One was George Kennan, who had earned a great name for himself through his activities in the libertarian movement ever since 1885 and, as an elderly man, still followed attentively the

[27] V. Kerzhentsev, "Russkaya revolutsia i Amerika" (The Russian Revolution and America), *Lietopis*, July-Aug., 1917.

destiny of the second Russian revolution.[28] If he could not have
replaced Root, he certainly would have been a great help as an expert on Russia.

The second forgotten man was William English Walling, an
American non-Marxist socialist who, after a trip to Russia, had
published in 1908 an enthusiastic and strangely prophetic book in
which he called the first revolution of 1905–1906 only the democratic "first act" of a forthcoming social revolution. He regarded
the Russian revolution of 1905 as "heir to the ages," descended
partly from primitive Christianity and partly from the Reformation.[29] Obviously, he was not overencumbered with knowledge of
Russian history, or he would have known that Russia was converted
to Christianity in the tenth and eleventh centuries by Byzantium,
the dogmatic orthodoxy of which was even then a far cry from
primitive Christianity, and that the Reformation never had touched
Greek Catholic Russia.

Nevertheless, his prediction regarding the imminence of the inevitable second act that was to revolutionize the very foundations
of modern thought and social order deserves serious consideration.
The following passage sums up very well his vision of things to
come:

As the Russians have to contend with world forces and are bringing
about world results, it is no ordinary war or revolution in which they
have engaged themselves. Already it has become a part of the social
struggle of all Europe; if it lasts many years it must ultimately become
a part of some future world upheaval of unprecedented magnitude, of
new and widespread world revolutions and world wars.

In 1907–1908 Walling was closer than Lenin to the notion of
the inevitability of a Russian social revolution. During the First
World War, however, as an "outcast" like his admired teacher Leo
Tolstoy always opposed to socialist parties, he became less prophetic
and much more moderate. After the November Soviet revolution

[28] The New York weekly *Struggling Russia*, Nov. 22, 1919, p. 519, printed
a letter from Kennan to the editor in which he condemned the "usurping
tyranny" of Bolshevism which had succeeded that of the czars.
[29] W. E. Walling, *Russia's Message*, New York, 1908, Preface and pp. 164-
165, 420, 438. A good Russian translation of this book appeared in 1910 in
Berlin.

he was already an ardent opponent of Soviet Machiavellism and its social program, of compulsory labor and the expropriation of the miserable peasantry.[30]

Despite his shortcomings Walling was an expert on urban and rural Russia and in June, 1917, would have brought to the Root Mission an understanding of and much useful knowledge about a country he had studied thoroughly.

Elihu Root's speech in Petrograd on June 15, 1917, at the presentation of his mission to the provisional government was friendly and well meant. But it was weak in saying not a word about past Russo-American contacts, particularly those that had helped to promote a libertarian movement in Russia; and the too extensive quotation from Wilson's addresses gave added coolness and lack of immediacy. The theme of continuation of the fight was clearly enough emphasized:

> One fearful danger threatens the liberty of both nations. The armed forces of a military autocracy are at the gates of Russia and the allies. The triumph of German arms will mean the death of liberty in Russia. No enemy is at the gates of America, but America has come to realize that the triumph of German arms means the death of liberty in the world; that we who love liberty and would keep it must fight for it . . .
>
> So America sends another message to Russia—that we are going to fight, and have already begun to fight, for your freedom equally with our own, and we ask you to fight for our freedom equally with yours.[31]

The response to Mr. Root was made by the new Russian Minister for Foreign Affairs, M. I. Tereshchenko. In fluent English, he quoted that part of the American Declaration of Independence

---

[30] Letter to the editor, in *Struggling Russia*, Nov. 22, 1919, pp. 524-525. Walling was in correspondence with Lansing concerning the task of the mission. He sent a telegram which read: "Immediate renunciation of no annexations no indemnities program by President may save Russia. Nothing else will." (See Baker, *op. cit.*, p. 76.)

[31] As quoted under the title "From the Oldest of Democracies to the Youngest" in the *Survey*, Vol. XXXVIII, p. 272 (June 23, 1917). In an address to the Russian-American Chamber of Commerce at Petrograd on June 21, Root said: "The Mission has no function to discharge in respect to industrial or commercial life. That was intentionally excluded from the scope of its duty. We came to Russia to bring assurances of the spiritual brotherhood of the two great democracies." (See Elihu Root, *The United States and the War*, Cambridge, Mass., 1918, p. 105.)

beginning with the "self-evident truths" and ending with the casting off of absolute despotism. He showed that the Russian democratic government was trying to dissociate itself from the war aims formulated on May 3 by the previous Minister, Paul Miliukov; and he was most consistent in his anti-imperialistic line when he told the American mission:

The Russian people have no wish of conquest of dominion and are opposed to those ideas in others, and first of all they will not allow any of those imperialistic desires which our enemy has formed, manifest or hidden, to come to good in whatever sphere he may have planned them, political, financial, or economic.[32]

He stood on the general precepts of the American Declaration and Wilsonism. In opposing transfers of territories or peoples without their consent—which went beyond anti-Germanism to include any imperialism—he spoke not only to the audience before him but to the Soviets of the Workers' and Soldiers' Delegates, to whom he did not wish to yield a monopoly on anti-imperialism. His final sentence is perhaps the last pro-American declaration by a democratic Russian minister:

These two great peoples, the free people of Russia and the free people of America, the great people of the United States, the oldest, strongest, and purest democracy, hand in hand, will show the way that human happiness will take in the future.

It is well known that President Wilson was much disappointed in the results of Root's mission. He even annoyed that elderly statesman by refusing to listen to a report; and did not consult Root or any member of the mission after its return from Russia.[33]

There is scarcely any doubt that Wilson in the summer of 1917 became aware of the necessity for a specific handling of the Russian issue—which was important as early as June, 1917, when democratic Russia was still in the camp of the Allies, although torn by inner tensions and war-weariness.

The longer the war went on after the return of Root's mission, the more anxious Wilson became about Russian affairs. The official

---

[32] As quoted in A. J. Sack, *The Birth of the Russian Democracy*, pp. 385-386.
[33] Jessup, *op. cit.*, p. 368.

activities and measures of the Petrograd embassy seemed to him to be insufficient. The recommendations of the mission on financial, technical, and welfare assistance were accepted as requiring implementation. But the President was much interested in the spiritual contact with Russia, in raising the morale of the Russian army, in influencing Russian public opinion and periodicals for a continuance of the mortal struggle.

Wilson decided on October 23, 1917, to send Edgar Sisson to Russia as his special representative with personal instructions. The letters of introduction were to Premier Kerenski and members of his cabinet; but the provisional government was overthrown by the Bolsheviks on November 7, eighteen days before Sisson arrived. His activities in Petrograd were independent of Ambassador Francis both in powers and in funds.[34]

Sisson was very active in obtaining publication in the Bolshevik newspaper *Izvestiya* of Wilson's famous speech of January 8, 1918, on the fourteen points before the Congress. This was an unheard-of success. A German translation was made for distribution among German war prisoners and to "fraternizing" German soldiers in trenches, and the Russian text was translated also into Polish and Ukrainian for distribution in millions of posters among soldiers and the people. Authority for this distribution was given to Sisson by Lenin personally,[35] who at that time was absorbed in the protracted Russian negotiations at Brest-Litovsk with the German, Austro-Hungarian, and the Turkish empires.

Of the whole text of the President's speech, the introductory part preceding the paragraphs on specific countries was most impressive. *Izvestiya* (Number 263, Petrograd, 1917) underscored with fat letters most of the following sections, which relate to the peace slogans of tormented Russia and the great issues of future international relations:

. . . The Russian representatives have insisted, very justly, very wisely, and in the true spirit of modern democracy, that the conferences they have been holding with the Teutonic and Turkish statesmen should be held within open, not closed, doors . . .

[34] Edgar Sisson, *One Hundred Red Days*, New Haven, 1931, pp. 17, 30.
[35] *Ibid.*, pp. 208-215.

There is, moreover, a voice calling for these definitions of principle and of purpose which is, it seems to me, more thrilling and more compelling than any of the many moving voices with which the troubled air of the world is filled. It is the voice of the Russian people. They are prostrate and all but helpless, it would seem, before the grim power of Germany . . . They call to us to say what it is that we desire, in what, if in anything, our purpose and our spirit differ from theirs . . . Whether their present leaders believe it or not, it is our heartfelt desire and hope that some way may be opened whereby we may be privileged to assist the people of Russia to attain their utmost hope of liberty and ordered peace.

. . . The day of conquest and aggrandizement is gone by; so is also the day of secret covenants entered into in the interest of particular governments . . .

In all these policies of Woodrow Wilson an important consideration was to avoid throwing Russia into the lap of Germany and to remain in contact with Russian public opinion, including the still lingering opposition. But as hope faded of a compromise with the new Bolshevik commissars President Wilson, in the second half of December, 1917, cabled to Sisson insisting that he break off relations with the Bolshevik authorities and avoid any entanglement with Russian diplomatic officers.[36]

Thus Russo-American peaceful democratic contacts neared their end in an accelerating tempo.

Let us now try to weigh the various intervening factors in the period of revolution. It certainly cannot be said that the rightness or wrongness of American political and diplomatic attitudes toward Russia was of decisive importance in motivating Russia's democratic revolution. That the impact of the United States was felt in times of peace was undeniable, and even in times of war and revolution it affected the moderate liberals, the democrats, and certain elements of the socialist camp. It would certainly have been of a much deeper and more lasting nature if there had been enough time for it to work. But this was not the case. The revolution of 1917 was an explosion of resentments and aspirations that had been dammed up for at least a century, from the days of Alexander I,

[36] Baker, *op. cit.*, pp. 412, 420; Sisson, *op. cit.*, p. 90.

by the antireform maneuvers of the old regime. Russian capitalism, unable to mature under governmental pampering and governmental control, produced an unripe ideological socialism untempered by extended experience with legal trade unionism. The old structure, deprived of an influential middle class, simply could not stand up.

To a certain extent it may be said that the failure—if it can be called that—of the March revolution was due to the fact that for the first time in history the Russian people were the center about which historical events were shaping in which they took a direct hand. There had been incidents of a similar nature in the past beginning with the expulsion of Polish interventionist troops in 1613 connected with the election of the first Romanov, Michael, as Czar; but the people, though always interested, had been silent in matters concerning themselves. Revolution and uprising in and after 1825, though in behalf of the people, had been basically aristocratic ventures, often regarded by the common people with mistrust rather than sympathy. During the 1870's—the preparatory years of the revolution—an attempt had been made toward a rapprochement between the leading opposition intelligentsia and the illiterate masses with the slogan and the practice of "going to the people" with general and political education and propaganda. Too often, however, these revolutionary missionaries had been arrested and denounced to the political police.

The revolution of 1905 had been a first, tentative, insufficiently organized attempt. It had consisted of a number of fiery local uprisings, rural and urban, with a few centers in both capitals, in important towns, in the Baltic provinces, Poland, and the Caucasus. In 1917 the village was replaced by its sons in the army and on the front, represented in the local "soviets." Now, for the first time, the intelligentsia had a platform on which they could appear in revolutionary cooperation with the people. But there was still a yawning abyss between the intelligentsia who led the revolution in the towns and the rural masses and the lower urban strata. The short period of quasi-parliamentary representation in the Duma from 1906 on— a decade of limited elections—could not change materially the social and political backwardness of these Russian masses existing side by side with a politically active and uncompromising intelligentsia.

The democratic March revolution was ripe enough not to need —and it did not have—any individual hero; the real hero of this upheaval was the people itself. But revolutionary Russia was not powerful enough or organized enough to resist the Germans from without, Bolshevism from within, and the czarist darkness from behind. For their part, the intelligentsia, after decades of participating directly and indirectly in the illegal underground activities of clandestine circles, had grown too rigid to reorientate themselves immediately after the collapse of czarism, to turn from the dogmatic intransigeance of the past to the sober, realistic policy of a full-fledged, middle-of-the-road democracy. They were conscious of the need for the change, but it just did not work out.

This rigid radicalism was a product of the enormous gap between the extraordinarily high level of the élite and the low plane of the illiterate common people. Under Catherine the Great the élite had been a very thin aristocratic layer; toward the end of czarism they had become much more numerous, embracing not only parts of the gentry, but parts of the clergy, the petty bourgeoisie, and the intelligentsia. And down to 1917 political activity centered in and around the élite and its specific orthodoxy.

Parties appeared in Russia in the first third of the nineteenth century. However, they were not parties in the parliamentary sense: they did not participate in shaping the country's political destiny: they did not share in governing it. They were the opposition, differing among themselves only in the ways in which they differed with the government. Thus Russia with its regulative idea of democracy versus autocracy was handicapped by illegal parties permeated with a spirit of ideological intransigeance and dogmatism. This meant an inherent unwillingness to compromise. In revolutionary maximalism, stemming from Bakunin and Tkachov, which the moderate Social Democrats vainly tried to reduce from the beginning of this century, Russia resembled France most, and England and the United States least.

After three hundred years of Romanov autocracy and only a decade of quasi-parliamentary schooling during the Duma years 1906 to 1916, Russia entered upon her democratic revolution in March, 1917. What chance was there for the formation of a group of political parties in a revolution against the old regime? Such an alliance was thinkable only in its negative stage, and only then did it actually work—especially during the preparatory years of 1915 and 1916. In that period the moderate monarchists and the radical anti-monarchists formed the famous progressive bloc of the Fourth Duma, where the monarchist chairman Rodzianko fought against Nicholas II and the Russian Girondist Miliukov became the ideological leader of a powerful patriotic opposition to a decaying monarchy. In the coalition the socialists of the Duma were scarcely distinguishable from the rest of the opposition. This absolutely negative stage survived czarism, but lasted only a few short weeks —from the first riots to the abdication of the Czar and his brother Michael.

Then serious dissension broke out among the revolutionary forces. The rift widened rapidly. Attempts at compromise were made, the most successful one smashing the July uprising of the Bolsheviks aimed at overpowering the provisional government. Also, the Mensheviks and Socialist Revolutionaries tried to form a united front with the progressive bourgeoisie to resist Bolshevism, particularly in the Moscow National Conference in August, 1917. But the Russian battle of Armageddon could not be prevented by belated patchwork compromises.

For all the outward institutional and legal similarity between democratic America and democratic Russia from March to November, 1917, there was nevertheless an inward social and cultural disparity that grew out of their wholly different pasts. In time, the difference could have been overcome and the parallelism turned to continuous cooperation; but the two countries had started on parallel courses at different original speeds, and they moved at different velocities. The force that unquestionably tended to draw them together throughout a hundred and forty years, and that became particularly strong during the period of the provisional government in 1917, was not strong enough to overcome the inertia that held them apart.

We do not wish to carry the mechanical analogy too far. However, something should be learned from the experience of almost a century and a half. In international politics, for a considerable time to come, these two bodies of different orientation were to pursue increasingly divergent aims.

Looking Forward

This book, I hope, has shown the political and ideological impact of the United States on the libertarian movement and reforms in Russia from the very beginning. At the same time it has reviewed a long span of American diplomatic relations with Russia from Francis Dana to David Francis and indicated how much more effective our diplomacy could have been had our diplomats had a greater knowledge of the country in which they represented the United States. They should have known that in Russian eyes the United States was ever the *enfant terrible* of the West, the fascinating, restless reformer and revolutionary, for long decades the sole standard-bearer of republicanism, and later the personification of economic progress and technological efficiency. American precepts, ideas, political thinking, and activities remained hidden in books and reviews to be enjoyed by the few who read them, while the many were not permitted even a remote acquaintance with the United States except for its economic, financial, and industrial achievements. There has been much criticism of secret diplomacy, especially the secrecy surrounding diplomatic negotiations and the concealment of certain articles in otherwise open treaties. But traditional diplomacy suffers from another vice: that of concealing itself politically from the country it represents and isolating itself from any understanding of the political conditions of the country to which the diplomat is accredited.. The tendency has been to surround career diplomats with more and more specialist attachés having expert knowledge in particular fields. There are military attachés, economic attachés, agricultural attachés, and many others; but there are no political attachés, men who not only know the language of the country but are thoroughly familiar with its political conditions, movements, and aims. This omission was particularly crucial for Russo-American relations after March, 1917, when Russia, on the rack and exhausted, experienced the terrific military and propaganda pressure of the German Empire from without and the unprecedented demagoguery of Bolshevik "diggers and levelers" from within.

The current of contacts and impacts running through about seven score years was interrupted in 1918. This break in Russo-American diplomatic relations lasted fifteen years, much longer than similar ruptures between the Soviet Union and the leading European powers following the Bolshevik victory. But even then only diplomatic relations and intercourse were severed; contacts and impacts of a political and ideological character continued, and may actually have been increased, just because of the enormous differences between the two powers after the short period of democratic identity. The resumption of diplomatic relations in 1933 did not eliminate or even decrease the ideological estrangement. Under the Soviet-American partnership as allies against Hitler Germany in the Second World War differences were submerged; but after the conclusion of hostilities in 1945 and the establishment of the United Nations, the cleavage reappeared on the surface, becoming most acute at the end of the 1940's. While diplomatic relations and collaboration in the United Nations continue, Soviet Russia and the United States have drawn poles apart ideologically and politically. These differences have been cast into sharp relief by the weakening of the third member of the Big Three, Great Britain.

In spite of all its weaknesses, international law still makes possible contact between countries whose mutual international relations have worn dangerously thin or have been broken, even though it be predominantly a legal nexus. This basic difference between international law and international relations in the constellation of Soviet Union and United States—a dichotomic constellation, in which the basin of international relations is permanently draining away while naked international law stands high and dry at its rim—stands out in the middle of the century more sharply than ever before.

The period of Russo-American relations that came to an end in 1918 is by no means a closed chapter. The institutions that sprang up, the events that occurred, the intercourse that took place—which we have tried to describe and analyze in this volume—project their influence beyond chronological boundaries; and some may even be revived if demanded by political expediency. Future historians of diplomatic and political relations between the United States and the Soviet Union will find they can take no short cut. They will not be able to start with 1933, when the Soviet Union received *de jure* recognition from the United States; they will have to retrace the winding path to the beginning of the nineteenth century.

Index

427